ADVANCES IN LIBRARY ADMINISTRATION AND ORGANIZATION

ADVANCES IN LIBRARY ADMINISTRATION AND ORGANIZATION

Series Editors: Edward D. Garten and
Delmus E. Williams

Volume 1:	Edited by W. Carl Jackson, Bernard Kreissman and Gerard B. McCabe
Volumes 2–12:	Edited by Bernard Kreissman and Gerard B. McCabe
Volumes 13–20:	Edited by Edward D. Garten and Delmus E. Williams
Volume 21:	Edited by Edward D. Garten, Delmus E. Williams and James M. Nyce

ADVANCES IN LIBRARY ADMINISTRATION
AND ORGANIZATION   VOLUME 22

ADVANCES IN LIBRARY ADMINISTRATION AND ORGANIZATION

EDITED BY

EDWARD D. GARTEN

University of Dayton Libraries, Ohio, USA

DELMUS E. WILLIAMS

University of Akron Libraries, Ohio, USA

JAMES M. NYCE

*School of Library and Information Management,
Emporia State University, Emporia, Kansas, USA*

2005

ELSEVIER
JAI

Amsterdam – Boston – Heidelberg – London – New York – Oxford
Paris – San Diego – San Francisco – Singapore – Sydney – Tokyo

ELSEVIER B.V.
Radarweg 29
P.O. Box 211
1000 AE Amsterdam
The Netherlands

ELSEVIER Inc.
525 B Street, Suite 1900
San Diego
CA 92101-4495
USA

ELSEVIER Ltd
The Boulevard, Langford
Lane, Kidlington
Oxford OX5 1GB
UK

ELSEVIER Ltd
84 Theobalds Road
London
WC1X 8RR
UK

First edition 2005

British Library Cataloguing in Publication Data
A catalogue record is available from the British Library.

ISBN: 0-7623-1195-9
ISSN: 0732-0671 (Series)

∞ The paper used in this publication meets the requirements of ANSI/NISO Z39.48-1992 (Permanence of Paper).
Printed in The Netherlands.

Working together to grow
libraries in developing countries

www.elsevier.com | www.bookaid.org | www.sabre.org

ELSEVIER   BOOK AID International   Sabre Foundation

CONTENTS

LIST OF CONTRIBUTORS

Melissa Cox Norris	University of Cincinnati Libraries, Cincinnati, OH, USA
Odin L. Jurkowski	Central Missouri State University, Warrensburg, MO, USA
Pamela Kindja Ladner	Mississippi Gulf Coast Community College, Gautier, MS, USA
Marsha Lewis	Voinovich Center for Leadership and Public Affairs, Ohio University, Athens, OH, USA
Tara Lynn Fulton	Lock Haven University, Lock Haven, PA, USA
Charles B. Osburn	School of Library and Information Studies, The University of Alabama, Tuscaloosa, AL, USA
Lilia Pavlovsky	Ewing, NJ, USA
Barbara Simpson Darden	Union, NJ, USA
Hugh D. Sherman	Voinovich Center for Leadership and Public Affairs and the College of Business, Ohio University, Athens, OH, USA
Betty K. Turock	Rutgers University, Somerset, NJ, USA
Mark L. Weinberg	Voinovich Center for Leadership and Public Affairs and the Political Science Department, Ohio University, Athens, OH, USA
Julia Zimmerman	Ohio University Library, Athens, OH, USA
Eleni A. Zulia	Voinovich Center for Leadership and Public Affairs, Ohio University, Athens, OH, USA

INTRODUCTION

The tension between what researchers can deliver, what they regard as reputable knowledge, and what practitioners "need to know" is one that is characteristic of all the "half" or "quasi" professions. We can, for example, trace out this tension in social work, nursing, and, to some extent, in business and architecture. But perhaps nowhere is the relationship between "science" and practice as problematic as it is in library and information science (LIS). There are any number of historical and ideological reasons we can invoke to account for this. However, no matter how we attempt to explain it or to "place" it into context (one gambit has been to tie this division to the collapse of University of Chicago's experiment in library science education), the fact is that it remains. Not only does it continue, it has become an invariant feature, a constant, in the intellectual landscape of the discipline. It is, we could also argue, a divide we see little hope of resolving in any kind of definitive way.

This divide reflects something about how we as citizens of the United States and members of a particular culture view knowledge. While we valorize "pure knowledge", we also regard it with some suspicion especially if it is difficult to make an argument that links this knowledge to the "real" world in any direct fashion. After all, for most of us, "real" knowledge is something that "does something" (or leads to something) real. In other words, to be "real" it has to have an effect that we ourselves can either measure or experience or both.

So in very typical American fashion we tend to assume that "real" knowledge is only "real" and legitimate if it enables us to do something "better". Here, of course, is the rub. It is often difficult to link scientific knowledge to practical results in the world we live in. Further, for most of us, it is almost impossible for us to link science, "better" and the everyday world unless we invoke technology as a the medium through which science expresses knowledge in the world.

This is not to say (as is often thought) that Americans are fundamentally anti-intellectual. But it does mean we want "value" in some empirical, pragmatic (demonstrable) fashion in return for our investment. It is this cultural fault line that divides practitioners from researchers, especially in LIS. On one hand, the kinds of arguments researchers put forth, i.e., that scientific knowledge is essentially cumulative and, with more time, effort, and money, science will eventually tell us everything we need to know about how to run "our shop". This kind of argument practitioners see, at worst, as self-serving. At best, it provides them with little guidance and knowledge about the contingent, problematic world they occupy. Nevertheless, we still look to science to help us make sense of the world and the social institutions we work within.

This volume of ALAO will not resolve this tension between science and practice. But from time to time, it seems appropriate to remind readers why what we publish volume to volume takes the form it does. The contributors to this volume (as well as to others that preceded it) have attempted to deal with this issue in one way or another. While the authors differ from each other by problem, by scale, and in methodology and theory, the question "What can science tell us about practice?" underlies what they have given us here.

There are of course, any number of answers to this question. But if LIS has any relationship to the social sciences at all, there are at least two questions we, as researchers should be able to help practitioners with. The first is to bring to the surface and to help practitioners make sense of those elements of their social world, which they take largely for granted but are crucial to understand the work practitioners do and the institutions within which they work. The second, and this is coupled to the first, is to ask and help practitioners address perhaps the most fundamental of all questions about institutions and social life. Attributed to Garfinkel, this question is, given the context, "What's really going on here?"

In the first paper, Charles Osburn acknowledges that the environment in which libraries function has changed, sometimes dramatically, over the last 25 years. Nevertheless, where one wants to argue that collection development should be community- or collection centered or some combination of both, discussions in this area have tended to disguise the fact that the methodologies and concepts that inform what the LIS community calls collection evaluation have not changed much over the past two or three decades. What Osburn proposes is not another tool or toolkit. Instead, he suggests that we need to reconsider what cause and effect means when it comes to collection development and evaluation. In effect, Osburn wants us to unpack two central concepts that lay behind how the LIS community thinks and writes about collection evaluation but that are seldom acknowledged. To put it another way, he wants to base these discussions on something other than common sense. This kind of analytic challenge, one that replaces folk categories and belief with a more precise understanding of what goes on in the world, can lead to more reliable knowledge how we build our collections.

Jurkowski and Lardner both take up issues related to distance learning and library services. Jurkowski's paper, a fairly rigorous study, asks questions about "fitness in relation to library services and distance education students. In other words, Jurkowski is concerned with the extent to which academic librarians (and libraries) serve the needs of their institution's distance education students? Through content analysis, interviews with librarians and student surveys, Jurkowski found that libraries do serve distance education students comparatively well but that there is room for improvement. What is counter-intuitive about his findings is that they seemed to be relatively constant regardless of the institution's size, the kinds (numbers) of services a library offered students or whom the author interviewed. Equally puzzling, none of his informants were able to articulate (or to come to a consensus) about how to improve the services in place. While these findings could be written off as artifact of a research design and how its data are interpreted, it may well be that Jurkowski here has touched upon a more important issue. It is one that again takes us back to the issue of common sense and category. It may well be that her informants all meant different things when they talked about things like "use" and "instruction". To put it another way, this research suggests that we in the LIS community are not as well-equipped analytically as we should be when it comes to the understanding variation in meaning and practice, especially when they underlie and cross cut central taken for grant categories like "service".

Ladner, in her study of Mississippi's Virtual Community College, raises the same issue but with another term. Ladner is not concerned here with "use" but rather with the meaning of the term "adequate" Ladner is particularly interested in what "adequate" means for students who use online services and how to collect data that can be used by library staff and university administrators to determine whether they are meeting the needs of the College's distance learners.

Pavlovsky's and Fulton's papers are linked together by a mutual interest in sense making. Fulton makes an argument that Weicke's notion of organizational sense making, when applied to libraries, can enable both researchers and practitioners to better understand what "leadership" is in this context. Fulton believes that Weicke's concept of sense making will enable us not just to get a better analytic "grip" on what leadership is but also what constitutes "failure" and "success" when we talk about leadership. The author then goes on to discuss six areas of leadership that she believes require either more study or that have been refractory to the research efforts so far. In both cases, Fulton argues that the notion of sense making could contribute much to the study of library leadership.

Pavlovsky addresses in her nice piece perhaps the most refractory of analytic problems that confront social scientists. In the broadest possible sense, she is concerned with what sense making can tell those who design, work within, and use the space within a public library. As she notes, the analysis of verbal language (and behavior), while difficult, does not raises issues of any significant magnitude for social science. This, the author goes on to say, is not true when we are dealing with the "language of things". Not only is it difficult to recover what things "mean" and "say" to others, the problem is magnified when we attempt to deal with public space, like that of a library, and when we have to deal with the problem of variation. In short, designers, staff and users bring to public space not just different understandings but also inscribe them differently in the public spaces of libraries. She also makes it clear that many of statements space "makes" concern the institution itself. Pavlovsky has attempted to untangle a set of positions that together hold together and differentiate what a library is and what information provision and retrieval is within the context of that public space.

The last three papers (Norris, Turlock & Simpson, and Weinberg et al.) deal more or less directly with pragmatic issues anyone who works within a library can identify with. Norris in her discussion of marketing in academic libraries takes on a series of analytical and pragmatic tasks. Her paper attempts to identify why the notion of marketing is so problematic within the academic library community. This has to do with association marketing has with the commercial world, the free market environment and the Madison Avenue-ization of both the United States and its universities. It also has to do with, as Norris points out, how those who work in academic libraries think about their libraries especially in contrast to public libraries. Norris argues that conventional separations made between academic and public libraries (differences in services and users) should not disguise the fact that all libraries are fundamentally in the same business, whether we like to admit it or not.

Weinberg et al., point out that the term "value" is not an unproblematic one for the librarian community. It is not just that what "value" means is open to debate. It is at present an issue of some debate about what skills, competencies, institution shifts, whether it be in staff, resources or structure, will yield "greater" value. In effect what Weinberg and his co-authors want to do is link "value" and the institution together. (His argument pays less attention to end users.) To do this, he invokes Mark Moore's Strategic

Triangle. The authors argue that this model will enable the library community to think "better" about "value" and institution and the connections that exist and/or should exist between them. It will as well provide a road path that any library can make use of to deliver "value" to its constituents.

Turlock's and Simpson's paper takes a look at minority library career paths. This paper looks at the "choke points" that occurred in the career of seven African-American women in the library community. They extrapolate from these career paths a series of lessons learned about minority success and failure in the library community. The paper then goes on to argue that initiatives like the ALA Spectrum scholarships can lead to minority retention and success for Afro-American women within the library community.

On a personal note, I would like to thank Del and Ed for inviting me to join them in editing ALAO. As time goes on, I hope that they (and ALAO readers) will not find that their confidence in me has been misplaced.

James M. Nyce
Co-Editor

COLLECTION EVALUATION: A RECONSIDERATION

Charles B. Osburn

Evaluation occupies both the beginning point and the end point in any management planning cycle, thus providing quality assurance and accountability while adjusting the course of future efforts of the enterprise. The purpose of the present essay is to advance a rationale for rethinking the library and information science (LIS) profession's ideas about the formal evaluation or assessment of collections that are established and maintained in libraries and information centers.

It is clear that the environment surrounding our libraries is far more complex and dynamic in the year 2005 than it was, for example, in 1975. In their recent analysis of this apparently deep social transformation, Alexander Bard and Jan Soderqvist refer to it (in terms that may be only slightly exaggerated) as a new social, cultural, and economic paradigm in the making, and identify the primary forces behind it as digitization and electronic networks. Among the major consequences of the social transformation they envision is that the new paradigm "will not be concrete, but fluid. It is not merely that we are developing new social norms; it is a matter of a completely new sort of norm" (Bard & Soderqvist, 2002, p. 22).[1] This conclusion affords useful insight into the relations between the library and its primary environmental concern, which is the community it serves, with special meaning for a reconsideration of the evaluation of the collections we develop and maintain.

Advances in Library Administration and Organization
Advances in Library Administration and Organization, Volume 22, 1–21
ISSN: 0732-0671/doi:10.1016/S0732-0671(05)22001-1

But the strategies the profession has employed for decades are less and less reflective of the nature of this changing societal environment and so are bound to become even less satisfactory than they have been. Discussed below, the traditional methodologies never did lead to conclusions that were readily applicable to management decisions, and now they no longer reflect the changing nature of relations among the information universe, the community, and the profession. Although our profession has applied great ingenuity for decades to the crafting of these approaches, their inherent inadequacies consistently have resulted in the frustration of more questions than answers. Much to the credit of methodologies designed during the past decade (the most frequently discussed in the literature today being LibQual+), they have placed the emphasis on community satisfaction, rather than on the collection. Still, such approaches work as intermittent projects with a telescopic focus that contain many of the weaknesses of current evaluation strategies, whether collection-centered or community-centered. The purpose of this essay is to describe a way to place a moving binocular focus on the community and the collection, although not to the exclusion of what can be characterized as the more conventional methodologies.

There is fairly wide agreement within the profession about the causes of the new environment in which library services are provided and about the variety of its manifestations in any given local setting. In fact, in most cases our profession has adjusted and continues to adjust to the changing conditions of its environment by adopting new procedures, policies, and even principles. And this has been accomplished with remarkable swiftness in the interests of seizing new opportunities for improved service while maintaining economies. Yet, despite a great deal of invention, testing, tweaking, and the application of powerful technologies, concepts behind the evaluation of collections remain locked in a status almost perfectly identical to that of 30 years ago. A strategy for evaluation that yields a reliable basis for decision-making and planning, other than one that is highly particularized, static, and detached from the point of contact between collection and community, remains at large.

We are in need of an approach to the assessment of the service afforded by our library collections that stands for more than a project whose product consists of a simple testimony to the past transformation of the information universe, to the past patterns of relevant community activity, and to collection growth. We would benefit, instead, from a view of evaluation that consists of a process commensurate with and integral to these phenomena, a process that incorporates the substance of cause and effect in a more dynamic mode.

DEFINITIONS

The definition of the collection employed in this essay accounts for it as an assemblage of information sources made accessible systematically in any format by the library or information center for the purposes of the community that is to intended to serve.

The word 'assemblage' in this definition indicates that the collection is pieced together from seemingly random parts according to some design, while the adverb 'systematically' connotes method and purpose in constituting the parts as a whole. 'Accessibility' refers to the relative convenience of consulting the collection, primarily by obviating travel to a remote physical location or an unduly frustrating delay in response. The 'community' is the population the library or information center intends to serve, including members of the host institution, whether municipality, university, school, or corporation, and others to whom the host institution chooses to extend its resources. The community consists of those who are both active library users and potential library users.

In summary, the collection represents the library's essential service, which is the direct access it provides the community with sources of information and knowledge. From the public's perspective, the library has been and continues to be perceived in terms of its collection, just as the noun 'library' implies, which is a significant consideration in understanding that institution's survival through the ages. The collection is the planned result of an on-going series of decisions called 'collection management'.

COLLECTION MANAGEMENT

The ultimate purpose of collection management is to render relevant parts of the information universe accessible to the community; to bring together people and ideas. The 'information universe' refers in this paper to the entire corpus of recorded information and knowledge, past and current, published and unpublished, in any format.

The definition I have followed for collection management during the past 25 years is as follows: collection management is the process of information gathering, communication, coordination, policy formulation, evaluation, planning, and budgeting that results in decisions about the acquisition, retention, and negotiation of access to information sources in support of the intellectual interests of a given community. It comprises various functions, 'collection development' being the final stage of that decision process as it relates to the aggregate of individual selection decisions. To fully appreciate these two concepts, which have been formulated in the course of more than 30 years, it is useful to remember that the collection is developed, which is to say that it is expanded and redesigned, whether by agents inside the library or by those outside the library, and whether the activity is organized or not. This essay has to do with collection management as an organized process that is administered from within the library.

Collection management is not a linear function. It is a multi-dimensioned process whose purpose is to convert the otherwise discrete entities called the collection, the information universe, and the community into an adaptive organism. It is the process of stewardship of a community good, and is, therefore, closely engaged with the community it serves. To the extent that collection management is central to internal library operations, it is a technical service. But, to the extent to which it functions as a sphere of communication enveloping the library and the community, it is a public service that is pivotal in library-community relations. In any case, it is a highly visible library service.

Among the many concerns of collection management, the liaison responsibility ranks in importance with that of selection, which is the ultimate formal decision of collection management to incorporate a specific source of information into the collection. In this context, liaison is intended to build mutual understanding between library and community, primarily to ensure that the development and maintenance of the collection shadow as closely as possible its changing environment. Information gathering for this purpose is largely an intelligence effort to gain insight into the motivations, intellectual interests, and means and patterns of the community's most likely connection to the information universe. Tangentially, the process of liaison incorporates the marketing of library management's aspirations, plans, challenges, opportunities, and limitations to the community as a means of fostering community understanding of the library.

Evolution of the conceptual model during the 20th century from that of 'acquisition' to 'book selection' to 'collection building' to 'collection development' and then to 'collection management' was extraordinarily rapid. Indeed, it would not be an exaggeration to suggest that the reworking of fundamental concepts that guide so critical an aspect of a social institution in the course of so few decades is astonishing. In some cases, however, acceptance of these concepts outpaced their practical application, as seen most obviously, perhaps, in the profession's approach to collection evaluation. But, precisely because of the rapidity of the introduction of the most recent of these conceptual models during an era of severe financial constraint and of the sweeping infusion of information technologies, the administrative endorsement, guidance, and support necessary to put them properly into practice rarely or never were forthcoming. This matter will resurface below as one of the general causes of logistical problems encountered in collection management.

The concept of collection management incorporates a system's view in describing how its component functions interact in the development and maintenance of information sources. This view depicts collection management as a purposeful subsystem within the library and the library as a subsystem in its elaborate environment or supra-system that is the host institution. Use of the word 'management' is intended to capture the reality of the function as a complex decision-making responsibility no longer involving just art and impression, but also requiring some science and a lot of communication as well. In the evolution of the models (acquisition to book selection to collection building to collection development, and now to collection management) one can see a subtle shift in what the profession increasingly considers the primary objects of librarianship: not books and technology, but people and ideas.

EVALUATION

In applying the word 'evaluation' and its cognates as they may be applied to library collections, it is useful to extract defining words and phrases from several standard dictionaries to arrive at the most relevant concepts. Thus, a definition for collection evaluation can be amalgamated: it is a determination or fixing of the value; a determination of the significance or worth, usually by careful appraisal and study. Similarly, a combined set of definitions for collection assessment, which is a designation of almost equal frequency, would be: to determine the importance, size, or value; and, for appraisal, another commonly used phrase, would be to assign a monetary value. The objective that stimulates the undertaking of this management activity in a given library ultimately determines the most appropriate definition of evaluation.

When applied to library services in general, evaluation is inherently complex and prone to disappointing results for at least these four reasons: the objects of analysis, as well as their relations to each other are forever changing; we have little or no control over either the information universe or the community we are trying to bring together in the most productive way;

there is usually a considerable hiatus in the cycle that separates formal evaluation from the revision of direction for the collection, and that action from the next evaluation project; and the goal of the project is too often ambiguous.

The purposes behind evaluation are quite varied, a condition that goes far to explain why collection evaluation so often leads to frustration. The most common among the purposes of demonstrating the value of the collection on some supposedly objective basis is to justify the expense of the collection and its continued development. This is accountability, which also figures in an effort to demonstrate benefits to or positive outcomes for the community consistent with the mission and goals of the host institution. But whatever other issues may be involved, the purposes of collection evaluation, one way or another, attempt to rate the quality of the collection as it stands, as measured against any number of possible standards.

Collection evaluation can also be used to formulate or to adjust policy, assess collection management personnel performance, plan staffing and budgeting, rank institutions, and inform consortial agreements. A concomitant value of the formal processes of collection evaluation is their potential to raise the library's visibility in the community and to demonstrate its attention to community interests.

As might be expected, the literature of librarianship is marked by a plethora of studies dedicated to collection evaluation, presenting a very rich variety of methodologies. In fact, this aspect of service evaluation in librarianship offers such an impressive spectrum of possibilities that it figures very prominently among the major contributions of librarianship, such as the organization of knowledge, to the other information professions. But the volume of such studies is markedly overwhelming in contrast to the weight of their practical value. Most of them base evaluation on the results or the product of collection management, which usually has meant the status of the collection per se and/or its quality as judged by the community. These two essential procedures can be referred to as the collection-centered evaluation and the community-centered evaluation, respectively. Surely no one can argue against the logic of studying these two objects since the collection is, after all, what we say we are evaluating, while the community embodies the reason for being of the collection.

The collection-centered evaluation is the more time-honored of these two objects of collection evaluation, reflecting an era when our profession was less outward oriented in spite of formal library mission statements that most likely stated otherwise. Evaluation of this type includes verification of quality by comparison of library holdings on several bases: standard bibliographies; expert impression provided by a consultant; both qualitative and quantitative comparisons with other libraries and with others of similar mission and supported by similar (but usually greater) resources; citation analysis; and the application of various formulas and standards that may be recognized by an external authoritative body, such as an accreditation agency. But these normative approaches have little to tell about the value of the collection in fulfilling the library's mission in the community specifically in question. Meanwhile, understanding the relation of collection size and growth, on the one hand, and collection quality on the other has always proved to be a particularly mysterious objective.

The community-centered evaluation involves study of both use made of the collection and user attitudes toward it. User studies most often are quantitative. They, too, include several bases for analysis that devolve from number and kinds of uses of the collection. Use of the collection can thus be identified by means of analyzing surveys of the user community, circulation and re-shelving data, database monitoring and reporting, interlibrary loan statistics, and whatever other movement of information can be identified and captured. The assessment of outcomes is perhaps the most significant conceptual basis for the evaluation of general library service quality advanced so far. But applying it convincingly to collection quality is a difficult case to make, yielding very tenuous and questionable results. For example, we have not yet determined how to demonstrate proof of the library's value to the community, other than through positive correlations between some kind of increased library activity and a desirable outcome in the community that may or may not really be related by cause and effect.

User studies, although driven by qualitative concerns at the outset, tend to be expressed in quantitative terms at the end because of their facile manipulability and apparent objectivity. Studies of the library user most often take the form of satisfaction surveys and focus groups, both of which may address a range of characteristics, such as motivation for use, information seeking habits or methods, patterns of use, impediments to use, and results of use. In the latter instance, some user studies assess outcomes that purportedly stem directly from consultation of the collection.

It may be helpful to bear in mind that each of the types of method itemized under the rubrics collection-centered and community-centered evaluation can be realized in practice through a considerably large number of schemes.

WEAKNESSES OF CONVENTIONAL APPROACHES

Given the many possible purposes for the evaluation of collections and the complexities of the collection management mission to make the most relevant parts of the information universe accessible to the community, it is no wonder that the conventional evaluation procedures produce more questions than answers. But problems even more profound are abundant: evaluation that is focused on the collection is antithetical to a library mission claiming service to the community; at best, such studies provide only a snapshot assessment, post facto and static, of the collection; and there are the still greater complexities of incorporating both leased segments of the collection and consortial agreements into the evaluation. On the positive side, collection-centered evaluation methodologies most often can confirm speculation only mildly while, on the negative side, only the extreme and blatant findings may be valid. But findings usually are not extreme and blatant; if they are, much damage has already been done.

Community-centered evaluation posits the more serious set of difficulties, of course, because it represents an attempt to fathom the human mind in some methodical way. Consequently, findings usually become highly ambiguous and dubious. In the first place, user motivation is largely unknowable, although we do know that it is relatively unstable. Not least among the many reasons for this lacuna in our knowledge is that our profession has not achieved an accepted definition of 'use' upon which to base a better understanding, while the concept of 'satisfaction', even if we could define it, would still be close to impossible to ascertain, for it is too closely interwoven into the fleeting moment. This problem is magnified by the typical user's unsophisticated awareness of the constitutive elements of his or her own cognitive process and related state of satisfaction, let alone the user's likely unwillingness to accept the challenge required to articulate it for someone else.

But the entire cascade of difficulties associated with trying to understand user and potential user motivation does not end even there. For, just as beauty may reside only in the eye of the beholder, information is information only as it influences the complex mind of the receiver, who gives it a context for meaning. Therefore, as Sanna Talja points out, "it is impossible to get unmediated knowledge about a person's cognitive skills or even information seeking behavior, because the ways in which they are accounted for are always mediated by culturally constructed interpretive repertoires" (Talja, 1996, p. 74). So, even looking over the user's shoulder, if such activity fell within logistical and legal bounds, it would likely be of little value. Then there is the too often overlooked fact that the words 'user' and 'community' do not reference the same population, for there is usually only a small overlap. Furthermore, as an example of just one consideration that should be fairly straightforward but turns out not to be, we do know that convenience plays a role in use and in satisfaction, although we cannot claim to know either the nature, relative importance, or other implications of that condition. And, again, the conventional studies yield only a static, snapshot perspective on an environment that is quite the opposite of that. When these considerations are taken into account, collection evaluation and collection management are badly disjointed.

THE ELUSIVE 'SILVER BULLET'

What we have been seeking in vain, it would seem, is a silver bullet. It is as though we have believed that by following a quantitative course, we would be able to achieve a truly objective, perhaps even scientific, evaluation. But we have not yet succeeded in accomplishing this. The author of our most thorough text on the general subject of collection management, Edward Evans, reports the current status of the usefulness of conventional methods of collection evaluation quite cogently with the conclusion that "There is much research to do before collection evaluation becomes an objective science. Everyone agrees that collection evaluation is a difficult task, and the results are highly subjective. Thus, the evaluator must be willing to live with what are, at best, tentative results" (Evans, 2000, p. 447). Yet these methods persist in the absence of any other.

Quantitative methodologies devised thus far have achieved wide use, very possibly by dint of a desire to emulate the evident successes of science and technology. But they prove disappointing in the context of collection evaluation because they either are too normative and subject to misinterpretation or are too narrowly focused. Disappointment follows from a number of inadequacies in the quantitative procedures: they address differing purposes of the collection; they operate in an environment driven by the vicissitudes of community motivations; they work in a divergent context of both individual and social epistemology; they are very weak in theory and lack predictive capacity; their data can easily be skewed by anomalous events; they do not fare well with the logistical and substantive problems of accommodating different disciplines; and, most significantly, they cannot account for the contexts of the information they do provide. In agreement with most who have engaged in and/or written about the conventional methodologies, Evans advises that "Because no one evaluation method is adequate by itself, a combined approach is most effective"(Evans, 2000, p. 447); but probably not much more. Taking that conclusion a step further, one could also find that the greatest single weakness of the conventional evaluation methodologies, even when combined, is their lack of capacity to be instructive about, or even reflective of, the dynamism inherent in the interactions and potential interactions of the community and the information universe via collection management. Sometimes it seems that our profession's manner of employing relevant technologies has changed in a negative sense that, whereas we used to adopt new technologies as means to improve performance of a given task, we now seem to be more of a mind to seek out new tasks to which we can apply the ever growing capacity of technology. Be that as it may, current technology can do little more than expedite conventional means of gaining fragmentary glimpses into the community, the user, use, and the collection. For with the application of technology, too often "Information is thrown at problems. The mechanical manipulation of information is believed to guarantee objectivity and untainted judgment—just like the camera and the photograph before it," as Bard and Soderqvist confirm. In this mistaken view, they say, "Subjectivity is synonymous with ambiguity, unnecessary complexity, and arbitrariness. It marks a deviation from the straight line and is therefore the heretical antithesis of technology" (Bard & Soderqvist, 2002, p. 81). Ironically, given the nature of what we are trying to accomplish through collection evaluation, it is subjectivity, not objectivity, that is the key; the collection is of value only as it relates in subjective, cognitive ways to the community. Furthermore, as Michael Hill points out in his book-length synthesis of the influence of information on society, "The problem of trying to conduct research on or with human beings is that very rarely can one set up a rigorous experiment...One has to use statistical methods which yield only results with a known probability of certainty" (Hill, 1999, p. 37). There is no silver bullet.

CONVENTIONS PERSIST

In view of fairly wide agreement within the LIS profession about the general unreliability and practical usefulness of what are labeled here as 'conventional' procedures for evaluation, it is somewhat surprising that we continue looking to them for guidance. One reason may be that we work in an environment that is highly dynamic and challenging, yet equally exhausting and unsettling, so we cling to what we know and to what works at least partially. "The past is a haven to the spirit which is not at ease in the present," Edward Shils reminds us (Shils, 1981, p. 207). More to the point, he argues that human beings tend not to "feel an urgent need to think up something new when there is already a pattern ready at hand. This is especially so when action in accordance with the given pattern has already shown itself to be serviceable" (Shils, 1981, p. 201). One possible explanation for our tenacious grip on these conventional strategies in collection evaluation may simply be that we have been able to get away with doing so because those outside the library seem to be impressed by our ingenious methods and satisfied with the volume of data we can produce. Or maybe they're just bedazzled. The present status of thinking about library collection evaluation can be analogized to the critical juncture leading to change in the putative scientific paradigm, and which Bard and Soderqvist also ascribe to society in general:

> When a large number of anomalies appear there are two possible courses of action. The first is to try to squeeze the new phenomena into the old system of explanations. This is what people have always done within science: patched up and repaired old theories... It holds for a while, bearably, but with time it becomes gradually more apparent that the predictions produced by the old theory are no longer of any use. And then we are confronted unavoidably with option number two: to admit that the old system has had its day, even if there is no new system ready to take its place. This precipitates a crisis. The importance of this crisis is that it signals a need for new thinking" (Bard & Soderqvist, 2002, p. 22).

Some 20 years ago a mantra circulating the business world proclaimed that, instead of attending to doing things the right way, emphasis should be placed on doing the right things. This was a catchy sound bite, intended to drop the jaw in profound epiphany. It made abundant sense since, obviously, it is not very productive to do the wrong things the right way, the stimulus for this insight being that business in that era apparently too often expended resources on going nowhere in terms of its goals. There remains the matter of identifying the right things to do. No one is likely to suggest seriously that there is one right thing to do to evaluate a collection any more than there is one right thing to do to gather information for the purposes of developing that collection. But some things are better than others. In commenting on the disjointedness of public policy development, Neill concludes that "It seems that in public policy issues, the invisible college is lacking" (Neill, 1992, p. 126).[2] The formulation and constant refining of library policy for the management of its collection arguably occupies a more advantageous position than many other public policy issues to benefit from a kind of invisible college planning strategy. Some of its strategic characteristics could be of use to library collection evaluation.

EVALUATION OF THE PROCESS

If the methods LIS has been applying to collection evaluation are generally unsatisfactory, then the issue before us is that of finding a better way to go about it; that is, identifying the right things to do. What is advocated here is that the process followed in collection management, as described above, be made the centerpiece of collection evaluation and supplemented, as deemed useful, by the carefully tailored conventional methodologies that focus on specific segments of the collection and the respective segment of the community it supports. It is unfortunate that collection management in many, if not most, libraries and information centers continues to be relegated to a secondary position as a soft function compared to most others. Soft in the sense that it usually is neither a tightly scheduled function, such as reference, interlibrary loan, and circulation, nor a quantifiable function like cataloging and instruction, nor even a locus determined function as are the aforementioned. A highly labor-intensive responsibility, collection management nonetheless too often is fitted in with other duties as time permits, most often by salvaging the time and energy that remain only after those other duties have been performed. This response to prevailing conditions has been enabled by the rationalizing truism that a collection does grow and assume new shape one way or another, that is to say, whether this happens by means of a purely acquisition-driven model or by means of a systematic process guided by a mission. As a consequence, collection management generally operates too much on borrowed time, and this situation will have to change. Other challenges incurred in the adoption of greater rigor in collection management are addressed below.

Most labor intensive among collection management activities is the liaison function. But to the extent that the liaison function may be formalized and expanded, it will add further demands and an extended dimension of complexity to collection management. If the collection is to represent the reasoned interests of an informed community collaborating with library personnel in the process, then it may be the single most important part of collection management; certainly it is the most influential force in selection. Ideally, collection management proceeds on the basis of collaboration between the community and the library, with the library managing the process. The library gathers intelligence about the community by various means,

most important among them personal interaction with as many representative members as practicable. As an integral component of this process,
collection management librarians keep the community apprised of new developments in the library, foremost among which are changing aspirations,
challenges, opportunities, and limitations. The underlying assumption is
that the library can improve its service by capturing some of the intellectual
capital of the community, particularly its knowledge, judgments, perspectives, values, expertise, insights, and experience about the community that
reside within the community, then introduce that information, which has
been developed within a given context, into the library's planning, policy
making, and procedures. But this must be a process, rather than a project,
for, as Neill reminds us, "Information about the values of others can never
be secure, since values change, not only over long periods but also sometimes overnight, and values held under one situation might not hold under
different circumstances." (Neill, 1992, p. 127).

The library in any setting is immersed in intellectual capital that can be
harnessed to the purposes of library management. Strategic concepts behind
this kind of liaison that informs collection management include stimulating,
learning about, defining, understanding, sharing, and acting upon the intellectual capital of the community. Narrowed to a focus on collection
management, intellectual capital consists of such attributes held by individual members of the host organization as can selectively be of value in
relevant policy, planning, and procedures. These are the principal concepts
of intellectual capital and knowledge management that are directly applicable to library management, in general, but in particular to collection
management.

The organized systematic use of this intellectual capital, which is called
knowledge management and is described primarily in the literature of business, thus concerns itself with the tacit knowledge held by individuals in the
organization, but not contained in databases or documents or any formal
records of the organization. As inferred from her review of the literature on
knowledge management, Mac Morrow finds that it operates on the basis of
knowledge conversion processes that stem from "a view of the organization
as a living organism rather than as a machine for information processing...
Ideals, values, emotions, insights, intuition, and hunches—all highly
subjective—are viewed as an integral part of knowledge" (Mac Morrow,
2001, p. 386).

This process is analyzed further by Herbert Snyder and Jennifer Burek
Pierce (Snyder & Pierce, 2002, p. 492), who emphasize that the conversion of
tacit knowledge held by individuals into an organizational or group asset is

the central purpose of knowledge management, rendering that kind of intellectual capital of great, even though intangible, value to the organization's potential. Mac Morrow adds that management of intellectual capital "encompasses customer relationships, that is, the value of an organization's relationships with the people with whom it does business, the value of processes, the value of trademarks, patents, and other intangible assets" (Mac Morrow, 2001, p. 392) and that the purpose of this is to "understand and exploit the role of knowledge in the process of managing organizations so as to cope effectively with rapid environmental change" (Mac Morrow, 2001, p. 396).

Adoption of this modus operandi in collection management would require maintenance of both formal and informal communications in an ongoing cyclical and substantive process. Insight into the deeper nature of this process can be drawn from Bertalanffy's summary of the systems view of social organizations. In the course of his description of general system theory, he observes that many systems in technology and nature proceed on a basis theorized by Norbert Wiener as 'feedback' in the then emerging field of cybernetics. Bertalanffy recounts that "The theory tries to show that mechanisms of a feedback nature are the base of teleological or purposeful behavior in man-made machines as well as in living organisms, and in social systems" (Bertalanffy, 1968, p. 44).

For the purposes of collection management, select intellectual capital of the host organization, that is to say its tacit knowledge, is the substance of this feedback process. It is found in human relationships that must be based on trust and respect. The process itself, according to business writer Thomas Stewart, is collaborative, customized, and nonlinear, employing "mysterious and almost inarticulate processes of research, alignment, assessment, support, stimulation, connection, storytelling, and judgment. People are trained in the use of explicit knowledge; they are counseled in the development of tacit knowledge" (Stewart, 2001, p. 125). This feedback loop in the system thus infuses into the library a very special kind of information, the community's intellectual capital, which can be garnered only in this way. The process leads to knowledge that helps determine specific collection management decisions because it concurrently provides an ongoing assessment of the collection management function.

The concept of looking to the community or the customer for some answers to our many questions about managing services in their best interests is not limited to the business world or even, within the library, to collection management. In a recent study, Richard Smiraglia traces the development of knowledge organization theory. He characterizes the early period of theory development, when tools of information retrieval began to be designed in the 17th century, as the era of pragmatism and rationalism. This pragmatic beginning prepared the way for a period of empiricism, beginning in the first quarter of the 20th century when patterns of information use began to be observed and analyzed. From that foundation, the current era, characterized by what Smiraglia calls historicist epistemology, emerged in the second half of the 20th century to emphasize the role of the user's cognitive functions in information retrieval. Smiraglia contends that "Epistemology provides us with key perceptual information about the objects of knowledge organization. Each perspective can contribute to understanding; collectively, a balanced perspective can be achieved" (Smiraglia, 2002, p. 344). He concludes that research on the nature of subject searching "suggests that cognitive aspects of user behavior are at least as important as the subject characteristics of the documents represented" (Smiraglia, 2002, p. 346). This line of thinking reaffirms the aforementioned shift of emphasis in LIS perspective from objects to ideas.

THE COLLECTION MANAGEMENT ENVIRONMENT

Anyone at all familiar with the output of the so-called information and knowledge industries knows well that they generate a very dynamic universe. It is characterized by the rapid development and expansion of new fields and the advancement of new modes of information creation and delivery via interconnected and innovative technologies. And all this occurs in the context of a fluctuating economy and an increasingly intense workload in the library. Meanwhile, the community served by the library, regardless of the community's size, is an equally dynamic entity, simply because it is comprised of diverse, intellectually active, human beings who, according to Doyle McCarthy, are swept along by "the 'autonomy' and 'force' of knowledge *in its own right*" (McCarthy, 1996, pp. 19–20; emphasis in the original). Sandra Braman theorizes the reasons behind this social phenomenon: "Because informational products and processes are constitutive of individuals, communities, and societies, they are constantly interacting with the social, cultural, political, economic, and ecological environments in which they are occurring and to which they refer" (Braman, 1995, p. 110). This is not necessarily chaos, but it is a condition of great complexity that constitutes a problem for those in the library who are developing and evaluating collections for the varied intellectual purposes of its community. And there is no simple solution to this problem.

As we have seen, the essence of human social life is change—evolution. The essence of that change lies in the meeting and solving of problems. Problems come from the outside, as a block in life's path, or from the inside, as an innovative idea (the problem being how to put that idea into practice). In either case there is a problem to be solved. If there were a problem-solving theory that could predict success, inevitable, and unvarying success, all the variables would need to be identifiable in order to be taken into consideration in the process of solution. To attempt to identify these variables is to step into a complex world in which the thoughts and emotions and beliefs of individuals are at play in situations where not even all the observable facts can be known. After years of scrutiny in psychology and cognitive science, the method or strategy of how to go about solving problems has been described for many disciplines and fields of work, but there is no theory of problem solving (Neill, 1992, p. 133)[2].

Bearing in mind that the mission of collection management is to maintain an appropriate intellectual congruence of the information universe with the community, it becomes evident that the liaison function can proceed successfully only to the extent that it is conceived and implemented as a highly dynamic process. And given these considerations, it is easily arguable that collection management process is best conducted as ongoing and commensurate with environmental evolution, thereby providing windows of assessment at any point. At the center of such a process is 'feedback' from the community to the library. In Bertalanffy's explanation of the systems view, this constitutes "the homeostatic maintenance of a characteristic state or the seeking of a goal, based upon circular causal chains and mechanisms monitoring back information on deviations from the state to be maintained or the goal to be reached" (Bertalanffy, 1968, p. 46). For collection management, the special value of applying this perspective to assessment lies in the fact that evaluation is both the beginning of the collection management cycle and its end point, because in this scenario evaluation is as integral to collection management as the selection function.

BROADER IMPLICATIONS FOR THE LIBRARY

Because collection management is central to library services and operations, the kind of intellectual synergy described here as drawn from the interactions of collection management and the community has the potential to foster a new library ethos, well beyond the specific functions of collection management. In their book on intellectual capital (IC), Johan Roos and his associates argue that "The concept of IC brings with it a whole new set of values about what is good and bad management, what is the right and the wrong thing to do in corporations" (Roos et al., 1998, p. 151). This benefit should be quite appealing to anyone who believes that the library too often seems to lose sight of the ultimate object of its efforts: its clientele and the community. In assessing present and future characteristics of organizational leadership, Stewart concludes that the successful leader "views business from the customer's perspective and ensures that commitments to customers are met; he creates effective teams, genuinely listens, and inspires people to commit to the organization's vision" (Stewart, 2001, p. 234). What matters in this context, he contends, "is getting the process right—making sure the right people are talking to each other about the right things," and understanding that the job is to "develop capabilities: not to plan the company's actions, but to increase its capacity to act, its responsiveness, its repertoire" (Stewart, 2001, p. 235). Infusion of the community mind into the corporate mind creates the foundation for a successful enterprise. In terms of the practical application of these management principles, Dale Zand, one of the earliest proponents of managing a corporation's intellectual capital, confirms that a group of people with different points of view and the capacity to alter points of view are most likely to solve problems and plan a better future, because "Exchanging ideas with people who think differently than we do stimulates the discovery of new knowledge...The manager in a knowledge organization must take the lead in establishing unconventional groupings. People with different ways of conceptualizing a problem stimulate new approaches to knowledge in each other" (Zand, 1981, p. 17). A collection management program that embraces the concepts and principles advanced by current theorists in relevant aspects of the business world can become one of the most significant influences toward, perhaps even a model for, organizational learning in general within the library.

As great an advantage as that would be, however, it does not represent the full potential of acknowledging and managing the intellectual capital available for use in developing and maintaining the best collection possible. Noted earlier was the definition of the fuller purpose of collection management liaison as the enhancement of mutual understanding between library and community, so the combined entity can collaboratively tailor the collection in the community's interests, while doing so in a way that is manageable by the library. This marketing aspect of collection management liaison contributes in another significant way to building a solid foundation for ongoing and substantive communication. Academic libraries, primarily the larger ones, took important steps in this direction by creating bibliographer positions, beginning especially in the early 1960s. But administration evidently did not provide the sustained guidance and support necessary to realize the potential of the structure that partially was in place. It was a good idea that lacked the necessary theoretical basis and plan, so never was fully realized. But the assignment of a higher priority to the liaison dimension of librarianship supported by a foundation constructed of intellectual capital management concepts can be made successful as well as transportable to all types of libraries. And the library can succeed, not only in managing the collection in a context of more reliable and useful information, but also in strengthening its support from the community. In their study of intellectual capital, Snyder and Pierce contend that its effective management should, indeed, produce that result. (Snyder & Pierce, 2002, p. 482).

Likewise, in his assessment of the deeper and longer-term advantages of the alliance that can be nurtured in this process, Stewart theorizes that knowledge becomes part of what the organization and its clients trade, creating a sharing basis for their association. He concludes that "Companies that learn with their customers (simultaneously teaching them and learning from them) come to depend on each other. Their people and systems— human and structural capital—mesh better than before" (Stewart, 2001, pp. 179–180). This scenario depicts at once the strategy and the spirit of the collaborative environment in which collection management and evaluation would do well to operate.

SUMMARY AND CONCLUSIONS

It would be a monumentally naive oversight not to acknowledge the serious logistical challenges accompanying adoption of the strategy for collection management and its evaluation advocated in this essay. The greatest challenges are associated with the quantity and quality of staff for the purpose, but equally so with the mindset of general library administration. They are broad concerns encompassing many implications. For example, Zand admonishes that since productivity in this mode of operation becomes intangible and resolution uncertain, "It is hard for the manager to know when people are working. It is also extremely difficult for him to know when he has accomplished something. His knowledge has been fused with the contributions of so many others that it is often meaningless to identify his contribution" (Zand, 1981, p. 6). And there are other challenges. Recasting the liaison function on the scale suggested here would likely even prove to be a change both broad and profound enough for the entire library as to constitute an added dimension of organizational activity. But is there a library activity more important than collaborating with the community in its best interests? It is not as though librarianship has failed to adapt to new directions of thinking in the course of the recent past, or that it has steered away from added responsibilities that may first have appeared impossible to accommodate. Quite to the contrary, librarianship has faced such challenges head on, only to discharge them ultimately with distinction. Experience of the past three decades demonstrates clearly that fundamental change, in fact, has been accommodated so frequently with success as to constitute a way of life in most libraries. This has been accomplished by adopting a new and often inevitable goal, identifying a priority for it, and then marshalling the resources, spirit, and ingenuity to implement that priority, which almost always required reordering the priority of responsibilities that had become traditional. If the library of the 20th century was able to introduce and successfully manage a technological infrastructure with its attendant organizational learning and new services, while adapting to greatly reduced purchasing power, surely the library of the present century can accommodate a more meaningful participation of the community in the management of more closely-tailored library services, especially in the management of collections.

Criteria applied to the evaluation of collection management, rather than to the evaluation of the collection per se, would emphasize matters of structure and process: they would place much weight on the presence of collection management policies and the involvement of the community in their creation; on the process for monitoring and revising policy; on the integration of policy in host institution planning and policy creation; and on the quality of communication. The criteria would give much attention to the library personnel who implement policy and manage the process, addressing matters such as quantity and quality of staffing relative to collection management assignments, the overall management structure of collection management, and, of course, the nature of an organized liaison activity. Other categories of criteria would likely develop, as well, as experience with the process grows.

This essay is not about abandoning what it characterizes loosely as the conventional approaches to collection evaluation. It is about employing an evaluation of the process of collection management as the centerpiece of collection evaluation, complemented peripherally by those other methodologies. The latter can thus be applied in a more meaningful context and guided by more realistic expectations, and they can be focused more narrowly for very specific purposes. As it currently is administered, collection evaluation tends to be an intermittent retrospective activity, lacking in vision. "Vision is a clear understanding of what makes the difference between success and failure, and how that translates into behavior and decisions"

(Stewart, 2001, p. 243). Library management, particularly collection management, needs to take leadership in nurturing the relations of library and community by putting greater stock in this idea. Several decades of experience in academic libraries have led me to the conclusion that the ultimate indicator of a library's success is to be found in the level of support accorded it by the host organization, relative to its support capacity.

About three decades ago, in an article on library theory and research, Brenda Dervin advocated refocusing from a set of 'attribute prediction' questions, which measure library activities by demographic or similar categories, to a consideration of the "*kind of view* we need to take of library activities in order to generate useful measures" (Dervin, 1977, p. 17, emphasis added). Questions so guided would include "how the librarian can intervene usefully with users presenting different situational needs at different points in time" and how the librarian can "enter the user's informing processes" (Dervin, 1977, p. 29). Her recommendation for library theory and research is quite pertinent to the reconsideration of collection evaluation recommended here.

Throughout this essay, it has been my intent to convince the reader that we can manage library collections more effectively to the extent that we are able to draw upon the knowledge embedded in the community we serve, doing so through a synergistic process that merges development and evaluation. And if we believe in the value of our service potential, then surely we also believe that the better our community understands what we are *trying* to do, what we *can* do and *cannot* do, and *why*, the more likely it is that adequate support will be forthcoming from the community and the host institution, or at least the kind of support that is based on a better understanding of our services. It is implicit in this essay that these strategies can be applied, in respectively appropriate ways, to all types and sizes of library. The evaluation of collection management is also the ultimate evaluation of the collection itself.

NOTES

1. Similarly, a decade earlier, Gernot (Wersig, 1993, p. 234) had observed a current of fundamental change of motivation in the science dimension of society: "This new kind of science is not primarily driven by the search for complete understanding of how our world works but rather by the need to solve or to deal with problems. Their outcome would not be statements how something works but strategies how to deal with problems. They are strategy-driven problem approaches... Problems occur because of complexities and contradictions."

2. The 'invisible college' is a concept in the sociology of science that describes a closed group at the frontier of their field that shares information in its advancement.

REFERENCES

Bard, A., & Soderqvist, J. (2002). *Netocracy: The new power elite and life after capitalism.* London: Reuters.

Braman, S. (1995). Alternative conceptualizations of the information economy. *Advances in Librarianship, 19,* 99–116.

Dervin, B. (1977). Useful theory for librarianship: Communication not information. *Drexel Library Quarterly, 13*(3), 16–32.

Evans, G. E. (2000). *Developing library and information center collections* (4th ed.). Greenwood Village, CO: Libraries Unlimited.

Hill, M. (1999). *The impact of information on society.* New Providence, NJ: Bowker-Saur.

Mac Morrow, N. (2001). Knowledge management: an introduction. *Annual Review of Information Science and Technology, 35,* 381–422.

McCarthy, E. D. (1996). *Knowledge as culture: The new sociology of knowledge.* London: Routledge.

Neill, S. D. (1992). *Dilemmas in the Study of Information. Exploring the Boundaries of Information Science.* Westport, CT: Greenwood.

Roos, G., Edvinsson, L., & Dragonetti, N. C. (1998). *Intellectual capital: Navigating in the new business landscape.* New York: New York University Press.

Shils, E. (1981). *Tradition.* Chicago: University of Chicago Press.

Smiraglia, R. (2002). The progress of theory in knowledge organization. *Library Trends, 50,* 330–349.

Snyder, H., & Pierce, J. (2002). Intellectual capital. *Annual Review of Information Science and Technology, 36,* 467–500.

Stewart, T. (2001). *The wealth of knowledge. Intellectual capital and the twenty-first century organization.* New York: Currency Press.

Talja, S. (1996). Constituting 'information' and 'user' as research objects: A theory of knowledge formations as an alternative to the information man-theory. In: P. Vakkari, R. Savolainen & B. Dervin (Eds), *Information seeking in context* (pp. 67–80). London: Taylor Graham.

von Bertalanffy, L. (1968). *General system theory. Foundations, development, applications.* New York: Braziller.

Wersig, G. (1993). Information science: The study of postmodern knowledge usage. *Information Processing and Management, 29,* 229–239.

Zand, D. (1981). *Information, organization, and power. Effective management in the knowledge society.* New York: McGraw-Hill.

AN ANALYSIS OF LIBRARY WEB SITES AT COLLEGES AND UNIVERSITIES SERVING DISTANCE EDUCATION STUDENTS

Odin L. Jurkowski

INTRODUCTION

Higher education, and in particular libraries, have changed significantly over the last decade due to the adoption of technological advancements such as the Internet and the World Wide Web. The multitude of ways patrons can interact with librarians and library resources has been only the latest step in a very long process which started with traditional snail mail and the phone. As educators, librarians have always been interested in using new tools to improve services. These services are increasingly being made available to patrons who do not physically enter a library building. This paper looks at what library services are currently being offered to students at a distance in order to better plan for the future.

Distance education has been of increasing importance to higher education and in particular library practitioners. While distance education was not a topic during my time as a student at Dominican University years ago, presently many library science programs around the country such as the Library Education Experimental Program (LEEP) at the University of

Advances in Library Administration and Organization
Advances in Library Administration and Organization, Volume 22, 23–77
Copyright © 2005 by Elsevier Ltd.
All rights of reproduction in any form reserved
ISSN: 0732-0671/doi:10.1016/S0732-0671(05)22002-3

Illinois in Urbana-Champaign are offering courses or entire degrees via a distance. Furthermore, the library science courses I presently teach at Central Missouri State University are either entirely online or hybrids with very few face-to-face class meetings.

Distance education is, however, part of a larger universe, and can be viewed as a sub-field of instructional technology. As defined by Seels and Richey (1994, p. 1) "Instructional Technology is the theory and practice of design, development, utilization, management and evaluation of processes and resources for learning." This definition from The Association for Educational Communications and Technology (AECT) ties together the educational and teaching aspect of academia in which libraries are an important part. As stated by Bateman (2003):

> Of particular interest to academic librarians is the field of educational technology. As educators themselves, they have been using technology for quite some time to educate faculty, staff, and students in information literacy. College and university librarians have also expanded their roles and have enhanced the faculty – librarian relationship by providing faculty support in the use of educational technology (p. 9).

Academic libraries tend to differ from other types of libraries in their approach to serving patrons in that they endeavor to teach students, faculty, and staff how to find information instead of simply providing it for them. By teaching students to be self-sufficient library users, students will be able to become lifelong learners and can function independently in libraries and in life in general. Cognizant of learning theories and the needs of the parent institution, a constructivist approach to serving academic library patrons is an example of the connection between library instruction and classroom instruction. As such, in the college or university environment, patrons of libraries are heavy users of technology.

Distance education involves students, faculty, and staff in a myriad of roles. A widely recognized definition is offered by Moore and Kearsley (1996):

> Distance education is planned learning that normally occurs in a different place from teaching and as a result requires special techniques of course design, special instructional techniques, special methods of communication by electronic and other technology, as well as special organizational and administrative arrangements (p. 2).

A slightly newer definition is offered by Simonson, Smaldino, Albright, and Zvacek (2000): "Distance education is now often defined as institution-based, formal education where the learning group is separated geographically, and where interactive telecommunications systems are used to connect learners, resources, and instructors" (p. 7).

The student in a distance education course naturally requires library services via a distance. The exact amount or the types of services these students require will vary depending on the institution, program, and individual class. To aid in understanding these requirements, the Association of College & Research Libraries (ACRL) (2000) states:

> Library resources and services in institutions of higher education must meet the needs of all their faculty, students, and academic support staff, wherever these individuals are located, whether on a main campus, off campus, in distance education or extended campus programs, or in the absence of a campus at all; in courses taken for credit or non-credit; in continuing education programs; in courses attended in person or by means of electronic transmission; or any other means of distance education (p. 1023).

ACRL also specifically states that "Distance learning library services refers to those library services in support of college, university, or other post-secondary courses and programs offered away from a main campus, or in the absence of a traditional campus, and regardless of where credit is given" (Association of College & Research Libraries, 2000, p. 1023). What those services must consist of will vary from institution to institution. Accrediting agencies, regional and program-specific, as well as other interested parties may encourage certain services, but there are no specific guidelines that detail a set list of minimum requirements. However, in general, the Association of College & Research Libraries (2000) suggests that this include reference assistance, user instruction, interlibrary loan, document delivery, access to reserve materials, adequate service hours, and more.

Distance education may be considered by some as a relatively new development, but in reality it has been around for quite some time. Many of the same services have already been offered in different formats. For instance, remote access to online catalogs is not a new concept. Book catalogs, the forerunners of card catalogs, were an early form of remote access. In the 19th century, a student living miles from the university could find out what the library owned by consulting the book catalog kept in his or her rooming house or study (Kalin, 1991).

Correspondence schools have been around since the 1880s, long before the computer and the Internet (Moore & Kearsley, 1996). Students received most of their materials though the mail. Since many of these students needed library services to complete assignments, librarians often supported these students by compiling printed bibliographies or research guides as well as providing copies of required readings and interlibrary loan services (Cooper, Dempsey, & Vanaja, 1998).

These services grew over time as institutions increased their offerings and required more of their students. Packages mailed to students began to include lecture notes, copies of reading materials, assignments, and other printed resources. Often the students would need to physically access a library, which led to making arrangements between libraries.

Because print resources dominated the library scene, the initial efforts of librarians to meet the needs of students focused on three areas (Derlin & Erazo, 1997, p. 103): "(1) access to printed material and a limited selection of other media such as records and films, (2) assistance in the search for appropriate printed material related to specific topics of interest, and (3) retrieval of printed material for the learner's use." As the traditional library was then still a physical repository of printed material, the library was challenged in performing these functions, being place- and time-bound.

All of this changed with the birth of the Internet in 1969 (Leiner, Cerf, Clark, & Kahn, 2000). The first applications that were developed were textual in their nature due to the limited bandwidth. The first library uses were for tools such as e-mail, gophers, and listservs.

Educators looking for new ways of reaching students looked toward the fledgling Internet. Bibliographic instruction using the Internet appeared in the early 1990s. Fairmont State College began using e-mail to teach bibliographic instruction sessions in 1994 (Burke, 1996), and the University of Illinois Libraries experimented in such offerings at around the same time (Vishwanatham, Wilkins, & Jevec, 1997).

Interaction with students began to change when the web was developed. Today, the library's web site is often viewed as the library in and of itself (Linden, 2000), and it is the student's point of contact from home. However, students from home see these web sites from a slightly different perspective. These students require instruction on what services are provided to them, how to access them, and in which ways personal assistance can be provided. They do not need a building map, but need, instead, to know, how to process interlibrary loan requests.

An interesting note is that all of these changes are actually increasing the need for librarians in order to design these web sites, organize the information, subscribe to indexes, and teach users how to access resources (Laverty, 1997). With more databases, students see an entire world of citations, and they tend to want everything. So the demand for interlibrary loans is actually increasing.

The task we now confront is determining which services are most important to students and where improvements can be made (Cooper et al., 1998). This is an area in which a discrepancy sometimes exists between the perceptions of patrons and those of library and administrative personnel. While much has been written about what services should be offered, little empirical data exists which shows what specifically is being offered, what should be offered, and what students want.

Library instruction is but one of a set of services that distance education must continue to review and improve upon. In the early days of libraries, the situation was quite different. It was not until the 1960s and 1970s that librarians began supplementing one-on-one teaching from the reference desk with classroom instruction (Engle, 1996). As an early adopter of web use, Engle used NCSA Mosaic on his Macintosh and created web pages that were distributed throughout his local network to multiple users simultaneously, one of the first examples of distance learning via the web.

This has led to present-day use of video conferencing (Balas, 2001) and streaming video (Crowther & Wallace, 2001) to interact with distance education students. Caspers (1998) experimented with interactive television as well as one-on-one reference via phone and/or e-mail, and she now uses web tutorials. This is leading towards new ways of reaching distance students, in some instances using full-scale course management software such as WebCT or BlackBoard to further enhance communication between librarians and students (Kesselman, Khanna, & Vazquez, 2000).

SIGNIFICANCE OF THE STUDY/PROBLEM STATEMENT

Little empirical data exists that shows what library services are being offered, what should be offered, and what students want. There is a need for continuing research on the types of services libraries provide to distance education students and what is readily available to students through the library web site.

The initial research questions included:

- What services do academic libraries offer to distance education students?
- How does this vary depending on the amount of distance education that the institutions offer?
- How are distance-education student needs being met? In what ways are the needs of these students assessed?
- How are decisions made for determining what services are provided?

There is literature that talks about how to design a good web site in terms of user interface, usability, esthetics, and other technical and design issues. There are other sub-fields that study what constitutes good library service to students. Similar discussions take place about library service to distance education students, adult learners, and higher education.

This study is the next step after talking about what library services distance education students should have. I have provided a snapshot of what services are actually being provided through academic library web sites today, interviews discussing how some of the decisions relating to what and how these services are offered are made, and student surveys to assess their needs. By looking at current library web sites at academic colleges and universities that serve distance education programs and doing a content analysis with follow-up interviews, I will have shown the variety of services offered, the services provided most often and those just emerging, and how libraries are trying to meet student needs. The results show that certain sizes of institutions offer more or different services than others, and certain services are more prevalent than others. Therefore, I will show that there is no consistency among libraries as to what services they offer, although there are certain services that have become standard.

I will then present information collected from interviews with select individuals involved with the development or oversight of these web sites or libraries in order to better understand the reasons choices have been made and policies put into effect. Student surveys will also provide a more rounded picture, with opinions of the importance and value of library services in real use.

THEORETICAL CONSTRUCT

This research can realistically be viewed from several viewpoints: instructional technology, education, library science, and distance education to name a few. There are components that contain references to theories of feedback, transactional distance, human–computer interaction, user interface, adult learning theory, andragogy, and more. Other areas include grounded theory and phenomenology (Budd, 2001), feedback and self-regulated learning (Butler & Winne, 1995), learning styles and web page design (Holtze, 2000), and information retrieval theory (Buckland, 1988).

A combination of theories can be beneficial (Walster, 1995). However, I have chosen to concentrate on constructivism. Constructivism looks at the role of the individual in building his or her own learning (Walster, 1995). It is a theory that learning builds on prior knowledge and proposes that learners actively construct their own understanding. Constructivism is the belief that individuals using their experiences as a foundation personally construct knowledge from internal representations (Walster, 1995). Library patrons do this as they use tools and services to research specific topics.

From my vantage point, there are two ways of perceiving how constructivism can be used to plan library services for distance education students. The first is expressed in terms of information, viewing the library as a cognitive tool, sometimes referred to as mind tools. The second is stated in terms of instruction from an information literacy viewpoint.

According to Jonassen and Reeves (1996, p. 693) cognitive tools "refer to technologies, tangible or intangible, that enhance the cognitive powers of human beings during thinking, problem solving, and learning. Written language, mathematical notations, and, most recently, the universal computer are examples of cognitive tools." The library web site contains the citations, articles, full-text information, organizational structure, and more that students need. This explains how patrons using library services can construct their own meaning from what they research in the library. Patrons learn as they independently seek out new information that builds upon what they have already discovered. The library becomes the scaffolding students require to grow in their individual fields.

As Moore and Kearsley (1996) point out, most distance education students are adults. Adults thrive in a constructivist atmosphere, and the web is well suited to help adults construct meaning (Wilson & Lowry, 2000). The web is both a rich source of information and a tool to access information. It also accommodates considerable variability in answers and perspectives, and requires personal judgment in determining the relevance and accuracy of information found.

The second main constructivist approach is in terms of library instruction. Librarians can use the medium for teaching patrons about the resources available, what would be appropriate, how to evaluate resources, and use the information found. Here we see the relationship between librarian and learner, and the librarian's role as guide, facilitator, and organizer. This also includes an understanding as to how patrons relate to library services that they see them as counterparts of traditional services that they can access through a web interface (in this case, how to access reference, bibliographic instruction, interlibrary loan, databases, and more in this newest environment). Traditional services are now offered in new and multiple formats. Students must make a cognitive shift in how they approach these similar services from an older print-based medium to newer electronic mediums. From this view we can better plan library instruction and benefit from using constructivist theories.

LIMITATIONS AND ASSUMPTIONS

As in any type of research there were some limitations and assumptions that had to be taken into consideration. To begin with, due to the nature of the medium, the research had to be conducted in as short a time frame as possible. Web sites constantly change, so this is effectively a snapshot of the things were at a specific point in time. Coding errors were also a possibility (Dewey, 1999). Other errors may arise from information buried deep in the site or from disorganization. This was limited as much as possible due to the fact that the author, a professional and experienced librarian, did all the coding. Furthermore, it was assumed that, if the researcher could not find the information in a reasonable amount of time, then the patron most likely would not have found it either. Finally, at the end of the study it was discovered that a few errors had occurred during coding. This, however, reflects the diversity of approaches and real-life situations that would occur.

There was also the possibility that some of these websites may have had certain information behind a password-protected section that the coder would not have access to. Studies have shown that librarians post as much information as possible so that answers readily available and pressure can be taken off library staff (Quinn, 1999). Furthermore, most often the only items behind password protection are citation and full-text databases and electronic reserves documents. Usually, these are accessed through a publicly viewable web page that states what is available and then prompts the user for a password. There were, however, two instances where a fully online institution had to be removed from the list during preliminary research.

The number of web sites to be evaluated was also limited. This required a sampling of possible institutions. The number was adequate to get an overall picture of the current status at colleges and universities, and was randomly chosen from different states around the country, from varying sizes of student populations, and from different types of institutions. The interview process was meant to supplement what was found in the quantitative analysis and a representation of the varying types of institutions selected.

SUMMARY

As individual courses and complete programs continue to be offered to students off campus, libraries have to redirect resources and redefine how patrons' needs can be met. This paper is meant to provide some basic answers: What library services are being offered to users at a distance? How are libraries determining the types of services to offer? Does the amount of distance education the parent institution offers impact library services? What other questions will arise after the research is completed? What are library services needs of distance education students, and do they mirror the needs that librarians believe them to be?

LITERATURE REVIEW

This research began with literature reviews that approached library web sites as sources of information. These are studies that used content analysis to study or evaluate web sites from various perspectives. This was followed by literature that approached the topic from an instructional viewpoint. From a constructivist perspective it can be seen how these two approaches can provide different ways of meeting student needs.

Library Web Sites as Sources of Information

There has been some research similar in approach to this study. They have involved the same methodology and have focused on web sites and libraries. These studies have looked at the types of features that are offered through library web sites. One such study was a content analysis of Ohio public library web sites (Mason, 1998). This was a study of 113 sites, with organization, scope, and presentation of links arranged topically. It basically showed that these libraries were at different stages of creating effective web sites. It is of interest to note that in her literature review, Mason found relatively few studies involving content analysis of web sites (Bates & Lu, 1997; Burt, 1997; Clyde, 1996; Neth, 1998). The coding sheet that Mason produced was fairly simple and short, but it demonstrated how one could be developed. It provided an example of approaches for evaluating web sites. Some of the questions asked were about external links, the organization of ready reference links, the categories of links, the number of links, annotations, and more (Mason, 1998).

Another interesting study was a content analysis of the web sites of the fifty state library agencies of the United States of America (Berendsen, 1998). This was a study of 50 web sites in order to see what the State Library of Ohio's web site should contain. The researcher listed 28 criteria on their coding sheet and from it created a frequency table. The research objectives were to aid in determining what content and design features the State Library of Ohio should include or exclude in its revised web site, and to identify content and design features of web sites of a particular genre (state library agencies). Their coding sheet asked about OPAC links, search engines, what's new information, mail to links, counters, internal search engines, address, hours, forms, mission statement, and more (Berendsen, 1998).

Meyers (2000) analyzed 37 United States botanical and horticultural library web sites. The intent was to determine the elements included in these web sites, to evaluate the sites based on their design, and to compare those results based on library type in order to provide a resource for future site development. Meyers' review of the literature revealed little current published research on similar studies, although there was an abundance of literature relating to web site design and evaluation. The data were analyzed in a standard frequency table. This was also done separately for each type of library, then for four different categories depending on size of collection, and then for four different categories depending on size of web site.

There were several studies that were related to this paper in one way or another. They each had interesting aspects to them and touched on some of the same issues, problems, areas, or topics. Tolppanen, Miller, and Wooden (2000) examined the web sites of 133 academic libraries from medium-sized universities. They examined all of their features in order to determine the core characteristics of the web sites for libraries at universities with populations of 6,000 to 13,000 students. They determined that the navigational and design aspects of library web sites need to be improved, and greater use of online instruction, tutorials, and virtual tours would be worthwhile endeavors to supplement traditional face-to-face bibliographic instruction. Dewald (1999), on the other hand, examined 20 web-based library tutorials to look at instruction over the web that focuses on one single area of distance learning. She determined that online library instruction should not completely substitute for personal interaction with students. Independent learning has its place, but librarians still need to be in contact in one form or another with students in order to have instant feedback and a transaction of ideas. Library tutorials were lacking in the amount of interaction involved.

Janes, Carter, and Memmott (1999) looked at 150 randomly selected academic libraries to answer two questions: what proportion of libraries conduct digital reference services, and what are the characteristics of those digital reference services? They also tried to explain how they would handle possible limitations if they could not find the information on the web site. They decided that if the searcher could not find such a service within 5 min, they would stop searching. They felt that if they could not find it in five minutes, then neither could a patron.

Agingu (2000) sought to determine how useful the library web sites of historically Black colleges and universities are as tools for disseminating information and providing services to users. They studied 65 web sites and 12 different items. They found that these libraries are lagging behind other libraries in the amount of services they provide, and do not have the variety of resources other institutions offer, such as web-based databases, electronic books and journals, and web-interfaced catalogs. It was recommend that parent institutions increase support for the library and hire additional staff with appropriate technical expertise.

Clyde (1996) did an early survey looking at library use of the Internet in Iceland and the ways in which libraries were using the web to provide information via a home page. This study consisted of a content analysis of home pages of public libraries and school libraries in 13 different countries.

King (1998) took a different approach. She examined the home pages of 120 ARL (Association of Research Libraries) libraries. She meant to present a picture of the types of elements that ARL library web pages most often incorporated. This included details about: backgrounds, document headers, document footers, document body (graphics, links, and text), page length, number of steps to library home page from parent institution web site, and domain name servers.

Stover and Zink (1996) examined 40 higher education library web sites at the time that the web was a new tool in libraries. They looked at some of the basics: number of links on home page, if the author was identified, how many screens did the home page comprise, how many bytes were there in the largest image, how many images were included, was there a link to the university or college home page, were there any typographical errors, when was the page last updated, was there a mechanism for comments, and was there a statement of purpose. In the end they concluded that many home pages were badly designed and neglected fundamental principles of information organization.

Library Web Sites as Sources of Instruction

From an instructional perspective, academic librarians and library web sites provide a large number of services to students. They provide instruction on how to find and use library resources. As the amount of information continues to grow and the tools for finding and obtaining information changes, this becomes an increasingly daunting task. This section will describe some of the studies that have touched on these perspectives as well as some general papers that describe the types of services that libraries should provide.

Cooper et al. (1998) from DePaul University sent out an informal e-mail survey and followed it up with telephone interviews with six faculty. They also monitored four electronic discussion lists, and attended panel presentations at conferences on distance learning. They found that faculty expectations about library skills that distance learners develop are founded on older assumptions about how students learn to use a library. Faculty expect distance learners to use an academic library, but then they make no distinction between the skills needed by a student on campus and one at a remote site. Most faculty believe that a combination of handouts (developed by themselves or by librarians) are sufficient to address students' needs in negotiating their options for library use.

Taylor (2000) surveyed library webmasters about aspects of their roles and job tasks. This survey was intended to discover how decisions were made and responsibilities were assigned to maintain the library web site. They found ($N = 82$) that the responsibilities for decision making about content were most often shared with managerial librarians, other librarians, and web committees, and were based on written policies developed by the library and the policies of the parent institution. Respondents reported problems with library committees, the slowness of decision-making, ill-defined roles, and concern that people were given responsibility without authority.

Stover (2000) completed a qualitative study to ascertain the opinions and attitudes of librarians toward the Internet as a tool for more productive reference services. They used a questionnaire on their web site and announced it on listservs. This study supported using both qualitative and quantitative aspects in unison, as their surveys included both Likert scale questions and open-ended essay questions.

Much of the related literature dealing with library web sites and distance library services is based on the experiences of the authors of the various studies and their opinions. These writings are based on day-to-day operations of those in the field, observations of what's going on around us and reflections from speaking with other practitioners. While not as rigorous as research projects, these papers do provide insights into the general perception of current practice.

So what are the library needs of distant learners? From one perspective the needs are the same for all library users regardless of location (Rodrigues, 1996). Distance learners need the same services as traditional students. They still need services such as circulation, interlibrary loan and document delivery, reference, and databases (Linden, 2000). They also need instruction in finding, evaluating, and using library resources. The differences, however, lie in the user's need to rely on technology for communication and access and the arrangements used to compensate for the distance between the library and its patrons. Sometimes the descriptions of services outlined in the literature lead to a bit more detail. There are specific services that distance learners should expect from their libraries, and there is a need for additional technology and/or organization to make services available to off campus clients that is distinctly different from those required to address traditional needs. Clients studying at distance need:

- the ability to search periodical indexes, abstracts, CD-ROMs, and bibliographic services such as ERIC;
- the ability to electronically check out books and renew them over the telephone (preferably toll free);
- the electronic delivery of photocopies, the results of literature searches, and government documents;
- microfiche duplication;
- access to answers to research questions;
- access to tables of contents from professional journals;
- the ability to internally track and deliver all interlibrary loan services;
- an electronic feedback system.

Furthermore, these distance learners want to know how to log on to the web site from their PCs at home or work, to make database selections, to conduct expanded database searches, and to obtain guidance as to which resources work best under which situations. They do not want to read manuals, but they do want access to encyclopedias, dictionaries, periodical full-text articles, catalogs, reviews, biographies, statistics, and information on how to evaluate authors, books, journals, and web sites (Niemi, Ehrhard, & Neeley, 1998).

Some of the literature goes beyond simply talking about these ideas and is based on new research. Some of this is tangential, providing complementary information and insight into the research process involved with libraries, web sites, and academia.

Studies such as one done by Pealer and Dorman (1997) have also gone further into evaluation of web sites in terms of content (currency, references, and readability), authorship (author credentials, bias), purpose, and esthetics (style, fonts, graphics, and layering). Other studies have been more extensive. Cohen and Still (1999) examined 50 library home pages at

Ph.D. – granting institutions and 50 at two-year colleges. Looking at web sites as information tools, reference tools, research tools, and instructional tools, they wanted to see how they fit into the structure of the parent institution and how well the library web site reflected the college/university.

Curl, Reynolds, and Mai (2000) studied asynchronous credit courses in libraries. Purdue University offered a course titled Information Strategies using WebCT and Subramanyam's circular model of the evolution of scientific information as the framework. They found a correlation between frequency of visits and grades earned, that students who used their own computers did better than those who used only computer labs, that computer skills that students brought to class were uneven, that students liked the flexibility, and that cooperative and collaborative learning was evident.

An interesting side note to this literature was that Lee and Teh (2000) found that studies of academic library web sites either exclusively used quantitative analyses or qualitative methods, concluding that there appears to be a lack of a mixed-method approach for the evaluation of academic library web sites that integrated the results of both kinds of studies. Therefore, this study was designed to add to the literature in terms of both research methodology and the specifics of library services to distance education students.

RESEARCH METHODOLOGY

The methods used in this research comprise three different approaches. A content analysis was completed to provide a quantitative perspective, and personal interviews and surveys were completed to provide additional perspectives. These interviews and surveys were completed in order to provide insight into the differences (or the lack of differences) found among library web sites and to determine how these websites are meeting the needs of distance education students. The surveys offered a student viewpoint. This section begins with a brief explanation of content analysis and then describes the research design and how the study was conducted.

Content Analysis

Content analysis is a research methodology used to quantify text, terms, and ideas within written documents. Allen and Reser (1990) describe it as a family of research methods that attempts to identify and record the meaning of documents and other forms of communication in a systematic approach. Most often used in a strict quantitative fashion, a large subpopulation of research has been using the term in a more general sense, not any less systematic but more inferential in nature.

Originally used for examining textual literature in newspapers and other fixed forms, it is now also used to objectify and organize electronic media such as web sites. Content analysis of traditional media, such as newspapers and broadcast media, assume some linearity or at least commonly accepted sequencing of messages. Hypertext by its very nature changes this approach; each person interacts with web sites in different ways, and, therefore, the final results may vary (McMillan, 2000). The rapid growth and change of the web also leads to potential problems in the third stage of content analysis, data collection, and coding.

One of the problems with looking at web sites is their dynamic and changing nature. Bauer & Scharl (2000) gives three possible options to sidestep potential shortfalls. The first approach is to complete a snapshot analysis. This allows a static view similar to traditional print-based media. Using this method, researchers analyze a large number of web sites at a given time. This allows comparison of individual criteria and the clustering of sites by any number of qualifications. The second approach is a longitudinal analysis, in effect a series of snapshot analyses allowing the researcher to see trends. This approach takes advantage of the dynamic nature of the web. The third option is a comparative analysis. By comparing web sites from one institution with those of competitors or similar types of institutions, the researcher can make note of the relative performance of the sites they are studying. This study uses both the first and the third options.

Krippendorff (1980, p. 21) defines content analysis as "a research technique for making replicable and valid inferences from data to their context." There are usually four steps. The first is data making: collecting data in an analyzable form which others would be able to re-evaluate. Text would be collected, speech or sounds would be recorded and then transcribed, and a collection would be formed. Second comes data reduction in order to ease computational efforts. It may be statistical, algebraic, or simply a question of omitting what turns out to be irrelevant detail. Third is inference, the reason for any content analysis, the task of finding relationships. Fourth is analysis. This is the identification and representation of patterns that are noteworthy and statistically significant.

Once the data is collected and organized, a statistical analysis is done in order to pull out important trends. According to Krippendorff (1980), the most common form of representation of data, serving primarily the summarizing function of analysis, is in terms of frequencies: absolute frequencies, such as the numbers of incidents found in the sample, or relative frequencies, such as the percentages of the sample size. Volume measures such as column inches, time, space, or other frequency-based indices have the same status in content analysis.

Interviews and Surveys

Interviews are often conducted in order to provide more background information or substance to a numerical finding. Explanations of why certain decisions were made as well as what elements or were not included in the website can then be added to the final analyses. This is meant to complement the data previously found. Bogdan and Biklen (1998) argue that this combination of approaches is ideal. Miles and Huberman (1994) state that qualitative data can be used to supplement, validate, explain, illuminate, or reinterpret quantitative data gathered from the same subjects or site. Indeed, combining quantitative and qualitative analyses seems to provide the best picture. A combination of numbers and words are both needed to really understand the world (Miles & Huberman, 1994).

It is not feasible to interview every single librarian that would fit in this study. Therefore, some type of sampling must be done. According to Maxwell (1996), purposeful sampling is often ideal for small samples. In this type of strategy, particular settings, persons, or events are selected deliberately in order to provide important information that cannot be obtained as well from other choices. Miles and Huberman (1994) describe a similar type of sampling that they call stratified purposeful. For this study, this method seems ideal, as it illustrates subgroups and facilitates comparisons.

However, this study has gone one step further. As is often true of qualitative methods, the data were also analyzed inductively. It could then be said that the research is grounded in the data (Bogdan & Biklen, 1998). This type of methodology is more open-ended, with probing questions yet flexible enough to develop as more information is gained as opposed to a preset and inflexible plan.

Procedure: Quantitative Content Analysis of Web Sites

The first part of this research consisted of a quantitative content analysis. Seventeen diverse library web sites were initially selected. While many of the studies found in the literature included a greater number of samples, they did not also include interviews and surveys. Furthermore, larger studies usually used smaller sets of content items for analysis.

Therefore, a smaller set of web sites was used in a more complex analysis and in combination with additional methods for this study. The web sites chosen were categorized by the amount of distance education offered to students: fully online institutions, traditional institutions now offering complete degrees via a distance, institutions offering at the most individual courses via a distance, and institutions not yet offering distance education to provide some comparisons. This initial number was realistically feasible with the understanding that additional sites would have been reviewed if the results warranted more data collection.

All of the institutions selected are regionally accredited, according to Peterson's (2002) Guide to Distance Learning Programs. Table 1 lists the library web sites that were coded for this study.

Table 1. Library Web Sites Coded.

Institution	URLs
(1) Primarily distance education institution	
(2) Full programs/degrees offered via distance education	
(3) Single courses offered via distance education	
(4) Little to none distance education	
(1) City University	http://www.cityu.edu/library/home.asp
(1) Nova Southeastern University	http://www.nova.edu/library/main/
(1) Touro University International	http://support.tourou.edu/virtual_libraries/index.htm
(1) The Union Institute	http://www.tui.edu/vermontcollege/templates/about_us.php?article_id = 39
(1) Walden University	http://www.lib.waldenu.edu/
(2) Central Missouri State University	http://library.cmsu.edu/
(2) Ferris State University	http://www.ferris.edu/library/
(2) Illinois Institute of Technology	http://www.gl.iit.edu/
(2) University of Illinois	http://www.outreach.uiuc.edu/aolibrary/
(2) University of Wisconsin–Madison	http://www.library.wisc.edu/
(3) Central Methodist College	http://www.cmc.edu/library
(3) Delta State University	http://library.deltastate.edu/
(3) Kentucky State University	http://www.kysu.edu/library/default2.html
(3) Northern Illinois University	http://www.niu.edu/libraries.html
(3) Southeast Missouri State University	http://library.semo.edu/
(4) Dominican University	http://domweb.dom.edu/library/
(4) Saint Anthony College of Nursing	http://www.sacn.edu/library

The coding of web sites was done during the month of September 2002. This time frame was necessitated due to the fact that web sites change frequently. This study was, therefore, a snapshot of specific services at that point in time. The researcher did all of the coding. Those items not found within a reasonable amount of time, five minutes, were checked off as not existing. In order to gain a better understanding of the experiences that the library users face, this researcher wanted to approach the sites from a student's perspective and coded all of the sites himself.

The coding was accomplished by browsing and searching selected library web sites, and then adding results to an electronic coding sheet. These results were then able to be moved into other statistical software and manipulated for analysis.

The coding sheet was developed to list the types of services that are offered (Table 2). The review of the literature provided some types of ideas

Table 2. Coding Sheet.

Institution	Name
-	URL
-	Date accessed
-	Type of institution (http://nces.ed.gov/IPEDS/COOL/Search.asp)
-	Size of institution (http://nces.ed.gov/IPEDS/COOL/Search.asp)
-	Degree or programs offered via distance
General information	Mission/vision
-	News (what's new)
-	New acquisitions
-	Internal search engine
-	Site map
-	Webmaster
-	Employee listing
-	List of subject specialists
-	Policies
Distance education	Page for distance learners
	Specified librarian for DE
	Strategies for distance learning effectiveness
Reference	Phone, toll free
	E-mail
	electronic form
	Chat
	Video conferencing
	Consultation, research assistance
	Online reference materials

Table 2. (*Continued*)

Institution	Name
Bibliographic instruction	Tutorials
	Class (credit/non-credit)
	Links to evaluation of resources
Interlibrary loan	Information about
	Materials mailed
	Electronic forms
Circulation	Books delivered
	Print materials copied and delivered
	Book renewal form
	Joint borrowers card
	Arrangement with other libraries
Databases	Indexes and full-text
	Online catalog
	E-books
	Journal holdings
	Subject web sites
Reserves	Electronic reserves
Feedback	Electronic feedback mechanism
	FAQ
Password protected site	Description

to think about, and an initial pre-review of library web sites provided some initial insight. The coding sheet was also left open to modification as the study progressed with the option to go back and re-review web sites if a major function was not initially included.

Procedure: Qualitative Interviews and Surveys

The second part of this research consisted of interviews and surveys. The researcher contacted four libraries after the quantitative analysis was completed. These sites were selected from representatives of web sites with low, medium, and high degree of service elements. This provided variation and explanation for the findings and also a better idea of what kinds of decisions were made at these institutions.

The interviews were conducted in October 2002. The telephone conversations were recorded so that transcripts of the conversations could be made. The interviews were open to any topic that the respondents wanted to discuss. The following is a generalized description of those interviewed during October 2002:

- Assistant Professor of Information Services at a small, private Midwestern college
- Distance Education Librarian at a medium-sized public university
- Head of Distance Education and Instructional Library Services at a large, private university
- Instructional Services Librarian at a large, public university

With this approach, questions and topics for discussion were developed prior to and after quantitative data analysis. Preparation for the interviews evolved as information was gathered and the interviews themselves were flexible depending on what the interviewee was willing and interested in discussing. Once the interviews were completed the transcripts were coded and analyzed for key words and ideas. Either themes were to emerge or the diversity of responses was to instead show a diverse set of approaches from libraries. Regardless of the specific results, additional interviews would have been considered if warranted

The third part of this research consisted of surveys of students enrolled in distance education courses. These surveys were conducted from the list of institutions where librarians were previously interviewed. Six faculties from three different institutions shared the survey with their students. This was done to gauge the satisfaction students have with their library web sites and overall distance services, and to provide a learner-based perspective.

Contacts were made at these institutions to find faculty who were currently teaching a distance education course. Surveys were distributed to students through their teachers by directing them to a web-based survey form. The form was created and posted on the author's personal web space at Central Missouri State University. The electronic form simplified the process, allowing immediate anonymous feedback from students without the costs and time involved with paper surveys.

A pilot study was conducted in September 2002 in order to gauge the amount of time that would be involved with a full study, to insure that the web-based survey form was working properly, and make sure that the methods chosen were feasible. Contacts for student surveys and library interviews were made through institution web sites.

CONCLUSION

Using both quantitative and qualitative approaches, this study consisted of a content analysis, interviews, and student surveys. The data collected will show in the next section what services are offered on academic library web sites, how those decisions are made, how student needs are being met, and in what ways these needs are assessed. The web sites chosen represent institutions that offer varying degrees of distance education to student populations, ranging from schools that only offer programs online, to others that offer a select number of degree programs or only a few courses. It is difficult in today's academic world to find institutions that do not offer at least a little distance education, and this trend may well grow in the future as the majority of schools will offer some combination of face-to-face courses and programs with other distance courses and programs. With this increase in distance learners, libraries will be fully involved in the distance world.

FINDINGS

The findings for this research were broken down into three main areas by the type of research conducted. This was done because the research required a specific order to be followed. The first was a quantitative approach using a content analysis of academic library web sites. This was followed by interviews of library personnel from a selection of those analyzed institutions, and then surveys of students enrolled in distance education courses from that narrower list.

Content Analysis

As the content analysis was conducted for the library web sites, the results were maintained in a spreadsheet file. This raw data was then available for manipulation and transfer to SPSS statistical software.

The first calculations conducted were to simply add up all of the individual content analysis items found for each institution. Table 3 shows this summary arranged for each institution from highest to lowest number of items found. This overview provides a snapshot of the range of variation from library to library and an easy way to visualize which institutions seemed to have the strongest overall student services.

Table 3. Total Number of Content Analysis Items Found for Each
Institution Library Web Site Evaluated.

Institution	Type of Institution[a]	Sum of Items
University of Illinois	2	31
Ferris State University	2	31
Illinois Institute of Technology	2	30
University of Wisconsin–Madison	2	29
Central Missouri State University	2	24
Northern Illinois University	3	24
Nova Southeastern University	1	22
Delta State University	3	22
Walden University	1	19
Southeast Missouri State University	3	19
Saint Anthony College of Nursing	4	15
Kentucky State University	3	13
The Union Institute	1	12
City University	1	12
Dominican University	4	8
Central Methodist College	3	8
Touro University International	1	6

[a]1 – Primarily distance education institution; 2 – full programs/degrees offered via distance
education; 3 – single courses offered via distance education; 4 – little to no distance education.

This table shows that there was a broad range of features found. The
highest was 31 items at both the University of Illinois and Ferris State
University, and the lowest was 6 at Touro University International. The
table also shows that there was no overall major grouping or standard, as
there appeared to be an even distribution from high to low with no large gap
or jump from one extreme to the next.

The next way of looking at the data involved finding the mean for each of
the content analysis items evaluated (Table 4). The mean is the arithmetic
average of the scores in a distribution ($\sum X_i/n$). These calculations were
done using SPSS. With an average institution size of 10,955 students, the
mean shown represents the percentage of institutions in the study that had
these features on their web sites.

The mean percentage of how often the item was found ranged from 100 to
0 percent. The only item that was consistently found 100% of the time was
online indexes and full-text databases. The items found 0% of the time were
pages that detailed strategies for distance learning effectiveness which would
be useful for distance learners to refer to, and video conferencing available
for reference and research purposes. Although these two items were not

Table 4. Mean Percentage of Content Analysis Items Found.

Content Analysis Item	Mean (%)
Indexes and full-text	100
Online reference materials	88.2
Online catalog	88.2
Employee listing	82.4
Journal holdings	82.4
Subject web sites	82.4
E-mail	76.5
ILL information about	76.5
ILL electronic forms	76.5
Policies	70.6
Tutorials	64.7
Webmaster	58.8
ILL materials mailed	58.8
Internal search engine	52.9
Page for distance learners	52.9
Book renewal form	52.9
Arrangement with other libraries	52.9
Electronic feedback mechanism	52.9
News (what's new)	47.1
Electronic Form	47.1
Books delivered	47.1
E-books	47.1
New acquisitions	41.2
Phone, toll free	41.2
Print materials copied and delivered	41.2
Site Map	35.3
Specified librarian for DE	35.3
Class (credit/non-credit)	35.3
Joint borrowers card	35.3
Mission/vision	29.4
List of subject specialists	29.4
Consultation, research assistance	29.4
Electronic reserves	29.4
Chat	23.5
FAQ	17.6
Links to evaluation of resources	5.9
Strategies for distance learning effectiveness	0
Video conferencing	0

found at any of the institutions analyzed, they had been found at other institutions during preliminary literature reviews and observation of sites. If the sample size was increased they might have been found in use, yet would certainly still have been at the bottom of the list. The table, therefore, shows which items are most common. The items least in use would be areas of improvement for institutions not yet providing those services or information.

Table 5 shows the percentage of items found overall for each type of institution. This was done by taking the individual items found and averaging them with others within their grouping. This provides a breakdown by the amount of distance education offered.

Surprisingly, institutions that were primarily distance education institutions did not have the strongest library web sites. The strongest were institutions that offered degrees from a distance followed by those that offered only individual courses from a distance. This was then followed by the primarily distance education institutions and then those that are not yet offering any distance education.

Table 6 provides a look at the most common content analysis items found by specific type or amount of distance education offered. Within each of the four categories, these items were found 100% of the time. This provided a different perspective, with the most common features being found varying among the different types of institutions. While there was consistency found for indexes and full-text databases, there were other areas that tended to differ.

Table 7 shows some of the most interesting correlations found after reviewing the data. Significant nonparametric Spearman correlations were found using SPSS for the content analysis items of amount of distance education offered and for size of institution. This is a measure of the relationship between two variables $(1 - 6 \sum d^2/n(n^2 - 1)$. It was found that the more that distance education was offered, the more likely that certain features were available on the web site: circulating books delivered to the student, reference available via e-mail, and interlibrary loan materials mailed directly to the students home instead of having to pick them up in person. As for the size of the institution, the larger the institution the more likely that it would provide the following services: books could be renewed online by student, reference librarians would be available for consulting, bibliographic instruction classes were offered in one form or another, bibliographic instruction tutorials were available online, synchronous chat software was in use for reference transactions, and most importantly the overall sum of content analysis items would be high.

Looking further into correlations, it was found that there appeared to be no significant correlation between the amount of distance education offered and the overall sum of items found (0.076). There was also no significant correlation between the amount of distance education offered and the size of the institution (0.238). What this appears to show, then, is that the amount

Table 5.   Percentage of Content Analysis Items Found at Each Type of
Institution.

Type of Institution	Items Found (%)
1. Primarily distance education	37.4
2. Offers degrees from a distance	76.3
3. Offers courses from a distance	43.2
4. Does not yet offer any distance education	30.3

Table 6.   Content Analysis Items that were found at 100% of the
Institutions by Institution Type.

Content Analysis Items	Amount of Distance Education			
	1. Primarily	2. Degrees	3. Courses	4. None
Indexes	X	X	X	X
E-mail	X	X		
News		X		
New acquisitions		X		
Internal search ENGINE		X		
Webmaster				X
Employee listing		X		X
Policies		X	X	
Page for DE students		X		
Online reference materials		X	X	
BI tutorials		X		
ILL info		X		
ILL forms		X		
Books renewed online		X		
Online catalog		X	X	
Journal holdings		X	X	
Subject web sites		X		X

of distance education offered does not make as much of a difference as to
the amount of services and information provided to distance education
students via a library web site as does the actual size of the institution. This
means that just because an institution offers distance education courses and
degrees does not mean that the library has necessarily increased or improved
its services to meet the needs of distance learner. The factor that seems to
make the most difference is simply the size of the institution, which may
relate to a larger staff and larger budgets. Those institutions with the largest

Table 7.   Significant Correlation Content Analysis Items for Amount of
Distance Education Offered and Size of Institution.

Content Analysis Items	Amount of Distance Education Offered	Content Analysis Items	Size
Circ books delivered	0.575	Renew books online	0.650**
Ref E-mail	0.574	Sum	0.618**
Ill materials mailed	0.507	Ref consult	0.606**
		BI class	0.603**
		BI tutorial	0.553
		Ref chat	0.510

Correlation is significant at the 0.05 level (2-tailed).
**Correlation is significant at the 0.01 level (2-tailed).

student populations tend to have the most features on their web sites. Figures 1 and 2 graphically demonstrate the correlation between size of institution and the sum of items found as well as the amount of distance education offered and the sum of items found, respectively. Figure 1 shows a plot of the size of each institution in regards to the number of students enrolled with the sum of their web site features from the coding sheet. SPSS software added a line showing the correlation and how it increased with institution size.

Figure 2 shows a similar plot with the same sum of features found, but with the amount of distance education offered. This time, no correlation was found, showing that the items were not related. The amount of distance education offered made no difference in the total number of web site features found.

From these results from the content analysis we have seen that there is an apparent lack of preparation by colleges and universities serving distance education students in terms of library services. Those larger schools with naturally larger budgets and staff tended to have stronger library web sites and services. In the next section, we will see that interviews and surveys found some additional issues.

Interviews

A total of four phone interviews were conducted during the month of October 2002, the first being a pilot study. All of those interviewed readily answered all of the questions I asked. The first, we'll call Maria, is Professor and Instruction Services Librarian at a large public university. The

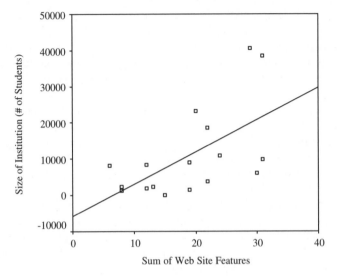

Fig. 1. Graph of Size of Institution Versus Sum of Web Site Features (Produced in SPSS).

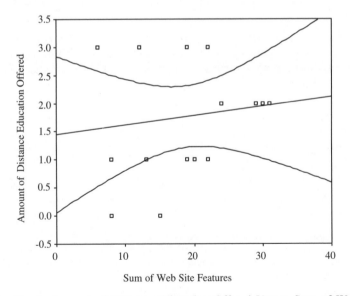

Fig. 2. Graph Amount of Distance Education Offered Versus Sum of Web Site Features (Produced in SPSS).

second, Sarah, is Head of Distance Education and Instructional Library Services at a primarily distance education university and has an Ed.D. in Educational Technology. The third, Kathy, is Assistant Professor of Information Services at a smaller college library and has multiple duties. The fourth, Paula, is Distance Education Librarian at a smaller state university.

The first point discovered came across immediately at the beginning of the interviews. There is quite a variety of ways that libraries are arranged and staffed to support distance education students, and there is still a good deal of flux as the environment continues to change. One librarian seemed to have a straightforward position in responsibilities and title. This new position, which is actually focused on a single purpose, has only been in existence for 10 months. The incumbent has been there 3 years after completing her MLS and previously worked as an Instructional Services Librarian. Other libraries still blend these positions together and have not yet increased staffing. This requires librarians to split their time between multiple duties and may not have the luxury of developing any one area as an expertise.

> Maria: I'm library instruction services librarian so I'm over library instruction and information literacy. And I'm also the coordinator for library services for distance education.

Other libraries have unusual circumstances and arrangements. Take, for instance, the combined academic and public library. While the distance education librarian works primarily with distance education students, there are still additional issues that she must deal with.

> Sarah: My title's head of distance and instructional library services... The library specifically is the library research and information technology center and is a joint use facility between the university and...Public Library System, and, as a result we (my department) do the bibliographic instruction for on campus, online, and distance students.

Finally, one smaller library was forthright and stated how many different responsibilities can be given to each person. She has the opportunity to really do the work of several positions.

> Kathy: I work as reference librarian. I also do the systems stuff which really is not very much... We have very little systems work to do anymore. I do maintain, developed and maintain the library's web page, in addition to many other duties here on the campus. We're a small school. We have to wear lots of hats.

The complexity of some of these institutions can mean that there are wide-ranging groups of people involved with providing services to distance education students. Smaller libraries may take on more responsibility, committees may range from informal to formal, and different people on the respective campuses may have a voice. Some libraries are making changes and adding staff.

> Sarah: Now we have a part-time person who deals with the day-to-day issues of web maintenance, but she's just overwhelmed and we are in the process of interviewing for a webmaster position. But I think a lot of the decisions about how it's going are more committee based.

> Interviewer (I): So that would mean you have in place policies and procedures and guidelines for...

> Sarah: I don't know so much of written down policies, I mean we've got policies for how we deal with the public. I don't think we have written policies in the department or the library, but the university has policies that say what colors we can use, what fonts we can use and so forth.

Other libraries have more internal structure and make decisions themselves.

> Kathy: I assume if you're going to say do you have a committee, we have our staff. And there's like six of us, seven of us that are full-time library staff.

> I: So it's like an informal committee?

> Kathy: Yes, it's an informal group process. I manage and maintain it.

> Libraries may also reach out to other departments on campus but do so in different ways. This interaction can take the shape of a variety of forms.

> Paula: There's not really a committee. It's basically just been me working with people. The bulk of our classes are in the university center for extended learning, and I've kind of worked in conjunction with them to see what services they thought were needed.

A concept that was held across libraries regardless of any other differences (sizes, budgets, and so forth) was the idea that distance education students should have equivalent library service as those provided students studying on campus. Interestingly, the services that these libraries did offer varied. Some did a better job than others, yet they all held to the idea of comparability of service provided as a common value. It was also interesting in that they all expressed it so strongly and in very similar ways. (Researcher emphasis is in italics.)

> Maria: Our goal is to provide library services and resources equivalent to those provided to on campus students.

> Sarah: We try to provide equal or equivalent services for all our students

> Kathy: We try very hard to treat them exactly as if they are a student in our library, only we communicate with them by phone or email.

Paula: We basically started with the premise that they should have access to at least all of the services that our students on campus have. And then we extended that. They're not available to come here and check out our book materials so we deliver our books to them for free.

All librarians interviewed also felt that they were meeting the needs of their distance education students. Some expressed this more strongly than others and some less. Nonetheless, they all felt that, regardless of the differences in services offered, that adequate library services are provided. Some of this may have been due to pride in their job, and some may have felt that they were doing the best job they could with the resources at hand. But, at that point in the interviews, it did not seem fair to conclude that a formal needs assessment is regularly done by any of the librarians or that they could really detail student needs satisfaction.

Maria: I think that we usually meet it pretty well.

Sarah: My library I think does very well. In fact I think it's one of the best libraries in the country in terms of that because we do BI for all students, for all distance students one way or another and it may be one shot, one hour but we do reach all of them.

Kathy: Our distance education students…have full access to our collection…We try very hard to treat them exactly as if they are students in our library only we communicate with them by phone or email. But that communication needs to be initiated by the student. We do not contact every single student. They do have to initiate the contact. We have done web searches, we've done database searches, we've done ILL searches and sent the materials down to those students for them to use. A couple of our programs do require research papers for every graduate. We have to be able to support that.

Paula: Just my impression. I'd say we probably meet their needs, gosh, probably fairly well. I wouldn't say excellent.

Another area of service that was emphasized by more than one person was the importance of bibliographic instruction. It was felt that creating a powerful web site, offering numerous services, providing a wealth of online resources, and librarians to support the students can only go so far. The impression was that it is the instruction of students in what resources are available and how to use them that is what is most important. If the students know they are there but do not know how to effectively access them, they are also of no use.

Kathy: What I'm working on, the big push or project right now is we've just moved bibliographic instruction into the English classes. So that's kind of a new thing. And as we do that we'll probably redevelop a little bit of our web page, because hopefully we're going to be creating better consumers.

Sarah: On a program by program basis. For the school of business we do online tutorials that are tied right now to a specific class that is being moved next term to require pre-service that all incoming students will have to do along with technology training. For the doctoral students (we have six doctoral programs in education), we have different approaches for each of the programs. It just varies. If the students don't come to campus and they're not online, then we are site based and go physically to the site... And, as a result, I think that bibliographic instruction is particularly important, and, if that piece is not there, all the other pieces for a distant student aren't very helpful.

Sarah: My library, I think, does very well. In fact I think it's one of the best libraries in the country in terms of that because we do BI for all students, for all distance students one way or another and it may be one shot, one hour but we do reach all of them.

Sarah: For BI, we probably provide better services for the distance students than we do for the on campus students because we assumed for a long time that students on campus had reasonable access and could ask for help, and we mandated that something be developed for the off-campus students.

There are also several different ways in which the determinations of services are made. Feedback is generally believed to be important, and librarians want to know what the students and teaching faculty want. Some approaches for collecting data that were cited include surveys, focus groups, working closely with those involved, educating those involved, and forming committees. One way that librarians thought would be useful is providing a form or an e-mail link on the library home page in order for patrons to send feedback at any time. However, those links seem to be generally ignored. This may be due to the fact that it is taken for granted and overlooked, or patrons are too busy and do not want to take the time for unsolicited feedback.

Maria: So it's the library, the online teachers, and the administrative unit that oversees distance learning which is within the continuing education department.

Maria: On every single page of every online course there's a link to the library home page, and on that home page there is a big link at the bottom, and I mean not just in tiny print, that says we welcome student comments and suggestions.

I: Do you get many comments or suggestions?

Maria: I don't. I get hardly any. It's very prominent on the page, but I get very few.

Maria: So we try to go to the outlying areas and meet with distance learning students, and we did do focus groups in April with distance learning students in Moab. And we met that time with the public librarians and the school media librarians or the people who are in charge of the computer labs in the schools. So we get a lot of good feedback there, and that helps.

Sarah: A couple of ways. We've done a couple of focus groups recently, one for faculty, one for students, and one for the general public. When we go out and do training we do a student satisfaction survey as sort of a touchy-feely, you know, do you feel like you learned something. And we're trying to implement a pre-test, post test now but that's on a program-by-program basis so that's just getting started and/or having something that requires the students to go and demonstrate that they learned how to do things. But that's more just assessment not getting their feedback. They have all those options for communicating when they're not happy.

Kathy: On a regular basis, through phone, email, fax, however, we need to do it. We are also in contact with the offices. We maintain an office on each of these campuses. We're in contact with those offices. And through these offices we get to the professors.

Maria: One thing that we've really been working on…assessment. That's always an issue. Is getting a really strong sense of student and faculty satisfaction with library services for distance learners per se.

Maria: We do [survey the students], but not enough. So that needs to be more regular. Supposedly, I don't have control of that, because supposedly it's part of the overall library services survey and that keeps getting delayed, so there needs to be more regular assessment.

Paula: We haven't done a formal survey of any kind just yet since we just started. I do travel to the classes and teach some classes off site so when I'm there I get some feedback and some informal feedback.

There are also some new services that are being worked on that may not be evident to faculty and students in their day-to-day usage of the library. Some are behind the scenes, some are works in progress, and some require more information to be gathered.

Paula: We have a new Ariel interlibrary loan system so we can deliver articles via email.

Ariel is an interlibrary loan hardware and software solution whereby the lending library scans in the requested article or other text document and transmits it to another Ariel station at another library via an Internet connection. The borrowing library can then print out the article on a laser printer and deliver it to the student.

Sarah: Iliad, Serials management, proxy difficulties.

Iliad is a software and hardware solution whereby articles or other text materials can be scanned in and placed on a library web server. Students are then notified via e-mail that the documents are ready to view and are provided a unique URL on which the images are stored. Students then have a certain number of days to view and print the documents before they are deleted from the server. Some libraries that have concerns about copyright complications in the future are moving toward this more complicated system. Technically, the libraries are not making copies and giving them to students. Instead, libraries are allowing students to see the documents that other libraries have purchased.

> Kathy: I think everything's kind of set and is sitting there right now. What I'm working on, the big push or project right now is that we've just moved bibliographic instruction into the English classes. So that's kind of a new thing.

> Paula: So we're looking at maybe getting an 800 number.

Several different types of problems emerged during the interviews. First are difficulties with getting print resources to distance education students. Articles and short documents can be faxed or scanned, but entire books have to be mailed and there are then additional costs associated with the mailing and greater complexity in terms of students having to return items. Second is the issue of copyright of video resources. While a teacher may show a video tape to an entire class in one physical room, most vendors do not want their videos converted to streaming video for distance students. This may change in the future, but for now teachers are either not allowed or must pay much more for those rights. Third is the issue of adjunct faculty. Many college and university libraries serve students that are taught by adjunct faculty that often do not stay in close contact with librarians. Librarians, therefore, are not aware of the needs of those students. Finally, there are issues involved with administrators and other departments on campus. While there have always been conflicts in one form of another between these groups, there are now more opportunities than ever to disagree.

> Maria: The only thing they might not be able to get are things that we don't normally have leave the building like reference sources or a print encyclopedia or something like that. But we help them find online equivalents when possible.

> Maria: The one thing we are still struggling with is e-reserve of media.

> Sarah: The University has a very large group of adjunct faculty who are not on campus and not easily accessible, and it's very difficult to get lists of these faculty from human resources…I've proposed several things to my VP, and he's gone nowhere with it. It's just dropped like a lead balloon…We would like to have our webmaster person have an understanding of cold fusion and be able to handle and to use more advanced applications…and we have run into a major roadblock with the office of information technology that says we can't hire somebody with those skills…and then they stonewall us.

> Paula: I think our biggest problem that we actually overcame was our library uses a barcode number to get into all of our resources. And for all the students the barcode number gets printed on the student ID card. For a long time they weren't issuing student ID cards to off-campus students,…but we finally did get a policy in place where they are now getting the cards printed and mailed to distance learners, so we did solve that problem.

The librarians interviewed also expressed interest in things that they would like to see happen, if possible. There were realistic concerns as well as wish lists for changes that they knew would not happen any time soon. The first issue is a need for new ways of reaching students for instruction. Second, is a perceived need for additional staff. Third, is a desire to develop greater resources on the web site. Fourth, is the development of electronic reserves.

> Sarah: In terms of services to distance students, I think that the challenge for working with them is that, you can have the document delivery, you can have the databases, but these configurations and ways of having them network with each other are getting to be, I think for the end user, more complicated. It is difficult for them to understand what they are accessing when they click on this,…and, as a result, I think that bibliographic instruction is a particularly important role and that, if that piece is not there, all the other pieces for a distant student aren't very helpful. But trying to get the faculty to collaborate in developing and offering these programs, to get them to have buy in, is hard…. There is tremendous resistance from the undergrades to add a required course,…so I think a lot of it is still about building bridges and working with various stake holders to try to keep building on what we have.

> Maria: We've wanted an entire position devoted to distance learning rather than having it tacked onto my job, but we haven't been able to fund that yet.

> Kathy: I would love to be able to develop for each department a web page of resources.

> Paula: Other than the chat reference that's probably the newest thing. We did recently have a change in our proxy server…and now we have an automatic one…That's made a big change in the volume of calls for people needing technical assistance. Other than that, next semester we are looking into starting an e-reserves programs.

In summary, the interviews show some of the reasons that services to distance education students are not as good as the librarians wish they were. Librarians are often overworked and do not have the staff, support, and money that they would like. While some issues are technical or dependent on other vendors, there are conflicts with their own campuses ranging from the administration to various other departments. Librarians would like to increase instruction to students and get more feedback, but they have not had the time to do so or, sometimes, the knowledge of how best to do it. The next section will look at student surveys in order to better understand the perspective of distance education students.

Surveys

Students enrolled in distance education courses at various institutions around the country were surveyed to get their impression of library services as well as to allow them an open forum for commenting on their thoughts and feelings (Appendix for a copy of the student survey form). The survey was developed to complement the content analysis using many of the same items. Students could, therefore, rate the importance of web site features. Between the two approaches, content analysis and survey, we found what services are being offered, and what services students actually want. The paper form was converted into a web-based form and placed on the researcher's personal web site. Results from the form were e-mailed to the researcher providing anonymity and ease for the participants.

A pilot survey was conducted during September 2002 with a single course from a single teacher. A response rate of 32% was returned. This was determined by the teacher replying that she e-mailed the URL of the survey to her class of 25 students. The response rate was calculated after counting the surveys that were electronically submitted.

During September and October of 2002 the rest of the student surveys were conducted with a primarily distance education university and a medium-sized public institution offering degrees via a distance. An unexpected difficulty arose with rest of the surveys, as a return rate was not able to be calculated. With more than one class completing the online survey and due to the nature of the web-based survey in its ease of completion for the students, immediacy, low cost, and anonymity, it also led to uncertainty in terms of returns. It was initially thought that teachers would be able to provide the number of students that were in the courses and a simple overall calculation could be made as was done with the pilot. However, the teachers were not as reliable with the data and it quickly became impossible to tell exactly how many total students received the survey URL. There were 68 returned surveys, but it could not be determined how many students did not respond.

Table 8 shows the results of the first seven questions on the survey. Respondents were primarily graduate students (89.6%), and most lived far from campus (75%) at a distance of 51 or greater miles, although other libraries were within 5 miles from home (57.4%). Most courses presently enrolled are web based (86.8%), and the majority never visits the campus library (57.4%), instead choosing to use library services from a distance on a weekly basis (67.4%).

The results of the remaining questions 8–21 are shown in Table 9 in order of highest to lowest mean score. The survey asked for a rating of very important to very unimportant which was converted numerically into 1–5, 5 being the highest and 1 being the lowest. Therefore, question 20 which asked for the importance of full-text databases resulted in the highest mean score

Table 8.   Student Information and Library Usage Results from Student
Distance Education Survey.

1. Classification	
Undergraduate	10.4%
Graduate	89.6%
2. Distance Living from campus library	
5 miles or less	8.8%
6–25 miles	13.2%
26–50 miles	2.9%
51 miles or greater	75.0%
3. Distance living from any other library you have access to and use	
5 miles or less	57.4%
6–25 miles	27.9%
26–50 miles	7.4%
51 miles or greater	7.4%
4. Number of distance education courses taken to date	
This is my first	11.8%
1–2	16.2%
3–5	35.3%
6 or more	36.8%
5. Type of distance education course presently enrolled in	
Web based	86.8%
Stored media	2.9%
Other	8.8%
6. Frequency of physical visits to campus library	
Never	57.4%
1–2 times semester	11.8%
1–2 times month	11.8%
Almost every week	19.1%
7. Frequency of use of library web site from home/work	
Never	4.4%
1–2 times semester	10.3%
1–2 times month	19.1%
Almost every week	67.4%

of 4.87 with 88.2% stating it was very important, 7.4% important, 2.9% neutral, and 0 unimportant or very unimportant. On the other end, the FAQ section reported the lowest mean of 3.42. This came about with 16.2% stating it was very important, 36.8% important, 27.9% neutral, 8.8% unimportant, and 2.9% very unimportant. Close to the low response for the

Table 9. Library Web Site Importance from Distance Education
Student Survey.

	Question	VI %	I	N	U	VU	Mean (1–5)
20.	Databases full-text	88.2	7.4	2.9	0	0	4.87
15.	Ref online mat links	70.6	25.0	2.9	0	0	4.69
9.	Internal search engine	72.1	23.5	2.9	1.5	0	4.66
22.	Links to sub web	58.8	30.9	4.4	1.5	1.5	4.42
11.	Distance learners page	55.9	30.9	11.8	0	1.5	4.40
21.	Print journal holdings	48.5	41.2	4.4	1.5	1.5	4.31
13.	Reference e-form	44.1	38.2	13.2	1.5	0	4.22
12.	Reference email	44.1	33.8	17.6	1.5	0	4.18
18.	OPAC	50.0	27.9	11.8	4.4	1.5	4.13
19.	E-books	38.2	27.9	25.0	4.4	0	3.93
17.	ILL forms	36.8	29.4	20.6	8.8	0	3.87
16.	BI tutorials	30.9	36.8	19.1	10.3	0	3.85
10.	Site map	39.7	29.4	14.7	7.7	7.4	3.82
23.	Electronic reserves	28.4	40.3	17.9	7.5	1.5	3.73
14.	Reference chat	30.9	29.4	23.5	4.4	5.9	3.63
8.	News	27.9	27.9	23.5	11.8	2.9	3.49
24.	Feedback form	14.7	42.6	26.5	8.8	2.9	3.49
25.	FAQ	16.2	36.8	27.9	8.8	2.9	3.42

FAQ is the Feedback Form at a mean of 3.49. This is an interesting find in that it corroborates the interviews. Librarians noted that the feedback form was seldom used, and students noted that they did not see the feedback form as important. While still regarded overall as useful, the data clearly shows which functions are deemed more important by students currently enrolled in distance education courses.

A Spearman correlation was conducted with the data using SPSS. The highest correlation found was −0.567 between frequency of physical visit and distance living from campus. This is logical and helps to ensure the integrity of the data, as one would assume that the farther students live from campus, the less likely they would visit the library in person. A second very high correlation found was 0.544 between the importance of electronic forms for reference and electronic forms for interlibrary loan. This also makes sense, as electronic forms on web sites make communication easier as compared to having to open up separate e-mail programs. Students who like using forms for one purpose tended to like them for another.

The final piece of the survey was open questions that asked students to comment and add opinions and other points they would like to make. The first question asked: "What is your general impression on library services to distance education students?" Of the students that provided some type of satisfaction level, 27 responded with some form of a positive answer such as "great," five with an adequate such as "ok," and four with negatives such as "inadequate," "slow," "not user friendly," or stating that "distance learners are ignored." There were several specific services or aspects of the library that students mentioned in their positive responses. Four students mentioned that having home access is wonderful so that they do not have to visit the library, two that they have noticed improvements over time, one for electronic reserves, two for the help desk, one for fast turn-around times, two for phone assistance especially with an 800 number, and one for mailing resources. Negative comments included four students complaining about not having enough resources especially in terms of full-text, and four students that they have had difficulty with searches and that accessing resources can be "overwhelming for new users."

Some of the more interesting comments on the general impression of the library web sites included the following. Note that spelling and grammar mistakes were not corrected. These are the exact quotes that they typed. Comments show the importance of library assistance, overwhelming web sites, and a greater need for full-text resources:

> "My general impression on library services to distance education students is that the library help department is a necessity."

> "My general impression is that using library services can assist distance education students. However, unless an individual is already comfortable navigating through the tremendous maze of information, the library and other online can be quite overwhelming."

> "Personally, my biggest need is full text journal articles…you can get some but others are limited by licensing and can not be provided on line. That is a problem. Finding full text journal articles on-line is nearly impossible (if you want them for free)."

> "It has been difficult for me to use, but a blessing when I can use it successfully."

> "I still prefer human contact, customer service by telephone is very important to me. Those handling phone calls have been wonderful, polite, extremely helpful."

The next question asked was "What are some of the strengths for library services to distance education students at your institution?" Twenty-four students responded that home access overall is the strength, eight was the phone help line, seven were the librarians and faculty, seven was interlibrary loan and the mailing of materials, three the convenience, three the speed of obtaining materials, and single responses of reserves, technical support, website navigation, tutorials, scholarly articles, specific databases, and on-line full-text materials.

Some of the more notable comments covered the strengths of the library web sites, from the amount of resources available to how important it is for distance students:

> "Without the library services for distance education I would not be enrolled."
> "The incredible amount of information that is available at a individual's fingertips."
> "The way they help you at the phone when you call them."
> "Actually, best library service I've seen...beating traditional libraries."

The next question asked: "What are some of the weaknesses for library services to distance education students at your institution?" The greatest weakness as reported by nine students is that not everything is online. Four responded that they have had difficulty with searches, four that the site is confusing and not user friendly, three that there is not enough personal support especially with time zone differences, three that delivery, access and support is not fast enough, two that there have been technical problems such as cumbersome logins, two about additional costs for delivery to distant students, two about not receiving enough instruction, two that the distance just makes it more difficult overall, and finally that the site is sometimes slow.

Some notable comments discussing weaknesses included lack of guidance, difficulty in obtaining all types of resources since everything is not full-text, and a greater need for personal support:

> "They do not specifically address the needs of distance learners, nor do they even really acknowledge distance learners."

> "The searches can get very complicated and may not ever get to the information one is after. In many cases the web searches seem to work better and easier."

> "The institution does not provide appropriate instruction and guidance for maximizing the benefit for distance education students."

> "Not all documents are full text."

> "book/journal holdings"

> "Getting copies of dissertations is difficult"

The final question asked: "What would you like to see changed/added? Additional comments?" Five students asked for more full-text, four for a more user friendly web site, three for more databases, three for more books online especially access to dissertations and theses, three for more phone lines or access to librarians via chat, two for greater instruction and training for new students, and finally for additional journals and library hours.

Some of the more notable comments about what students would like changed included a need for more help and instruction, more full-text, better search engines and organization, and individualized assistance:

> "Making remote access easier to understand to connect to the library from your own personal computer. The instructions are confusing and most of the time, I can't get it to work."

> "More help for new students who are in the distance education program!"

> "There needs to be a regular and ongoing, systematic training program initiated for all distance education students.... Additionally, online library tutorials, technical assistance, and 'real-time' personal help should be provided for distance education students."

> "More data bases, better search engine, more full text materials on line."

> "The material of the entire library be put online."

> "A way for students to be able to participate in a "real-time" chat session with a librarian, if the student has questions that need to be answered. That way the student will not have to call long distance to get their questions answered or wait for a reply by e-mail."

CONCLUSION

The three data sources to this paper (content analysis, interviews, and surveys) were able to show strengths, weaknesses, and areas of opportunity for growth. Together they corroborated many of the same findings:

- services were adequate overall but there is room for improvement;
- additional instruction is needed and there is no clear consensus on how to do that;
- additional feedback from students and faculty is needed, but again no clear solution has been found;
- that distance students need to be treated as a distinct group separate from on-campus students.

The content analysis uncovered a set of services that seems to be drawn more along lines of school size and finances rather than the types of students the libraries serve. The interviews offered a consistent view that librarians feel they are serving students well, although hints of frustrations shown through in terms of politics, relationships and what they would like to do but cannot. The surveys provided a student perspective. Students seemed happy with services as well overall, but will probably never be completely happy until 100% of what the library owns in print is online. They also want more instruction, easier sites to navigate, more personal attention via phone/e-mail/chat, and search engines and databases that are more user friendly. The next and final section will discuss these findings in relation to each other and offer concluding remarks and areas for further study.

DISCUSSION OF FINDINGS

The final section will present main findings from this research within the context of the initial research questions. Suggestions will be made for future research and implications for practitioners and educators.

What Services do Academic Libraries Offer to Distance Education Students?

The first research question asked about the actual services being offered by academic library web sites at the time this study was conducted. This data was primarily obtained by conducting a content analysis. Further corroboration was found from interviews and student surveys. Niemi et al. (1998) spoke about what services are needed, but this study has now taken a further step and quantified exactly what is being offered and what students want.

Of those services offered to distance education students, the one key resource that was available 100% of the time is full-text resources. This consistency shows the state of libraries and the importance of such features. In less than a decade since the development of the web, library web sites, and full-text resources have become standard. Following close behind this were online catalogs (88.2%) and links to online reference materials (88.2%).

Students confirmed the importance and high use of full-text resources, resulting in the highest mean score of 4.87 out of 5 with 88.2% stating it was very important, 7.4% important, 2.9% neutral, and 0 unimportant or very unimportant. During open-ended questions, students' negative comments focused on not having enough full-text resources.

On the other extreme, the items found 0% of the time were web pages that detailed strategies for the effective support of resources in support of distance learning, and the capacity to make video conferencing available for reference and research purposes. These items were found during preliminary study construction, but were not found within the sample of web sites chosen. FAQ (17.6%) and links to evaluation of resources (5.9%) were also at the bottom of the list.

As for students, the FAQ section reported the lowest mean of 3.42 out of 5. This came about with 16.2% stating it was very important, 36.8% important, 27.9% neutral, 8.8% unimportant, and 2.9% very unimportant. Close to the low response for the FAQ is the Feedback Form at a mean of 3.49. It is also interesting to note that even the lowest response questions from the student surveys were still remarkably high.

Furthermore, there was a broad range of features found throughout the web sites analyzed. The highest was a total of 31 items at both the University of Illinois and Ferris State University, and the lowest was a total of 6 at Touro University International. It also showed that there was no overall major grouping or standard as there appeared to be an even distribution from high to low with no large gap or jump from one extreme to the next.

How Does this Vary Depending on the Amount of Distance Education that the Institutions Offer?

Probably the most important finding in this research was that the types of library services offered to distance education students were not reflective of the degree to which distance education programs are offered on those campuses. The deciding factor was the size of the institution. A Spearman correlation of 0.618 between size of the institutions student body and the sum of their selected web site features was found. The larger the school (and, therefore, the larger the library's budget and staff) the more likely that they offer a greater number of services. However, this is also a disheartening outcome, as more and more institutions are offering distance education courses and programs. One would like to believe that institutions offer services and provide the framework for students based on student needs. It appears that many institutions are jumping into distance education unprepared. Surprisingly, institutions that were primarily distance education institutions did not have the strongest library web sites. The strongest were traditional institutions that offered degrees from a distance followed by those that offered only individual courses from a distance. This was then followed by the primarily distance education institutions and, finally, those that are not yet offering any distance education.

This conflict between mission and services was uncovered statistically using a Spearman correlation. The correlation between the amount of distance education offered and the overall sum of items found was 0.076.

Additionally, there was also no significant correlation between the amount of distance education offered and the size of the institution (0.238). This means that just because an institution offers distance education courses and degrees does not mean that the library has necessarily increased or improved their services to meet distance learner needs.

It was found, however, that the more that distance education was offered, the more likely that certain features were available on the web site: circulating books delivered to the student, reference available via e-mail, and interlibrary loan materials mailed directly to the student's home instead of having users pick them up in person. As for the size of the institution, the larger the institution the more likely that it would provide the following services: books could be renewed online by student, reference librarians would be available for consulting, bibliographic instructions classes were offered in one form or another, bibliographic instruction tutorials were available online, and synchronous chat software was in use for reference transactions. And in general the overall total sum of web site features was found to be higher at larger institutions.

However, it was interesting to note that during the interviews, each librarian felt that they were meeting student needs well. Each institution seems to have an apparent niche. Although different, each library provides a unique collection of services to meet their students' needs.

How are Distance Education Student Needs being met? In what Ways are the Needs of these Students Assessed? How are Decisions made for Determining what Services are Provided?

This next section details student needs, and how it is determined what those needs are. It is broken down into the following areas: equivalence, needs assessment, instruction, and computer interfaces and navigational design.

Equivalence

Equivalence is the idea that distance learners should have equivalent library services to those offered students on campus. During interviews for this study each of the librarians stated that this is their library's goal. Students responded during surveys that they still want more full-text online. It seems that they will probably never be 100% satisfied until 100% of what they are looking for is online.

The greatest weakness as reported by students is that not everything is online, although they did speak up about other deficiencies they felt strongly about. Several responded that they had the following complaints:

- difficulty with searches
- confusing and non-user-friendly sites
- not enough personal support, especially with time zone differences
- delivery, access and support is not fast enough
- technical problems such as cumbersome logins
- additional costs for delivery to distant students
- not enough instruction
- distance just makes it more difficult overall
- site is sometimes slow

Some of the more notable comments about what students would like changed included a need for more help and instruction, more full-text resources, better search engines and organization, and individualized assistance.

Other student comments included lack of guidance, difficulty in obtaining all types of resources since everything is not full-text, and a greater need for personal support. Librarians want to offer equivalent services, but require money, staff, and institutional support and collaboration. Determining user needs varies considerably from institution to institution, with some librarians making more decisions on their own, and others acting as part of larger committees.

This study has shown that, while it is true that distance learners need the same services as other learners, students in these programs are adamant about weaknesses in delivery and access and support issues, and do need a larger array of full-text resources. Libraries also need to provide additional staff and money for creating and supporting those services. There appears to be a disconnect between what some libraries are offering and what some students are expecting. Distance students may need the same services, but providing them requires additional resources and development.

Needs Assessment

Another common theme during interviews was the idea that student feedback is important, and that librarians need to be proactive in getting it. Paper forms, electronic forms, and other passive forms of collecting opinions seemed to be ineffective. Librarians need to get out to the classrooms, talk with the faculty and students, and basically find a way to force dialog with those involved in these programs. Students agreed that these electronic forms were not important although they did seem to be open to providing feedback. A more personal approach such as using focus groups may open up dialog between users and librarians.

The FAQ section reported the lowest mean of 3.42 for questions they were asked. This came about with 16.2% stating that FAQ's were very important, 36.8% important, 27.9% neutral, 8.8% unimportant, and 2.9% very unimportant. Close to the low response for the FAQ is the feedback form at a mean of 3.49. This is an interesting find in that it corroborates the interviews. Librarians noted that the feedback form was seldom used, and students noted that they did not find the feedback form that effective or useful. Students did not state how they could make their needs known otherwise.

From the statistical findings and the interviews with librarians, it is evident that a more formal needs assessment program is needed throughout many libraries. Although many libraries do have mechanisms in place to determine what services to offer and what patrons want, much of this is done informally or without any real assessment program. Waiting for comments via a suggestion box or a web-based comment form provide little information. There is a great deal of literature that speaks about assessment in general and assessment in terms of libraries (Colborn & Cordell, 1998; Hiller, 2001; Niyonsenga & Bizimana, 1996). Assessment can be conducted via paper surveys or web-based surveys. Focus groups can be formed, and formal committees within the library and within the college or university can also provide feedback. This study shows the importance of formal needs assessment. The problem lies not in the lack of knowledge of needs assessment, but in actual implementation and awareness.

Instruction

From an instructional design point of view, it is clear that, as designers of services and web sites, librarians need to continually analyze the instruction that they provide. Good instruction begins with an analysis of the audience, students in this case. Design of instruction takes place, followed by program development, and then actual use. Finally, evaluations are conducted, and the entire process is analyzed again and modified.

It was interesting that an increased need for instruction did not appear from the content analysis results or the survey statistics. However, it was very evident that it is an important issue when participants are allowed to speak freely within interviews and open-ended questions on the surveys. Both librarians and students felt that personal assistance and user instruction are even more important, not less, as students move further away, and as technology increases. This shows that a combination of quantitative and qualitative approaches to data collection is important in order to ensure that all viewpoints are expressed. As a student wrote on the survey, "the institution does not provide appropriate instruction and guidance for maximizing the benefit for distance education students."

Students consistently wrote that more personal assistance was needed. Even though technology has been rapidly improving and interfaces have been simplified, the amount of technology and the multitude of databases available can be overwhelming. Students need support to find out how to most effectively use library resources. Students within this research study stated that they have had difficulty with searches and that accessing resources can be "overwhelming for new users." By emphasizing personal assistance to make learning how to use library resources relevant to the student, a constructivist approach becomes evident. Even though it may be easier to post web pages and provide canned instruction for distance students, it becomes clear that with the changing technology and more information available, adult students still need personal assistance. Formal instruction that is tied to the student's research questions and personal interests makes for much more useful instruction. By being able to make connections to their own interests, a constructivist approach helps students to learn better. Additionally, different learning styles add another layer of complexity to instruction, requiring that multiple approaches to library instruction be used to reach all students.

One of the main issues that arose from this study was the problem with reaching distance students for library instruction. This came across both from the students and the librarians. Wiggins (1999) states that highly structured instruction in forms such as video, workbooks, web pages, computer assisted instruction, or pathfinders is not enough. Students need to take that information one step further with individualized support in order to better understand why they are doing something instead of just how. The key is to balance rules, facts, and information that can be transmitted easily, with additional support and communication. That may be in the form of face-to-face workshops, phone, e-mail, chat, asynchronous discussions, or with new technologies as they are developed. It seems clear that many libraries are still struggling with how to best reach their students and need to use appropriate instructional design techniques for ideal instruction.

The use of new tools such as asynchronous computer mediated communication (CMC) enables all members of a group to be in touch. Just as these tools are widely used in distance education courses, they can also be utilized for library instruction and assistance. Library instruction and library reference requires similar types of two-way interaction and feedback to ensure that both librarian and student understand what the other is thinking and that the information to be found meets the needs of the search. As adult learners, our library patrons have a great deal of personal experience to draw upon, like how to make decisions for themselves, and they often have family responsibilities that keep them busy. This has direct consequences to the types of library services and support that will be preferred.

Computer Interfaces and Navigational Designs

There was a very noticeable need for improved navigation, organization, and interface design of library web sites. Obviously there has been a great deal of improvement since the first library web sites were created, and it seems that most libraries are continually revising their structures each and every year. However, there is still room for improvement. Students have asked for improved interfaces and easier searching. Although some of this is out of the hands of librarians, as commercial vendors have all but taken over the actual databases themselves, there is still room to continue teaching students how to work with what is available. Furthermore, information of database options and the structure of the library web site itself can still be improved upon. This brings us back to user instruction, better organized library web sites, and onscreen instructions and navigation guides before they even connect to the databases. As one student commented: "Making remote access easier to understand to connect to the library from your own personal computer. The instructions are confusing and most of the time, I can't get it to work."

Students had responded that they have had difficulty with searches, that library sites are confusing and not user friendly, that there is not enough personal support especially with time zone differences, that delivery, access and support is not fast enough, and that there have been technical problems such as cumbersome logins.

Practitioners and educators should take advantage of work already done on learning styles and web page design (Holtze, 2000), as well as information retrieval theory (Buckland, 1988). Tolppanen et al. (2000) examined the web sites of 133 academic libraries from medium-sized universities. They determined that the navigational and design aspects of library web sites need to be improved, and greater use of online instruction, tutorials, and virtual tours would be worthwhile endeavors to supplement traditional face-to-face bibliographic instruction.

This research has not only confirmed what others have said about navigational issues, but spoken directly to student issues in regards to the overwhelming number of choices they now have to make, and how an increased number of databases makes it difficult for students to determine where to start.

Future Research Directions and Implications for Practitioners

There are several areas that now appear to offer additional research opportunities. The first area is on database and full-text resources for distance education students. In this paper it was discovered that databases and full-text resources are now common. However, it seems that there could be quite a large difference between institutions. Future research could look into both quantity and quality of full-text offerings.

Additional questions have arisen as to instruction of distance education students in terms of library services. What is the most effective way of reaching these students for bibliographic instruction? Both librarians and students asked for additional interaction. There are many different approaches. These include web based independent instruction, face-to-face class sessions, interactive television, and personalized service through e-mail, chat, and phone. This is an area that librarians have not studied in school and have, therefore, had to learn on the job.

Another question deals with student ages, backgrounds, and generational differences. How do these differences impact how they use and perceive the library and the type of instruction and assistance they want? Are different techniques going to work better for one group compared to others? Will a variety of assistance means have to be offered?

What is it that students are actually using? We learned the types of services they want, but how many of them use their public library or a closer college library instead? How much of their research consists of using web sites as opposed to subscription databases with peer-reviewed articles? In terms of faculty usage, how much library work do faculty require of their students and how many of them simply provide students with course packets and other materials?

Furthermore, how can we get various areas of the campus to work together better? Librarians interviewed discussed frustration with other campus units or departments. In what ways can we improve the library image and library influence on the institution? How can the library take more control over its function? Would more of a systems approach with shared individuals working across departments better meet library needs, especially in terms of things of a technical nature?

Practitioners, on the other hand, continue to have issues with staffing deficiencies and with campus politics. There is a greater need for advocacy on campus and greater emphasis on relationships with other departments. There is also an apparent disconnect between college missions and their support and funding of libraries. Additional resources must be spent to improve library services to distance education students before the time and effort is spent on creating distance courses.

Areas of improvement for libraries serving distance education students, therefore, include introduction of more full-text resources, expansion of electronic reserves to include media beyond simple text, closer working relationships with adjuncts, better relationships with administration, increased staffing, improved navigation on library web sites, and increased instruction for students to counter the ever-increasing amount of information that is available. To that end, libraries will have to continue to integrate the library throughout the institution and improve their interactions with all departments, faculty, staff, and students.

The librarians interviewed also expressed interests in things that they would like. The first issue is a need for new ways to reach students for instruction. The second is a perceived need for additional staff. Third, there is a desire to develop greater resources on the web site. Fourth, there is a need to develop further the electronic reserves program.

CONCLUSIONS

This research has provided interesting insight into the provision of library services to distance education students. While answering many questions, and opening up additional avenues for continued research, it has also offered an insight into how research data might be gathered via electronic means.

Technology has had a continued effect of blending beyond borders. From the classroom, to the library, to home, and to work, academia is continually pushing the envelope in terms of access and communication. Teachers and librarians, now more than ever, must make a concerted effort to work together in meeting the needs of today's "tech savvy" students. At the same time, we must realize that students need more help than they care to admit or at least more than they voice. The more services that are offered, the more that technology can provide, the more guidance is needed.

REFERENCES

Agingu, B. (2000). Library web sites at historically Black colleges and universities. *College and Research Libraries, 61*(1), 30–37.

Allen, B., & Reser, D. (1990). Content analysis in library and information science research. *Library and Information Science Research, 12*, 251–262.

Association of College & Research Libraries. (2000). Guidelines for distance learning library services. *College & Research Libraries News, 61*(11), 1023–1029.

Balas, J. (2001). Online treasures: Distance services: Researching today's state-of-the-art technology. *Computers in Libraries, 21*(4), 56–58.

Bateman, B. (2003). Educational technology: A guide to resources on the web. *College & Research Libraries News, 64*(1), 9–12.

Bauer, C., & Scharl, A. (2000). Quantitative evaluation of web site content and structure. *Internet Research: Electronic Networking Applications and Policy, 10*(1), 31–43.

Berendsen, N. (1998). *A content analysis of the web sites of the fifty state library agencies of the United States of America.* Unpublished master's thesis, Kent State University, Ohio.

Bogdan, R., & Biklen, S. (1998). *Qualitative research in education: An introduction to theory and methods.* Needham Heights, MA: Allyn & Bacon.

Buckland, M. (1988). *Library services in theory and context.* New York, NY: Pergamon Press.

Budd, J. (2001). Information seeking in theory and practice: Rethinking public services in libraries. *Reference & User Services Quarterly, 40*(3), 256–263.

Burke, J. J. (1996). Using e-mail to teach: Expanding the reach of BI. *Research Strategies, 14*(1), 36–43.

Butler, D. L., & Winne, P. H. (1995). Feedback and self-regulated learning: A theoretical synthesis. *Review of Educational Research, 65*(3), 245–281.

Caspers, J. (1998). Hands-on instruction across the miles: Using a web tutorial to teach the literature review research process. *Research Strategies, 16*(3), 187–197.

Clyde, L. (1996). The library as information provider: The home page. *The Electronic Library, 14*(6), 549–558.

Cohen, L., & Still, J. (1999). A comparison of research university and two-year college library web sites: Content, functionality, and form. *College & Research Libraries, 60*(3), 275–289.

Colborn, N., & Cordell, R. (1998). Moving from subjective to objective assessment of your instruction program. *RSR: Reference Services Review, 26*(3–4), 125–137.

Cooper, R., Dempsey, P., & Vanaja, C. (1998). Remote library users – needs and expectations. *Library Trends, 47*(1), 42–64.

Crowther, K., & Wallace, A. (2001). Delivering video-streamed library orientation on the web: Technology for the educational setting. *College & Research Libraries News, 62*(3), 280–285.

Curl, S., Reynolds, L., & Mai, B. (2000). Reality check: Asynchronous instruction works!. *College & Research Libraries News, 61*(7), 586–588.

Derlin, R., & Erazo, E. (1997). Distance learning and the digital library: Transforming the library into an information center. *New Directions for Teaching and Learning, 71,* 103–109.

Dewald, N. (1999). Transporting good library instruction practices into the web environment: An analysis of online tutorials. *The Journal of Academic Librarianship, 25*(1), 26–31.

Dewey, B. (1999). In search of services: Analyzing the findability of links on CIC university libraries' web pages. *Information Technology & Libraries, 18*(4), 210–213.

Engle, M. O. (1996). Using World Wide Web software for reference and instruction. *Internet Reference Services Quarterly, 1*(2), 7–15.

Hiller, S. (2001). Assessing user needs, satisfaction, and library performance at the University of Washington Libraries. *Library Trends, 49*(4), 605–625.

Holtze, T. (2000). Applying learning style theory to web page design. *Internet Reference Services Quarterly, 5*(2), 71–80.

Janes, J., Carter, D., & Memmott, P. (1999). Digital reference services in academic libraries. *Reference & User Services Quarterly, 39*(2), 145–150.

Jonassen, D., & Reeves, T. (1996). Learning with technology: Using computers as cognitive tools. In: D. Jonassen (Ed.), *Handbook of research for educational communications and technology* (pp. 693–719). New York, NY: Simon & Schuster Macmillan.

Kalin, S. (1991). Support services for remote users of online public access catalogs. *RQ, 31,* 197–213.

Kesselman, M., Khanna, D., & Vazquez, L. (2000). Web authorware and course-integrated library instruction: The learning links project at Rutgers university. *College & Research Libraries News, 61*(5), 387–390.

King, D. (1998). Library home page design: A comparison of page layout for front-ends to ARL library web sites. *College & Research Libraries, 59*(5), 458–465.

Krippendorff, K. (1980). *Content analysis: An introduction to its methodology.* Beverly Hills, CA: SAGE Publications Inc..

Laverty, C. Y. (1997). Library instruction on the web: Inventing options and opportunities. *Internet Reference Services Quarterly, 2*(2–3), 55–66.

Lee, K., & Teh, K. (2000). Evaluation of academic library web sites in Malaysia. *Malaysian Journal of Library & Information Science, 5*(2), 95–108.

Leiner, B., Cerf, V., Clark, D., & Kahn, R. et al. (2000). *A brief history of the Internet.* Retrieved October 7, 2001. Available: http://www.isoc.org/internet-history/brief.html.

Linden, J. (2000). The library's web site is the library: Designing for distance learners. *College & Research Libraries News, 61*(2), 99–101.

Mason, S. (1998). *Using links to facilitate access to Internet resources: A content analysis of Ohio public library web sites.* Unpublished master's thesis, Kent State University, Ohio.

Maxwell, J. (1996). *Qualitative research design: An interactive approach.* Thousand Oaks, CA: Sage Publications, Inc.

McMillan, S. (2000). The microscope and the moving target: The challenge of applying content analysis to the World Wide Web. *Journalism & Mass Communication Quarterly, 77*(1), 80–98.

Meyers, M. (2000). *A content analysis of US botanical and horticultural library web sites.* Unpublished master's thesis, Kent State University, Ohio.

Miles, M., & Huberman, M. (1994). *Qualitative data analysis: An expanded source book.* Thousand Oaks, CA: Sage.

Moore, M. G., & Kearsley, G. (1996). *Distance education: A systems view*. Belmont, CA: Wadsworth Publishing Company.

Niemi, J., Ehrhard, B., & Neeley, L. (1998). Off-campus library support for distance adult learners. *Library Trends, 47*(1), 65–74.

Niyonsenga, T., & Bizimana, B. (1996). Measures of library use and usersatisfaction with academic library services. *Library & Information Science Research, 18*(3), 225–240.

Pealer, L., & Dorman, S. (1997). Evaluating health-related web sites. *Journal of School Health, 67*(6), 232–235.

Peterson's (2002). *Guide to distance learning programs*. Lawrenceville, NJ: Thomson Learning, Inc..

Quinn, B. (1999). Missing links: A survey of library systems department web pages. *Library Hi Tech, 17*(3), 304–315.

Rodrigues, H. (1996). The role of the library in distance education. *Microcomputers for Information Management: Global Internet working for Libraries, 13*(1), 21–30.

Seels, B., & Richey, R. (1994). *Instructional technology: The definition and domains of the field*. Washington, DC: Association for Educational Communications and Technology.

Simonson, M., Smaldino, S., Albright, M., & Zvacek, S. (2000). *Teaching and learning at a distance: Foundations of distance education*. Upper Saddle River, NJ: Merrill.

Stover, M. (2000). Reference librarians and the Internet: A qualitative study. *Reference Services Review, 28*(1), 39–49.

Stover, M., & Zink, S. (1996). World Wide Web home page design: Patterns and anomalies of higher education library home pages. *Reference Services Review, 24*(3), 7–20.

Taylor, M. (2000). Library webmasters: Satisfactions, dissatisfactions, and expectations. *Information Technology & Libraries, 19*(3), 116–124.

Tolppanen, B., Miller, J., & Wooden, M. (2000). An examination of library World Wide Web sites at medium-sized universities. *Internet Reference Services Quarterly, 5*(2), 5–17.

Vishwanatham, R., Wilkins, W., & Jevec, T. (1997). The Internet as a medium for online instruction. *College & Research Libraries, 58*(8), 433–444.

Walster, D. (1995). Using instructional design theories in library and informationscience education. *Journal of Education for Library and Information Science, 36*(3), 239–248.

Wiggins, M. (1999). Instructional design and student learning. *RSR: Reference Services Review, 27*(3), 225–228.

Wilson, B., & Lowry, M. (2000). Constructivist learning on the web. *New Directions for Adult and Continuing Education, 88*, 79–88.

APPENDIX. STUDENT WEB SURVEY FORM

Library Services to Distance Education Students Survey

This survey is being conducted as part of the research for a dissertation done by a doctoral student at Northern Illinois University. All information provided will be kept anonymous and confidential. Please refer to the consent form before completing the survey. Thank You.

| 1. Classification | _____ Undergraduate |
| | _____ Graduate |

2. Distance living	_____ 5 miles or less
from campus	_____ 6–25 miles
library	_____ 26–50 miles
	_____ 51 miles or greater

3. Distance living	_____ 5 miles or less
from any other	_____ 6–25 miles
library you have	_____ 26–50 miles
access to and use	_____ 51 miles or greater

4. Number of	_____ This is my first
distance education	_____ 1–2
courses taken to	_____ 3–5
date	_____ 6 or more

5. Type of distance	_____ Web based
education course	_____ Interactive TV
presently enrolled	_____ Stored Media (CD-ROM, Videotape, etc.)
in	_____ Other

Library Usage

6. Frequency of physical visits	_____ Never
to campus library	_____ 1–2 times/semester
	_____ 1–2 times/month
	_____ Almost every week or more

7. Frequency of use of library	_____ Never
web site from home/work	_____ 1–2 times/semester
	_____ 1–2 times/month
	_____ Almost every week or more

Library Web Site Importance

This section will explain the types of features that you would like to see in a library web site for distance education students. Please rate the following

library web site areas in terms of importance according to the following
Likert scale:

VI   Very Important
I   Important
N   Neutral
U   Unimportant
VU   Very Unimportant
n/a   not applicable/have not used or does not exist

8. News/What's New	__VI __I __N __U __VU __n/a
9. Internal Search Engine	__VI __I __N __U __VU __n/a
10. Site Map	__VI __I __N __U __VU __n/a
11. Distance Learners Page/Section	__VI __I __N __U __VU __n/a
12. Reference e-mail	__VI __I __N __U __VU __n/a
13. Reference electronic form	__VI __I __N __U __VU __n/a
14. Reference chat	__VI __I __N __U __VU __n/a
15. Reference online materials/links	__VI __I __N __U __VU __n/a
16. Bibliographic instruction tutorials	__VI __I __N __U __VU __n/a
17. Interlibrary loan electronic forms	__VI __I __N __U __VU __n/a
18. Online Catalog for books	__VI __I __N __U __VU __n/a
19. E-books	__VI __I __N __U __VU __n/a
20. Databases	__VI __I __N __U __VU __n/a
21. Print journal holdings list	__VI __I __N __U __VU __n/a
22. Links to subject specific web sites	__VI __I __N __U __VU __n/a
23. Electronic reserves	__VI __I __N __U __VU __n/a
24. Feedback form	__VI __I __N __U __VU __n/a
25. Library FAQ	__VI __I __N __U __VU __n/a

Please answer the following questions with short answers:

26. What is your general impression on library services to distance education students?

27. What are some of the strengths at your institution?

28. What are some of the weaknesses at your institution?

29. What would you like to see changed/added? Additional comments?

DISTANCE EDUCATION STUDENTS' PERCEPTIONS OF LIBRARY SUPPORT SERVICES: MISSISSIPPI PUBLIC COMMUNITY AND JUNIOR COLLEGES

Pamela Kindja Ladner

INTRODUCTION

The first university was founded in Italy during the early 1110 s. Since that time, education has not changed much. Early college education was based on communication, a continuous dialogue between teacher and learner. College education today is based heavily on communication with the only real change, in some instances, being the method in which the teacher and learner communicate.

Until the mid-19th century, teachers and students were meeting face-to-face. Beginning in the early 1990s, instructional films, satellite broadcasts, videotapes, teleconferencing, and then the computer emerged to enhance the educational process. With the advent of the Internet, colleges and universities were jumping on the bandwagon to provide learning opportunities at a distance.

Advances in Library Administration and Organization
Advances in Library Administration and Organization, Volume 22, 79–112
Copyright © 2005 by Elsevier Ltd.
ISSN: 0732-0671/doi:10.1016/S0732-0671(05)22003-5

Distance education proved popular among students who were restricted due to location, employment, and family responsibilities, and was especially helpful to anyone with family and time constraints (Busacco, 2001). The growing enrollment consisted primarily of non-traditional students who had jobs, family obligations, travel obligations, or who were geographically bound (Culpepper, 2001). "Today's communications technology is enabling institutions of higher education to reach populations in a variety of settings such as businesses, colleges, hospitals, and prisons" (Niemi & Ehrhard, 1998, p. 65).

The Mississippi Virtual Community College (MSVCC) began its first semester of operation in January 2000 with an enrollment of 1382 (State Board for Community and Junior Colleges, 2000). The Spring 2001 enrollment grew to 5349; an approximate 387% rise. "As a result of this dramatic enrollment increase and interest in the program, the State Board for Community and Junior Colleges (SBCJC) is continually reaffirming its commitment to the project. Part of that ongoing commitment was the collection and distribution of data, which enhanced all aspects of the MSVCC" (State Board for Community and Junior Colleges, 2000, p. 4), including library support services.

Academic libraries were struggling to provide services to off-site users (Lebowitz, 1997). Most academic libraries had very few resources for the distance learner. Many librarians had mixed emotions about the rapid addition of large numbers of electronic resources, but it became a responsibility not a choice (Culpepper, 2001). Due to the decrease in state funding and increase in the cost of electronic resources, it was imperative to reevaluate the services and resources to determine if the students' needs were met; if not, adjustments needed to be made (Libutti, 1999). The capacity to provide more and better services was counterbalanced by the rising demands of patrons and the overwhelming array of options (Rumble, 2000).

"Like traditional younger learners, distance adult learners require ancillary services, especially library services, to help them conduct research and fulfill their assignments" (Niemi & Ehrhand, 1998, p. 65). Distance learners accessed electronic databases through their personal computers. The librarian's role was to assist these learners by demonstrating how to use the electronic resources and how to conduct successful searches (Lebowitz, 1997). The only way that librarians were able to determine if the Mississippi public community and junior college distance education students perceive that they are receiving needed library support services was to conduct surveys.

Statement of the Problem

The Mississippi Virtual Community College experienced tremendous growth since its first semester of operation in the Spring of 2000 and continues to expand. Between Spring 2000 and Fall 2002, student enrollment in MSVCC increased from 1382 to 12,594 students or by 811%. This reflected an increase from 29 courses to 163 courses; from 53 sections to 569 sections. Mississippi public community and junior colleges' participation in MSVCC and students' enthusiasm for this type of instruction was evidenced by the growth of Internet-based distance learning: by Fall 2002, over 12,000 students enrolled in these classes. Figs. 1–3 show the growth of online instructions. While experiencing this growth, the system remained true to its mission of providing an accessible, affordable, quality education for people in the state of Mississippi. An assessment of library support services is needed to determine if distance education student's needs are being met as part of the system's mission to provide a quality education for people in Mississippi.

Purpose of the Study

Through the Mississippi Virtual Community College, Mississippi's public community and junior colleges offer students the opportunity to achieve

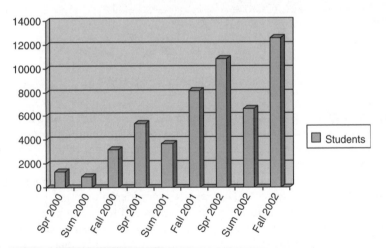

Fig. 1. Students Enrolled in MSVCC Online Courses.

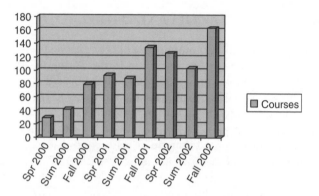

Fig. 2.   Courses Offered through MSVCC.

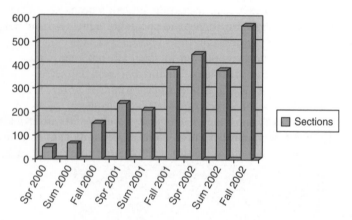

Fig. 3.   Sections Offered through MSVCC.

their educational goals through on-line classes in addition to traditional classes. Potential students face a vast array of educational opportunities to choose from and sometimes a never ending entanglement of administrative issues when entering into distance education activities.

Studying distance learning options holds promise for providing more and better educational services. The primary consideration of future studies should be the enhancement of student services while not compromising the integrity of the institution of educational program. Addressing old and new issues should be the focus in order to continue Mississippi public community and junior colleges' progress.

So the study asked the question: do Mississippi public community and junior college distance education students perceive that they are receiving adequate library support services?

Significance of the Study

Although there are no immediate benefits to participants, there are long-term benefits for the large number of Mississippi public community and junior college students taking online courses. The study will provide administrators and library staff members with the data necessary to determine if they are meeting the needs of the distance learner. The results will enable administrators to make meaningful changes and/or additions to the support services offered to the students.

LITERATURE REVIEW

Today's community colleges are in transition as they resolve to respond to a changing environment. The mission of the community college is to provide accessible, affordable, high-quality education by keeping the learner's needs at the core. It is imperative that community college leaders recognize and meet the changing needs of the learner in order to fully prepare their students for the future. "One way of expanding access to quality, timely instruction is the use of the Internet to bring instruction to the student rather than requiring the student to come to the instruction" (League for Innovation in the Community College, p. viii). Institutions of higher learning are turning to the use of the Internet to deliver courses to students at a distance, as well as to enhance educational programs that are delivered on campus (Palloff & Pratt, 1999).

The fastest growing segment of education is distance learning. Distance education can be defined in numerous ways, but according to O'Leary (2002) it can be defined as education delivered to remote locations using technology. Technology is what many have said is the only constant in our work today (O'Quinn & Corry, 2002). As technology changes, the need to change becomes increasingly important in order to stay current with today's offerings.

Evidence shows that the growth in distance education courses and enrollments has been phenomenal. "According to the U.S. Department of Education, distance education programs increased by 72% between 1995

and 1998" and "in 1998, institutions offered a total of 54,000 online education courses, with 1.6 million students enrolled" (Tulloch, 2000, p. 58).
These numbers reflect an increase from roughly 86 to nearly 1200 programs
(Beck, 2003). Experts estimate that, by the year 2007, approximately 50% of
learners enrolled in higher education will take courses through distance
education (Kascus, 1994).

What is Distance Education?

Distance education is not a new phenomenon, but the use of the Internet
and the World Wide Web has drastically changed the manner in which
education is presented (Willis, 1993). For over a 100 years, postsecondary
institutions have offered correspondence courses. A traditional correspondence course, also known as independent study, provides lesson materials to
the students by mail. Upon completion of the course, the student is granted
college credit that may be applied to a degree program (Conaway, 2002).

"Distance education is defined as a collection of innovative approaches to
the delivery of instruction to learners who are remote from their teacher"
(League for Innovation in the Community College, 1996, p.viii). It is a
process that uses a variety of technologies to overcome the time or place
boundaries that separates teacher and learner. The range of interpretations
runs from sending an instructor some distance from the main campus to
teach a group of students face-to-face to providing all instruction and
interaction via the World Wide Web (Hyatt, 1998). The U.S. Congress
Office of Technology Assessment defines distance learning as the "linking of
a teacher and students in several geographic locations via technology that
allows for interaction" (Cartwright, 1994, p. 30).

The History of Distance Learning

The concept and application of distance education has been in existence for
over 200 years (Duvall & Schwartz, 2000). In the United States, distance
education can be traced back to the 1700s with the beginning of a print-
based correspondence course. By the 1870s, these courses gained international recognition. In the early 1900s, universities and private schools were
offering correspondence courses to elementary, secondary, higher education, and vocationally oriented learners.

Cable TV and video teleconferencing became more widely available in the
1980s enabling distance learning programs to evolve (Fleischman, 1998). In

1995, Jones International University opened its virtual doors becoming the first completely web-based degree-granting university, and in 1999 it was the first online university to receive accreditation (O'Leary, 2002).

Today the Internet and compressed video allow distance learning to occur in real time (Valentine, 2002). Live video instruction is the most popular and fastest growing delivery mode of instruction in the United States (Ostendorf, 1997).

Purpose

Distance learning programs around the world were designed to offer a clear alternative to the conventional classroom that was considered inappropriate for the numbers and characteristics of the students to be served. Distance education should reach a large portion of the world population and should enable students to learn at any time and in any place. Distance learning is about access to educational opportunities for those who do not wish, or who are not able, to attend programs offered on-site (Fulcher & Lock, 1999).

Distance Learners

Qureshi, Morton, and Antosz (2002) selected seven characteristics that seem to define the majority of distance education students; yet relatively recent research suggests that the demographics of distance learners may be changing. The characteristics Qureshi, Morton, and Antosz selected were maturity, value learning, experienced, motivated, realism, and ingrained strategies. Palloff and Pratt (1999) reinforced the characteristics defined by Qureshi, Morton, and Antosz. They stated that students are adult by definition (maturity), are all engaged in a continuing process of growth (value learning), bring a package of experience and values (experienced), usually come to education with set intentions (motivated), bring mature expectations about education itself (realism), often have competing interests (employment, family, and social life), and possess set patterns of learning (developed or ingrained strategies).

Advantages

Distance education has created enormous opportunities for the expansion of educational opportunities, especially at the higher education level.

Advantages of using the Internet for delivering distance education courses include connectivity; flexibility; ability to offer needed courses, even with a limited number of students; and interactivity (Kerka, 1996).

Barriers

Although the area of distance education is promising, there are still many barriers to overcome. Qureshi et al. (2002) states that the several barriers, such as home responsibilities, job responsibilities, and lack of self-confidence or interest, may affect the performance of an individual. Such barriers include situational – circumstances in the individual's life such as family and work, geography, childcare, etc.; institutional – organizational policies, procedures and support services; and dispositional – attitudes towards self and learning (Qureshi et al., 2002).

Disadvantages

The lack of a healthy, supportive learning environment such as the library may hinder the performance of an individual. Distance education students may experience greater frustration because they are not aware of the resources available to them or do not know how to use them. Oberg and Henri (1999) reported that distance education students might express feelings of disadvantage in their learning experience if they do not acquire access to the main library and its services (Oberg, 1999).

The lack of knowledge required for determining the accuracy, consistency, and quality of information on the Internet can also be a disadvantage (Conaway, 2002). Students without proper instructions may not be able to evaluate the accuracy of online information (Busacco, 2001). Therefore, they must be taught how to distinguish between credible and non-credible information, and librarians are well qualified to do this (Libutti, 1999). Without library support services, the distance education learner is being denied a top-level educational experience (Roccos, 2001).

Support Services for Distance Education

In the increasingly digitized world of higher education, student support services such as library services often lag behind the infusion of technology.

As distance education became a prominent feature on the landscape of higher education, a variety of needed student support services were destined to follow (Wagner, 2001). As distance education grows, so does the need for quality student support services (Gubbins, 1998) in a user-friendly format, so students can be nurtured, encouraged, and supported throughout their academic careers (Wagner, 2001).

Although many consider the library to be the heart of an institution, instruction for using the library is not incorporated into traditional courses or distance education courses (Lebowitz, 1997). To complete their course of study, students need books, research materials, and someone to explain where to find them. The availability of library services for distance education students adds to the quality of education received and ensures that distance education courses are comparable to those taught on campus (Perraton, 2000). ACRL guidelines (2000) states, "the library services offered to the distance learning community should be designed to effectively meet a wide range of informational, bibliographic, and user needs. The exact combination of central and site staffing for distance library services differ from institution to institution."

A library is not a place, it is a service. Library services are an essential element that distance learning programs must provide (O'Leary, 2002). Library support services should be available to all students at any time, day or night. Library personnel are information suppliers whether or not the user is in the building.

In the field of distance education, there is an opportunity for librarians to promote their role as information specialists by establishing effective support services (Kirk & Bartelstein, 1999). It is inevitable that as distance learning expands, librarians become stronger and more important players as information tutors (Casado, 2001). Distance education provides a challenge to academic libraries and their management (Dugan, 1997). The library is pressured to be the innovator in establishing services and providing research materials to distance learners, and often without additional funding (Culpepper, 2001).

Added to this is the problem of providing equal opportunities for acquiring research skills needed for information literacy. Without training in the use of the library web page and electronic resources, distance learners are denied a quality educational experience (Roccos, 2001). Another major issue identified is the responsibility of ensuring that students acquire the skills needed for information filtering and analysis, and critical thinking (Lebowitz, 1997). Many libraries provide bibliographic instruction on the use of resources. One of the objectives of this instruction is to prepare students to become independent, self-directed information seekers, and analysts, a variation on the theme of "give a man a fish, feed him for a day; teach a man to fish, he feeds himself for a lifetime" (Dugan & Hernon, 1997, p. 3).

Unlike traditional younger students, adult learners require more ancillary services to help them conduct the research required for their assignments (Niemi & Ehrhard, 1998). The role of librarians is to assist these learners by providing support for them. Students must have the ability to search databases, indexes, and abstracts to answer research questions. Therefore, students should be taught how to locate resources that match their information needs (Wittkopf, Orgeron, & Del Nero, 2001).

The library information needs of the distance learner are no different from those of the on-campus student (Lebowitz, 1997). However, the lack of adequate funding to support distance education programs can result in inequitable services provided for on-campus and off-campus students and the dependence by the off-site and/or provider library on other libraries to provide services (Ryan et al., 2000). An institution must make an economic commitment to provide ancillary services to the distance learner.

"Distance educators seem to have a clear understanding that student support services are integral. However, there is surprisingly little hard knowledge about what works, and why" (Rumble, 2000, p. 233). Students deserve the same level of support whether they are in a traditional or non-traditional course. They deserve additional help in dealing with administrative, technical, and personal problems related to the course (Moore & Kearsley, 1996). Providing student support if and when it is needed is critical to the success of the distance education program.

Marie Kascus and William Aguilar (1988) argued that if a campus library assumed all responsibility for its off-site students, the development of the service would be at the expense of the on-campus library program. Dugan and Hernon (1997) determined that, while the on-campus program may suffer because of the effort needed to support a distance education program, the distance education students still did not receive the same services as the on-campus students. The distance education students lacked immediate access to and availability of materials and a face-to-face experience with a librarian concerning information access, filtering, and analysis.

The principal question in this research asked if MSVCC online students self-report that they were satisfied with the support services provided by the learning resources center, specifically the library. Support services in question include: the availability of a library within a reasonable distance, access to library resources, the delivery of needed materials, instruction in the use of library resources, and communication between library staff members and students. Support services must be comparable to those given on-campus students "and should include instruction in the use of library resources, printed and electronic; quick turnaround time for requested material not available in the library; quick response time to library related questions; and quick response time to non-library related questions" (Lebowitz, 1997, p. 307).

Related Research Studies

Burge (1991) analyzed two studies that explored the relationships among libraries, distance educators, and distance learners and found that librarians were totally isolated from the distance education environment. Due to the results of these studies, Burge stressed the urgency for librarians to play a more participatory role and to re-establish themselves as educators.

In 1994, The University of Tennessee conducted a survey and verified that the library was meeting the needs of the distance learners even though the students did not utilize the electronic resources available. The students received other kinds of library help, such as the interlibrary loan of books (Casado, 2001).

Weiser (1999) conducted a study that found a number of virtual libraries that support distance education, such as the University of Phoenix Library. Findings from this study indicated no significant differences in academic performance between distance learners and their on-campus counterparts. Distance education students were able to locate needed resources for assignments, even if they were not exactly sure where to locate them.

Teaster and Blieszner (1999) found that students were satisfied with this new medium, but they felt they needed more support and guidance in order to be able to take full advantage of the distance learning experience. They found that over half of the students were willing to take another course of this nature.

Fergusin and Wijekumar (2000) conducted a study of students at Indiana University of Pennsylvania and found that 75% of the students were extremely satisfied with the distance education course(s) and the services they received. Ninety percent of the students rated the technology aspect of distance learning as satisfactory.

Two surveys conducted by Murray State University in Spring 2000 and Spring 2001 revealed that 68% of students used the library for preparing some assignments. The most popular venue, used by 43% of the students, was access to online resources provided by MSU. Library resources were very helpful for 54% of the student population. Approximately 25% found library resources to be only somewhat helpful. Eight percent of the students were totally dissatisfied. Survey results also indicated that 84% of the students used books in research and 67% used journals. Online resources were used by 66% of the students. As a result of these surveys, some changes were made in subscriptions from print to electronic format to better meet the needs of the students. Library-generated materials (brochures, guides, and newsletters) have become more available to customers by becoming part of the library homepage. "Meeting service expectations of clientele that are somewhat dissatisfied can be accomplished by staff training and through publicity materials" (Culpepper, 2001, p. 67).

Future of Distance Learning

Virtual universities composed of a web of educational providers that collectively distribute services at the time, place, pace, and learning style of each individual student forms the foundation for higher education (Busacco, 2001).

Management theorist Peter Drucker predicted that 10% of existing colleges and 50% of independent colleges will close by the year 2025. Drucker concluded that "the traditional university becomes a wasteland within the next 25 years" (Dunn, 2000, p. 35). As the number of degree-granting institutions grows, the number of traditional campuses declines. Busacco (2001) confirmed this concept stating that some of today's existing independent colleges are closed, merged, or significantly altered in mission (Busacco, 2001).

Dunn (2000) offered the following conclusions and predictions for higher education: the number of degree-granting institutions increases, while the number of traditional universities decreases; university degrees are available at all levels through the use of information technology; courseware products bypass the institution and are provided directly to the learner; the distance between distance and local education is blurred; students are encouraged to move directly from high school to graduate programs; home-school leads to home-college; outsourcing of university functions occur; colleges and universities are responsible for paying taxes; two types of institutions exist, degree and certificate-granting institutions; distinctions between public and private institutions disappear; colleges and universities band together to deliver courses to students; accreditation is based more on educational outcomes; faculty revolt against the use of technology to deliver courses; the U.S. government continues to certify institutions for financial aid; and courseware applications cover 50% of all credits.

With predictions like these, colleges and universities must plan now for the future while remembering that students are vessels to be filled.

CONCLUSION

Effective distance education programs do not just happen; they evolve (Palloff & Pratt, 1999). For years, distance education was considered experimental, even questionable. Now, distance education is considered to be an increasingly important facet of education (Ryan et al., 2000). Many institutions are trying to position themselves so that they can offer online courses instead of losing them to competition. In order to effectively meet their students' demands to provide a wide variety of resources, while hampered by limited funding, community colleges are relying on past and present experiences of other institutions.

"The literature points out that there is a market for library resources and services wherever distance education is delivered" (Culpepper, 2001, p. 69). Librarians cannot overlook the opportunity to promote their resources, create new services, become more involved in the educational process, and to teach research skills. Low visibility of library services seems to be a general weakness that needs to be addressed (Fulcher, 1999).

NEED FOR THE SURVEY

In January 2000, the Mississippi Virtual Community College (MSVCC) began operation with an enrollment of 1382. A Spring 2001 enrollment of 5349 students reflected an approximate 387% expansion (MSVCC). As a result of this dramatic increase, State Board for Community and Junior Colleges (SBCJC, 2001) decided to collect and distribute data, which could be used to enhance all aspects of MSVCC, including library support services.

This study proposed to utilize archival data to determine the quality of library support services offered to distance education students. The instrument sought to determine quality and integrity issues associated with traditional and online learning.

Subjects

All participants in this study were enrolled in at least one MSVCC online course during the Fall 2001 semester. Each student was asked to complete only one survey even if he/she was taking more than one course. Of the class entries, 2309 of the 4781 (approximately 48%) non-duplicated head count responded to the survey.

Delimitations

The delimitations were: (1) the study was delimited to those students enrolled in at least one MSVCC online course and (2) the study was delimited to the self-report of student satisfaction issues related to the quality of library services.

Limitations

The following limitations were imposed: (1) differences existed in library support services provided by the 15 Mississippi public community and junior colleges in Mississippi, (2) the study was limited to the questions and answers that were asked on the survey, (3) the data used for this study were archival data that were collected by the State Board for Community and Junior Colleges in Fall 2001 and (4) the study was limited since the researcher was unable to differentiate the data by college.

Instrument

Descriptive and self-perception questions were included in the survey. Descriptively, the instrument provided demographic pictures of MSVCC students. Self-perception sought the students' self-report of their experiences. A copy of the IERC Committee's MSVCC Student Services Survey appears in Appendix A.

Procedures

In keeping with the MSVCC online medium, all surveys were conducted online. The survey was disseminated to the college Distance Learning Coordinators through links, emailed to all MSVCC Affiliated instructors, and announced on the MSVCC blackboard. The survey was conducted once during the semester, with each student receiving one questionnaire. Fifty-eight (58) questions were presented to MSVCC students. Two thousand three hundred nine (2309) individual student responses were collected. At the time of the survey, approximately 10,000 students were registered in online courses, but each student was asked to complete only one survey, even if he/she was registered in more than one class. SBCJC retrieved the completed surveys from the server and compiled the information into a software program.

ANALYSIS OF DATA

All the data were incorporated into a SPSS statistical software file. The data were then analyzed using frequencies, percentages, means, and standard deviations.

Overview

An analysis of the library resources sector of the Fall 2002 MSVCC Student Survey indicated that Mississippi public community and junior colleges' Learning Resources Centers were doing a good job of serving the virtual community college students in providing access to library materials (Appendix B). The "averaged ratings" showed that the high majority (87%) of MSVCC students using the library resources and instruction rated the services as adequate.

Research Question One

The first research question asked was whether the online courses offered through MSVCC required library resources. The choices given were "strongly agree," "agree," "disagree," "strongly disagree," or "not applicable." A breakdown of the responses to this question is found in Fig. 4.

Survey results indicated that 52% of the students self-reported that library resources were required for their online course. The researcher felt that this question was very misleading since it did not provide a "yes" or "no" response. Survey participants may have been unsure of how to answer this question. It was interesting to note that 20% of the respondents either "disagreed" or "strongly disagreed." Whereas, 28% felt this was "not applicable." Because of the wording of the question, the researcher can only

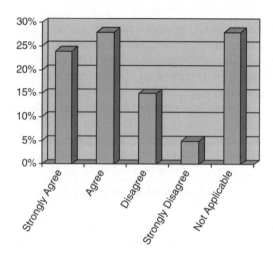

Fig. 4. Research Question 1: The Course(s) that I am Currently Taking Required
Library Resources/Research.

assume that 48% of the respondents reported that their online course(s) did
not require the use of library resources.

The most identifiable concern was the 48% of students who indicated that
no use was made of library resources. Individual faculty were targeted to
educate and inform them of the benefits of the resources offered and to
encourage them to make more assignments which require students to take
advantage of those library resources.

Research Question Two

The second survey question asked whether distance education students self-
reported that they were able to effectively use library resources. The choices
given were "strongly agree," "agree," "disagree," "strongly disagree," or
"not applicable." A breakdown of the responses to this question is found in
Fig. 5.

An analysis of the results has indicated that 58% of the respondents felt
that they were able to effectively use library resources; whereas, 13% were
not able to effectively use the resources. As a note, 29% of the students
surveyed thought the question was not even applicable.

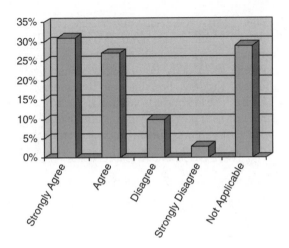

Fig. 5.   Research Question 2: I Learned to Effectively Use Library Resources.

Research Question Three

The third survey question asked whether distance education students self-reported that instruction for using library resources was made available. The choices given were "online through MELO," "handouts," "faculty instruction," or "librarian." A breakdown of the responses to this question is found in Fig. 6.

MELO provides an online tutorial as well as access to a librarian 24 hours a day, 7 days a week. Forty-one percent of the respondents selected MELO as their choice for receiving instruction in the use of library resources. Because of this information, community college librarians have already made the decision to continue supporting the MELO project.

Faculty instruction was also a favorite choice with 30% of the respondents reporting that the faculty provided instruction in the use of library resources. Librarians should realize that the training sessions provided to the instructors proved beneficial in terms of filtering the information through the teacher to the student.

The use of online and print handouts for instruction in the use of library resources reached 15% of the respondents, and the librarian assisted 14% of the respondents with this endeavor.

An analysis of the results indicated that the distance learning student was able to make use of the instructional methods offered. In an effort to better

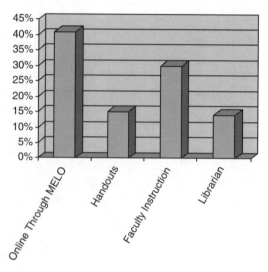

Fig. 6.   Research Question 3: Library Information was Provided in the Following
Way.

serve these students, librarians and faculty should stress the availability of
additional instructional support materials such as the online orientations,
videos, DVDs, and CD-ROMs.

Research Question Four

The fourth survey question asked whether distance education students self-
reported that they were satisfied with instruction received for using library
resources. The choices given were "strongly agree," "agree," "disagree,"
"strongly disagree," or "not applicable." A breakdown of the responses to
this question is found in Fig. 7.

Most students (87%) felt that instruction for library resources was made
available to them and they had effectively learned to use the resources. Only
11% of the respondents indicated that instruction for use of library materials was inadequate, although 2% indicated that such instruction was
"not applicable" for the particular course taken.

Some of the online instructors received training via the Community College Network. All of the instructors attended faculty orientation workshops
and were provided library handbooks and brochures, which identified

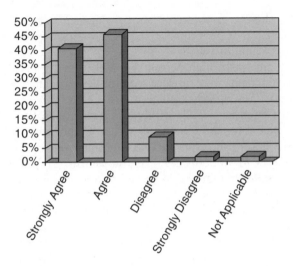

Fig. 7. Research Question 4: The Instruction for Library Material was Adequate.

library and learning resources and services available for all constituents of the College, regardless of location. Group e-mails were implemented for notification of changes and/or additions to the existing resources. The intention of providing instruction for faculty was to increase the faculty knowledge of the library and learning resources available to the distance learner and to help them integrate these resources into their courses. Also, an online orientation and a physical brochure which reflects library resources and services was made available for online students and faculty members.

Each student enrolled in an online course was emailed the link to the MELO website where an online orientation was located. This orientation included information about MAGNOLIA and MELO, as well as contact information about each community college library. A "Distance Education Library Orientation," in the form of a CD, DVD, or VHS was available for student checkout at all libraries. This in-depth orientation provided more detailed information to the student in hopes of encouraging them to utilize the available resources.

Research Question Five

The fifth survey question asked whether distance education students self-reported that offline library resources were delivered in a reasonable length of time. The choices given were "strongly agree," "agree," "disagree," "strongly disagree," or "not applicable." A breakdown of the responses to this question is found in Fig. 8.

Although there was a high percentage in the "not applicable" section, 34% of the respondents were satisfied with the delivery rate of books and/or magazine articles not provided online.

Mississippi Community College Libraries have established a Reciprocal Lending Agreement for the Mississippi Virtual Community College. It was created by the library directors in 2001 and approved by the community college presidents in March 2002. This document established a lending agreement for statewide library cooperation. Reciprocal lending is not intended to substitute for the provision by each community college of adequate library resources and services to support students, but it was created to increase access to library resources by the member libraries, to maximize use of the combined collections of the member libraries, and to support the Mississippi Virtual Community College. Students may conduct online searches of the individual libraries for books which he/she may need for an assignment, and request the book from the nearest community college library. Participation in the agreement by college libraries was voluntary.

In addition to the mutual loan agreement for the MSVCC program one other consortia agreement was in place for the participating community

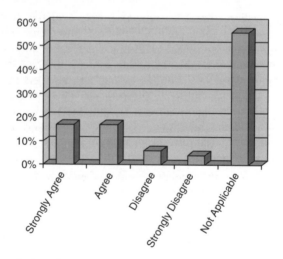

Fig. 8. Research Question 5: If I Needed Resources which were not Online, the Resources were Delivered with a Reasonable Period of Time.

colleges. MCCLIP is an agreement between Mississippi State University and 13 Mississippi community college libraries and was completed by Letters of Agreement on April 6, 2001. MCCLIP helped facilitate cooperation and sharing of resources between Mississippi's community college libraries and Mississippi State University libraries. The partnership allowed all libraries to share resources, excluding electronic resources.

SUMMARY

Distance learning has a well-developed history in the Mississippi Community and Junior College System. Progressive participation in distance education was seen as an integral mechanism for achieving the mission of the system; providing opportunities for continuing education in academic, technical, vocational, and adult education, and providing leadership in civic, cultural, and economic growth.

Through MSVCC, Mississippi's public community and junior colleges offered students the opportunity to achieve their educational goals through on-line classes in addition to the traditional on-campus offerings. The growth and popularity of online classes and the resulting growth in online enrollment provided the impetus for this study.

This chapter presents the researcher's conclusions and recommendations after gathering and analyzing the archival data. As mentioned previously, the survey instrument included descriptive and self-perception explorations. Descriptively, the instrument provided demographic pictures of MSVCC students, but due to restrictions set by SBCJC, the researcher was unable to utilize this data. A copy of the IERC Committee's MSVCC Student Services Survey appears in Appendix A.

Questions 1–10 under Section VI – Library Resources were analyzed for this study. The researcher used survey question 1 under library resources to answer research question 1. Survey question 5 under library resources was used to answer research question 2. Survey question 7 under library resources was used to answer research question 3. Survey question 6 under library resources was used to answer research question 4. Survey question 3 under library resources was used to answer research question 5.

All participants in this study were enrolled in at least one MSVCC online course during the Fall 2001 semester. Each student was asked to complete only one survey even if he/she was taking more than one course. Of the class entries, 2309 of the 4781 (approximately 48%) non-duplicated head count responded to the survey.

An analysis of the library resources sector of the Fall 2002 MSVCC Student Survey indicated that Mississippi public community and junior colleges' Learning Resources Centers were doing a good job of serving the virtual community college students in providing access to library materials. The "averaged ratings" showed that the high majority of MSVCC students (87%) using the library resources and instruction rated the services as adequate.

The study provided administrators and library staff members with the data necessary to determine if they are meeting the needs of the distance learner. The results enable administrators to make meaningful changes and/or additions to the support services offered to the student.

RECOMMENDATIONS

An important component in promoting overall student satisfaction and retention is the quality of support services provided to the student. It is important that online learners feel that they are part of the college community and are provided with the same support services as traditional students. Therefore, the researcher offers the following recommendations to assist in this endeavor: (1) develop an online publication to inform distance learners of new and existing library resources; (2) create a Learning Resources Centers bulletin board for distance learners to post any issues, concerns or ideas that might aid the enhancement of the distance education program; (3) the MELO project should be continued, expanded, and supported by all colleges participating in the MSVCC; (4) funding should be in place to employ a librarian and/or other staff whose sole responsibility is MELO; (5) each college should contribute library funding to create an electronic collection of resources to be used by MELO; and (6) community college libraries should work together to enhance the community college experience for distance learning students.

CONCLUSION

The survey questions as they have appeared on this survey have not provided the library directors with the information needed to determine student satisfaction with learning resources. A revised survey (Appendix C) needs to be implemented immediately in order to truly assess the quality of resources available to the students. Librarians also need to survey faculty members (Appendix D) to determine any shortcomings in order to promote faculty use of the many library resources available.

As was evident with any survey data, there existed room for improvement and advancement in MSVCC endeavors. However, colleges, faculty, administration, and staff associated with MSVCC should be encouraged by the current data. Future revisions of survey methods are planned in order to better assess all areas of service (Appendices C and D).

REFERENCES

ACRL Distance Learning Section Guidelines Committee. (2000). Guidelines for distance learning library services. *College & Research Libraries News, 61*(11), 1023.

Beck, E. (January/February, 2003). Distance education: A global perspective. *Adjunct Advocate, 10*(3), 12.

Burge, E. (1991). *Relationships and responsibilities: Librarians and distance educators working together* (Opening keynote address for the Off-Campus Library Services Conference). Albuquerque, NM: Ontario Institute for Studies in Education.

Busacco, D. (2001, February). Learning at a distance: Technology and the new professional. *ASHA Leader, 6*(2), 4.

Cartwright, G. P. (1994, July/August). Distance learning, *Change [on-line], 26.* Available: EbscoHost/Academic Search Elite.

Casado, M. (2001, April). Delivering library services to remote students. *Computers in Libraries, 21*(4), 32.

Conaway, C. (2002, 1st Quarter). Virtual University. *Regional Review [on-line], 12.* Available: EbscoHost/Academic Search Elite.

Culpepper, J. C. (2001). Pragmatic assessment impacts support for distance education. *Collection Management, 26*(4), 59.

Dugan, R. E., & Hernon, P. (1997, July). Distance education: Provider and victim libraries. *Journal of Academic Librarianship, 23*(4), 315.

Dunn, S. L. (2000, March/April). The virtualizing of education. *Futurist, 34*(2), 34.

Duvall, C. K., & Schwartz, R. G. (2000). Distance education: Relationship between academic performance and technology-adept adult students. *Education and Information Technologies, 5*(3), 177.

Fleischman, John. (1998). Distance learning and adult basic education. *Ohio: Ohio State University.* Available: ERIC/ACVE.

Fulcher, G., & Lock, D. (1999). Distance education: The future of library and information services requirements. *Distance Education, 20*(2), 313.

Gubbins, J. (1998, Spring). Help line: The ultimate in distance support. *Online Journal of Distance Learning Administration, 1*(1). Available: http://www.westga.edu/~distance/gubbins11.html.

Hyatt, S. (1998, Spring). Distance learning in the millennium: Where is it going? *Online Journal of Distance Learning Administration, 1*(1). Available: http://www.westga.edu/~distance/hyatt11.html

Kascus, M. (1994). What library schools teach about library support to distance students: A survey. *American Journal of Distance Education, 8*(1), 20–35.

Kascus, M., & Aguilar, W. (January 1988). Providing library support to off-campus programs. *College & Research Libraries [on-line], 49.* Available: EbscoHost/Academic Search Elite.

Kerka, S. (1996). Distance learning, the Internet and the World Wide Web. *ERIC Digest (ED295214) [on-line]*. Available: ERIC/ACVE.

Kirk, E. E., & Bartelstein, A. M. (1999, April). Libraries close in on distance education. *Library Journal, 124*(6), 40.

League for Innovation in the Community College. (1996). *Learning without limits: Model distance education programs in community colleges*. Mission Viego: League for Innovation.

Lebowitz, G. (1997, July). Library services to distant students: An equity issue. *Journal of Academic Librarianship [on-line], 23*. Available: EbscoHost/Academic Search Elite.

Libutti, P. O. (Ed.) (1999). *Librarians as learners, librarians as teachers: The diffusion of Internet and expertise in the academic library*. Chicago: Association of College and Research Libraries.

Moore, M. J., & Kearsley, G. (1996). *Distance Education: A system's view*. Belmont: Wadsworth Publishing Company.

Niemi, J. A., & Ehrhard, B. J. (1998, Summer). Off-campus library support for distance adult learners. *Library trends [on-line], 47*. Available: EbscoHost/Academic Search Elite

O'Leary, M. (2002, March). E-global library advances the virtual library. *Information Today, 19*(3), 19.

O'Quinn, L., & Corry, M. (2002, Winter). Factors that deter faculty from participating in distance education. *Online Journal of Distance Learning Administration, 5*(4). Available: http://www.westga.edu/~distance/jmain11.html.

Oberg, D., & Henri, J. (1999). Changing concerns in distance education for teacher-librarianship. *Education for Information, 17*(1), 21.

Ostendorf, V. A. (1997). Teaching and learning at a distance: What it takes to effectively design, deliver, and evaluate programs. *Teaching By Television, 71*, 54.

Palloff, R. M., & Pratt, K. (1999). *Building learning communities in cyberspace: Effective strategies for the online classroom*. San Francisco: Jossey-Bass Publishers.

Perraton, H. D. (2000). *Open and distance learning in the developing world*. New York: Routledge.

Qureshi, E., Morton, L. L., & Antosz, E. (2002, Winter). An interesting profile-university students who take distance education courses show weaker motivation than on-campus students. *Online Journal of Distance Learning Administration, 5*(4). Available: http://www.westga.edu/~distance/ojdla/winter54/Qureshi54.htm.

Roccos, L. J. (2001, Fall). Distance learning and distance libraries: Where are they now? *Online Learning of Distance Learning Administration, 4*(4). Available: http://www.westga.edu/~distance/ojdla/fall43/roccos43.html.

Rumble, G. (2000). Student support in distance education in the 21st century: Learning from service management. *Distance Education, 21*(2), 216.

Ryan, S., et al. (2000). *The virtual university: The Internet and resource-based learning*. Sterling: Kogan Page.

State Board for Community and Junior Colleges. (2000, Fall). *The Mississippi virtual community college: Fall 2000 survey results*. Jackson: State Board for Community and Junior Colleges.

State Board for Community and Junior Colleges. (2001, Spring). *The Mississippi virtual community college: Spring 2001 survey results*. Jackson: State Board for Community and Junior Colleges.

State Board for Community and Junior Colleges. (2001, Fall). *The Mississippi virtual community college: Fall 2001 survey results.* Jackson: State Board for Community and Junior Colleges.

Teaster, P., & Blieszner, R. (1999). Promises and pitfalls of the interactive television approach to teaching adult development and aging. *Educational Gerontology, 25*(8), 743.

Tulloch, J. (2000, Nov). Sophisticated technology offers higher education options. *The Journal, 28*(4), 58.

Valentine, D. (2002, Fall). Distance learning: Promises, problems, and possibilities. *Distance Learning Administration, 5*(3). Available: http://www.westga.edu/~distance/ojdla/fall53/valentine53.html.

Wagner, L. (2001, Fall). Virtual advising: Delivering student services. *Distance Learning Administration, 4*(4). Available: http://www.westga.edu/~distance/ojdla/fall43/wagner43.html.

Weiser, A. (1999, May). PA approves Phoenix campuses. *Library Journal, 124*(8), 19.

Willis, B. (1993). *Distance education: A practical guide.* Englewood Cliffs: Educational Technology Publications.

Wittkopf, B., Orgeron, E., & Del Nero, T. (2001). Louisiana academic libraries: Partnering to enhance distance education services. *Journal of Library Administration, 32*(1), 439.

APPENDIX A. MSVCC STUDENT SERVICES SURVEY

I. Student Profile

1. How many classes are you taking through the Mississippi Virtual Community College?

    One   Two   Three or more

2. How many previous on-line courses have you completed?

    None   One   Two   Three or more

3. Your academic standing:

    Freshman   Sophomore   Associates or   Don't Know
                                          Higher

4. Your race:

    Asian/Pacific   Black, Non-Hispanic   Hispanic
    Islander
    Native   White, Non-Hispanic   Prefer Not to Say
    American

5. Your gender:

    Female   Male   Prefer Not to Say

6. Your age group:

Under 18	18–19	20–21	22–24
25–29	30–34	35–39	40–49
50–64	65 and Over		

7. Your martial status:

Single	Married	Divorced/Separated
Widow/	Prefer Not to Say	
Widower		

8. Your general major field:

Academic	Technical	Vocational	Don't Know

9. What is your primary reason for taking online classes?

    Transportation Issues
    Class was not available or a regular classroom section was not open
    Online classes fit my work/job hours better
    Family/home (including childcare) responsibilities
    My advisor recommended online classes
    A friend recommended online classes
    I enjoy computers and the Internet. I wanted to try taking classes
      this way
    I have previously taken online classes and the experience was
      positive
    I thought this would be an easy alternate to regular classes
    Other

10. If online classes were not available, would you have enrolled in a regular
    classroom course?

    Definitely would have taken a regular class
    Probably would have taken a regular class
    Probably would not have taken a regular class
    Definitely would not have taken a regular class

11. Based on your experience so far, how would you rate the quality of
    instruction provided in online classes?

Excellent	Good	Average	Fair	Poor

12. Based on your experience so far, how do you feel the quality of online instruction compares with traditional courses you have taken?

Online instruction is better than traditional classroom instruction
Instructional quality is about the same online as in the traditional classroom
Traditional classroom instruction is better than online instruction

II. Student Services

1. I had access to adequate support and assistance in registration.

    Strongly Agree   Agree   Disagree   Strongly Disagree
    Not Applicable

2. College procedures were adequately described or provided to me.

    Strongly Agree   Agree   Disagree   Strongly Disagree
    Not Applicable

3. Advisement services were provided to me to assist in course selection and placement.

    Strongly Agree   Agree   Disagree   Strongly Disagree
    Not Applicable

4. Contact was easily made with the instructor.

    Strongly Agree   Agree   Disagree   Strongly Disagree
    Not Applicable

5. Student services were available to me throughout the time period of the course.

    Strongly Agree   Agree   Disagree   Strongly Disagree
    Not Applicable

III. Interaction and Communication

1. I had adequate interaction with the course materials.

    Strongly Agree   Agree   Disagree   Strongly Disagree
    Not Applicable

2. I had adequate interaction with the instructor.

    Strongly Agree   Agree   Disagree   Strongly Disagree
    Not Applicable

3. I had adequate interaction with other students.

Strongly Agree   Agree   Disagree   Strongly Disagree
Not Applicable

4. The discussion groups were supportive of the learning experience.

Strongly Agree   Agree   Disagree   Strongly Disagree
Not Applicable

5. The chat rooms were supportive of the learning experience.

Strongly Agree   Agree   Disagree   Strongly Disagree
Not Applicable

6. I adequately felt a part of a learning community.

Strongly Agree   Agree   Disagree   Strongly Disagree
Not Applicable

IV. Course Evaluation

1. This course is what you expected.

Strongly Agree   Agree   Disagree   Strongly Disagree
Not Applicable

2. The course site was well organized and easy to navigate.

Strongly Agree   Agree   Disagree   Strongly Disagree
Not Applicable

3. The content of the course presentations contributed to my learning.

Strongly Agree   Agree   Disagree   Strongly Disagree
Not Applicable

4. The textbook supported the course presentations and was
    appropriate.

Strongly Agree   Agree   Disagree   Strongly Disagree
Not Applicable

5. The supplemental materials contributed to the learning experience.

Strongly Agree   Agree   Disagree   Strongly Disagree
Not Applicable

6. The course evaluations were fair and supported the learning experience.

    Strongly Agree   Agree   Disagree   Strongly Disagree
    Not Applicable

V. Instructor Evaluation

1. The instructor designed the course to accomplish stated objectives.

    Strongly Agree   Agree   Disagree   Strongly Disagree
    Not Applicable

2. The instructor contributed to my learning experience.

    Strongly Agree   Agree   Disagree   Strongly Disagree
    Not Applicable

3. The instructor promptly responded to request for assistance.

    Strongly Agree   Agree   Disagree   Strongly Disagree
    Not Applicable

4. The instructor was prepared for conducting classes through distance learning.

    Strongly Agree   Agree   Disagree   Strongly Disagree
    Not Applicable

5. The instructor worked with me to insure a quality learning experience.

    Strongly Agree   Agree   Disagree   Strongly Disagree
    Not Applicable

6. The instructor was fair in grading.

    Strongly Agree   Agree   Disagree   Strongly Disagree
    Not Applicable

V. Library Resources

1. Did the course you are taking require library resources/research?

    Yes   No

2. How have you made use of library resources?

    Online   In Person   Telephone   Not at all

3. Which of the following electronic resources have you used?

    Magnolia   MELO   Online   Library Catalogs
    Other

4. For your online course assignments, did you use books and magazines
    which were not online?

    Yes   No

5. How often did you use online library services?

    Very Often   Often   Sometimes   Very Little   Not at all

6. Were offline resources delivered to you in a reasonable amount of time?

    Yes   No

7. Was instruction for using library resources made available to you?

    Yes   No

8. How was instruction for using library resources made available to you?

    Online (MELO)   Handouts   Faculty Instruction
    Librarian

9. How would you rate the adequacy of instruction for library materials?

    Adequate   Fair   Needs Improvement

10. Were you able to effectively use library resources?

    Yes   No

APPENDIX B. LEARNING RESOURCES DATABASES

MSVCC students have access to a number of online learning resources.
Included in these resources are databases provided through MAGNOLIA,
MELO, and the online library catalogs of all fifteen Mississippi community
and junior colleges. MSVCC consortium libraries are interlinked through
a network created in 1996 from funds appropriated by the Mississippi
Legislature in 1995. The $29,000,000 created the infrastructure both each
campus and the network that has linked the libraries of each institution.
    MAGNOLIA, Mississippi Alliance for Gaining New Opportunities
through Library Information Access, is a statewide consortium, which is

funded by the Mississippi Legislature. MAGNOLIA provides online databases for publicly funded K-12 schools, public libraries, community college libraries, and universities and university libraries in Mississippi. Students can use the MAGNOLIA databases by accessing the links provided by their community college library or from their home/remote computer by securing a user name from their library. The databases include EBSCOhost, FirstSearch, Gale's Info Trac, Grolier, SIRS, and Wilson Biographies.

The Mississippi community college library directors were commissioned by their presidents to develop an adequate library services program that would support the needs of the MSVCC students and faculty. In March 2000 Mississippi Electronic Libraries Online (MELO) was created under the leadership of librarians at Copiah-Lincoln, Northeast, and Mississippi Gulf Coast Community Colleges to meet the academic resource needs of distance learning within the community colleges.

MELO is an electronic environment that mirrors the traditional library through online databases, electronic books and journals, and scholarly websites. It strives to collect, store and organize information on a broad range of subjects. By encouraging cooperative efforts of the Mississippi Community Colleges and by promoting economic delivery of information, MELO supports the needs and interests of students and faculty. Content for the collection is examined for its currency, usefulness and relevancy within the scope of appropriate academic materials.

MELO is available to all students and faculty through the MSVCC web page found at http://www.msvcc.org. MELO's homepage provides links that give general information such as hours, addresses, and contact information for each community college library. It also includes links to proprietary databases and selected websites appropriate for each subject discipline.

MELO databases may be accessed directly at http://www.colin.edu/databases.htm and include *Issues & Controversies, Today's Sciences, Magill-On-Literature* and others. *Issues & Controversies* is a *Facts on File* product that offers authoritative information from opposing viewpoints about current and historical issues. *Today's Science* is a widely recognized reference science database. *Magill-On-Literature* is a standard source of information that gives reviewed analysis and brief plot summaries of the most studied works in literature. Other databases found on this page include all of the MAGNOLIA databases bringing the student quick access to a wide range of research material. The databases are available with unlimited simultaneous remote access to the distance student with pertinent contact information given at the website. In May 2002, training sessions were held for staff members from the libraries of the participating MSVCC institutions. The training sessions were designed around the use of the MELO databases and provided the library staff members with the ability to return to their respective institutions and teach their faculty and students how these resources could help in the virtual classes.

Online reference help is provided through MELO's homepage that gives the student access to 24/7 'live chat' reference services. Through this service students have access to a trained librarian any day 24 h a day. Other methods of obtaining reference help include links on MELO that provide email addresses, electronic reference form, and telephone numbers for all community college libraries. Reference help is also available by phone or in person at each library.

APPENDIX C. REVISED MSVCC STUDENT SERVICES SURVEY

1. I am enrolled in:

    [ ] Online classes only
    [ ] Both online and on campus

2. The online course(s) that I am currently taking require(s) library resources/research:

    [ ] Yes
    [ ] No (If no, do not continue with the survey).

3. I used library resources in the following ways (mark all that apply):

    [ ] Online
    [ ] In person
    [ ] By telephone
    [ ] Not at all

4. I used online services and resources:

    [ ] Very often (daily)
    [ ] Often (more than once weekly)
    [ ] Sometimes
    [ ] Very little

5. I learned about online libraries and how to use their resources from:

    [ ] Campus Library Online
    [ ] MELO
    [ ] Handouts
    [ ] Faculty Instruction
    [ ] Librarian

6. I used the following electronic resources:

    [ ] MAGNOLIA (EBSCOhost and others)
    [ ] MELO (MS Electronic Libraries Online)

7. I needed books and magazines for online classes which were NOT available online.

    [ ] Yes
    [ ] No (If no, go to question 9)

8. Resources that I could not get online, I requested from a community college library and received them in a timely manner.

    [ ] Strongly agree
    [ ] Agree
    [ ] Disagree
    [ ] Strongly disagree
    [ ] Not applicable

9. I learned to effectively use library resources.

    [ ] Strongly agree
    [ ] Agree
    [ ] Disagree
    [ ] Strongly disagree
    [ ] Not applicable

APPENDIX D. MSVCC FACULTY SERVICES SURVEY

1. The course(s) that I teach online require(s) library resources/research.

    [ ] Yes
    [ ] No

2. I used library resources to prepare my online courses.

   [ ] Yes
   [ ] No (If no, do not continue with the survey).

3. Instruction for using library resources has been made available to me.

   [ ] Yes
   [ ] No

4. Library instruction was provided in the following ways:

   [ ] Individual instruction by library personnel
   [ ] Group instruction for distance learning instructors
   [ ] E-mail or other online instruction

5. Check the following electronic resources that you use or you require your students to use online:

   [ ] MAGNOLIA Products (EBSCOhost and others)
   [ ] MELO (MS Electronic Libraries Online)
   [ ] Online Library Catalogs

6. I can effectively use library resources.

   [ ] Strongly agree
   [ ] Agree
   [ ] Disagree
   [ ] Strongly disagree
   [ ] Not applicable

7. How do you rate library support to you and your distance education students?

   [ ] Very Good
   [ ] Good
   [ ] Adequate
   [ ] Needs Improvement

ORGANIZATIONAL SENSEMAKING AS A THEORETICAL FRAMEWORK FOR THE STUDY OF LIBRARY LEADERSHIP

Tara Lynn Fulton

Why do leaders act the way they do? How do they consider a multitude of factors and options, and then decide how to move the organization forward? How do they adjust to changing clientele demands and community perceptions, and integrate them meaningful into plans for library collections and services? What mechanisms do library leaders use to influence others in the organization? If these questions fascinate you, read on.

In this paper I explain one way we might look at library administration—through the lens of a theoretical framework called organizational sensemaking. I chronicle some of the work already done in business and higher education settings to show the framework's potential value within our own field, and I share with you a study I conducted as an example of how one might use organizational sensemaking. For those of you who might want to consider conducting research from the organizational sensemaking perspective, some insights are offered about ways you might get started. For practitioners, organizational sensemaking may give you a new way in which to understand both your own leadership and the leadership of those around you.

Advances in Library Administration and Organization
Advances in Library Administration and Organization, Volume 22, 113–156
Copyright © 2005 by Elsevier Ltd.
ISSN: 0732-0671/doi:10.1016/S0732-0671(05)22004-7

OVERVIEW OF ORGANIZATIONAL SENSEMAKING

A Vignette

Marion has just taken on the directorship of a joint university/public library. You, as her protégé, are interested in observing how she approaches the new venture. You are curious about what information she will gather, whose advice she will seek, how she will figure out the expectations others have of her and the library, how she will prioritize the many challenges before her, and how she will negotiate her leadership role with the staff. In other words, you want to study Marion's organizational sensemaking.

Definition

Organizational sensemaking is one of several frameworks which apply cognitive science concepts to the study of organizations. "Sensemaking is a set of ideas emanating from the fields of psychology and organization studies that seeks to reveal how individuals construct meaning, interpret their world, and function within it" (Sutherland & Dawson, 2002, pp. 52–53). Those who study organizational sensemaking are interested in "how people in organizations think about their experiences and how they act in conjunction with their thoughts" (Gioia & Sims, 1986, p. 2). One of the major scholars in the area of sensemaking, Gioia, defined it as follows:

> Sensemaking is perhaps one of the few terms in the social and organizational sciences that means literally what it says: sensemaking refers to the concern with making sense of events and experience. ... Sensemaking is meaning construction. It is the process whereby people attempt to construct meaningful explanations for situations and their experiences within those situations (Gioia, 1986b, p. 61).

Sensemaking thus involves "the non-obvious analysis of things that at first blush appear patently obvious" (Gioia & Mehra, 1996, p. 1227). It asks the question: "How do [people] create a meaningful day-to-day world out of the many complex events taking place in a modern organization?" (Gioia, 1986b, p. 50).

Properties of Sensemaking

In his seminal book entitled Organizational Sensemaking, Karl Weick (1995) offered a set of seven properties that characterize sensemaking. They "serve as a rough guideline for inquiry into sensemaking," and they "suggest what sensemaking is, how it works, and where it can fail" (Weick, 1995, p. 18). While on first reading these properties seem somewhat obtuse, their relevance and meaning become clearer as one reads on.

1. Sensemaking is grounded in identity construction and maintenance. Sensemaking study begins with the individual doing the sensemaking. The sensemaker constructs images of oneself and one's organization, and is affected by the images others have (Weick, 1995, pp. 18–20). Organizational members are continually redefining their sense of themselves and the organization based on feedback from the environment.
2. Sensemaking involves reflection on elapsed experience. "To talk about sensemaking is to talk about reality as an ongoing accomplishment that takes form when people make retrospective sense of the situations in which they find themselves and their creations" (Weick, 1995, p. 15). In other words, the researcher gets participants to tell stories about their experiences and actions – what they thought about, why they did what they did.
3. Sensemaking involves enactment—not just the perceptions and thought processes of those in organizations, but how those perceptions and thoughts are manifested in action. Sensemaking involves "an effort to tie beliefs and actions more closely together" (Weick, 1995, p. 135). People are seen as being part of the environment, and thus they create their own constraints and opportunities to some degree (Weick, 1995, p. 31). Sensemaking is ongoing, not a one-time event. One is always in the process of making sense. One's actions in one phase of sensemaking come back to influence future sensemaking; i.e. sensemaking involves "creation as well as discovery" (Weick, 1995, p. 8).
4. Social contact is crucial to the construction and perception of problems during sensemaking. People do not "make sense" in isolation, but rather in dialogue with others. Attention is paid to talk and conversation, because "people actively shape each other's meanings and sensemaking processes" (Weick, 1995, p. 41).
5. One attempts to make sense of a phenomenon that stands out from the flow of ongoing events. Organizational sensemaking commences when there is some kind of shock that stimulates people to pay attention and to initiate action (Weick, 1995, p. 84). It is when we are interrupted from the normal flow of events, such as when milestone incidents occur, that we react emotionally and sensemaking is triggered (Weick, 1995, p. 45).
6. The sensemaker looks for cues in the environment—surprises, novelties, elements that do not fit. Weick described sensemaking as being about

how individuals attend to cues in the environment, filter them, select them, interpret them, and link them, as well as how interpretations and meanings are revised and made more explicit through action (Weick, 1995, p. 8). While extracted cues provide points of reference, context is very important in determining how an individual will make sense of the situation (Weick, 1995, p. 51). There is a recognition that different people in an organization will have different interpretations of and reactions to the same event (Weick, 1995, p. 53).

7. The sensemaker searches for plausible explanations rather than accurate ones. Interpersonal perceptions are often just as important in organizations as whatever might be "real" in an observable sense (Weick, 1995, pp. 56, 59). Accuracy is "nice but not necessary in sensemaking" (Weick, 1995, p. 59). Rather a "good story" that is coherent, reasonable, credible and/or memorable may be more important to "energizing and guiding action" (Weick, 1995, pp. 60–61).

Weick tied these seven elements together in the following summary of sensemaking process:

> Once people begin to act (enactment), they generate tangible outcomes (cues) in some context (social), and this helps them discover (retrospect) what is occurring (ongoing), what needs to be explained (plausibility), and what should be done next (identity enhancement) (Weick, 1995, p. 55).

HISTORY, VALUE, AND NATURE OF ORGANIZATIONAL SENSEMAKING RESEARCH

History of Sensemaking as a Theoretical Framework

"One of the most important developments in organization science during the past 20 years has been the growing interest in how organizational members conceptualize and make sense of their organizational worlds" (Porac, Meindl, & Stubbart, 1996, p. ix). Sensemaking as a theoretical framework for the study of organizations evolved from changes within the fields of sociology, psychology, and organizational theory. It represented a melding of concepts that were moving along parallel paths. Gradually during the 1970s the strands began to intersect and come together.

During the 1960s developments within sociology "called into question a strictly realist view of the world" (Porac et al., 1996, p. x). A field evolved which was called social constructivism or social interactionism, because it started from the premise that

> there can be no objective social or organizational reality because reality is a product of perceptual and interpretive processes. ... In a significant sense, then, perception and interpretation are all that matter. Perception and interpretation *define* reality (Gioia, 1989, p. 222).

Social constructionists believe that individuals actively interact with, construct, and shape their environments and their realities. "Social reality, insofar as it is recognized to have an existence outside the consciousness of any single individual, is regarded as being little more than a network of assumptions and inter-subjectively shared meanings" (Burrell & Morgen, 1979, pp. 28, 31).

Within this tradition, organizations also came to be seen as social constructions: Berger and Luckman's (1967) The Social Construction of Reality served as the core text on the sociology of knowledge from the constructivist view. According to them, organizational members create the realities they inhabit. As Gioia (1986a, p. 348) articulated it: "organizational reality is a socially constructed one, forged out of consensus of vision and action that exists largely or completely in the minds of the organizations' members". Based on language and face-to-face interaction with others, we each internalize particular meanings about events, roles, and other aspects of organizational life. Through interaction, power is negotiated and roles are defined, and thus leadership itself is considered to be a socially constructed phenomenon (Smircich & Morgan, 1982, p. 258).

In 1979 Weick wrote a book entitled The Social Psychology of Organizing, which introduced the term sensemaking, and, as he called it, a "new way of talking about organizations" (1979b, p. 234). It clearly embraced a social constructivist framework. In it he claimed that people invent organizations in order to reduce the equivocality of everyday experience and to create coherent, stable meanings (Weick, 1979b, pp. 12–13); they develop consensus about the meaning of behaviors, events, and actions (Weick, 1979b, p. 165).

Meanwhile, during the 1970s social cognition and information processing models of organizations were also evolving in the field of psychology and being applied to the study of management. The publication of Fiske and Taylor's (1984) text on social cognition was a major step in the evolution of the field. Fiske and Taylor defined social cognition as the study of "how people make sense of other people and themselves" (1984, p. 12). Social cognition is interested in the perceptions, thinking and reasoning behind behavior (Fiske & Taylor, 1984, pp. 9–10). "The growing interest in cognition, both within and between organizations, has coincided (not accidentally) with the increasing legitimacy of a constructionist point of view among organizational scholars" (Porac et al., 1996, p. x).

The broader field in which sensemaking fits is sometimes referred to as managerial and organization cognition. These scholars are interested in how managers absorb, process and disseminate information about the issues, opportunities, and problems facing their organization (Walsh, 1995). They are interested in how managers reason and "figure things out," but not necessarily in logical terms (Isenberg, 1986, pp. 242–243). Focus is on knowledge structures, which are variously referred to as cognitive frameworks, implicit theories, interpretive schemes, mental models, organizational ideologies, thought structures, frames of reference, industry recipes, perceptual filters, belief structures, and more (Walsh, 1995, pp. 284–285). In studying cognitive aspects of organizations, Weick proposed that "the researcher's job is to spot the thinking people in an organization, see what they're thinking about, and examine how those thoughts become amplified or diffused through the organization" (1979a, p. 43). In articulating the need for sensemaking as a theoretical framework, Gioia and Sims asked the fundamental question: "Does the discipline of management really understand the complex internal and social influences that affect and drive organizational behavior?" (1986, p. 5).

Thus, sensemaking as a framework ties the cognitive perspective and social constructivism together (Pfeffer, 1981, p. 3). Managerial and organizational cognition combines the sociologist's interest in beliefs and social practice with the psychologist's interest in decision-making, perception and leadership (Porac et al., 1996, p. xi). Weick recognized the convergence of these strands, and is the one who articulated and named the framework of organizational sensemaking. Weick's 1995 book, Organizational Sensemaking, is the preeminent, seminal work in the field. The book offered a systematic conceptualization of sensemaking as a framework for the study of organizations (Gioia & Mehra, 1996, p. 1228) and precipitated a more coherent and consistent stream of original research.

Sensemaking and the Study of Leadership

Organizational sensemaking has been used as a framework to study many elements of organizational life and organizational communication. In this paper I focus on its application to the study of leadership. Weick contended that "people try hardest to build meaning around those actions to which their commitment is strongest" (1995, p. 156), i.e. those for which they bear heavy responsibility. Thus it is natural that sensemaking scholars have looked especially at managers and management teams.

A basic postulate of the organizational sensemaking literature is that leaders simultaneously study and enact their environments—that managerial thought and action are inseparably woven together (Weick, 1983, p. 222). Leaders influence how organizations enact their environments in that they "choose which aspects of their environments to attend to, and their world views, interests, and biases shape these choices" (Miller, 1993, p. 128).

> Successful members of organizations are typically proficient processors of information and creative architects of meaningful experience. They engage in active attempts to make sense of the myriad of information cues that surround them. They forge understanding out of some very limited and ambiguous cues, and on the basis of that understanding, they act (Gioia & Sims, 1986, p. 2).

Daft and Weick (1984, p. 285) noted that information converges at the top management level, and strategic action is formulated there. From the leader's perspective "the effectiveness of one's organization, as well as the fate of one's own career, often hinges on the mastery of the ability to turn thought into act" (Gioia, 1986a, p. 336).

Management is both an art and a science, requiring analysis, organizing, and deciding, but also intuition, insight, and perception (Gioia, 1986a, p. 339). Sensemaking is good for studying what goes on in the heads and hearts of leaders as they deal with both daily organizational life and with the crises and surprises that inevitably surface. "[L]eaders, by nature of their leadership role, are provided with a distinctive opportunity to influence the sensemaking of others" (Smircich & Morgan, 1982, p. 269). Leaders define reality for others—"leadership actions attempt to shape and interpret situations to guide organizational members into a common interpretation of reality" (Smircich & Morgan, 1982, p. 261). Managers influence the sensemaking processes of organizational members through creation of vision, through management of symbols, and by setting policies and rules about how, what and when they communicate (Smircich & Stubbart, 1985, p. 730). "The cognitive approach to the study of organizations, then, appears to be fruitful for examining the process by which the management of meaning is accomplished" (Pfeffer, 1981, p. 8).

Sensemaking scholars are interested in encouraging "a more informed, more reflective, more self-conscious practice of organization" (Smircich & Stubbart, 1985, p. 733). Ultimately it is hoped that a better understanding of sensemaking will make better leaders. Sensemaking "primes people to be more self-conscious about some of the things they and their associates do automatically when they are puzzled," and thus may lead, according to Weick (1995, p. 182), to more subtlety, and richness of practice. We might hope that a leader's awareness of his/her own sensemaking would alter the dialectic between thought and action, that reflection on sensemaking will improve sensemaking.

Nature of Sensemaking Research

Weaver and Gioia (1994) pointed out that, while theorists sometimes struggle with bridging theoretical views to daily life, ordinary people "manage to succeed tolerably well at it on a fairly regular basis" (1994, p. 572). Sensemaking scholars generally seek to make their work accessible to practitioners, and to write in ways that retain the natural rhythm and feel of their participants' words. Weick described the ways in which sensemaking scholars

- "rely on what participants say and do,"
- "make an effort to preserve action that is situated in context,"
- consider "density of information and vividness of meaning" to be as crucial as precision, and
- produce findings that are "described in terms of patterns rather than hypotheses" (1995, p. 173).

"[T]he richness of one's language is a crucial resource in sensemaking," (Weick, 1995, p. 90).

Weick's sensemaking concept is most compatible with what is known as "interpretative" social science research, according to Hatch and Yanow (2003, p. 75). Interpretivism seeks

> to understand the fundamental nature of the social world at the level of subjective experience. It seeks explanation within the realm of individual consciousness and subjectivity, within the frame of reference of participants as opposed to the observer of action (Burrell & Morgen, 1979, p. 28).

Social scientists from this paradigm seek to "understand the social world from the point of view of those living within it, using constructs and explanations, which are intelligible in terms of the common-sense interpretation of everyday life" (Burrell & Morgan, 1979, p. 246). "Interpretive research explores what strategists were thinking, why they acted as they did, what they wanted to accomplish. Interpretive studies seek to understand the strategists' thoughts and actions at a personal level" (Smircich & Stubbart, 1985, p. 733).

Interpretivism was a reaction against the emphasis on objectivity in research, believing instead that the human element is important—"what is meaningful to people in the social situation under study" (Hatch & Yanow, 2003, p. 66). "[I]nterpretive research is not a quest for ultimate truth, but for a plausible, authoritative, verisimilitudinous and interesting analysis that enriches our understanding of social phenomena" (Brown, 2000, p. 50). It is representative of what Thayer (1988, pp. 232, 238) referred to as more relevant, more humane, more grounded, and non-hegemonic approaches to the study of leadership.

Therefore, the most compatible research methodologies for studying sensemaking fall into the qualitative rather than the quantitative tradition. Sensemaking scholars tend to use more case studies and life story accounts than surveys and data sets (Weick, 1995, p. 172). Weick noted that sensemaking work tends to focus on a small number of cases that are "chosen more for their access to the phenomenon than for their representativeness" (1995, p. 173). Sensemaking is not about proving hypotheses, generating propositions, or creating causal explanations, but more about real life settings (Weick, 1995, p. 173), partially because "cognitive variables are difficult to measure in the field" (Porac et al., 1996, p. xix).

Qualitative research has several oft-cited strengths for the study of organizations. Qualitative research has a unique ability to address the dynamics of situations, and the perceptions of organizational members. It is also good for studying inductive, incremental, emergent, or iterative processes. Qualitative research allows one to look at aspects of leadership that are not readily accessible to quantification, and is more sensitive to organizational context (Bryman, 1996, pp. 288, 289). As Thomas, Gioia, and Ketchen put it: "the strategic sensemaking process has a significant subjective component that only qualitative methods are well-suited to assess" (1997, p. 322). Qualitative research is generally seen as providing a more holistic, in-depth, and localized look at management.

Many theoretical foci exist within the study of sensemaking, and there is an attendant variety of methodological technique used (Porac et al., 1996, p. xiii–xiv).

[M]ethodological breadth indicates that no single method is sufficient to capture the full range of sensemaking within and between organizations. ... An important aspect of the modern attitude toward cognitive research in organizations is the willingness of

researchers to explore multiple methods to triangulate the complexity of sensemaking
process and structures (Porac et al., 1996, p. xiii).

Given the importance of language to sensemaking, it is not surprising that
interviews, conversations, and texts are the most important data sources for
sensemaking research. In-depth, open-ended interviewing is by far the most
common form of data collection for sensemaking scholars. Interview protocols are used to elicit people's accounts of events and their interpretations of
what events mean. People are asked to describe how situations came to be
and why they evolved the way they did.

Second to interviews, the most common methodologies involve participant observation and other ethnographic techniques. Ethnography involves
"immersion in the social context being studied" as the researcher "enters a
new cultural (organizational) domain with little familiarity about its inner
workings" and then strives to understand that social world (Gioia & Chittepeddi, 1991, p. 435). Ethnographic techniques allow researchers to examine interactions, performance, and communications that reflect managerial
sensemaking (Hannabuss, 2000, p. 406).

There has also been some use of organizational texts such as transcripts,
corporate reports/memos, media accounts of events, diaries, and archives
(for example, Balogun & Johnson, 1988; and Gephart, 1993). Texts allow
the researcher to trace the real-time progress of sensemaking processes
rather than relying on the kind of retrospective accounts that interviews do
(Gephart, 1993, p. 1467).

A write-up of sensemaking research is likely to include one or more of
three techniques: a) narratives, b) thematic analyses, and/or c) visual model
building. I will discuss each of these in turn.

People think narratively; in stories, they share an ongoing flow and sequence of experience (Weick, 1995, p. 127). The sensemaking scholar wants
readers to share directly how people reconstruct and make meaning of events
(Weick, 1995, p. 127). Narratives are "one of the natural cognitive and
linguistic forms through which individuals attempt to order, organize and
express meaning" (Mishler, 1986, p. 106). Jonas, Fry, and Srivastva (1989)
encouraged examination of "the raw materials of the sensemaking process by
taking seriously the words that executives use to convey meaning" (1989, p.
213). Narrative analysis asks questions such as "How do stories tie together?," and "How do they relate to each other?" (Mishler, 1986, p. 100).

In drawing out the similarities between individual stories, qualitative researchers, including sensemaking scholars, look for themes and patterns that
hold true for many of the participants in the study. They go beyond

description of individual cases to look for insights that apply across cases and which might add to our theoretical understanding of sensemaking. In data analysis, scholars look for connections, shared elements of sensemaking, as well as differences between participants. Typologies and charts are frequent means by which such patterns are expressed in the literature.

In addition to text, visual depictions of various kinds are used in sensemaking research. One approach is the use of cognitive maps. "Organizations exist largely in the mind, and their existence takes the form of cognitive maps" proclaimed Weick and Bougon (1986, p. 102). A cognitive map is a graphic representation of a person's or group's knowledge structure – "the concepts and the relations a participant uses to understand organizational situations" (Weick & Bougon, 1986, p. 106). It shows the spatial relationships between concepts, how the person classifies things, and how the person abstracts and simplifies a chaotic world (Weick, 1990a, pp. 1, 8). Cognitive maps may be gleaned from questionnaires, interviews, documents, or transcripts (Weick & Bougon, 1986, p. 113), or the researcher might ask participants to render their own. Maps are particularly useful for studies of sensemaking, because they can capture socially constructed realities, tacit values, metaphorical thinking, inconsistencies, and non-rational elements of thought (Weick & Bougon, 1986, p. 124). Maps can trigger memory, reveal gaps in thinking, highlight key factors, categorize, show the scale of various priorities, and show routes to change (Fiol & Huff, 1992, pp. 275–277).

"Studying sensemaking is by no means unproblematic as it involves dealing with context-specific, evolving, and often contradictory interpretations" (Vaara, 2003, p. 868). It is not for the faint of heart, for those with tight research production deadlines, or for those who prefer the clarity of unambiguous methods and outcomes. Given this brief overview of some methodologies used in sensemaking research, let us now look at what has been learned from these literatures so far.

WHAT WE ALREADY KNOW: EXISTING LITERATURE ON SENSEMAKING

Sensemaking Processes

How do people in organizations come to understand and make sense of the organizational experience? This is the basic question posed by Gioia (1986b), and the answer he provided revolved around symbols, schemas, and scripts.

Symbols are signs or other representations, which signify something broader (Gioia, 1986b, p. 50). A symbol "stands for some other object, entity or concept;" it "serves as a meaningful representation of some significant element of organizational experience" (Gioia, 1986b, p. 52). Symbols include words, objects, events, stories, metaphors, architecture, and rituals (Eisenberg & Riley, 1988, p. 131).

In our attempts to make sense of a new situation (draw meaning from it, understand it), we draw on previous experience stored in memory (Spreitzer, Shapiro, & Von Glinow, 2002, p. 206). When organizational members put bits of information together in particular combinations, they start to form conceptions of how things relate (Weick, 1979a, pp. 61–62). All organizational members, Gioia and Poole posited, begin with schemas—"some generalized cognitive framework that an individual uses to impose structure upon, and impart meaning to, social information or social situations in order to facilitate understanding" (1984, pp. 449–450). For example, each of us has a schema for a "good supervisor," against which we judge our bosses (Lord & Foti, 1986, p. 25). Schemas "guide answering the questions central to sensemaking efforts: 'What or who is it?,' 'What are its implications?,' and 'How should I respond?'" (Harris, 1994, p. 309).

Schemas are used "to organize and make sense of social and organizational information or situations" (Gioia & Manz, 1985, p. 529). Schemas act as filters through which we select salient environmental cues and ignore others, and they provide a mechanism by which we explain actions (Sutherland & Dawson, 2002, p. 53). "[T]he human ability to attend selectively to information, disregarding unimportant stimuli in favor of those that our preexisting store of knowledge indicates as important ... speeds and advances our capacity to remember, reason, solve problems, and act," yet it is also potentially an Achilles heel (Johnson, Daniels, & Huff, 2001, p. 80).

Schemas are developed from experience, helping to explain the differences between experts and novices (Lord & Foti, 1986, p. 33). What distinguishes experts from novices, then, is the development of "highly elaborate schemas resulting from many experiences with a particular issue or area of concern" (Harris, 1994, p. 311). Isenberg described managers as "highly experienced people operating within a familiar environment" (1986, p. 252). He found that schemas provided a number of important elements to managers' thinking, including:

1. bringing solutions forward almost unconsciously, serving as the basis for what is called managerial intuition;

2. creating a dense web of knowledge that allows managers to act even under uncertainty, and;
3. allowing managers to categorize things and make inferences (1986, pp. 248–254).

[D]iagnosis of organizational schemata is a powerful means for researchers to understand much of what goes on in organizations" and "how its members arrive at the conclusions they do" (Weick, 1979a, p. 53).

Within specific organizational settings, these schemas are translated into scripts—"a schematic knowledge structure held in memory that specifies behavior or event sequences that are appropriate for specific situations" (Gioia & Poole, 1984, p. 449). Scripts are a particular kind of schema—schemas that guides action (Gioia, 1986b, p. 57). Scripts provide a framework for understanding organizational action and dynamics (Gioia & Poole, 1984). Scripts represent the working knowledge we all have of how our organizations function, such as how meetings are conducted or how performance appraisals are done (Gioia & Poole, 1984, p. 450). Scripts can be learned from first hand experience or vicariously through observation or communication; part of the important role of training in organizations is the transfer of these scripts (Gioia & Manz, 1985, p. 534).

Scripts help to explain some of the unconscious nature of many organizational behaviors. Much of what goes on in organizations is familiar, habitual, rehearsed (Weick, 1979a, p. 66)—we operate on a kind of "autopilot" at work (Sutherland & Dawson, 2002, p. 53). Since many of our actions are unconscious and repetitive, scripts are the way we structure knowledge in memory so that we can carry out a sequence of events or actions (Gioia, 1986b, p. 50). Situational cues call forth these scripts and trigger certain kinds of responses (Gioia, 1986b, p. 57). So-called "standard operating procedures" are examples of scripts (Weick, 1995, p. 46).

Sometimes new information or events are readily assimilated into our existing ways of thinking, but the study of sensemaking becomes interesting when the individual is confronted with a situation that requires new ways of thinking and responding. Novel situations may require the rethinking of scripted behavior (Gioia & Poole, 1984, p. 454). When confronted with the inexplicable, our sensemaking processes become more conscious in an effort to resolve or explain the discordant information (Sutherland & Dawson, 2002, p. 53). Technology changes are examples of situations in which old patterns and scripts no longer work, and sensemaking is triggered

(Barley, 1986). Sensemaking scholars look at those underlying processes, often as a backdrop to the times when these processes fail and the organization is forced to think and act in new ways.

Collective Sensemaking

"The establishment of common understanding is important to an organization, because it enables organizational activities to become routinized and it helps organizational members achieve a level of commonality and continuity that facilitates organizational action" (Greenberg, 1995, p. 185). This process of coming to common understanding is often referred to as collective sensemaking.

As with individual sensemaking, symbols are a key element in collective organizational sensemaking, especially in the role they play in communication leading to shared meanings (Eisenberg & Riley, 1988). An example of a symbolic representation is the organizational chart. Organization charts depict the organization graphically, showing "communication relationships, lines of authority, chain of command, levels within the organization, superior-subordinate relationships, etc." (Weick, 1979b, p. 14).

Language is a critical tool in bridging between cognition and action (Donnellon, 1986) and a critical tool in social influence (Pondy, 1978, p. 91). Language and symbols are important elements in the development of shared beliefs and meanings (Pfeffer, 1981, p. 9). In fact, "an important practical implication of sensemaking is that, to change a group, one must change what it says and what its words mean" (Weick, 1995, p. 108). From the cognitive perspective, leaders use language and symbols to influence organizational members' interpretations of events and compliance with norms (Pfeffer, 1981, p. 1). Especially in problematic, poorly understood, abstract, ambiguous or unsettling situations, leaders use symbolism to guide meaning of the group and work toward consensus (Frost & Morgan, 1983). Managers' rhetoric is analyzed by sensemaking scholars for its use in persuading oneself and others, in negotiation of viewpoints, and in making decisions.

Meetings are one place where collective sensemaking is calculated to occur. Meetings are seen as central places for argumentation to take place: they maintain the organization by providing a way to make sense, communicate, and make decisions (Weick, 1995, pp. 142–144). "Participants exchange opinions, perceptions and judgments" in meetings, thus allowing them to negotiate common frames of reference and to reach collective agreements (Daft & Lengel, 1986, pp. 560–561).

Both storytelling and sensemaking are interpretive practices, and "sensemaking is often accomplished through storytelling" (Gephart, 1991, p. 35). "[T]he truth of a story lies not in the facts, but in the meaning," and they are part of the sensemaking process (Gabriel, 2000, p. 4). Stories offer "valuable windows into the emotional, political, and symbolic lives of organizations, making them powerful tools for the study of organizational members' experiences" (Gabriel, 2000, p. 2). Stories may be used to entertain, persuade, educate, blame, warn, reassure, or justify, among other uses (Gabriel, 200, pp. 22, 32). Stories have value in coaxing others to accept changes and in coping with rapid change (Boje, 1991, pp. 118, 125). Boje proclaimed that "in organizations, storytelling is the preferred sensemaking currency of human relationships" (1991, p. 106). Organizational members "tell stories about the past, present, and future to make sense of and manage their struggles with their environment" (Boje, 1991, p. 124).

Symbols are used to create shared meanings (Smircich, 1983, p. 55). Rituals and slogans, for example, "give form and coherence to the experience of organization members" (Smircich, 1983, p. 55). Ultimately we constitute organizational reality through symbols (Eisenberg & Riley, 1988, p. 136). Through them, "meaning is communicated and understood" (Gioia, 1986b, p. 51). Symbols articulate the values and aspirations of the organization (Gioia, 1986b, p. 67). An important skill for leaders to develop is the effective management of these symbols (Gioia, 1986b, p. 67).

Schemas at the organizational level are sometimes referred to as interpretive schemes. Interpretive schemes are "the cognitive schemata that map our experience of the world, identifying both its relevant aspects and how we are to understand them" (Bartunek, 1984, p. 355). They represent shared "assumptions about why events happen as they do and how people are to act in different situations" (Bartunek, 1984, p. 355). They are often taken-for-granted and unarticulated, yet they provide continuity and a sense of structure (Ranson, Hinings, & Greenwood, 1980, pp. 5–6). Interpretive schemes include mutual understandings about roles, authority relations, rules, etc. (Ranson et al., 1980, p. 5). A sense of commonality of experience facilitates coordinated action (Smircich, 1983, p. 55). "Organizations preserve knowledge, behavior, mental maps, norms, and values over time" which become shared, even though "individuals come and go" (Daft & Weick, 1984, p. 285).

"Organizational ideologies and cultures function for groups as do schemas and scripts for individuals" (Louis & Sutton, 1991, p. 62). Harris defined organizational culture as "shared beliefs, values, and assumptions that guide sensemaking and action in organizations." (1994, p. 309). "Schemas are the repository of cultural knowledge and meanings and the source of the consensual sensemaking characteristic of culture" (Harris, 1994, p. 310). They include traditional ways of doing things, appropriate behaviors, defining characteristics of subgroups, what the boss is like, and how roles are defined (Harris, 1994, p. 313).

Organizational Structure

Since sensemaking as a framework evolved partially from the 1970s literature on organizations as socially constructed entities, it is not surprising that an early focus of the sensemaking literature was on organizational design. Weick stated boldly that "organization and sensemaking processes are cut from the same cloth. To organize is to impose order, counteract deviations, simplify, and connect, and the same holds true when people try to make sense" (1995, p. 82). "[T]he organization is an instrument to do things, a means, a consciously constructed tool" (Weick & Bougon, 1986, p. 104). Organizations are a concept by which "people attempt to make sense of their world" (Burrell & Morgan, 1979, p. 260).

Organizations are stronger when organizational members share values, rules of behavior, and norms that become crystallized and stabilized in organizational structures (Gray, Bougon, & Donnellon, 1985, p. 89). Nonetheless, a key to understanding the relationship of sensemaking to organizational design is the recognition that sensemaking scholars view organizational design as a continuous activity, as an emergent process, rather than as an enduring entity (Weick, 1993b, p. 347). Organizations are not static structures; rather they are "better understood as dynamic, conscious, and subconscious processes through which meanings are constructed and destroyed" (Gray, Bougon, & Donnellon, 1985, p. 83). Thus, "organizational structures are less prescribed and permanent than roles, titles, and organization charts imply" (Gray, Bougon, & Donnellon, 1985, p. 94).

Ranson et al. (1980) represented one of the early works coming from the social interactionist perspective that was later described as representing the organizational sensemaking perspective. The authors proposed a theoretical framework for understanding how structures take shape and change over time (1980, p. 3). They postulated that structure is "continually produced and recreated by members," changing over time as members' interpretive schemes and context changes (Ranson et al., 1980, p. 1). The values, purposes, and interests of key members of the organization shape structure and are also embodied in structure (Ranson et al., 1980, pp. 7–8). They found that interpretive schemes served as an important source of stability during times of change, and that a change in schemes was critical for restructuring to occur (Ranson et al., 1980, p. 12).

Weick's (1979b) book, The Social Psychology of Organizing, was a key to the early work on sensemaking and organizational design. Organizing, he said, involves the creation of rules and conventions which provide recipes and blueprints to organizational members on how to interpret what is happening and how to get things done (1979b, pp. 3–4). In the mid-1980s authors began to build upon Weick's early work and make explicit connections between leader sensemaking and organizational structure/design. Several classic works on sensemaking evolved at this time. They looked, for example, at

- How ideas of organizational designers translate to organizational structures, and why organizational members respond to structures as they do (Brief & Downey, 1983);
- Why design decisions are the result of purposeful choices by human actors whose cognitions influence those decisions (Downey & Brief, 1986);
- How organizational members' interpretive schemes, emotions, and actions can affect what kind of organizational structure results, and the role of the leader in privileging some schemes over others (Bartunek, 1984);
- How existing role relationships can mediate between technological changes and organizational designs (Barley, 1986); and,
- How people create workable, meaningful organizational structures after an environmental disaster—organizational structures that are fluid, ad hoc, small, informal, and local (Lanzara, 1983).

Leader Role

Sensemaking as a framework fits into a general shift during the 1970s and 1980s in how scholars were thinking about leaders' roles, and in part it fueled that change in thinking.

Smircich and Morgan's (1982) now classic work, "Leadership, The Management of Meaning," represents an early contribution to sensemaking studies. In it the authors contended that "leadership lies in large part in generating a point of reference, against which a feeling of organization and direction can emerge," and that "leadership involves a process of defining reality in ways that are sensible to the led" (1982, pp. 258–259). As Thayer expressed it:

> A leader at work is one who gives others a different sense of the meaning of that which they do by recreating it in a different form, a different 'face,' in the same way that a

pivotal painter or sculptor or poet gives those who follow him (or her) a different way of 'seeing'—and, therefore, saying and doing and knowing in the world. A leader does not tell it 'as it is'; he tells it as it might be, giving what 'is' thereby a different 'face.'... The leader is a sense-giver (1988, pp. 250, 254).

Gioia and Chittipeddi defined sensegiving as "the process of attempting to influence the sensemaking and meaning construction of others toward a preferred redefinition of organizational reality" (1991, p. 442).

Thus, leadership is a form of social influence (Pondy, 1978). A primary role of leaders, according to Pondy, is "putting very profound ideas in very simple language" (1978, p. 95). A leader's ability to make subtle, creative use of language may be an important factor in his/her effectiveness, credibility, and ability to influence meaning creation, according to Pondy (1978, p. 93).

[T]he image of the executive as a 'sense maker' has replaced the former mindset that focused on solving problems, making rules, policing systems, adjudicating conflicts, and commanding the action of others ... Ultimately their job is to construe the world for themselves and others so that collective action and meaning is possible (Jonas, Fry, & Srivastva, 1990, p. 45).

Accordingly, skill in defining a reality that can gain a consensual following constitutes the essence of leadership" (Gioia, 1986b, p. 67).

Leader Decision-Making

Up until the late 1960s and 1970s, the literature on leader decision-making had been dominated by a so-called "rational choice" model. The rational choice model discussed decision-making in terms of calculation, maximizing choices, probability, and judgment (Porac et al., 1996, p. xii). Cognitive emphasis in the study of organizations evolved partially from literature that began to move away from strictly rational models of organizational action (Porac et al., 1996, p. ix). In the late 1970s interest evolved in uncertainty, ambiguity, and judgment bias in decision-making and in other more naturalistic views of decision-making. Cognitive theorists contend that managers deal more often with non-linear, ill-structured, and messy matters than the scenarios used in rational choice model analysis imply. Sensemaking in organizations "is inherently a fluid, open, disorderly, social process" (Choo, 1998, p. 67).

These scholars are interested in what managers do naturally rather than what they should do. Leaders' actions, they claim, are not normative: for example, leaders do not necessarily look for optimal solutions (Daft & Lengel, 1986, p. 36). Classic decision-making models propose a linear process from clarifying goals to assessing the situation to evaluating options to selecting a course of action (Isenberg, 1984). Managers must use classical rational decision-making approaches, but managers often act while thinking and incorporate intuition in their decision-making (Isenberg, 1984). Managers' reasoning processes are not strictly logical: rather they were characterized by plausible reasoning and probabilistic thinking (Isenberg, 1986, pp. 240–242). Isenberg found leaders frequently "bypass rigorous, analytical planning altogether" (1984, p. 82).

Researchers may be disappointed if they look for managerial thought to be conducted in lengthy, private sessions of contemplation, contended Weick (1983). Rather, managerial thought is woven into action, is done in conjunction with action, for example while leaders are supervising, writing reports, touring, or conducting meetings (Weick, 1983, pp. 222–223).

A number of sensemaking authors have alluded to the importance of non-rational elements in sensemaking, i.e. the role affect (emotions, beliefs, values, etc.) might play in organizational life (Gioia, 1986a, pp. 344, 349). There is particular interest in this phenomenon among organizational cognition scholars (Park, Sims, & Motowidlo, 1986, p. 216). "There is nothing 'objective' about the sensemaking process"; it "cannot be disentangled from the team members' own personal experiences, expectations, assumptions and values," according to Spreitzer et al. (2002, p. 206). "Affect influences on managerial judgments are subtle, insidious, and pervasive. We need to know more about how they operate" (Park et al., 1986, p. 231).

An abiding interest of sensemaking scholars is in how the acquisition and processing of information affects top management issue interpretation and sensemaking. Managers' beliefs about the environment, and how they scan and interpret that environment, affect organizational decision-making (Daft & Weick, 1984). Managers need to consider their own beliefs and whether they match the reality of their current situation, and must consider modifying their approach if they are to succeed (Daft & Weick, 1984, p. 294).

Strategic Change

Out of the interest in decision-making and organizational change, a new stream of literature developed during the mid-1980s applying sensemaking to the study of strategic change. Gioia, in the conclusion to his volume entitled The Thinking Organization provided a most articulate description of the interplay of sensemaking and organizational change:

> Another useful way to view adaptation to change is as a process of making sense of new experience. ... The sensemaking perspective implies consideration of the social

construction processes that people use to cope with change. The changing reality with
which people must often deal stems from the way they make sense of internal and
external events. Therefore, the impetus for change depends on the way meaning is
attributed to events (1986a, p. 352)

Due to environmental uncertainty, rapid change, and shifting organizational boundaries, strategic planning came under attack in the early 1980s, and
more emphasis was placed on continuous strategic thinking, which is consistent with the sensemaking framework (Fiol & Huff, 1992, p. 273). Where
rational choice models tend to focus on the content of strategic change,
sensemaking as a theoretical framework is useful because it looks at the
emergent, process aspects of change implementation (Ericson, 2001, p. 110).

The sensemaking literature on change is focused heavily on the connection between executive thought and strategic action.

It is now clear that any comprehensive portrayal of strategic management will not evolve
without accounting for these cognitive activities ... [T]he underlying assumption of
cognitive approaches to strategic management is that such cognitive processes are linked
to organizational action (Thomas et al., 1997, p. 300).

Managers have been found to have relatively stable strategic ways-of-thinking, which are not easily changed (Hellgren & Melin, 1993, pp. 61–62).
Ways-of-thinking involve a "set of values, assumptions, beliefs, ideas and
thoughts about leadership and strategic development of organizations"
(Hellgren & Melin, 1993, p. 63). Managers must learn to recognize incom-
patibility between their way-of-thinking and the strategic needs of the organization (Hellgren & Melin, 1993, p. 62).

Also during the mid 1980s, interest developed in what was called strategic
issue diagnosis. "Strategic issue diagnosis describes the individual-level,
cognitive process through which decision-makers form interpretations about
organizational events, developments and trends" (Dutton, 1993, p. 339). In
scanning the environment, organizational members choose to allocate their
attention toward particular issues, based upon which they build the strategic
agenda for the organization (Dutton, 1988, p. 127). According to Dutton
(1993), strategic issue diagnosis involves active, conscious, intentional effort,
yet it also relies heavily on automatic, unreflective, habitual elements. In
processing information, top-level managers often rely on heuristics to save
time (Dutton, 1993). However, this ability to operate in automatic mode
can lead to complacency, resistance to change, and blind spots, and, therefore, to inaccurate or inappropriate interpretations and responses (Dutton,
1993, p. 352).

Nystrom and Starbuck (1984, p. 278) focused on beliefs, and the ways in which they help determine how information is collected, ignored, and filtered, thus ultimately guiding strategic action. [P]revailing beliefs in an organization often must be "disconfirmed clearly and dramatically" before strategic change can happen (Nystrom & Starbuck, 1984, p. 283). Therefore, managers must influence and manipulate beliefs (Nystrom & Starbuck, 1984, p. 283). "Strategic problems arise largely because the top managers in those organizations hold onto outdated and unproductive beliefs," contended Nystrom & Starbuck (1984, p. 280). As summarized by Milliken and Lant, "[t]his growing body of research is beginning to provide us with insights into how managers' strategic choices may be systematically influenced by contextual characteristics, by managerial characteristics, by managers' cognitive limitations, and by the characteristics of the issues they confront" (1991, p. 130).

Gioia and Chittipeddi asked the question: "What is the nature of strategic change and the CEO's role in instigating it?" (1991, p. 433). They noted that "the study of interpretation and meaning systems, and the processes whereby those systems are altered, is of fundamental importance to the study of strategic change" (1991, p. 435). Gioia and Chittipeddi found that the initiation of strategic change can be viewed as a "process whereby the CEO makes sense of an altered vision of the organization and engages in cycles of negotiated social construction activities to influence stakeholders and constituents to accept that vision" (1991, p. 434). Key to the findings of that study was the fact that a captivating vision provided a symbolic foundation on which to build new interpretative schemes (Gioia & Chittipeddi, 1991, p. 446). Gioia and Chittepeddi concluded that

> the CEO's role during this period might best be seen as one that involves calling into question an obsolete interpretive scheme, framing a new interpretive scheme in understandable and evocative terms, proving guidance for action toward the incipient change, and exerting influence to accomplish it (1991, p. 444).

Related studies have investigated:

- The value of symbols in influencing people to embrace strategic change (Gioia, Thomas, Clark, & Chittipeddi, 1994);
- The importance of organizational identity and image to employees' ability to reconceptualize their organization (Gioia & Thomas, 1996); and
- The linkages between cognition, strategic action, and organizational performance (Thomas et al., 1997).

Robbins and Duncan (1988) theorized about the process by which CEOs create and utilize visions to initiate strategic change. They defined vision as "the shared, aspired future state for the organization which identifies the organization's values, sets priorities for goals and objectives, and sets the guidelines by which these goals and objectives will be pursued" (1988, p. 206). Visions "represent a shared set of beliefs about the organization's aspired role" (Robbins & Duncan, 1988, p. 206). "Within each individual organization, the vision will take on a unique form... The concept of strategic vision is a way of explaining why two similar organizations in the same industry may take different strategic directions" (Robbins & Duncan, 1988, p. 225).

In strategy literature, a key element related to sensemaking is the importance of top managers' shifting their mental models to account for industry changes and to renew their organizations. Porac, Thomas, and Baden-Fuller (1989) found that the mental models of organizational strategists affected their perceptions of the competitive environment, which in turn affected strategy. Beliefs about the identity of the organization relative to competitors, suppliers, and customers and beliefs about what it takes to compete influenced the strategic actions taken (Porac et al., 1989, p. 399).

Bartunek (1988) wrote a piece on the dynamics of organizational reframing. She proposed a model of the stages individuals must go through if they are to truly accept and feel comfortable with new frames—not reject them or merely pay lip service to them. According to Bartunek, individuals must reframe the way they think if the organization is to transform successfully, and leaders are key to this success. Information plays an important role in developing understandings in organizational members, and leaders must recognize the importance of feelings in how information is interpreted if they are to be successful in helping individuals to change (Bartunek, 1988, pp. 146–147).

Bartunek, Lacey, and Wood (1992) illuminated the social cognition processes that create conflict when new schemas are introduced, and how the dynamics unfold when change is initiated. It is advisable for leaders to uncover the implicit assumptions and expectations of both leaders and organizational members (Bartunek et al., 1992, pp. 206–207). Organizational members need time to make sense of the change—construe it, categorize it, and seek exemplars from past experience see, for example, Bartunek et al., 1992, p. 207). Change agents, they said, have an overly optimistic image of how actions will play out, and need to be more realistic about how smooth implementation of change is likely to be (Bartunek et al., 1992, pp. 207, 220). Likewise, Fairhead (1998) found that, when collaboration is allowed to emerge gradually, everyone involved is given time to adjust their perspectives and ways of working, resulting ultimately in a less painful but more fundamental organizational change.

Balogun and Johnson (1998) analyzed the political and social processes which effect implementation of planned change initiatives, especially what facilitates and obstructs change. Since one cannot predict how organizational members will make sense at various stages of change, they cautioned leaders to attend to the unintended outcomes of change.

One example of a study of stages of sensemaking during strategic change is Isabella's (1990) study of how managers construe organizational events as an organizational change unfolds. She interviewed managers to find out how their cognitive structures changed through the process, and how their perspectives shifted as change unfolded. Isabella (1990) identified four stages by which managers construe events as change unfolds—anticipation, confirmation, culmination, and aftermath.

Leaders must also be aware of the key roles played by middle managers and colleagues in the change process. The role of coworkers may involve rehearsing responses, testing reality, venting anger, clarifying the scenario, bolstering self-confidence, and clarifying arguments (Volkema, Farquhar, & Bergmann, 1996). Balogun (2003) found that middle managers serve as role models, providing coaching and support to staff, and communicating with them formally and informally about what a change means. Middle managers play a key role in interpreting the vision of senior leaders into tangible change steps that allow employees to make sense of the change (Balogun, 2003).

Studies on sensemaking have also revealed insights about the dynamics involved when a variety of workgroups are involved in organizational innovation and change. Considerable attention has been paid in the literature to the idea that managers come from different "thought worlds" or cultures from frontline employees and technical specialists, and the resulting differences in their sensemaking (e.g. Barley, 1986; Dougherty, 1992; Drazin, Glenn, & Kazanjian, 1999). They have different goals, different knowledge bases, different cultures, different ways of interacting, and different ways of operating (Dougherty, 1992, pp. 179–180). It is, therefore, incumbent upon leaders to "proactively foster collaborative action" and cross-fertilization in order to encourage learning and innovation across the organization (Dougherty, 1992, p. 191). When individuals from different professional groups are brought together, their frames, beliefs, and behaviors are modified in interaction with others, which fosters collective sensemaking and creativity (Drazin, Glenn, & Kazanjian, 1999, pp. 291, 293). Fairhead found that a "real-life alien role model" can serve as a powerful force for paradigm shifts in thinking, culture, and identity (1998, p. 104). In fact, in that study, top management played a relatively minor role in orchestrating changes; front-line staff used storytelling and other sensemaking devices to orchestrate their own collective learning and make innovation possible (Fairhead, 1998, p. 94).

Success and Failure

Consistent with the social cognition perspective on managerial problem sensing, cognitive scholars are interested in what managers notice and how they construct meaning (Kiesler & Sproull, 1982, p. 548). Emphasis is on where managers can go awry in these processes (Kiesler & Sproull, 1982). According to sensemaking scholars, the failure of organizations often results from cognitive biases that affect sensemaking processes. People and organizations must gather information, sample from it, select what information to use, and then integrate the information (Fiske & Taylor, 1984, p. 249). Within this process inferences are made that result in biases.

Starbuck and Milliken (1988) have become a core text in the processes of sensemaking. They analyzed executives' perceptual filters and the influence these filters have and do not have on organizational outcomes. In the process of observing and trying to understand the environment, perceptual filters are "the processes that amplify some stimuli and attenuate others, thus distorting the raw data and focusing attention" (Starbuck & Milliken, 1988, p. 40). Some perceptual filters they mentioned include information overload, stereotypes, habits, and values. Perceptual filters can create blind spots that prevent leaders from solving problems (Starbuck & Milliken, 1988, p. 52). Leaders are known to apply existing frameworks when radically new, creative solutions are needed, for example, and to fail to account for risk factors. Rightly or wrongly, leaders receive the credit for success, but "when the results are bad, executives get blamed for perceiving erroneously, for making analytic mistakes, or for taking inappropriate actions" (Starbuck & Milliken 1988, p. 35).

Sensemaking scholars caution managers about cognitive biases, which can lead to flawed sensemaking and thereby derail planning efforts. These biases may include oversimplifying factors, overconfidence in assessing options, underestimating risks, exaggerating problems, subjective judgments, selective recall, pretension, self-deception, illusion of control, selective perception, wishful thinking, hindsight bias, excuses, prior hypotheses, complacency, self-serving bias, self-justification, and rationalizations (Barnes,

1984; Das & Teng, 1999, pp. 760–761; Huff & Schwenk, 1990; Kiesler & Sproull, 1982; Schwenk, 1988, p. 44; Sutherland & Dawson, 2002, p. 57).

The good news is that heterogeneous management teams, careful environmental scanning, reward systems, and styles of decision-making that encourage questioning of assumptions can all be used to mitigate against the effects of biases (Milliken & Lant, 1991, p. 147).

Organizational Learning and Knowledge Management

Some sensemaking scholars are also organizational learning scholars—they are interested in how organizations use information to generate knowledge, how they interpret information, and how they decide what is significant. Choo (1998) studied organizations as sensemaking communities and concluded that "organizations are keenly aware that their ability to survive and evolve is determined by their capacity to make sense of or influence their environments and to constantly renew meaning and purpose in light of new conditions" (1998, p. 66). In other words, organizations need to learn. This learning involves scanning the environment, creating a knowledge base, identifying significant issues, and constructing meaning so as to act (Choo, 1998, p. 67).

Thomas et al. (1997) started with the premise that "the sensemaking process is the essence of the learning process for organizations" (1997, p. 308). They developed a model of strategic sensemaking and organizational learning consisting of four elements (scanning, interpretation, action, and performance) with four processes linking them (controlling, information processing, formulating strategy, and implementing strategy). They found that repetitive sensemaking cycles through these processes and elements offer the organization opportunities to integrate feedback from the environment and modify its actions accordingly (1997, p. 308).

Recently the literature has evolved into interest in how organizations create and manage knowledge in order to learn. According to Lehr and Rice, organizations must gather the knowledge individuals have, pool it, organize, and analyze it, and then disseminate it (2002, pp. 1060–1061). These related directly to Weick's notions of enactment, selection, and retention, and thus sensemaking is a very compatible theoretical framework from which to look at knowledge management (Lehr & Rice, 2002, p. 1064).

Choo (2001) found that organizations need to gather the right amount of data, the right type of data, accurate and timely data, and a continuous flow of data, but they must also be concerned with how that data is filtered and analyzed within the organization. In the processes of sensemaking the organization selects the issues most important to the organization's agenda, and create shared meanings and goals, thus influencing decision-making and knowledge creation (Choo, 2001, p. 200).

Occasions for Sensemaking

Gioia observed that, "in any organizational experience, a person's most pressing cognitive task (whether explicit and conscious or tacit and unconscious) is to make sense of the situation, to account for it, or to understand it in meaningful terms" (1989, p. 221). As discussed earlier, one of the major properties of sensemaking is that it is triggered when something happens that is out of the ordinary, unexpected—a disruption of routine that requires complex analysis and response (Weick, 1995, p. 87). When there is a novel situation, a discrepancy between expectations and reality, or a deliberate initiative calling for thought, organizational members must shift from automatic "habits of mind" to active, cognitive engagement (Louis & Sutton, 1991, p. 60). Unique and unfamiliar situations create occasions for sensemaking (Weick, 1995, p. 90). Therefore, it is not surprising that scholars have chosen to focus sensemaking studies on extreme or unique situations in organizations.

Louis's 1980 study on socialization was the first to specify sensemaking per se as the central core of a study. He studied newcomer sensemaking upon entering an unfamiliar organizational setting. "Newcomers need situation- or culture-specific interpretation schemes in order to make sense of happenings in the setting and to respond with meaningful and appropriate actions" (Louis, 1980, p. 233). He noted the disorientation, surprise, and sensory overload that accompany the experience of learning the ropes, coming to understand the culture, and gaining acceptance as an insider (1980, p. 231).

Crises and disasters are other forms of extreme or unique situations. Over the course of his career, Weick (1990b, 1993a) analyzed several disasters from a sensemaking perspective, and a number of other authors have followed suit. For Weick (1988), crises are not just events that happen to people—people also enact the environment and thus influence the nature and severity of the crisis (1988, p. 305). Crises impose severe demands and constraints on sensemaking, but at the same time, adequate sensemaking strategies can keep the crisis from getting out of hand (1988, p. 305).

New technologies, because of their inherent equivocality, require ongoing sensemaking and restructuring in the organization (Weick, 1990a, p. 2). They are "moving targets for learning" and at the same time trigger strong emotions and stress (Weick, 1990a, pp. 10, 23). They create "an unbroken string of tough decisions" and place constant demands on complex, abstract cognitive processes (Weick, 1990a, p. 14). Thus they serve as an excellent context in which to study sensemaking. For example, Eisenhardt (1990) studied how managers make fast, high-quality, strategic decisions within fast-moving, high-technology environments and found that they require conflict resolution, confidence, analysis of alternates, real-time information, and an intuitive grasp of the business.

ANALYSIS OF ONE STUDY OF LEADER SENSEMAKING

Purpose of the Study

In order to appreciate fully the value of organizational sensemaking as a theoretical framework, it is helpful to analyze the contributions of one such study. I invite you now to peek into a study I conducted a few years ago (Fulton, 2001), in which I conducted site visits and extensive interviews with seven Chief Information Officers (CIOs) who were merging library and computer center operations on their campuses. My study looked at the hopes, values, ideas, philosophies, and opinions of leaders as they made strategic decisions in the creation of new, merged organizations.

I focused my study on the sensemaking processes these CIOs used to decide on an organizational structure for the merged unit. The overarching purpose of the study was to understand how leaders go about envisioning a new organization and realizing those visions in terms of organizational structure. It looked at sensemaking as it relates to organizational structure, organizational vision, and strategic change. Several sensemaking questions framed my study:

- How do the preferences, assumptions, frames of reference, mindsets, and interpretative schemes of CIOs influence their restructuring process?
- How do CIOs sort through, filter, weave together, and perhaps even manipulate the many factors that influence their thinking?
- How do leaders decide what information to gather, what to pay attention to, and who and what will influence those choices?
- What images, mental models, implicit theories, and cognitive structures do CIOs have about where their organizations are going that affect the actions they ultimately take in creating a new order?

- How do CIOs frame and interpret social and environmental cues in order to construct options/choices that fit, that are plausible?
- What are the salient situational factors for leaders in deciding on an organizational structure?

In order to do this, I obviously had to ask the participants in the study to tell me the whole story of how they came to be CIOs, what was going on within both organizations at the time, how they came to choose the structure they ultimately chose, and what they were thinking about and feeling throughout the experience. Since I stayed on each campus for several days, and made at least one follow-up visit after doing preliminary analysis of the data, I had plenty of opportunity to go back to the CIOs to ask for clarification and elaboration as needed. I used a combination of qualitative methodologies (phenomenology and grounded theory) to analyze each case separately and then to look for overall themes and patterns. Each CIO's sensemaking processes were unique, and at the same time, there were similarities.

Findings: Mapping Vision to Structure

Structure is one means by which these CIOs manifested their visions, symbolized their visions, and actively worked towards those visions. Four mechanisms were identified by which leaders embedded their visions in new organizational structures: wholesale mapping, establishing a toehold, isolating the vision, and beginning with leadership. Leaders who had the most auspicious conditions were able to set their sights higher and push all at once for a new paradigm (wholesale mapping); coincidentally those who aspired to higher levels of integration tended to adopt newer organizational forms. The other three strategies represent ways in which leaders balanced idealism and pragmatism in their sensemaking processes. These CIOs were conscious of the need to temper their own perspectives about what they would *like* to have happen because of realities around them. In these riskier situations, they settled for a slower pace of change by (a) starting with one area that was ready for change (toehold), or (b) isolating the vision to certain areas within the organization, such as those most in need of an overhaul, or (c) focusing first on change at the management level (beginning with leadership). They made choices that fit the institution and the situation, yet also moved toward their visions and/or towards integration.

1.	Where?	Vision of the organization's role and reputation
2.	Why?	Goals for the reorganization
3.	How much?	Degree of integration
4.	When?	Evolution vs. revolution
5.	Who?	Role of the leader
6.	How?	Process for deciding on a structure
7.	What?	Selection of an overall structural type
8.	In what way?	Determining groups and matching individuals to roles

Fig. 1. Vectors of Choice in the Restructuring Process.

Findings: Vectors in Sensemaking during Reorganization

I was able to identify eight questions each CIO had to answer in order to make a final determination of structure. I called these the eight vectors of choice in organizational restructuring (Fig. 1). These eight vectors are at the heart of CIO sensemaking in the merger context.

A causal process, moving from making sense of the situation to vision to structure, was verified in most cases, but not all. In almost all cases vector 1 happened very early on and the process ended with vector 8, though not always, and there was considerable variation in the relative timing of vectors 2 through 7. Some of the vectors happened more or less simultaneously, or at least in quick succession. In other cases, significant thought time or process lapses punctuated the flow from one vector or set of vectors to the next.

Findings: Stages in Sensemaking during Reorganization

As CIOs worked through the vectors, five major stages of sensemaking emerged in this study.

Scripts and Givens
All of the CIOs came into their positions with strong beliefs about one or more of the vectors that made them unlikely to change their perspectives significantly. "Givens" represent sensemaking at that "earlier, more tentative stage prior to interpretation when the sensemaker grapples with the question: 'is it still possible to take things for granted?' And if not, 'what next?'" (Weick, 1995, p. 14). For example, several of the CIOs had previous negative experience with radical top–down change and were determined to use an evolutionary process that involved significant input and buy-in.

Environmental Scanning/Issue Identification
A significant component of the process for these CIOs was the environmental scanning activity that started during the interview and lasted up to about a year. Scanning the environment is a particularly critical element for leaders new in their positions. For a new leader, sensemaking activities include getting an overall impression of the institution, comparing this university to previous places of employment, and getting feedback about constituent needs (Gioia & Chittipeddi, 1991, p. 442). Early on in their tenure, CIOs were looking at external factors (e.g. the institutional culture, resource availability, and technology trends) to identify those that were likely to be important to their organization. They also looked internally for information about staff strengths, sources of resistance, and readiness for change. In their descriptions of their own behavior, they used phrases such as being aware, paying attention, anticipating, reading the winds, looking at trends, gauging forces, and assessing needs. Hosking referred to this process as "issue identification" in which the individual asks the question, "What is going on?" (1991, p. 97). As much as their situation allowed, CIOs took time to observe and listen carefully before committing to definitive actions. Vectors 2 and 5 usually involved significant environmental scanning.

Selection
A third category included vectors that turned out to be key selection points or "forks in the road" of change for a particular situation. CIOs sorted out the various factors that were affecting them, and filtered out the most salient ones. They asked the core question of what, if anything, they should do about the immediate situation (Hosking, 1991, p. 97). "Selection activity matches solutions with people, problems, and choices" (Weick, 1979b, p. 202). Vectors 3 and 4 often fell in this category.

Implementation/Action/Enactment
Vectors 6, 7, and 8 generally represented enactment processes in which CIOs translated their planning and sensemaking processes into action. These actions then set a course for the rest of the integration process at each institution.

Performance/Refinement
Thomas, Clark, and Gioia (1993) labeled the final process in strategic change as "performance," and this fit my study as well. For these CIOs, performance of their new organization was going to be constantly changing, and so they spoke in terms of continual evolution and refinement of the new structure. CIOs clearly concluded that restructuring is not a one-time decision, but is rather an inductive, emergent, iterative, incremental process. The CIOs talked about building confidence, waiting for evidence, constant repositioning, tinkering, tweaking, modifying, making adjustments, and "evolution not revolution." They all ended up talking in terms of implementing a custom solution, seeing how it worked, and altering the strategy incrementally as needed, which is typical of "enacting organizations" (Daft & Weick, 1984, p. 292).

These vectors and phases were at the highest level of interpretation, but most of the study stayed very close to the real life stories of CIOs. For example, Fig. 2 shows the factors faced by one CIO and how that factor affected the final structure.

Findings: Miscellaneous Insights and Revelations

As discussed, sensemaking research attempts to meld the theoretical and the practical in meaningful ways for readers. Sensemaking is such a rich framework, it allowed me to tease out many insights into leader sensemaking in this context. Therefore, my study is of interest to anyone interested in insights such as the following:

• How leaders signaled change, rewarded progress, and made it meaningful;
• Leaders' analysis of what motivates people and how they framed issues to engage particular individuals or groups;
• Why leaders chose their management team members as they did;
• How leaders bridged the us/them culture rifts within the organization;
• How leaders' own ethics, philosophies, background, and personalities affected their sense of what the right choice was for their institution at that time;

Factor		Reorganization effect
Early merger		No non-traditional models
Strong incumbent directors		Maintain hierarchy
CIO lacks technical background		Postpone some actions
Provost leaving		Solve immediate problems
Union		Proceed cautiously
Entrenched librarian culture		Wait for buy-in
CIO vision of information literacy		Create instruction unit
Financial exigencies		Make use of existing staff

Fig. 2. One CIO's Sensemaking about how Factors should Influence Reorganization.

- Why leaders who had a mandate to serve as change agents could operate more freely than those in constrained conditions;
- Why trust, respect, and empathy were critical to the success of a new organization;
- What was made possible when leaders believed that resistance is a natural part of the change process rather than a problem to be solved;
- How leaders dealt with ambiguity and uncertainty in organizational innovation;
- What individuals and groups leaders involved in decision-making, and what roles they played in influencing the leader's perceptions and actions; and
- How leaders thought about the pace and the process of change.

Findings: Metaphor of the Journey

More than any other single theme in these CIOs' stories, the overwhelming image conveyed was one of journey, and more specifically journey on the frontier. In the interview transcripts I found numerous references to "moving forward," "moving in a direction," "finding my way," and "moving ahead." They talked about phases and plans and pushing. These leaders were excited by the opportunities ahead, yet cognizant of the dangers, hardships, and risks along the trail. When they accepted the position, they experienced a sense of anticipation, of challenge, of opportunity, and of uncertainty. CIOs described restructuring as looking out to the horizon and guiding a group toward that vision, but not along a straightforward path. All encountered barriers, detours, and diversions, but also glorious unforeseen opportunities and discoveries.

The stories of these seven leaders are the story of realizing the vision and dreams of each. The opportunity to create a new organization, to explore a new frontier, is an exciting and risky one. It involves continuous balancing of vision, context, and situation – sensemaking and sensegiving. These CIOs' experiences were not about the magical moment of making a decision, not about calculating probabilities of success of alternate solutions, and not about a linear or even clear progression from vision to structure. Rather, the essence of their sensemaking might best be described as the willful creation of organizational evolution.

The CIOs I interviewed expressed many times how unique an opportunity it was for them to think back on that time in their lives and analyze why they felt, thought and did what they felt, thought and did. In sharing their stories in depth, this study was unique in providing a "you are there" look at leader sensemaking.

WHAT WE STILL WANT TO KNOW; A RESEARCH AGENDA FOR LIBRARY LEADER SENSEMAKING

The acknowledged founder and contemporary leader of the movement to study sensemaking, Karl Weick, characterized sensemaking as "not yet a body of knowledge... a developing set of ideas with explanatory possibilities" (1995, p. xi). While work has continued in the last 10 years, there is still much we can learn. Riggs (2001, p. 7) and others have bemoaned the dearth of literature on library leadership, and in particular the lack of empirical studies. In this section I talk about eight areas I see as particularly fruitful ways we can use the organizational sensemaking framework to understand library leadership in particular.

One obvious line of inquiry is the degree to which library leaders consider business models to be applicable in library settings. According to Zaccaro and Klimoski (2001) there is a need to study leadership within individual contexts, which can better capture "the cognitive, interpersonal, and social richness of this phenomenon" (2001, p. 3). Sensemaking might be used to look at when directors do and do not draw on business models, and the ways in which they might consider library settings to be unique. Some autobiographical sensemaking analyses could be interesting in this regard, as would studies based on individual and focus group interviews. It could be useful to replicate some of the research on decision-making, strategy, and special situations as discussed above to see and whether library leaders suffer from similar distortions in thinking and preconceived notions, whether library leaders use similar or different theories-in-practice, scripts, assumptions, etc. Even within librarianship, it is often inferred that leadership is different depending on whether one is in a university, a school, a corporation, or a community. But to what degree are the sensemaking processes of leaders really that different in these settings, and why?

Second, we have seen work recently on sensemaking in specific professions, such as doctors (Sutherland & Dawson, 2002) and police (Maguire, 2002). As Sutherland and Dawson noted, sensemaking provides a framework in which to look at the lifeworlds created and inhabited by professionals, including their values, their professional identities, and how their reactions to changes in practice might affect their behavior in terms of service quality (2002, p. 52). Hellgren and Melin called for research that looks at "the dynamic interaction between dominant ways-of-thinking, organizational cultures and industrial wisdom in different sectors" (1993, p. 67). Much work has already been done about what is unique in organizations comprised heavily of professional workers, as is the case in libraries, but it has been normative in nature rather than focusing on how leaders make sense of these contexts. Weick observed that professionals have higher levels of discretion in their jobs, and he speculated that this will lead to different sensemaking processes (1995, pp. 176–177). But professional managers of professionals are no doubt very unique sensemakers, indeed. I would like to see interviews with so-called Generation X-ers and Millennials to learn how managers can better tap into their skills. Similarly, participant observation could be used to study whether these younger generations make sense of leadership roles in different ways than do their mostly Boomer directors. Also, we have been only partially successful in bridging the traditional rift between librarians and staff. The testimonials of successful leaders could serve as exemplars for other leaders struggling with these and related personnel matters.

Third, when one attends library conferences or talks with library consultants, one hears a lot about teams, collaboration, and new models of organization—what Sweeney (1994) called the "post-hierarchical library." The "post-hierarchical library" is redesigned to minimize bureaucracy in order to focus on customized user service and to be flexible, responsive, and adaptable (Sweeney, 1994, p. 63). Rather than directing others and making decisions, the leader in the "post-hierarchical library" plans, coordinates, coaches, motivates, supports, and fosters relationships (Sweeney, 1994, p. 62). Teams are becoming increasingly important in library organizations (Spreitzer et al., 2002). In her textbook for school media specialists, Donham pointed out that they "must exert leadership, yet still be collaborative and collegial" in working with others at the school (1998, p. ix). We could afford to understand a lot more, for example, about the exact mechanisms used to share leadership, to mentor, or to lead self-managed teams. The sensemaking framework has the potential to shed light on the different skills, attitudes, and behaviors needed from leaders in this new environment. Daft and Lewin (1993) articulated the need for more work in this area: "Managers facing today's difficult environment are engaged in organizational experiments without the guidance and benefit of theories and models that would characterize the new paradigm" (1993, p. I).

Fourth, Weick noted that more research is needed on the influence of information technology on organizational practice (1995, p. 177). Within the field of information sciences, Kuhlthau (2004) and Dervin (1983, 1999) have used sensemaking as a theoretical framework for the study of information seeking behavior. I believe librarianship is a particularly intriguing setting in which to study sensemaking in this regard. So much of what library leaders contend with is the integration of new technologies. Needham went so far as to say that "libraries are at an intersection of great danger and even greater opportunity" because of the proliferation of networked information (2001, p. 133). New technologies require library leaders to "recognize, accept, and adjust to the constantly changing environment" and to break away from established structures, policies and procedures (Riggs, 2001, p. 9). Leaders need to develop new approaches and new tools, and they especially need "to inspire people and institutions to work together in a cooperative rather than competitive way" (Needham, 2001, p. 135). Libraries are often particularly risk-averse, and library leaders need to know how to encourage others to take calculated risks (Riggs, 2001, p. 10).

Technology is driving unprecedented change in libraries, which in turn increases the importance of leaders to help organizations to reshape themselves (Riggs, 1998, p. 55). It is especially critical that leaders develop compelling visions to bridge between the library's present and its future and to move the staff to action (Riggs, 1998, pp. 57–58). Riggs (2001, p. 11) called for library leaders to be more innovative, creative, and entrepreneurial, and we have seen how sensemaking has been used as a framework to study these qualities in organizations. As Riggs concluded, "[w]e need more transformational leaders in the library profession" (2001, p. 14), and, we need library leaders who can "redefine the paradigm" (Needham, 2001, p. 138).

A key leadership role for the school media specialist, for example, is in advocating change through technology (Donham, 1998, p. 177). More ethnographic observations of these processes could assist us in becoming more efficient and effective in managing these changes. Researchers might elicit cognitive maps of library leaders in particular circumstances involving new technologies, especially in terms of how they conduct sensegiving to the staff who cope with, integrate or troubleshoot new technologies.

Fifth is the area of leadership preparation and education. Recent difficulties in recruiting new leaders led Albritton and Shaughnessy (1990) to conclude that the profession was "experiencing a leadership gap, making focus on leadership development even more critical" (1990, p. 202). Bartunek, Gordon, and Weathersby (1983) drew particular attention to the importance of management development programs in helping managers to hone complex sensemaking skills, including abstract reasoning, social understanding, tolerance for ambiguity, dealing with divergent viewpoints, and flexible approaches to decision-making. Quite a bit is known and written about the qualities needed in library leadership. A list of competencies and responsibilities is provided in Hernon, Powell, and Young (2003). What they found to be less clear is how relevant leadership development opportunities such as those sponsored by the Association of Research Libraries, LAMA Management Institutes, or the Harvard Institute are to leaders in developing these qualities (2003, p. 171). A thorough investigation of exactly what sensemaking skills participants developed at such institutes would be illuminating. Sensemaking as a framework offers an opportunity to conduct in-depth interviews with attendees during and after such programs, so we can gauge better how to create curricula that offer maximum transference to real-life leadership situations. Action research on sensemaking is another possibility, following the model Boland (1984) used in which he designed an exercise to help library managers to envision future scenarios as part of planning.

Mentoring has also been an important vehicle for training library managers. Mentoring provides a form of socialization into library leadership (Chatman, 1992, p. 493), and sensemaking has been a valuable framework from which to study those taking on new roles (Louis, 1980). Mentors instill values, confidence, and a sense of reality and what is important; mentors serve as guides and sources of positive reinforcement and emotional support as proteges encounter new situations and dilemmas (Chatman, 1992). What was most helpful to me was when mentors talked me through how they made sense of particular sets of circumstances—I was able then to vicariously hone my own skills by analyzing their experiences with them.

Interviews about such sensemaking encounters between experienced and new library managers could provide rich insights for future generations of leaders.

Sixth, Weick articulated the need for more research on collective sensemaking (1995, p. 181). At conferences and meetings library leaders learn to view their practice at their home libraries differently based on the collective wisdom shared in these forums. Within librarianship we need to move beyond "how I done it good" stories to analyses such as Pye's (2002), which look at how generations of leaders make sense of context and adapt accordingly. "Organizations must develop information processing mechanisms capable of detecting trends, events, competitors, markets, and technological developments relevant to their survival" (Daft & Weick, 1984, p. 285). I would argue that library leaders could be more effective in using faculty liaison structures, professional development opportunities, and assessment strategies to ensure that we are adapting to change. We must stay abreast of information dissemination and use patterns, for example, if we are to remain competitive in an Internet environment, and we need to put more resources into research and development to ensure our place among information providers and information experts. Industry-level studies of sensemaking can serve as excellent models for work on library leadership on this broader level.

Seventh is the area of communication. "Perhaps no area of library leadership receives so much criticism as the area of communication" (Hanson, 1991, p. 38). "For too long the vision that library personnel have had of library leaders has been tarnished by those leaders' inability to give clear directions, to convey information concisely, to make requests that result in timely action or, in some cases, to communicate library needs to the outside world" (Hanson, 1991, p. 43). Hanson noted that "every library job description emphasizes communication as a job requirement" (1991, p. 39). Since communication and sensemaking are so integrally intertwined, it is easy to see why sensemaking makes a logical framework from which to analyze successful and unsuccessful communication strategies. As in other settings, sensemaking can provide useful insights into the ways in which library leaders can more effectively articulate vision, facilitate change, and engage successfully in sensegiving through memos, meetings, speeches, and stories.

Last, when library leaders read professional literature, they are ultimately hoping to gain insights into what methods are effective and what paths are likely to be destructive. Sensemaking has already proven a useful framework for looking at leader success and failure in other settings, and promises similar applicability to librarianship. Some questions that fascinate me in this regard include:

- How do library leaders decide which trends are worth attending to, and how effective is their environmental scanning?
- How does resource availability affect leader sensemaking?
- How do leaders learn to make use of a variety of leadership styles and to apply them appropriately in different circumstances?
- How is the first year as a library director different in terms of sensemaking? What is the role of the "honeymoon period?"

These are just a few of the areas I would propose as ones for further research. You may have others. I concur with Isenberg that "this intimate relationship between managerial understanding and managerial action remains one of the most intriguing areas of inquiry for management scholars to explore further" (1986, p. 259). I hope some of you will join me in taking up this challenge.

REFERENCES

Albritton, R. L., & Shaughnessy, T. W. (Eds) (1990). *Developing leadership skills: A sourcebook for librarians*. Englewood, CO: Libraries Unlimited.

Balogun, I. (2003). From blaming the middle to harnessing its potential: Creating change intermediaries. *British Journal of Management, 41*(1), 69–83.

Balogun, J., & Johnson, G. (1998). Bridging the gap between intended and unintended change: The role of managerial sensemaking. In: M. A. Hitt, J. E. Ricart I Costa & R. Nixon (Eds), *New managerial mindsets: Organizational transformation and strategy implementation* (pp. 55–82). New York: Wiley.

Barley, S. R. (1986). Technology as an occasion for structuring: Evidence from observations of CAT scanners and the social order of radiology departments. *Administrative Science Quarterly, 31*(1), 78–107.

Barnes, J. H. (1984). Cognitive biases and their impact on strategic planning. *Strategic Management Journal, 5*(2), 129–137.

Bartunek, J. M. (1984). Changing interpretive schemes and organizational restructuring: The example of a religious order. *Administrative Science Quarterly, 29*(3), 355–372.

Bartunek, J. M. (1988). The dynamics of personal and organizational reframing. In: R. E. Quinn & K. S. Cameron (Eds), *Paradox and transformation: Toward a theory of change in organization and management* (pp. 137–162). Cambridge, MA: Ballinger.

Bartunek, J. M., Gordon, J. R., & Weathersby, R. P. (1983). Developing complicated understandings in administrators. *Academy of Management Review, 8*(2), 273–284.

Bartunek, J. M., Lacey, C. A., & Wood, D. R. (1992). Social cognition in organizational change: An insider/outsider approach. *Journal of Applied Behavioral Science, 28*(2), 204–223.

Berger, P. L., & Luckman, T. (1967). *The social construction of reality: A treatise on the sociology of knowledge.* Garden City, NY: Doubleday.

Boje, D. M. (1991). The storytelling organization: A study of story performance in an office-supply firm. *Administrative Science Quarterly, 36*(1), 106–126.

Boland, R. J., Jr. (1984). Sensemaking of accounting data as a technique of organizational diagnosis. *Management Science, 30*(7), 868–882.

Brief, A. P., & Downey, H. K. (1983). Cognitive and organizational structures: A conceptual analysis of implicit organizing theories. *Human Relations, 36*(12), 1065–1090.

Brown, A. D. (2000). Making sense of inquiry sensemaking. *Journal of Management Studies, 37*(1), 45–75.

Bryman, A. (1996). Leadership in organizations. In: S. R. Clegg, C. Hardy & W. R. Nord (Eds), *Handbook of organization studies* (pp. 276–292). Thousand Oak, CA: Sage.

Burrell, G., & Morgan, G. (1979). *Sociological paradigms and organizational analysis.* London: Heinemann.

Chatman, E. A. (1992). The role of mentorship in shaping public library leaders. *Library Trends, 40*(3), 492–512.

Choo, C. W. (1998). *The knowing organization: How organizations use information to construct meaning, create knowledge, and make decisions.* New York: Oxford University.

Choo, C. W. (2001). The knowing organization as learning organization. *Education+Training, 43*(4/5), 197–205.

Daft, R. L., & Lengel, R. H. (1986). Organizational information requirements, media richness, and structural design. *Management Science, 32*(5), 554–571.

Daft, R. L., & Lewin, A. Y. (1993). Where are the theories for the 'new' organizational forms?: An editorial essay. *Organization Science, 4*(4), 1–6.

Daft, R. L., & Weick, K. E. (1984). Toward a model of organizations as interpretation systems. *Academy of Management Review, 9*(2), 284–295.

Das, T. K., & Teng, B. S. (1999). Cognitive biases and strategic decision processes: An interpretative framework. *Journal of Management Studies, 36*(6), 757–778.

Dervin, B. (1983). *An overview of sensemaking research: Concepts methods and results to date.* Seattle: University of Washington School of Communication.

Dervin, B. (1999). On studying information seeking methodologically: The implications of connecting metatheory to method. *Information Processing and Management, 35*(6), 727–750.

Donham, J. (1998). *Enhancing teaching and learning: A leadership guide for school library media specialists.* New York: Neal-Schumann.

Donnellon, A. (1986). Language and communication in organizations: Bridging cognition and behavior. In: H. P. Sims & D. A. Gioia (Eds), *The thinking organization* (pp. 136–164). San Francisco, CA: Jossey Bass.

Dougherty, D. (1992). Interpretive barriers to successful product innovation in large firms. *Organization Science, 3*(2), 179–203.

Downey, H. K., & Brief, A. P. (1986). How cognitive structures affect organizational design: Implicit theories of organizing. In: H. P. Sims, D. A. Gioia & Associates (Eds), *The thinking organization* (pp. 165–190). San Francisco, CA: Jossey Bass.

Drazin, R., Glenn, M. A., & Kazanjian, R. K. (1999). Multilevel theorizing about creativity in organizations: A sensemaking perspective. *Academy of Management Review, 24*(2), 286–307.

Dutton, J. E. (1988). Understanding strategic agenda building and its implications for managing change. In: L. R. Pondy, R. J. Boland & H. Thomas (Eds), *Managing ambiguity and change* (pp. 127–144). Chichester, UK: Wiley.

Dutton, J. E. (1993). Interpretations on automatic: A different view of strategic issue diagnosis. *Journal of Management Studies, 30*(3), 339–357.

Eisenberg, E. M., & Riley, P. (1988). Organizational symbols and sensemaking. In: G. M. Goldhaber & G. A. Barnett (Eds), *Handbook of organizational communication* (pp. 131–150). Norwood, NJ: Ablex.

Eisenhardt, K. M. (1990). Speed and strategic choice: How managers accelerate decision making. *California Management Review, 32*(3), 39–54.

Ericson, T. (2001). Sensemaking in organisations: Towards a conceptual framework for understanding strategic change. *Scandinavian Journal of Management, 17*(1), 109–131.

Fairhead, J. (1998). Paradigm change and leveraged learning during the Rover—Honda collaboration. *Creativity and Innovation Management, 7*(2), 93–106.

Fiol, C. M., & Huff, A. S. (1992). Maps for managers: Where are we? *Journal of Management Studies, 29*(3), 267–285.

Fiske, S. T., & Taylor, S. C. (1984). *Social cognition.* New York: McGraw Hill.

Frost, P. J., & Morgan, G. (1983). Symbols and sensemaking. In: L. R. Pondy, P. J. Frost, G. Morgan & T. C. Dandridge (Eds), *Organizational symbolism* (pp. 207–236). Greenwich, CT: JAI.

Fulton, T.L. (2001). Integrating academic libraries and computer centers: A phenomenological study of leader sensemaking about organizational restructuring. (Doctoral dissertation, Pennsylvania State University, 2002). Dissertation Abstracts International 62 (12), 4085A (UMI No. 3036035).

Gabriel, Y. (2000). *Storytelling in organizations: Facts, fictions, and fantasies.* Oxford, UK: Oxford University.

Gephart, R. P., Jr. (1991). Succession sensemaking and organizational change: A story of a deviant college president. *Journal of Organizational Change Management, 4*(3), 35–44.

Gephart, R. P., Jr. (1993). The textual approach: Risk and blame in disaster sensemaking. *Academy of Management Journal, 36*(6), 1465–1514.

Gioia, D. A. (1986a). Conclusion: The state of the art in organizational social cognition. In: H. P. Sims & D. A. Gioia (Eds), *The thinking organization* (pp. 336–356). San Francisco, CA: Jossey Bass.

Gioia, D. A. (1986b). Symbols, scripts, and sensemaking: Creating meaning in the organizational experience. In: H. P. Sims & D. A. Gioia (Eds), *The thinking organization* (pp. 49–74). San Francisco, CA: Jossey Bass.

Gioia, D. A. (1989). Self-serving bias as a self-sensemaking strategy: Explicit vs. tacit impression management. In: P. Rosenfeld & R. Giacalone (Eds), *Impression management in the organization* (pp. 219–234). Hillsdale, NJ: Lawrence Erlbaum.

Gioia, D. A., & Chittipeddi, K. (1991). Sensemaking and sensegiving in strategic change initiation. *Strategic Management Journal, 12*(6), 433–448.

Gioia, D. A., & Manz, C. C. (1985). Linking cognition and behavior: A script processing interpretation of vicarious learning. *Academy of Management Review, 10*(3), 527–539.

Gioia, D. A., & Mehra, A. (1996). Review of the book Sensemaking in organizations. *Academy of Management Review, 21*(4), 1226–1230.

Gioia, D. A., & Poole, P. P. (1984). Scripts in organizational behavior. *Academy of Management Review, 9*(3), 449–459.

Gioia, D. A., & Sims, H. P., Jr. (1986). Introduction: Social cognition in organizations. In: H. P. Sims Jr. & D. A. Gioia (Eds), *The thinking organization* (pp. 1–19). San Francisco, CA: Jossey Bass.

Gioia, D. A., & Thomas, J. B. (1996). Identity, image and issue interpretation: Sensemaking during strategic change in academia. *Administrative Science Quarterly, 41*(3), 370–403.

Gioia, D. A., Thomas, J. B., Clark, S. M., & Chittipeddi, K. (1994). Symbolism and strategic change in academia: The dynamics of sensemaking and influence. *Organization Science, 5*(3), 363–383.

Gray, B., Bougon, M. G., & Donnellon, A. (1985). Organizations as constructions and destructions of meaning. *Journal of Management, 11*(2), 83–98.

Greenberg, D. N. (1995). Blue versus gray: A metaphor constraining sensemaking around a restructuring. *Group & Organizational Management, 20*(2), 183–209.

Hannabuss, S. (2000). Narrative knowledge: Eliciting organizational knowledge from storytelling. *ASLIB Proceedings, 52*(10), 402–413.

Hanson, C. D. (1991). The language of library leadership: Effective communication. In: D. E. Riggs (Ed.), *Library communication* (pp. 38–54). Chicago, IL: American Library Association.

Harris, S. G. (1994). Organizational culture and individual sensemaking: Aschema-based perspective. *Organization Science, 5*(3), 309–321.

Hatch, M. J., & Yanow, D. (2003). Organizational theory as an interpretive science. In: H. Tsoukas & C. Knudsen (Eds), *Oxford handbook of organization theory* (pp. 63–87). Oxford, UK: Oxford University.

Hellgren, B., & Melin, L. (1993). The role of strategists' ways-of-thinking in strategic change processes. In: J. Hendry & G. Johnson (Eds), *Strategic thinking: Leadership and the management of change* (pp. 47–68). Chicester, UK: Wiley.

Hernon, P., Powell, R. R., & Young, A. P. (2003). *The next library leadership: Attributes of academic and public library directors*. Westport, CT: Libraries Unlimited.

Hosking, D. M. (1991). Chief executives, organising processes, and skill. *European Review of Management Science, 41*(2), 93–103.

Huff, A. S., & Schwenk, C. R. (1990). Bias and sensemaking in good times and bad. In: A. S. Huff (Ed.), *Mapping strategic thought* (pp. 89–108). New York: Wiley.

Isabella, L. A. (1990). Evolving interpretations as a change unfolds: How managers construe key organizational events. *Academy of Management Journal, 33*(1), 7–41.

Isenberg, D. J. (1984). How senior managers think. *Harvard Business Review, 62*(6), 81–90.

Isenberg, D. J. (1986). The structure and process of understanding: Implications for managerial action. In: H. P. Sims & D. A. Gioia (Eds), *The thinking organization* (pp. 238–262). San Francisco, CA: Jossey-Bass.

Johnson, P., Daniels, K., & Huff, A. (2001). Sense making, leadership, and mental models. In: S. J. Zaccaro & R. J. Klimoski (Eds), *The nature of organizational leadership* (pp. 79–103). San Francisco, CA: Jossey Bass.

Jonas, H. S., Fry, R. E., & Srivastva, S. (1989). The person of the CEO: Understanding the executive experience. *Academy of Management Executive, 3*(3), 205–215.

Jonas, H. S., Fry, R. E., & Shrivastva, S. (1990). The office of the CEO: Understanding the executive experience. *Academy of Management Executive, 4*(3), 36–48.

Kiesler, C. A., & Sproull, L. (1982). Managerial response to changing environments: Perspectives on problem sensing from social cognition. *Administrative Science Quarterly, 27*(4), 548–570.

Kuhlthau, C. C. (2004). *Seeking meaning: A process approach to library and information services* (2nd ed.). Norwood, NJ: Ablex.

Lanzara, G. F. (1983). Ephemeral organizations in extreme environments: Emergence, strategy, extinction. *Journal of Management Studies, 20*(1), 71–95.

Lehr, J. K., & Rice, R. E. (2002). Organizational measures as a form of knowledge management: A multitheoretic, communication-based exploration. *Journal of the American Society for Information Science and Technology, 53*(12), 1060–1073.

Lord, R. G., & Foti, R. J. (1986). Schema theories, information processing, and organizational behavior. In: H. P. Sims & D. A. Gioia (Eds), *The thinking organization* (pp. 20–48). San Francisco, CA: Jossey Bass.

Louis, M. R. (1980). Surprise and sensemaking: What newcomers experience in entering unfamiliar organizational settings. *Administrative Science Quarterly, 25*(2), 226–251.

Louis, M. R., & Sutton, R. I. (1991). Switching cognitive gears: From habits of mind to active thinking. *Human Relations, 44*(1), 55–76.

Maguire, E. R. (2002). Community policing, loose coupling, and sensemaking in American police agencies. *Justice Quarterly, 19*(3), 503–536.

Miller, D. (1993). The architecture of simplicity. *Academy of Management Review, 18*, 118–138.

Milliken, F. J., & Lant, T. K. (1991). The impact of an organization's recent performance history on strategic persistence and change: The role of managerial interpretations. *Advances in Strategic Management, 7*, 129–156.

Mishler, E. G. (1986). *Research interviewing: Context and narrative*. Cambridge, MA: Harvard University.

Needham, G. (2001). The concept of leadership in technology-related organizations. In: M. Winston (Ed.), *Leadership in the library and information science professions: Theory and practice* (pp. 133–144). Binghamton, NY: Haworth.

Nystrom, P. C., & Starbuck, W. H. (1984). Managing beliefs in organizations. *Journal of Applied Behavioral Science, 20*(3), 277–287.

Park, O. S., Sims, H. P., Jr., & Motowidlo, A. J. (1986). Affect in organizations: How feelings and emotions influence managerial judgment. In: H. P. Sims & D. A. Gioia (Eds), *The thinking organization* (pp. 215–236). San Francisco, CA: Jossey Bass.

Pfeffer, J. (1981). Management as symbolic action: The creation and maintenance of organizational paradigms. In: L. L. Cummings & B. M. Staw (Eds), *Research in organizational behavior*, Vol. 3 (pp. 1–52). Greenwich, CT: JAI.

Pondy, L. R. (1978). Leadership is a language game. In: M. W. McCall Jr. & M. M. Lombardo (Eds), *Leadership: Where else can we go?* (pp. 87–99). Durham, NC: Duke University.

Porac, J. F., Meindl, C., & Stubbart, C. (1996). Introduction. In: J. R. Meindl, C. Stubbart & J. F. Porac (Eds), *Cognition within and between organizations* (pp. ix–xxiii). Thousand Oaks, CA: Sage.

Porac, J. F., Thomas, H., & Baden-Fuller, C. (1989). Competitive groups as cognitive communities: The case of Scottish knitwear manufacturers. *Journal of Management Studies, 26*(4), 397–416.

Pye, A. (2002). The changing power of explanations: Directors, academics and their sensemaking from 1989 to 2000. *Journal of Management Studies, 39*(7), 907–926.

Ranson, S., Hinings, B., & Greenwood, R. (1980). The structuring of unstructured organizational structures. *Administrative Science Quarterly, 25*(1), 1–17.

Riggs, D. E. (1988). Visionary leadership. In: T. F. Mech & G. B. McCabe (Eds), *Leadership and academic libraries* (pp. 55–65). Westport, CT: Greenwood.

Riggs, D. E. (2001). The crisis and opportunities in library leadership. In: M. Winston (Ed.), *Leadership in the library and information science professions: Theory and practice* (pp. 5–17). Binghamton, NY: Haworth.

Robbins, S. R., & Duncan, R. B. (1988). The role of the CEO and top management in the creation and implementation of strategic vision. In: D. C. Hambrick (Ed.), *The executive effect: Concepts and methods for studying top managers* (pp. 205–236). Greenwich, CT: JAI.

Schwenk, C. R. (1988). The cognitive perspective on strategic decision-making. *Journal of Management Studies, 25*(1), 41–55.

Smircich, L. (1983). Organizations as shared meanings. In: L. R. Pondy, P. J. Frost, G. Morgan & T. C. Dandridge (Eds), *Organizational symbolism* (pp. 55–65). Greenwich, CT: JAI.

Smircich, L., & Morgan, G. (1982). Leadership: The management of meaning. *Journal of Applied Behavioral Science, 18*(3), 257–273.

Smircich, L., & Stubbart, C. (1985). Strategic management in an enacted world. *Academy of Management Review, 10*(4), 724–736.

Spreitzer, G. M., Shapiro, D. L., & Von Glinow, M. A. (2002). Helping transnational team members to sense trust: A counterintuitive approach to leadership. In: H. Sondak (Ed.), *Research on managing groups and teams: Vol 4: Toward phenomenology of groups and group membership* (pp. 203–233). Stamford, CT: JAI.

Starbuck, W. H., & Milliken, F. J. (1988). Executives' perceptual filters: What they notice and how they make sense. In: D. C. Hambrick (Ed.), *Executive effect: Concepts and methods for studying top managers* (pp. 35–66). Greenwich, CT: JAI.

Sutherland, K., & Dawson, S. (2002). Doctors at work. *International Studies of Management and Organization, 32*(2), 51–69.

Sweeney, R. T. (1994). Leadership in the post-hierarchical library. *Library Trends, 43*(1), 62–95.

Thayer, L. (1988). Leadership/communication: A critical review and a modest proposal. In: G. M. Goldhaber & G. A. Barnett (Eds), *Handbook of organizational communication* (pp. 231–263). Norwood, NJ: Ablex.

Thomas, J. B., Clark, S. M., & Gioia, D. A. (1993). Strategic sensemaking and organizational performance: Linkages among scanning, interpretation, action, and outcomes. *Academy of Management Journal, 36*(2), 239–270.

Thomas, J. B., Gioia, D. A., & Ketchen, D. J. (1997). Strategic sensemaking: Learning through scanning, interpretation, action and performance. *Advances in Strategic Management, 14*, 299–330.

Vaara, E. (2003). Post-acquisition integration as sensemaking: Glimpses of ambiguity, confusion, hypocrisy, and politicization. *Journal of Management Studies, 40*(4), 859–885.

Volkema, R. J., Farquhar, K., & Bergmann, T. J. (1996). Third party sensemaking in interpersonal conflict at work: A theoretical framework. *Human Relations, 49*(11), 1437–1454.

Walsh, J. P. (1995). Managerial and organizational cognition: Notes from a trip down memory lane. *Organizational Science, 6*(3), 280–321.

Weaver, G. R., & Gioia, D. A. (1994). Paradigms lost: Incommensurability vs. structurationist inquiry. *Organization Studies, 15*(4), 565–589.

Weick, K. E. (1979a). Cognitive processes in organizations. In: B. M. Staw & L. L. Cummings (Eds), *Research in organizational behavior*, Vol. 1 (pp. 41–74). Greenwich, CT: JAI.

Weick, K. E. (1979b). *The social psychology of organizing* (2nd ed.). Reading, MA: Addison Wesley.

Weick, K. E. (1983). Managerial thought in the context of action. In: S. Srivastava (Ed.), *The executive mind: New insights on managerial thought and action* (pp. 221–242). San Francisco, CA: Jossey Bass.

Weick, K. E. (1988). Enacted sensemaking in crisis situations. *Journal of Management Studies, 25*(4), 305–317.

Weick, K. E. (1990a). Technology as equivoque: Sensemaking in new technologies. In: P. S. Goodman & L. Sproull (Eds), *Technology and organizations* (pp. 1–44). San Francisco, CA: Jossey Bass.

Weick, K. E. (1990b). The vulnerable system: An analysis of the Tenerife Air Disaster. *Journal of Management, 16*(3), 571–593.

Weick, K. E. (1993a). The collapse of sensemaking in organizations: The Mann Gulch disaster. *Administrative Science Quarterly, 38*(4), 628–652.

Weick, K. E. (1993b). Organizational redesign as improvisation. In: G. P. Huber & W. H. Glick (Eds), *Organizational change and redesign* (pp. 346–379). New York: Oxford University.

Weick, K. E. (1995). *Sensemaking in organizations*. Thousand Oaks, CA: Sage.

Weick, K. E., & Bougon, M. G. (1986). Organizations as cognitive maps: Charting ways to success and failure. In: H. P. Sims, D. A. Gioia & Associates (Eds), *The thinking organization* (pp. 102–135). San Francisco, CA: Jossey Bass.

Zaccaro, S. J., & Klimoski, R. J. (2001). The nature of organizational leadership: An introduction. In: S. J. Zaccaro & R. J. Klimoski (Eds), *The nature of organizational leadership* (pp. 3–41). San Francisco, CA: Jossey Bass.

UNDERSTANDING THE ROLE OF VALUES IN LIBRARY DESIGN

Lilia Pavlovsky

INTRODUCTION

It has been suggested that "space and artifacts constitute systems of communication which organizations build up within themselves" (Gagliardi, 1992a, b, p. vi) and reflect the cultural life within that organization. This is a study of how the "landscape" of a public library ("Library X"), as an information retrieval system, relates to the values of the people who created it. The efforts here are geared towards understanding the physical instantiation of institutional culture and, more specifically, institutional values as they are reflected through the artifact.

Statement of the Problem

Information retrieval (IR) systems can be intimidating to users. In this context, an information retrieval system is loosely defined as a place that is intentionally created for a user population to which they can go for particular types of information. It is also not clear why some systems do not appeal to the populations for whom they are designed. It is speculated that mismatches exist between the actual design of systems and how those systems are perceived and navigated by users.

Advances in Library Administration and Organization
Advances in Library Administration and Organization, Volume 22, 157–274
Copyright © 2005 by Elsevier Ltd.
All rights of reproduction in any form reserved
ISSN: 0732-0671/doi:10.1016/S0732-0671(05)22005-9

It is suspected that designers and users of IR system are perhaps misunderstanding each other's goals through their respective understanding of the information-seeking environment. It is not clear how or at what point such misunderstandings occur. Since the physical environment is typically the first point of entry into the information system it becomes the focal point for this study. It is the place where the users interact with information providers either directly or through objects that were placed into the system with certain objectives in mind.

It is in this space that objects that are perceived to be of value to users are placed. In turn, users are expected to locate such objects and use them for their information-seeking objectives. Both information providers and users have distinctly separate yet inextricably intertwined priorities that converge within the public space of the IR system. Such priorities and values are the focus of this investigation.

Research Goal

The goal of this study is to define, describe, and understand values as they are instantiated within the artifact (the information system) as well as how they are articulated in the institutional text that fundamentally defines the artifact. Gagliardi (1992a, b, p. 9) writes "...the social scientist finds himself entirely at ease when analyzing written or verbal communications, but flounders in the attempt to grasp the language of things." Part of this study is focused on classifying and understanding the language and the meaning of the artifacts in the public space of a library. Since artifacts do not exist outside the social groups that create them, the other part of this study will focus on analyzing and discussing the institutional text that defines the role of information provision within an institutional context.

Research Questions

This study will address the following research questions:

1. How can the physical and intellectual space of an information system be characterized with respect to the types of values that it represents?
2. What are the values of the information providers?
3. What is the relationship between the values discovered?

4. What do the values that are discovered suggest about perceptions of users and use of the system?

This study takes an interpretive approach towards understanding how environments and text can reveal institutional value structures. The role of values in system design is unclear and this project sets forth to understand this role as well as to create a methodological approach that addresses this issue.

LITERATURE REVIEW

This is a review of the literature that defines environments as being socially constructed entities. Within this context I will present studies that have examined the symbolic aspects of artifacts. Environmental aspects of library design will also be examined.

Defining Space

The impact of physical environments is not often viewed with the same amount of significance as cultural, social, or institutional environments, yet a large proportion of resources are allocated towards the development and maintenance of physical settings (Canter, 1975). Most spaces are designed with functional issues in mind. This should not suggest that symbolic meanings are not present. People do not only experience space in a functional way. Some suggest that spaces become what they are because meanings are appropriated to them (Parker Pearson & Richards, 1994a, b, c). The way we divide space is "…probably the most fundamental manifestation of how we divide reality…" (Zerubavel, 1991, p. 6). This division is culturally bounded.

"The relationship between spatial form and human agency is mediated by meaning. People actively give their physical environments meanings, and then act upon those meanings" (Parker Pearson & Richards, p. 5). By appropriating function to an object, one also appropriates meaning. Meaning, however, is not universal. Often concepts "…such as utility or comfort" are taken as being universal principles even though they are "culturally specific, relative values." (Parker Pearson & Richards, pp. 6–7).

Where there is space there are borders that define it. Physical allocation of space, as well as classification of functions within, facilitates environmental control. Boundaries can be fixed or fluid, physical, or negotiated.

Boundaries serve to stabilize social relationships (Jackson, 1984) and, from sociological perspectives, can be viewed as outcomes of social agreement about where they should be. Boundaries serve to define the natural land-scape in social terms – they transform natural space into public space.

Environmental meanings stem from familiarity with the way the environment is structured as well as from an understanding of physical and social boundaries. Jackson's point suggests that cultural knowledge is important in evoking a feeling of familiarity in environments. The premise presented in this research is that even though information providers may intend for a system to be utilized in a certain way by a certain group of people, it may not actually end up being utilized in that way. This notion stems from the idea that if creators' values underscore the creation of an environment (and it is assumed that they do) then there may be elements in that environment that are unfamiliar to those for whom it is designed.

Zerubavel (1991) discusses the complexity of drawing the "fine lines" that distinguish various elements of the social world. To define something is to give that thing a boundary; an act that is first mental before it is instantiated in physical form (Zerubavel, p. 2). Understanding how those lines are drawn, Zerubavel claims, will enable us to understand the social world that created them. The creation of any entity suggests both a conscious and a tacit effort to determine what should go into that entity and what should not.

With respect to information systems, boundaries define what goes in and what stays out of the system (Turner, 1987a, b). Boundaries define the system's scope. If they are set too broadly, then the system becomes overly complex. If they are too narrow, then it becomes trivial (Turner, p. 105).

Symbolic Nature of Artifacts

Space is defined not only with respect to the borders drawn around it but also by the artifacts placed within. Artifacts are physical entities that are "products of human nature" (Gagliardi, 1992, p. 3) and exist independently of their creator. To study artifacts is to study what has been referred to as "a fundamental category of experience: space" (Gagliardi, p. 4). Artifacts are both functional and symbolic. They are used and they are interpreted (Gagliardi).

In the literature there is a tension between architectural perspectives on space and those of social scientists studying that space. Hall (1976, p. 160) states that, "architects traditionally are preoccupied with the visual patterns of structures – what one sees. They are almost totally unaware of the fact that people carry around with them internalization of fixed-feature space learned early in life."

In this context, environments need not be viewed as being of one culture. Instead, it is suggested that a variety of value structures, norms, rituals, beliefs, etc. exist within the boundaries of an institution not unlike those suggested by Shibutani's (1955, 1986) notion of "reference group." This concept emerges from the observation that "...people who occupy a common habitat do not necessarily share a common culture" (Shibutani, 1986, p. 109). Instead, it is posited that "modern mass societies are made up of a bewildering variety of social worlds (Shibutani, p. 109). The social worlds can coexist in one physical domain, such as an institution. This idea further suggests that differing value structures can coexist within an institutional context though they may not necessarily be given equal prominence within the physical space of the environment.

Although this is not a new idea, it is one that has not had much attention in studies of institutional culture (Gagliardi, 1990). "The idea that concrete forms can incorporate mental and value structures has been asserted by various writers, students of symbolism, art historians, and anthropologists" (Gagliardi, p. 28). The archeological study of relics suggests the notion that certain understandings of cultures can be interpreted from the study of physical expressions of that culture. Institutional image and its instantiation in physical form is an important element of institutional identity.

Berg and Kreiner (1990) examine buildings (architecture) as artifacts that reflect institutional values. They suggest that some buildings are actually designed to evoke a certain type of behavior within (e.g. places of worship) given certain physical cues that are encountered outside and inside. Buildings are also viewed by Berg and Kreiner (p. 49) as "totems" and symbols of "strategic profile." Selection of sites and décor is done very carefully in a conscious effort to represent the organization's value structure. It is also said that design in décor and architecture does affect how organizations themselves are viewed and preferred over their competitors. Berg and Kreiner (p. 61) conclude that meaning can be "'read' from physical aspects of an artifact."

Thomas (1996) similarly suggests that buildings can be "read" by those who interact within them. Thomas (p. 9) studied a variety of library environments with the perspective that "...interactions between people and institutions arise in social situations created through communication..." and that "libraries have within them embedded social, political, and cultural values which are recoverable in aspects of their material presentation."

Thomas found that the different institutions reflected different values, depending upon their positions, ideology, purpose, functions, etc. The complexity of institutional values is underscored as it is reflected in day-to-day practices. "Even though these practices provide clues for library users, architectural and environmental aspects of facilities may go largely 'unseen' as a part of the 'woodwork' by library staff members who encounter them on a daily basis" (Thomas, p. 465). Thomas suggests that culture is that which is often taken for granted by its members and perhaps, that librarians may not quite "see" their environment from the same perspective as their users.

Berg and Kreiner (1990, p. 62) further note that "...corporate buildings are seldom left to speak for themselves. They are described, reviewed, and interpreted over and over again in direct communications from the organizations. In such communications a custom-made code is established, a rudimentary code which links a specific message to that particular building directly, and, a code which will not be applicable to other corporate buildings." The implication of this observation is the idea that the inhabitants of the building have some element of control over the environment through organized rhetoric.

Rosen, Orlikowski and Schmahmann (1990) argue that physical design of space is also a way in which institutions can use space to attain discipline and control. Space is also used as a demarcation of status.

In a study of computer systems, Ciborra and Lanzara (1990, p. 149) propose the following premise: "...computer-based information systems are embodiments not of just data flows and work routines, but also of organizational cultures and archetypes." Ciborra and Lanzara introduce the concept of "formative contexts" that suggests interaction unfolds in two directions.

What Ciborra and Lanzara suggest is that seemingly benign "plastic" systems can change institutional realities in permanent ways. Systems modify behavior not only in physical ways but also in basic, culturally driven ways that are taken for granted. Their research addresses the taken for granted elements of institutional culture that in this case are behaviors of individuals in the throes of change. They argue that people have deep rooted, pre-existing notions of institutional arrangements, situations, etc. Systems are not static artifacts, and the current way of examining them must change. Their agenda proposes a need to focus beyond economics and efficiency toward how systems relate to cognitive and institutional frameworks.

Scholz (1990) also points to the existence of complex relationship between social and technological factors. His effort is to understand how information is processed within the institution in relation to cultural factors. An institution is seen as an interaction between subjective (symbolic) and objective (empirical objects and events) realities. The seemingly objective functions of a system are made subjective by people who give meaning to those functions.

Sassoon (1990) found specific elements such as color to be linked to institutional ideology. Dougherty and Kunda (1990) studied how photographs can portray organizational culture. Institutional cultures can also be found in stories and texts that are created by the leaders of those institutions. In turn the myths and stories are instantiated in artifacts and symbols within the institutions.

Raspa (1990) studied how the Domino's pizza culture is very carefully presented in images created by its CEO and integrated within the operating environments of the franchises. The notion of metaphor is introduced as a mechanism by which an institution's culture can be described and interpreted.

Larsen and Schultz (1990, p. 300) present themselves as "cultural Geiger counters" in their study of bureaucracy of The Danish Ministry of Domestic Affairs that has been metaphorically converted to a Monastery. The metaphor was used as a tool in the research process (as presented in Morgan's (1986) work as well) to enable the researchers to get at what they considered to be the more "fundamental features of the culture" (Larsen & Schultz, p. 300). Although the usage of the metaphor in the study of symbolic elements within institutions may provoke a variety of biases, it still provides a lens through which to view elements from a different perspective.

Perspectives on Library/System Design

It is difficult to present a cohesive body of literature on the topic of library and system design. At first glance, it would appear that the two literatures are unrelated. Yet in a broader context, when the subject matter is addressed at a basic level (as opposed to system specifics) it becomes easier to see the relationships between the "systems" and the "library" literatures.

A Departure from User Studies – Examining the System

Over the last several decades there has been a shift in the literature from a "system" oriented perspective to a "user driven" one. Dervin and Nilan

(1986) identified this shift in perspective, and research continued to build on the ideas presented in their review. The trends they observed were focused on the importance of defining and understanding information-seeking processes in sociological, cognitive, affective, and behavioral areas (e.g. Kuhlthau, 1991; Dewdney & Ross, 1994; Chatman 1991, 1996; Belkin & Vickery, 1985; Dervin, 1980; Taylor, 1986; Bodker, 1991). Much research has fallen out of this model that highlights users' requirements, perspectives and behaviors – the users' point of view.

Systems have been examined with respect to their ability to fulfill the users' requirements in terms of specific search behaviors (e.g. Chang & Rice, 1992); thought processes and problematic situations (e.g. Belkin, 1980, 1987); affective/emotional elements (e.g. Kuhlthau, 1991); and elements/conditions that affect users outside of the system which could be potentially responded to by the system (e.g. Chatman, 1991, 1996; Dervin, 1980).

The system is typically regarded as a tool that contains potentially relevant information items. The system's objectivity is not often questioned, nor is its configuration with respect to how, by definition and default, it tends to impose a particular framework upon its respective environment as pointed out by Boland (1987). By definition a system defines and shapes activities within its boundaries, yet this particular effect of the design is not often investigated.

Lyytinen (1987, p. 4) states that "despite impressive advances in technology...IS misuse and rejection are more frequent than acceptance and use." Some research points out that systems are not always used to capacity (e.g. Borgman, 1996), if at all (Chatman 1991). It is possible that the technologies, as powerful as they are, are not the only solution to a system's problems. It is also possible that "...little is really known about what design is or how people go about doing it" (Turner, 1987a ,b, p. 97). Turner (p. 97) points out the "...problem of understanding design is not unique to information systems" specifically citing problems in architecture and engineering.

Many information systems fail because of "...conceptual problems, data problems and people problems" (Lyytinen, 1987, p. 35). Lyytinen and others (Banbury, 1987) strongly argue that any arrangement or change of a system will affect how that system will be absorbed (or rejected) into the community. In order to account for these issues, researchers need to take into account the "cultural, social, political, and moral aspects of system design (Lyytinen, p. 5). Systems are embedded in a social and cultural milieu and that relationship needs to be understood.

Library Design

There is a large literature that discusses various aspects of library design. Primarily, the focus is on standards (architectural; design elements; technical issues) and anecdotal experiences. The purpose of this section has been to pull out the literature that is most closely related to the topic of this project. This review is not intended to be an exhaustive discussion of all the literature because this is not possible given the diversity and scope of the topics addressed.

The impact of physical environments is often not assigned with the same amount of significance as cultural, social, or institutional environments, yet substantial resources are allocated towards the development and maintenance of physical settings (Canter, 1975). In short, use of space remains a relative mystery (Sommer, 1969a). In library and information science literature there is a distinct focus on how information resources are used but not as much attention has been placed on how the systems themselves impact use (Thomas, 1996).

Bazillion and Braun (1994) suggest that libraries should be teaching instruments and call for libraries to "move beyond their custodial role and to become an integral part of the teaching process" (p. 14). Others note the challenges faced in the process of design (Jones, 1993) where the focus is on elements of design, structure, lighting, etc. The "human element" (Jones, p. 221) focuses on physical elements that are convenient ("no revolving doors, no turnstiles"); accessibility ("accessible to users of all ages, irrespective of any disabilities") (p. 222); and other factors revolving around measurable elements such as increases in demand, furniture design, etc. Line (1998) presents the position that libraries have gone from the "bulk" service attitude towards designing systems around people. Rather than design around groups, individual facts need to be taken into account. Yet it is not clear how, exactly can a system can be made to do everything for everyone.

Many factors influence how libraries are designed and redesigned. Sutton (1996) points out that as technologies and work habits change so does design. "Click-free" zones have been introduced into library environments with the advent of portable computers. Other spaces those are separate from the primary library space that support collaborative work is another example. Libraries are also involved in user training as a result of technological growth (Sutton 1996). It is argued that library space should adapt to changes in user work behaviors.

Jones (1993, p. 214) lists "flexibility, cabling, lighting, environmental controls, accessibility and user-friendliness" as factors that should be considered in library design. Flexibility itself presents an issue because some argue that it is futile to project into the future while others disagree and say that being open to change is the only approach that should be considered. For example, keeping things like flooring accessible is an idea suggested because it facilitates access to the wires, cables, etc. Martin (1992) also suggests that librarians should take long term needs into account – they should think very carefully about how much enclosure is necessary, and new technologies should be integrated incrementally (Martin, 1992). Jones also raises the importance of security, as investments in technology increase, as being a criterion of concern.

A recurrent theme in this literature is how to make a library aesthetically pleasing and practically useful, as well as appealing to a wide range of clientele (Rizzo, 1992). Rizzo suggests that libraries mean different things to different people and that those elements should somehow be incorporated in a good design. A public library is a "study hall...workplace... distribution center...cost center...a part of the community...a museum...a part-time parent...a store...an evolving organism...something more...." (Rizzo, p. 325) He points out that design needs to follow the providers' understanding of the institution's purpose on both local and ideological levels. Such values and ideals need to be translated into form.

Issues in library design are often paradoxical. First, there is a need to maintain order and variety while maintaining control over the content and the people who use it. (Lushington, 1993). What really falls out of this brief discussion of library design literature is that there are many factors that are directly competing with one another in the public space. Libraries are attempting to cover a lot of ground with respect to defining themselves in relation to their services.

A *Georgia Librarian* (Winter, 1993, p. 98) issue featured library design. Architectural firms were asked to share some of their experiences in working with librarians and libraries. One firm placed an emphasis on visual control, maximization of space, security, energy efficiency, cost, and flexibility for technological growth. Another commented on the flow of people in relation to materials as being a complex issue in design. Yet another noted that the library should reflect the unique needs of the community within which it is built. Some discussed the need to combine technology, user-friendliness and storage space into one environment. Some tended to focus more on program objectives and merge those into a design the fits into a profile that fits the community. The challenge of designing libraries in contemporary times stems from that need to balance the realities of the world and the library ideology based in the notion that access should be provided for all.

"Libraries often have stronger personalities than other building types..." stated Thomas O. Ramesey (1993, in The Georgia Librarian, p. 100) due to their understandings of the groups and communities they serve.

Designing public libraries is not an easy task because the designers must consider the diversity of its clientele and its role within the community (Curry & Henriquez, 1998). "While public libraries provide for group functions, customers also expect them to be sanctuaries for individuals seeking refuge from social, political, and psychological distractions: quiet, more private areas should also be available. Library customers vary in age, education, ethnic background, and aesthetic preferences, but, despite this kaleidoscope of users, a public library building must somehow address the needs of all community members" (Curry & Henriquez, p. 81).

Curry and Henriquez examined the experiences of both architects and librarians pertaining to their participation in the library design process. One finding noted that librarians tended to emphasize the need for flexibility while the architects emphasized the need to focus on a single vision of what the space should be. Interestingly, they also found that librarians were much more apt to get their ideas from touring other libraries and similar institutions (such as bookstores) while architects were more focused on creating innovative concepts for the place in question. "One architect felt strongly that the project librarian had visited too many libraries resulting in a "wish list" of features, which could not all be integrated into a new building with unity and originality" (Curry & Henriquez, p. 88).

The other significant difference in the perception of building design is summarized in the following statement: "The architects continued to see the building in much more static, symbolic terms throughout the process. They described what the building "is," while the librarians described what the building "does" (Curry & Henriquez, p. 89). The emphasis of the architects is on the form while the librarians focus on function. Intner (1999) strongly emphasizes that form most definitely should follow function and that the key to this whole process is the professional who determines what the function is or should be. If form truly follows function, then form also reflects the choices and ideas determined by the information professional.

One common thread of the "library and architects" literature tends to be the notion that potential miscommunication between librarians and architects is a common problem (Connor & Patton, 1995). This could account for the variety of questionable designs found in some library spaces. The design process is really one of creating and realizing priorities from both the information professionals' perspective and architectural constraints and design issues. What might be an architect's objective in design may not be one of the library's objectives. "Often a fine building architecturally can be a difficult building for the librarian" (Havard-Williams & Jengo, 1987, p. 160).

Rohlf (1986, p. 100) argues that form does not always follow function with respect to the design of libraries "despite the well-meaning intentions of both the architect and other project designers." The reality of designing libraries is that there are many groups involved, including librarians, architects, interior designers, administrators, consultants, and probably others. Problems arise when architectural zeal overpowers the librarians' knowledge of function. The end result is a form that hinders function. Problematic areas include overbuilt facades, poor lighting, inadequate furnishings, graphics, poor location of tables/chairs; cumbersome signage; conflict between architectural dimensions (based on four-foot measures) and library furniture dimensions (shelving based on three-foot measures); inadequate heights for work stations; inadequate supervision of construction work, among others (pp. 101–105).

Rockwell (1989) points out that the way an architect views space is fundamentally different from the way a librarian views the same space. Rockwell (p. 307) describes "the architects' vocabulary" as being "...full of words like statement and integrity and look" while librarians are concerned with reference and circulation functions.

Lushington (1976, p. 92) argues that "flexibility has become the greatest 'cliché' in library design. The universal rush to embrace this concept has led in many cases to a deliberate avoidance of good functional design." He points out that it is often the medium sized library that suffers from poor design features because large library design principles are often inappropriately applied to medium sized environments.

Another observation made by Lushington is that many libraries are still designed with outdated criteria. An example he gives is that of pedestrian entry in suburban settings that are modeled upon urban library designs. Few libraries "...invite automobile customers to use their facilities by being visible from the road and providing covered walkways and minimal distances from car to entrance (Lushington, p. 93). Other design elements that could use improvement include doors that are often too cumbersome for smaller patrons (kids); and bookshelves that are often designed and placed in ways that break up the collection in unanticipated ways, making them difficult to navigate.

People affect the shape of an environment and the environment, in turn, affects how people travel and act within it (Parker Pearson & Richards, 1994a, b, c). Spaces are carved from the landscape and artifacts are arranged with purposes and in an effort to create a meaningful space. Parker,

Pearson, and Richards (p. 6) point out that it may be difficult for us to see symbolism and function (or utility) as co-mingled and conjoined.

Built environments are a physical manifestation of someone's ideology and design. Personal space, on the other hand, is technically the distance an organism places between itself and others (Sommer, 1969a, p. 247). Personal space is transient as it accompanies its owner, while physical space is fixed. People, in general, tend to keep certain social distances between them. In situations where familiarity prevails the distance might be less than in a random encounter on the street.

In public settings personal distance is dictated by spatial arrangement of seating, corridors, ways of getting up and down (stairs, elevators), ways of commuting (e.g. subways), and so forth. Personal space has invisible boundaries (Sommer, 1969a) while physical space has, more or less, invariable and stationary boundaries. Individuals, as centers of the personal space, carry with them goals, objectives, and, in general, a frame of reference (Shibutani, 1955) which ultimately defines them as who they are. Physical spaces, on the other hand, have already been designed and built with goals and objectives in mind for the functionality of that environment. Elements of design carry with them the notion of intent to affect motion and navigation through built environments.

The interaction between individual space and physical space can be an effortless endeavor or one full of frustration and confusion depending upon how well the two "understand" each other. Studies of personal space examine territoriality (e.g. Sommer, 1969b) or spatial marking (Sommer, 1969a; Becker, 1973). Becker utilizes the concept of spatial "jurisdiction" to suggest that people mark spaces differently in environments where they are transients than in those where they are not.

Sommer (1969b) studied how space was utilized in a library setting and how the actual environment regulated interaction among patrons. He found that some patrons preferred privacy while others wanted a more social environment. He also discovered that there are many tactical maneuvers that patrons employ in order to attain their spatial objectives. Social stimuli were found to be distracting in situations that required concentration on tasks. Social stimuli were also found to be a motivational element for patrons to use the library. Territory was "marked" by seat selection and placement of personal objects.

Becker's (1973) study defines territorial demarcation by users of public spaces to be more jurisdictional than territorial. The idea here is that, since the person is a transient in an environment such as a library, territorial marking is relatively limited.

Environments can signify status (Konar, Sunderstrom, Brudy, Mandel, & Rice, 1982) where "… 'status' usually refers to the value placed on a member of an organization or social system by comparison to other members…visible symbols of status, which represent where an individual fits in an organization, are common in most organizations." p. 562). Criteria presented are accessibility (privacy associated to status); floor space (high ranking people had more); furnishings; layout (higher status individuals in government and the private sector were more likely to arrange their workspaces so as to face the visitor across his or her desk, they also had more windows) and personalization of workspace.

Curry and Schwaiger (1999) examined environmental design issues in libraries as they pertained to teenagers. They point out the fact that teenagers, by definition, are a difficult group to understand as they are caught up in a developmental whirlwind. Planning space for their requirements is a challenge. "Adolescence is a period where there is a developmental drive for autonomy and independence, and this drive for independence is linked to why young adults value places that they can call their own" (Curry & Schwaiger, p. 10). Often, young adults will not accept a space as their "own" if that space was designed by adults who have their own preconceived notions pertaining to what they feel that teens want. Curry and Schwaiger suggest bringing the teens into the design process as an effort to allow them to identify with the space. The authors' perspective strongly urges libraries to be responsive and to make an effort to understand what teens value in such environments. Status here shows a relationship between age and environment that, in some ways, suggests status.

It is further noted in the literature that many libraries do not involve students in the design process (Brown, 1992). He also argues for incorporating the students' "uninhibited, fresh outlooks…" to the process (Brown, p. 31). The argument for involving users in the design process is really an effort on the part of those who design and build libraries that place user values into the system.

Graham (1998, p. 72) suggests that even though the modern library has gone through a process of evolution since its predecessors were built, there are still certain elements that have "persisted since the origins of the separate book storage space." The library building symbolizes the values that "we place on learning and culture, whatever use we subsequently make of it" Graham (p. 72).

Concepts like use, comfort, convenience, etc. are often considered to be "universal" when, in reality they are "…culturally specific, relative values" (Parker Pearson, & Richards, p. 7). Though Parker Pearson and Richards analyze personal living spaces (homes) as cultural constructs, the basic principles they apply to that analysis might well be considered in the examination of public space.

Most spaces are designed with functional issues in mind. That does not necessarily mean that symbolic meanings are not present. People do not only experience space in a functional way, and some would suggest that spaces become what they are because meanings are appropriated to them (Parker, Pearson, & Richards, 1994a). Spaces do not just exist. They are attributed values (this is a good/bad place); they become cultural institutions where stories are collected to compile histories or other documentation of event. The "culturally constructed elements of a landscape are thus transformed into material and permanent markers and authentications of history, experience and values" (Parker, Pearson, & Richards, p. 4).

Everyday actions create and sustain space. "The relationship between spatial form and human agency is mediated by meaning. People actively give their physical environments meanings, and then act upon those meanings" (Parker, Pearson. & Richards, p. 5). Spaces are apportioned in ways that have meaning for the occupants. By appropriating function to space, one simultaneously appropriates meaning, thus suggesting that the meaning, even at the most literal level, should be understood by occupants.

"Buildings communicate," writes Eaton (1991, p. 519). And, not only do library buildings communicate but so do the materials within them. Users are affected "...by messages coded in the building itself, in its architecture, decor, lighting, and furnishings, as well as in signs" (Eaton, p. 519). Eaton argues that the library environment (as can any environment) communicates to users in both a cognitive and affective way and that both aspects of the users' experience should be considered in design and maintenance.

Thomas (1996) suggests that people react differently to the same architectural forms. In a sense, architecture evokes meaning, and she argues that library designers need to be more sensitive to the possibility that "....libraries may be 'choosing' some types of users and discouraging library use by others" (Thomas, p. 3).

Comments on Findings in the Literature Review

The perspectives discussed in this review were derived from multi-disciplinary contexts. There is no one literature that connects values of information providers to library design, per se. However, there is enough evidence in related literature that suggests clearly the possibility of doing so. The effect of the designer's choices on the shape of the system appears to be an issue that warrants investigation. The link between institutional values and values in the physical space of the information environment exists, but little empirical evidence exists that actually defines and supports the facets of such a relationship.

THEORY

This study will examine how institutional values relate to the values reflected by the public space of a library environment. The public space is the "constructed environment of the organization" (Schein, p. 3) that includes both artifacts and public documents. In theoretical terms, the elements being investigated revolve around the notion of how the process of organizing and structuring space reflects the cultural values of the organizers.

Just as users are engaged in a sense-making process (Dervin, 1992) during their quest to reduce uncertainty in their situations, organizations also engage in a similar process, albeit from a different perspective (Weick, 1991).

Sense-Making from an Institutional Perspective

Sense-making in organizations is grounded in the creation of identity (Weick, p. 22). Individuals within the organization act within a particular sociocultural context that is bounded by the rules and visions of the institution. Although an organizational member is still an individual, in an organizational context he or she works within the parameters set forth by the collective. The individual's role is a dual one, where that person is his or her own agent as well as a representative of the institutional value and belief system (Weick, p. 23). Individuals "simultaneously try to shape and react to the environments they face" (Weick, p. 23). As institutional members and proponents of institutional culture and norms, librarians and other individuals responsible for the operation and design of the system, create a system that essentially reflects those values and norms.

Another facet of sense-making is the notion of retrospect (Weick). The present is really a moment that culminates a particular history of a particular environment. When any individual (sense-maker) within an institution needs to make a decision he or she basically makes that decision within a historical context created by the institution over time while bringing in elements of the future. Decisions are not necessarily made in situations where uncertainty is lowered by demands for more information.

Winograd and Flores (1986) similarly pointed out that one cannot ask how objects are defined without understanding the role of tradition in the process. People and situations exist "…within a pre-understanding determined by the history of our interactions with others who share the tradition" (Winograd & Flores, p. 7). The way that people see things depends on their "traditions," or world-view. How librarians create, define and discuss their world is also bounded by tradition. Part of this investigation is an effort to describe the traditions that shape the environment in relation to the values that emerge from those traditions.

The notion of "retrospect" (Weick, p. 24) in organizational sense-making suggests that any one individual is not necessarily responsible for any one element that exists within the information system – be it a physical entity or an institutional rule. The role of information provision does not need to be examined in the present but as a culmination of concepts and ideas that are based in historical evidence. The process of creating an organizational reality is not one that exists in any particular moment in time. Librarians don't just do their tasks as a knee jerk response to a situation that is focused in a present context. Their actions are inextricably linked to the library's fundamental belief system that is grounded in institutional and professional ideologies, policies, rules and norms. Weick postulates, the stronger and more defined the value and belief structure is within an institution the more the guidance it provides to the individuals acting within.

Objects exist in environments. These objects can be meaningful or not depending on if and how they are perceived, ordered, and named. Once meaningful order is created, it is considered as being socially constructed. In turn, the socially created world becomes a constraint upon its creators in that it serves as a framework of rules that maintain order and give distinct boundaries to the environment. Environments are "enacted" (Weick, p. 30) by people, meaning that certain elements out of a potentially infinite range of possibilities are brought to the foreground and given "life" and meaning. The relevance of this to the library environment is particularly evident when thinking about the nature of library collections. On the one hand, information providers define and bring into a system a variety of information bearing objects that they feel are potentially useful to the user community. On the other hand, those objects serve as constraints that ultimately define the system in terms of content/subject matter and, at the same time, affect the actions of information providers with respect to classifying and organizing that environment in a meaningful way. Information objects are "enacted" by individuals who are part of an institutional history. In turn, the cultural values create a framework within which those objects are enacted.

As much as sense-making is often viewed as an individual process, Weick reminds us that it is also a very social one. Even though individuals make choices, in an institutional context they are made within previously established social norms and boundaries. It is a given that in some way the choices made will have to be "implemented, or understood, or approved by others" (Weick, p. 39). This becomes an interesting issue in the library environment because the "other" is a group that is not resident within the institution, but is a critical factor in the decision-making processes of the library. A collection development librarian works within her institutional constraint (budget, space, etc) as well as within constraints that are related to users, and the knowledge and perception the library has about users. The librarian's decision is made in relation to a socially constructed "other." "Sense-making is never solitary because what a person does internally is contingent on others. Even monologues and one-way communications presume an audience" (Weick, p. 40). This element of the sense-making theory brings the user into the system in a theoretical way.

Institutional sense-making is an ongoing process. It is assumed that people are always in the middle of doing something that is essentially a frame temporarily extracted from a larger continuum of action. If a person is in the middle of doing a project, then his vision is basically focused on elements in his ongoing environments that affect those projects.

A response to the reference question is a frame that is merely a moment in time extracted from a larger process, such as reference service. And reference service is a part of the process of organizational ideology that frames the importance of such a service, and so forth. It is suggested that everyday action is linked to a value system that is part of a larger frame. This element of the sense-making theory puts action within a contextual frame.

Finally, Weick writes that plausibility is more of a goal in the sense-making process than accuracy. "The strength of sense-making as a perspective derives from the fact that it does not rely on accuracy, and its model is not object perception. Instead, sense-making is about plausibility, pragmatics, coherence, reasonableness, creation, invention, and instrumentality" (Weick, p. 57). The sense-making theory, as a theoretical framework, suggests that the process of information retrieval and its result are negotiable and not always based in precision or exact response.

These principles of institutional sense-making have been applied to an information provision environment in the following way. Once information providers enact a process or product, a tangible outcome results. That outcome, for the purposes of this study, will be examined as an artifact within the public space of the information system. These outcomes are inextricably linked to the social context from which the information provider community is derived. This project will attempt to explain the relationship between outcome and social context. The providers' plans and efforts to define themselves in the institutional context also serve as cues in understanding the goals and ideals of the community that, in turn, are instantiated within the processes and products of information provision.

Artifacts

Information providers create a context of information provision that involves making sense of their environments in relation to a defined user community. The artifact, or the system, is the result of their efforts. It is also assumed that the values of information providers are instantiated in the artifact. This section will briefly discuss how artifacts are viewed in this study.

An artifact is, as Gagliardi (1992, p. 3) writes, "...(a) product of human action which exists independently of its creator; (b) intentional, it aims, that is, at solving a problem or satisfying a need; and (c) perceived by the senses, in that it is endowed with its own corporeality or physicality. In this sense, the information system is viewed as an artifact and my objective is to understand how values shape and define that artifact as well as what priorities are projected by that artifact.

Artifacts can be considered as physical expressions of cultural values. Gagliardi suggests that artifacts have both practical and hermeneutic dimensions. The system is both a functional unit and a product of human action. The information system can be viewed as an entity with a functional purpose. It is a place where one goes to get information, a book, read the paper, etc. At another level, the information system is a purposefully designed physical environment that embodies and reflects the beliefs and efforts of the people who created it as well as assumptions about the people for whom the system is designed. Values underscore and guide the processes of institutional creation and maintenance. Artifacts embody some part of those values and assumptions.

Information providers make choices that create rules (such as policies, procedures, etc) and they make choices that affect the order of the information system. Their rules govern their choices and, in turn, those choices serve as guidelines for action within the environment. The choices providers make are also constrained by internal and external forces (e.g. finance, space, ideology, etc). Systems cannot include everything. The act of selection is a value-laden process that is further embedded within an institutional sense-making framework

Arranging Physical and Cognitive Space

Just as physical space represents thoughts, purpose and evokes, meaning and action, so does the construction of the cognitive elements of an information retrieval system. In a way, placing concepts, words, thoughts, and ideas in logical order is not unlike the arranging space in the physical domain.

The purpose of such classification and demarcation is to make order out of an otherwise chaotic world. Order, however, is often taken for granted. Boundaries appear fixed only because our minds perceive them as being so. How the world is "cut up" is really an action that is bounded by social norms and rules.

A library is an example of a place that creates an image of order. The way any library is organized is only one alternative out of a potentially limitless possibility of choices. Zerubavel (1997, p. 3) points out that "the way we draw lines" varies considerably from one society to another as well as across historical periods within the same society. He further suggests that, to understand social order, it is critical to understand how those lines are drawn. Finally, those lines are only real and visible to the social entity that creates them and to those who understand their purpose.

Classification is both a personal and social act. Zerubavel (1997) writes that "[a]fter all, the way we happen to draw the line between "classical" and "popular" music or between "drama" and "comedy" is remarkably similar to the way others do, despite the fact that it is neither natural nor logical" (Zerubavel, 1997, p. 53). The act of creating an information system is part of a larger social/historical context. The process of making sense within the institution is relative to the institution, in a collective sense, as well as to the constituents of that institution for whom it is designed. Those who create order make the choices that define that order.

Where there is classification and division in a social environment, it is not uncommon to find "border disputes" (Zerubavel, 1997, p. 64). Zerubavel (1997, p. 64) writes that such boundary disputes can range from legislative battles over speed limits to "academic debates over the boundaries between species."

Research in IR literature points out that people can't find what they seek in IR systems. Such problems are typically viewed as retrieval problems (e.g. the system didn't produce because the search strategy was off; the user didn't use the right key words; something technical went wrong, etc.). Perhaps it is also possible to view these problems as emerging from a mental "border dispute" between users and providers. The problem of system use need not reside only at the point of contact a user makes with the system. This proposed theoretical framework facilitates examination of borders that are created by information providers. In short, the battles fought on the grounds of the information system might well be cognitive ones that arise out of some kind of misunderstanding that arises pertaining to how the system presents itself to users and their interpretation thereof.

Culture, Artifacts, and Values

The purpose of this section is to show the relationship between artifacts, culture and values. Schein's (1984) model will be used in a modified form (see Figure 1) to discuss and integrate the theoretical elements previously discussed into one framework. Culture is defined as:

> ... the pattern of basic assumptions that a given group has invented, discovered, or developed in learning to cope with its problems of external adaptation and internal integration, and that have worked well enough to be considered valid and, therefore, to be taught to new members as the correct way to perceive, think, and feel in relation to those problems (Schein, p. 3).

Culture exists within the norms and structures that are taken for granted and that constitute a groups' existence. Part of a group's culture can be found in the visible elements of its environment that exist as visible artifacts. Schein (p. 3) defines these artifacts as "the constructed environment of the organization, its architecture, technology, office layout, manner of dress, visible or audible behavior patterns, and public documents such as charters, employee orientation materials, and stories." From the study of artifacts one can begin to understand how a group constructs its reality and gain insight into "how" the reality is constructed in that specific way. To begin to understand why a group does certain things one needs to examine the values that define and are defined by the group.

Values are typically unobservable but they can be inferred from objects and behaviors that exist within the context in question. Institutional values are, more often than not, articulated in some way. The value system

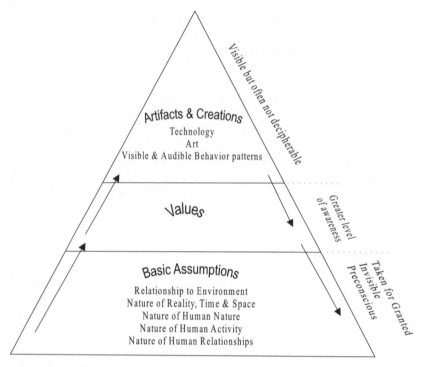

Fig. 1. Cultural levels, adapted from Schein, 1984.

is the result of conscious thought and rationalization of the group's everyday reality. Values result from "…what people say is the reason for their behavior, what they ideally would like those reasons to be" (Schein, 1984, p. 3).

But to truly understand a culture, its tacit, unspoken and taken for granted elements need to be discovered. Values, once enacted, often result as a "…underlying assumption (s) about how things really are. As the assumption is increasingly taken for granted, it drops out of awareness" (Schein, 1984, p. 4).

Such assumptions are very powerful because it becomes less possible to confront and debate something that is considered so fundamental to the belief system of the group that it is virtually unchallengeable. For instance, if one were to ask a librarian why one should read one would most certainly be considered odd, at best. Yet, this notion exists as a basic value as well as an assumption of the library environment. A value that is non-debatable is probably best considered as a cultural assumption, while a debatable statement is probably best defined as a value (Schein, 1984).

METHODOLOGY

Objectives, Definitions, and Assumptions

The first objective of this investigation is to identify values that are reflected in the physical space of a library and the texts produced by the library about itself. The second objective is to classify and analyze the values discovered. In order to answer the research questions, it was determined that the sources of data would be twofold. First, in order to characterize the physical/intellectual space of the library I would require access to the physical environment. Second, I needed to identify and gain access to institutional documents that would potentially contain statements from which institutional values could be derived.

Although use is not studied in this investigation it is always assumed that the environment is designed for users and, therefore, must reflect certain values and assumption that information providers make about users. Methodologically, this limits my investigation to only those areas that are directly accessed by users.

Information providers, based on theoretical premises presented, are not viewed as only those people who are currently working at the library. The term "information providers" is used generally to represent all the people who, in the past and present, had some input into the design and function of the system. It is assumed here, that, over time, the institutional identity is made more concrete in organizational documents that essentially define the visions, functions, processes, goals, objectives, and future directions of the institution.

Setting

The site selected for this study is a public library located in central New Jersey. This specific site was selected for several reasons: it was convenient; the administration was supportive, thus alleviating many issues of access; and the administrative organization was excellent, so documentation was readily available. Furthermore, the actual physical space was small enough to be investigated within a reasonable period of time.

Access

In general, access did not present any problematic issues since most of the objects being investigated were part of the public domain. None of the information requested contained any sensitive material. Human subjects were not a consideration in this project since the objective was to understand how human values are embedded in the physical/textual environment rather than in human behavior. Unexpectedly, the primary obstacle in this study was that of information overload. Library X holds so much information about itself, its history, its users, etc. that it was important to be specific with respect to what information was relevant to this study. The issue of overload was resolved as the parameters of the study became more focused.

Researcher's Role

The primary obstacle encountered was trying to distance myself from my knowledge of libraries and the issues within. Having once been a manager of an information center as well as a student, I found I had many preconceived notions about how information space should be designed, what the issues were, etc. Even though it was sometimes difficult to hold biases in check (particularly when sometimes it is difficult to see one's own biases), my a priori knowledge was more of an asset because it enabled me to get right into the environment without having to learn the ropes of an unfamiliar territory. Fortunately, my experience was outside of public libraries, thus putting me in a more objective position with respect to the issues within.

Attaining distance from the subject matter was a challenge in that it was unclear how much distance was necessary. With time and with the help of outside literature, a comfortable distance was attained. The outside literatures served as different lenses from which the library could be viewed.

Research Approach

The research questions and issues in this study required a qualitative approach. The primary objective is twofold: (1) to identify values and priorities as they are reflected in a physical artifact; and (2) to identify the values/priorities represented in institutional documents that specifically defined the elements of the public space. The data structure would emerge from the sources examined rather than configured into predetermined categories.

This approach is in line with what is commonly known as "grounded theory" (Glaser & Strauss, 1967) in that the work attempts to provide a naturalistic description and interpretation of the environment.

This study does not strive to verify or dispute any extant theory on values. Instead, the goal is to highlight, define, and organize values discovered in an information environment and to interpret the meaning of those values within the constraints of the context investigated.

This study aligns with the symbolic interactionists' (e.g. Blumer, 1969; Becker & McCall, 1990) premise that people respond to things in terms of what those things mean to them. In studying artifacts one has to assume that objects are intentionally selected and placed in a way that is believed to have some kind of impact on those who will potentially interact with those objects.

Meaning arises from "...the process of interaction between people" (Blumer, p. 4). This is an interesting issue considering that this study does not focus on human action, per se, but the relics or by products thereof. The artifacts that are studied are very much alive in the sense that they were placed there by information providers who intended for those artifacts to have meanings to those who would potentially use them in the library. This perspective suggests that the artifact is actually a medium through which providers and users interact.

The providers' views and values are more formally articulated in institutional documents. Those documents also represent the ideological as well as functional visions of the institution as it relates to serving the user community. Even though users are typically not present in the planning processes, their points of view are defined by providers who through various channels (studies, surveys, personal knowledge) have learned about this community. This is not to suggest that such knowledge is correct but rather that it does exist and that the users' perspective is kept in mind during the process of creation and maintenance of systems and services.

Ethnography and Fieldwork

This project is a case of study that employs techniques that are most closely, but not exclusively, aligned with the ethnographic method. A single definition of what ethnography is does not really exist (Wolcott, 1995) because there is no consensus with respect to what the objective of ethnography really is. Culture, as Geertz (1973) points out, is not particularly exotic and is perhaps most likely found in the most mundane elements of everyday life. It was this particular characterization of culture that influenced my choice of subject.

In order to define and understand values in the context of a library environment it became necessary for me to spend some time doing fieldwork describing how values are presented within a physical space. Where my study deviates from ethnographic research is in the fact that I do not study the actual social interactions that occur within the library.

Although my approach is not typical, it is also not unique. Thomas (1996) examined the architectural and environmental design elements of a variety of libraries. Thomas' research also takes an ethnographic perspective justifying it as a method that allows the researcher to examine an environment first-hand in order to catch a glimpse of the culture of everyday life.

The primary approach used could be labeled as an archeology of every day life or perhaps even an ethno-archaeology. Regardless of the label, what is of relevance is that there is an effort here to introduce the human factor into an inanimate object. Although physical spaces cannot talk (literally) they do convey information as people travel through them. A conversation of sorts, laden with messages, albeit unspoken, results between the human traveler and the artifact. In turn, that artifact represents the objectives of its creator(s).

Since people create those objects and systems of organization and classification I have to assume that certain criteria were used in the process. Certain objects were chosen over others. Certain things were placed in various locations for various reasons. Where there are choices, there are always values.

Operationalizing the Methodological Approach

It is neither easy to focus when doing fieldwork nor is it particularly easy to "read" an environment (Thomas, 1996) when that environment does not talk back. Once the basic parameters for this study were defined my objective was to get into the field and start describing the artifacts found within. With fieldwork, frameworks and approaches tend to change and develop over time. At first the physical space was an overwhelming environment to systematically describe. Lack of focus characterized the early stages of the project.

Eventually, I requested access to the library after hours so that I could take pictures of the environment that would supplement my descriptions of it and the drawings and maps that I had collected from the library. I was given permission and took several hundred pictures that were developed and classified in a notebook in sections that were labeled according to the structure that will be further discussed in this section. This strategy removed any activity from the built environment and allowed me to finally focus on the artifact.

With respect to the documents, I made a decision to include only formal documents that defined the various roles, visions, and activities of the library. Collecting the documents was a relatively straightforward matter in that all I needed to do was to define the nature of the document and the administrative staff would produce it for me. Other documents that were heavily relied upon in this study were architectural drawings of the library space as well as other maps given to me by the administrative personnel. Background information was gleaned from meeting minutes.

The Artifact and the Institution – Breakdown of Data Sources

This study focuses on two particular elements that are believed to define the information system: the artifact and the institution. The public space of the information system is the artifact. The institutional perspective is found in institutional documents. Figure 2 illustrates the two primary areas of concern of this investigation as well as outlines the types of data sources and analytical approach used.

The Artifact

The artifact (the actual system open for user navigation) was divided into two categories of "space" – the physical environment and the "intellectual" space. The physical environment is defined as the actual physical configuration of the public space of the information system. The intellectual environment refers to how objects in that space are classified and organized.

The physical design was classified into the following categories adopted from Berg and Kreiner's (p. 41) model and pictured in Figure 3.

1. Architecture, referring to the overall physical space;
2. Interior design, referring to what is inside the building, such as layout, color schemes, furniture, etc;
3. Visual identity, refers to visual material, logos, colors, etc. and,
4. Institutional design, which refers to how the institution's products are packaged and "sold" (in this case presented). These categories will be expanded to include all products of institutional efforts such as systems of classification, access, customer service, and so forth.

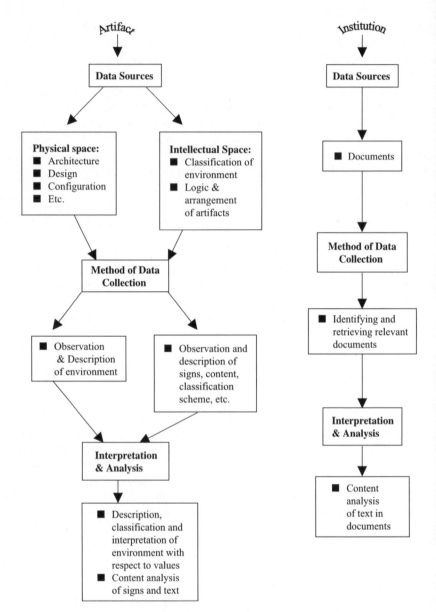

Fig. 2.   Sources of Data and Analytical approach.

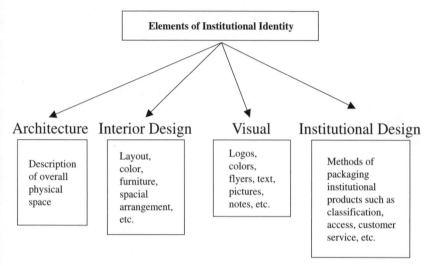

Fig. 3. Categories used to describe Library X *(Adapted from Berg & Kreiner)*.

This general framework was useful in keeping the data in a manageable format. The physical space was described and a "text" of sorts was created. My description of the environment, maps, and photographs served as the primary sources for this text.

The data for this portion of the study was collected over the period of a year. The library's space was broken down into sections, and I proceeded to spend time within each section noting how each was presented to users. A large portion of time was committed to accurately describing items within the sections, their arrangement, and potential relationship to one another. These were recorded as field notes that included pictures, descriptions, and comments pertaining to the objects presented. Field notes were supplemented with materials collected from the administrative offices that included maps, plans, etc. Furthermore, I photographed each section in as much detail as possible and created a notebook of photographic details of the information environment.

The Institution

The documents that were collected for this project were primarily those that were policy oriented, ideological, or geared to explain the library to users.

Table 1.   Sources of Data – Documents.

Type of Document	Type of Data
Primary	
"Extra" institutional	
1. First amendment	Professional values as set forth by the American
2. 14th amendment	Library Association and adopted by Library X
3. Library bill of rights	in their "Materials Selection Policy"
4. The freedom to read statement	
5. Statement on labeling	
6. Freedom to view statement	
Institutional	
1. Mission statement	Information pertaining to how Library X believes
2. Reference policy manual	the system should be run; information they feel
3. Circulation policy and regulations	is important for users to know; general rules,
4. Materials selection policy	policies, procedures and plans all of which reveal
5. Library exhibit policy	priorities
6. Library user bill of rights	
7. Library X code of conduct	
8. Guardians' responsibilities for youths	
9. Long range plan	
10. Library user's guide	
11. Circulating collection	
12. Development policy	
Secondary	
Institutional	
Minutes of Board of Trustees meetings	Historical background; general orientation to issues

Table 1 itemizes the types of documents that were used in this study. The documents were examined individually and organized with respect to the area of the library to which they pertained.

Most of the documents collected were products of Library X. Some, such as the mission statement, were in a state of transition and, therefore, both the old and new mission statements were included in the analysis. Other institutional documents collected and analyzed were policy manuals produced by Library X. Documents from the American Library Association were also analyzed since they were adopted by Library X in their Materials Selection Policy. Library X also had a long-range plan that was included in the data. The collection of documents was a relatively straightforward process that included asking the library director for the primary documents.

Once the documents were collected the content of their text was analyzed with respect to extrapolating values from the text and placing them into tables. The values that were derived from documented sources were relatively explicit in that more often than not, they were stated directly in the text of the document. In some cases interpretation was necessary to extrapolate what was the purpose/priority of a particular statement, rule, policy, etc.

Values

My approach in defining values was to keep the initial definition simple and broad. Values are the "...criteria for judging what is worthwhile" (Williams, 1979, p. 20). Values are further defined as:

> ...an organized set of preferential standards that are used in making selections of objects and actions, resolving conflicts, invoking social sanctions, and coping with the needs or claims for social and psychological defenses of choices made or proposed (Williams, p. 20).

Schein's (1984) work points out that one can learn about how groups construct their reality in a specific way from organizational artifacts. To understand why a particular reality is the way that it is, one needs to examine the values that define and are defined by the group. Schein argues that institutional values are often articulated. They result from decisions and choices made both on a macro and micro level within the institution. Some values result from the rationale, while others are tacitly embedded in assumptions about how things are or should be. In the first stage of the study, values were identified with respect to what was perceived as being important within the context studied. In the initial part of the investigation the primary question that guided my attempt to extrapolate values was "what is valued here?" In other words, I looked for concepts that represented what I believed to be important (a priority) or of value to the environment in question. In the documents these concepts were more explicitly stated while in the artifact they were more tacitly represented.

The following section essentially generates a list of concepts that are identified as being valued within the environment being investigated. Once the items that are valued were organized, they were placed into a spreadsheet format that enabled me to see in what domain those concepts occurred. Through this process of organization, core values were identified. The final discussion examines the relationship between the concepts identified.

EXAMINING THE ARTIFACT

NOTE: Due to space limitations this section has been shortened. Tables of extracted values/priorities have been consolidated and included in the Appendix.

The Physical Environment

Architecture

Library X is a brick structure located on the grounds of the township's municipal complex. It would be difficult to distinguish the building as a library from the other buildings if it were not for the words identifying it as such appearing on the façade at the right of the entrance foyer. Parking that is most convenient to the library is limited. Though there are other places to park, people need to drive into other sections of the municipal park where they can leave their cars.

The interior space of the library is rectangular. The public environment is characterized by open space that includes seating, book stacks and other information resources. General areas are not bounded by walls but by signs, filing cabinets, etc. that distinguish the areas. Walls and doors bound staff and administrative areas. The service stations are typically surrounded by counters, desks, or other objects that suggest the notion that passage beyond a certain point is for authorized personnel. The building has large windows on the front, back and right side that are visible from the public space. The ceilings are high with lighting embedded within the ceiling tiles. Table 5.1 breaks down the values/priorities reflected in the layout of the general architectural layout.

There is an effort on the part of the library to distinguish itself from the rest of the complex. Distinction can be both functional and ideological. On a function level, simply "Library XYZ" would have been sufficient to identify the building and its purpose. Instead, the library chose to place its logo, an abstraction of a book and a mind. Reading is a value that is highly regarded in the library world and Library X brings that to the forefront (literally) of its physical façade.

On a functional level there are subtle suggestions to users as to what they should be doing with respect to their behavior within the library environment. Certain groups are favored over others with respect to how and where they can park. This is also an attempt to maintain order in an equitable way. Some rules are more flexible than others.

Interior Design

Transitional Space (the Entranceway). Thomas (1996, p. 148) points out in her study of library architecture that the entrance vestibules present a great opportunity for the information providers to "…articulate policies, to provide directions to users, and to promote reading or library activities." She also noted that "…signs and posters were offered in abundance in those areas." This initial step into Library X's space is no exception.

Before the users enter the main area of the library they are presented with a large amount of information. There is an effort to communicate the following: where to park; library hours; where to return library materials; how returns should be classified into categories and, respectively, into bins labeled "children's," "adult," "videos," etc.; meeting schedules; where to smoke; where to walk; that security is an issue; what the primary sections of the library are; the automated information kiosk is prominently displayed; convenience items (baskets to carry books); art displays; community program displays; prices of stamps; phone card solicitations; letters of patron praise; a list of library benefactors; what is considered to be popular reading material by the library; the library logo; and the categories of users are defined (e.g. children, adults, etc.).

From the main corridor, a user can (assuming that he looks up) see the library's total configuration and have access to information pertaining to the organization of the environment. From this initial location one can glean much information from the environment as well as the values/priorities of Library X, summarized in Table 5.2.

The priorities of Library X are reinforced within the small confines of the entrance vestibule. Reading, community, and importance of being affiliated with the library are underscored. The notion of security is introduced early on the user's passage into the system. The presence of electronic detectors and gates is obvious. Furthermore, the presence of a security guard during peak hours is clearly visible from the entranceway as well. Although the space of the library is public and ideally "belongs" to everyone, there is always an undertone of the necessity to maintain order in that space. Not all users are to be trusted and the library must maintain a system that is reasonably secure and protective of a publicly owned resource.

This initial point of entry is a transitional space because it is a sort of "twilight zone" (Underhill, 1999, p. 46) between the outside and inside. The assumptions being made by information providers, at this point, is that users will stop, look and orient themselves to the environment during those initial steps. Underhill discusses this important yet often misunderstood space. The nature of his subject differs from that of a library environment (he studies merchandising environments), yet the goals of the two occasionally intertwine. His primary premise is that customers typically do not come to a screeching halt the second they enter the store. Instead, he says that, when customers get inside, "…they're busily making adjustment…adjusting their eyes…craning their necks…ears and noses and nerve endings are sorting out the rest of the stimuli…there's a log going on…I can pretty much promise you this: These people are not truly in the store yet" (Underhill, 1999, pp. 46–47).

Space in the Main Portion of the Library. The public space consists of several sections. As one enters the library, the main reading area that includes adult reading materials as well as magazines and other popular reading materials are directly ahead of the main foyer. To the left is a section devoted to a variety of media services. To the right, past the circulation desk is the reference services area. Finally, in the far-right corner the children's section can be found. Each of these sections is clearly labeled, and the signage is visible from most areas in the central part of the library.

Administrative offices as well as other processing services are located on the left side of the building. There are doors that signify passage from the public space to the organizational space beyond. The area between private and public space is clearly delineated and the territory of information providers is clearly marked.

The reference desk is bounded on four sides by counters and filing cabinets, with the exception of two spaces utilized for librarians' exiting and entering into that space. Counters and filing cabinets border the main reference desk. The configuration makes it clear that users are not allowed behind the reference desk because it is a work area designated for reference staff. The way that the reference desks are designed primarily forces interaction to occur from one particular side. Rather than having circular access, by design, linear (one sided) access to patrons appeared to be preferred. The way that objects are organized and placed upon counters defines where the "front" is and shows patrons where to queue up for service. Media Services and Circulation had no opening in any of the counter space that divided public from private space. In the children's services area the librarian is stationed at a desk. This formation gives the provider ready access to the environment as well as makes for a more informal set up, where the librarian is more integrated within the environment.

The rectangular shape characterizes Library X's design. The stacks, tables, and place for computer terminals are situated in either a north/south rectangle or in an east/west rectangular format. The exception to this rule is found in the "New Books" section, where the stacks are angled 45°. The books on the stacks can be seen clearly from the main entrance and the stacks are scattered in a way that optimizes this visibility.

There is a seating arrangement in the central reading area. It was interesting to note that most of the time people seated in this section never sat next to each other. Typically some alternative seating arrangement was observed. The chair that was isolated from the others tended to be occupied more frequently. The placement of the chair offered privacy by situating a plant right next to it as well as its placement away from the rest. Another cluster of "comfortable chairs" is situated in the front section of the library near the "new books" area. There are four chairs that are placed in a circular arrangement with square tables between every two chairs.

In general, most of the seating areas for users have tables, chairs, and a few study carrels. In the study area located at the back of the library there were 53 chairs. More often than not users would situate themselves so that they could spread their work materials out. There was also a considerable amount of territory marking, (Sommer, 1969b) observed as people would place coats, hats, umbrellas, etc. on the table and chairs so as to occupy the space and assumingly discourage others from using it.

Part of the "Young Adult collection" is located near the rear of the library behind a portion of the Adult collection. It is marked with both a large blue commercial sign hanging from the wall as well as a hand made sign that looks like a craft projects. There are figures of boys and girls holding the banner which reads "Young Adult." The collection is labeled with pink construction paper signs that read "Young Adult Collection Fiction Paperback" outlined in pink glitter. This collection appears to be geared toward teenaged girls.

The young adult/children's section is located in the far right corner of the library building. It is distinguished from the other sections by color, design, and shape of objects within. A large orange giraffe sits on top of one of the book stacks and can be seen from a distance. The stacks are shorter than standard since its intended users are not of adult height. There are many circular and curvilinear shapes found within this environment as well ranging from chairs that are shaped like people and positioned in a reclining setting, tables, rounded cubicles and many interesting shapes of objects ranging from a ship's wheel to stuffed animals and toys within the environment. There is also a unisex washroom available as well as a Baby Changing station in that section.

The study carrels in the children's area are circular and colorful. The insides are white and are cylindrically shaped, including the built in black seat. Also in the children's area one can find a large stuffed gorilla sitting on the stacks; wall hangings including tapestry like colorful forms, as well as paintings. Plants are also situated in strategic locations. Children's artwork is found on the wall outside the children's area.

The lighting (mostly fluorescent) in the library is variable and often very dark in areas where it would be expected that more light would be better, such as in the study carrels. The lights are very high into the ceiling so that by the time light gets down into the public spaces it is relatively diffused. There are many large windows in the library but the roof extends far beyond the walls thus creating a situation where the soffits actually block some of the light, particularly in the back area. Between some stacks it is dark.

The noise level in the library is usually high. The central portion of the library is carpeted while the walkways around it are not. The uncarpeted area is basically a rectangular passage around the main area (adult collection section on the map). This space typically has fewer artifacts in the way and occasionally a display of artwork is placed around the perimeter of the walkway. If one is sitting at one of the tables or chairs, typically one is on a carpet. Yet, even when it is quiet, the sound of heals clicking on the parquet floors is audible. Office staff must walk via such paths to get into the administrative side of the library. The restrooms, meeting rooms, and telephones are also located off the "main thoroughfare" thus facilitating steady traffic between these areas and the rest of the library. The end result is noise. There is a certain amount of "white" noise in the library including whirring machines, talk, ventilation systems, etc. Often something would pierce through the typical level of noise, creating a disruption.

With the exception of the children's area the overall interior is designed using a muted color scheme. Browns, greens, and beiges, are common colors. More colors are brought into the environment by the objects that are housed within the space. In fact, between the colors of the papers hung on walls, the book spines, the exhibits and signs there is an enormous range of color diversity. It is not color that is put in a place for a reason, but the colors emerge randomly depending on the nature of the artifact.

The values/priorities are summarized in Table 5.3. The most prominent values that emerge from examining the physical design of the library are those of organization and order. Another priority that emerges from examining the physical environment is that of circulation and use of resources. The placement of chairs and tables suggests efficiency and maximization of space. The notion of efficiency also appears in terms of how the stacks are arranged in order to maximize display of resources.

The effort to distinguish public from private space appears to be a priority. There is a distinct difference between the way the children's and adult areas are designed. There is a strong value placed upon making the library an inviting place for children. Vivid colors versus dull, earth tones; curvilinear furniture versus geometric; bright space versus darker lighting; interesting artifacts versus none or little ornamentation of the adult space. The young adult section is lost somewhere between the two, as they appear to fall into the "twilight zone" (Zerubavel, 1991) of social definition as they represent the ambiguous area between adult and child. There is also a strong value placed on personal creativity and creation of art by children, as evidenced in the corridors and hallways displaying such objects.

Visual. Even before the user enters the public space, a visual presentation of Library X's image, in the form of a logo, is prominently displayed on the building façade. The logo is a very basic sketch of an open book where the left side is made to look like a head with a design within the head, while the right is a blank page. Underneath it the name of Library X is written. The description of the logo is as follows:

> The book is the basic foundation of a library. The open book with the profile looking outward represents the free flow of ideas and a look towards the future. The open mind and eye symbolize our desire to learn. The open letter of "[the name of Library X]" run together, reinforcing the theme of a free flow of ideas, and the assimilation of our culture – past, present and future. (Source: Library X document).

This image is repeated on all library documents, circulars, etc. It also characterizes the nature of the products and services within. There is a strong value placed on the book and learning.

The public space is cut up and organized through the use of signage. Sections are labeled by either user type (Young Adult, Adult, Youth Services); service type (Reference, Circulation, Media Services); type of materials (books, tapes, magazines); or classification of information objects (e.g. Science Fiction, Mystery, Romance, etc). There is space allocated for a variety of functions (e.g. Meeting Rooms, Quiet Study).

The signage of the library is colored, but it is not clear as to what the rationale is behind the different colored of signs. Almost every element in this space is labeled in some way. Rooms are labeled in terms of the types of use that are intended (e.g. "Quiet Study, "FOR INDIVIDUAL STUDY ONLY,"). Rule oriented signs are also posted (e.g. "NO SMOKING," "No Food or Drink)." Others tell users to be "Quiet." Other signs offer assistance ("ASK FOR A COZY BLANKET AT THE MAGAZINE WINDOW! PROVIDED BY THE FRIENDS OF THE LIBRARY").

An entire section of a bulletin board is dedicated to work/job related postings ranging from: "Ask for these Employment Newspapers At the

Magazine room: [lists papers]." While others advertise newspaper employment, to resources for jobs such as "Help wanted ads from 64 Sunday Newspapers on Microfiche Weekly!"

Other posters are instructional in nature such as one that attempts to teach users about the "American Business Disc" and another that provides a *Business Week* "Best-Seller List" near the business reference section. Other signs are directional, attempting to help users find things in the library, or informational like one that says that "As of February 15, 1995, the reserve fee will be 50¢. Some reflect the nature of a specific collection while others describe the function of a particular service. One can find many posters created by the American Library Association that promote reading. The "READ" posters feature a variety of celebrities promoting libraries and literacy or others that imply that "cool" kids, athletes, and other notable characters read.

One can also find theater schedules, discount tickets for various Broadway shows, and *News Bulletins for the New Jersey Bar Association*. There are signs everywhere. Some of the bulletin boards in the main corridor have a sign labeling them as "Information Center." On them there are posters and letter that range from advertisements to announcements pertaining to "men's health issues." Some contain book jackets for various books in the library. Others display reports for schools or other issues pertaining to education and schooling.

Near the tax returns, taped on vertical file cabinets are posters advertising tax amnesty "guaranteed to stop perspiration," information on how to file tax returns either manually or electronically. Another pillar is dedicated to vocational and military options for students (e.g. navy, vo-tech post high school, army, etc). Virtually no space remains uncovered by signs or other wall hangings. On the door of the librarians' office there is a poster of a hand in a star "Reach for a star. Ask a Librarian." The signage in the Media center tends to be either descriptive or rule oriented advising users of rules, protocols of use and fees.

The priority of the information providers appears to be to ensure as much equality in access as possible through vehicles such as fee structures and loan duration. It would appear that the more complex, a technology is, the more it costs. A higher value is placed on those objects, though it does not necessarily follow that such objects are the most valued within the context of Library X's reality.

The values of the information providers that are reflected in the visually oriented artifacts tend to fall into two categories: ideological and functional. Ideological values are those that present the visions and ideologies of information providers in a symbolic form, such as in the logo. The actual logo does not state these values, but it is assumed that its form will symbolize the meaning of the design and will determine the values intended. The values presented in this section with respect to the logo were derived from the information provider's own description of the logo. Reading, cultural assimilation, open mindedness, free flow of ideas, and learning are what the providers believe they are all about.

Other ideological types of messages are round in "READ" posters that highlight the value and importance of reading as well as in other materials that highlight the importance of the role of the librarian like the "reach for a star, ask a librarian" cited earlier in the act of individual achievement.

On a functional level the visual elements of the library are efforts to offer direction and guidance for users with respect to the use of various artifacts. The signage tends to be less instructional and more dogmatic in that it stipulates rules and guidelines for borrowing materials as well as costs associated with borrowing those materials. Other signage is directional, an effort that attempts to classify the library into sections that are perceived to fit the areas of demand. Basically, this is an act of labeling the artifact into sections of perceived utility.

Informing users appears to be a high value in the library if one were to assume that the number of signs correlates in some way to the belief that more information is better. The content of the signage tends to be very general and the pillars so cluttered that nothing particularly stands out. There appears to be no particular focus that guides the content of the leaflets and flyers.

In some ways many of the signs posted are vehicles of communication with users. There is information that is considered to be of potential relevance to users; there is an effort to "teach" users about the importance of library use, there is also an appeal to the users' comfort and convenience, there is also an effort made to orient the user to the system as well as to advise users of the institutional values that govern use. Table 5.4 summarizes the previously discussed values that were derived from examination of the visual artifacts in the information space.

Intellectual Configuration of Space ("Institutional Design")
The public space of the library holds the essence of what is created by information providers for users. The artifacts found within are both physical and intellectual. What is meant here by "intellectual" is the nature of the system's logic that is essentially a human logic. This logic represents how information providers via an information system collect and organize objects in ways that they believe make sense to users.

The Central Area. Objects are "highlighted" for users in terms of perceived interest by providers. The "card catalog" (labeled as such) is really a row of online terminals providing formal access to the system. The information kiosk, prominently displayed offers location related information to users. It is not particularly clear upon looking at it what its purpose is. Collections contain artifacts that cater to a variety of interests and needs ("popular" materials, rental books, biographies, mysteries, new fiction, non fiction, large print books, language books, etc.).

The whole "front-line" of resources is geared towards popular interest and thus, it is assumed that items will circulate at a higher rate if presented in this fashion. This is a relatively common approach to "marketing" resources and merchandise (Underhill, 1999). The primary value, with respect to the configuration of this space, appears to be the marketing of products and circulation (Table 5.5).

Popular Fiction/Paperback Reading Area. Directly behind the front line of information resources are the magazine section and the popular paper-back book collection. The magazines are organized alphabetically while the paperbacks are in special sections. Headings include "Romance," "Star Trek," "Movies/TV," "Science Fiction," "Fiction," "Western," "Spy Adventure," "Horror," "Mystery," and "Romance." It is possible to find items under these headings in the main collection, but, for the most part, this is a high circulating popular fiction collection. I was informed that these items are not contained in the main catalog and, therefore, are circulated based on users' predisposition toward the subject matter. Furthermore this collection indicates that providers believe it to have popular appeal as it is placed in the most central location of the physical environment.

It appears that the priority of information providers is to place the books that are perceived to have the highest level of demand in the forefront of the library as well as in the paperback reading area. Circulation and use are the priorities that are in close conjunction to this type of configuration. The general holdings of the library are not given this level of distinction in that they are housed in stacks that do not allow for much visibility of the items. The assumption appears to be that the primary access point to this collection will be the catalog. Table 5.6 summarizes the values for this area:

Media Services. Media services functions as a control center and distributor of objects classified as "media," objects defined as "tapes, CDs, and software." The word "media" is subdivided within the institutional context to mean "tapes, CDs, and software." In this case it can be seen that format affects classification and distinction. Within the section there is further subdivision of categories to include Contemporary Cassettes, Contemporary, Country Cassettes, Contemporary Compact Discs; Holiday Compact Discs, Musical/Soundtrack/Comedy, Country; New Age Compact Discs, Contemporary Compact Discs. It is not very clear what, exactly, is meant by the label "contemporary" other than that it is something presumed to have an appeal to people in a current point of time.

The cassettes are organized in alphabetical order. The assumption, with respect to this type of organization, is that the user will figure out how objects are ordered and is readily able to find the cassette of choice. Groups, such as "Foreigner" and so forth are filed under "F" for the name of the group. But something like "Peter Gabriel" is filed under "G" for the artist's last name. This seems logical since authors are typically filed by last name, but it is not entirely consistent with respect to filing under the first letter of the artists' name. Eventually, by looking at other objects in the collection, one should be able to see that the preference in ordering the units is by using the performer's last name. Such rules are not specifically spelled out, and it is probably through serendipity or prior experience that the user figures out the logic of this environment. The assumption here is that users can be taught by the system. There is also reliance upon users' prior familiarities with the method of organization (as perhaps found in a music store).

Such configuration of objects is fairly straightforward and probably requires a minimal effort to maintain. On the other hand, this type of very general classification assumes that when a seeker examines a CD entitled "Sound of Music" that he will know that it, and others in that section are considered to be "Musicals." Furthermore, in that section the sign "Musical/Soundtrack/Comedy" suggests that there is a difference between the three categories – which indeed there is. But, to someone who may not understand that difference, it may not be very clear.

Within the videotape collection, more specific categories are found such as "Drama," "Western," "Science Fiction," "Horror," and so forth. There is also a section for "New Releases." The model is similar to what one would encounter at a local video store. Thus, the user, assuming he had some experience renting videos, would basically have a mental model of this type of structure. This structure also presumes some knowledge of popular culture in that, if one were not tapped into the movies in the mainstream, they would not know what, exactly, was meant by "New Releases."

Probably the most prominent priority that is reflected by the organization of the media services environment is that of appeal to the popular perceptions on how media items are typically ordered and displayed. The items are classified by object type and then simply put into alphabetical order. The objective appears to be an effort to present an environment that is easy to use and familiar to users based on assumptions that they have visited music stores and browsed through the collection there. This section contains popular and expensive objects that are potential targets for theft. The library reduces this risk by housing the actual artifact in a secure room that is accessed by users via a counter in the media services area. Table 5.7 highlights the values in the organization of media services.

Youth Services
Situated in the opposite corner of the library from the Media Services is the Youth Services area. "Youth Services" is broken down into two categories on the main sign: "Children" and "Young Adults." The distinction between these categories is represented in design as well as in the nature of the respective collections. The nature of library work done by young adults differs from that of toddlers and younger school aged children.

There are two distinct areas reserved for these two categories. The children's area is much larger, more colorful, and contains more holdings than the young adult area. The young adult area is situated along the back wall of the library. A green banner that is hand painted with the words "young adult" marks it. The section contains a collection of paperback books that are marked by signs written on pink paper in glitter. Many of the items within seem to be directed towards teenagers, specifically teenaged girls. This area is segregated from both the children's and the adult area. The types of books (mostly stereotypically "teenager" items with titles such as *Dreams, Sweet Valley High*, etc.) are placed rather on standard shelves.

In the children's area, each stack is marked by a commercially produced Peanuts^{TM} poster, which indicates what can be found in a particular section. Each poster also contains Dewey Decimal numbers that correspond to general subject headings. Parts of the collection are color-coded. New books are prominently displayed, as are other books in the collection. Not all books rest in the standard vertical position on the shelf. Many stand on tables on their own or are leaned against an object so as to allow them to stand out in the environment. More of the book is visible to users – something that might make it more appealing or at least more noticeable to users.

There appears to be a strong effort in this department to emphasize and focus on the educational aspects of not only the content of the resources but of the information-seeking process as well. Although the area is much more compact than the adult section, its arrangement is similar. The primary difference is in how the sections are labeled and the fact that all services (circulating collection, reference, media and entertainment and even restrooms) are located, physically in the same place. Furthermore, there is a librarian specialized in children's services stationed in the area.

Although the children's collection, with respect to its intellectual organization, may be as complex as the adult collection, its use is potentially simplified by the fact that navigation, access, reference and retrieval are all located in a bounded and contained area. The area even contains its own exhibits and artwork. The only service that requires passage beyond the boundaries of this area is circulation. The environment, being both organizationally and aesthetically interesting appears to be conducive toward information-seeking, lounging, "hanging out," enjoying a story or interacting with others. The physical elements support the social ones as well as intellectual pursuits. The assumptions made about user behaviors, as they are seen in the physical space are realistic for the targeted population (children). The services are tailored according to those assumptions.

The priorities associated with the intellectual configuration of the children's area are that education can/should be fun and that the library should be easy to use. What is most noticeable as a priority is the manner in which the objects are displayed and the efforts that the providers make toward educating the children about the system. Although the organization of the objects is relatively standard (e.g. Dewey system, alphabetical, etc), the priority in the placement of objects is to facilitate ease of use and appeal to their target audiences – children or parents of those children. The books are displayed in a variety of ways, and the space is large enough so that the user does not feel overwhelmed by the artifacts contained within. At the same time, there is a "protective" feel to the environment that reflects the providers' need to control traffic and resources in this area. This element of exclusivity suggests an effort to lend a sense of ownership to the users regarding this space. In all there is no question that children are a priority.

With respect to the young adult collection, it is difficult to say what the priorities might have been with respect to its development. The books in the isolated area seemed to be more geared towards teenaged girls, an action that suggests that perhaps information providers felt that the girls were more likely to read than boys. The collection is somewhat odd in that it contains a series of paperbacks that randomly display a book that typically has a picture of a female on the cover. Table 5.8 summarizes values in the youth services area.

Reference

The reference area holds a myriad of different collections that essentially do not circulate. There are exceptions to this rule as noted in the Reference Manual. Here one can find items ranging from telephone books to mail order catalogs to tax forms (that are for public distribution). There is a business reference section and a general reference collection. Vertical files are also located in the Reference Department.

The reference area is a very busy environment. It is anticipated that users will work there, ask questions, utilize parts of the collection that are not located in the central portion of the library, browse, and interact with a variety of materials and computer oriented resources. All areas of the collection are organized in ways that are best seen fitting to the nature of the material. The standard reference collection is, for instance, classified numerically and can be located through the catalog. Other portions are organized by subject matter, or alphabetically or simply placed for users to examine (such as items on the bulletin board). It is in this area that users can expect to interact with the system via a human being – the reference librarian.

This environment is very different from the central area where items are often out in the open and relatively simple, almost intuitive, to find. In the reference area there is an organized chaos of information resources that surround the central hub of the area – the reference desk. It is impossible to see everything that is available in the reference area simply because of the volume of information.

It is assumed that users will understand the meaning of the word "Reference," particularly since the term is really a "system" term for an area where help can be obtained. What could be potentially confusing to users not familiar with this concept is the relationship between the reference collection and reference services in that the former is a non-circulating print resource while the latter is a human interface for the system.

It is also not clear when one enters the reference area how the various portions of the collection can be accessed. How, for instance, does one find out that there are catalogs, annual reports, or phone books at the library? How do people learn about the fact that tax forms can be obtained at the library? It is assumed by the system that such items will be used and are of value, for why else would they be there? As an intellectual space, the reference area is complex in its services, responsibilities, and retrieval methods.

There is an entire section labeled as "Business Reference" that is separated from the other reference collection. Related materials and documents and other collections (e.g. annual reports of companies and organizations) can be found close by to supplement the primary reference resources. Table 5.9 outlines the priorities/values inferred from the reference area.

The priority of the reference area is the provision of information in an interactive environment. Information is posted everywhere and the librarian, given the way the role is situated in the space, is identified as the authority. It is one of the more formal arenas within the library space where users come face to face with the librarians. The primary emphasis is on interaction, assistance and the use of resources as identified in information-seeking contexts.

DOCUMENTS: INSTITUTIONAL VALUES

Adopted Documents from Outside of Library X

The second part of the data collected for this study involved the analysis of documents that were considered to be relevant to the definition of organizational values and norms. This section discusses those documents in terms of the values that are presented within the documents adopted from professional organizations.

Although most of the policies that govern Library X are created by Library X, some are adopted from the professional organizations to which Library X belongs. In this case, the primary source of guidance for general visions and rights is the American Library Association (ALA). In its "Materials Selection Policy," Library X adopts the following policies: 1st and 14th Amendments; ALA Library Bill of Rights; ALA The Freedom to Read; ALA Statement on Labeling; EFLA and ALA The Freedom to View; NJLA People's Library Bill of Rights. These statements are found on the American Library Association's website in the section entitled "Intellectual Freedom." They will not be discussed in detail here though the values represented within are summarized in Table 5.10.

The statements presented are not bounded by any sort of monetary, geographic, etc. or other constraints. They are basically a representation of an organizational/professional ideology. This sort of ideology sets a framework or even a creed, for institutional affiliates (such as Library X) to follow. The notions, however, are certainly subject to local interpretation and implementation.

The basic value system represented in the previous documents promotes intellectual freedom and takes a stand against censorship. From this position, fundamental library values can be seen. The values discussed in this section, thus, are ideological in nature. They represent a code or a level towards which the institution strives.

Through membership in the larger organization and via the mechanism of adoption, Library X has determined that the above referenced creeds are of value to its operation and, in turn, to its users. The ALA statements define an ideological structure for Library X that, in turn, guides the organization's planning process for the creation and maintenance of the system. These values are based in the library profession's view of what it should be to the public and what it should do to protect the publics' rights. Such rights are based in the foundations of democracy and incorporated into a library perspective by the American Library Association and, through adoption, by Library X.

Mission

In an organizational context the mission statement provides an over-arching "vision" that affects the development and enactment of policies, rules and procedures. A mission statement is "an organization's 'raison d'être' – its reason to be…the primary thrust of an organization's mission statement is external: it focuses on customers, markets, and fields of endeavor…many mission statements reveal not simply purpose, but philosophy…" (Higgins, p. 157). A closer look at Library X's mission statement reveals how the information providers define themselves and their purpose as well as their philosophy, with respect to the values embedded within.

During the course of this investigation, Library X's mission statement underwent a change. This section will discuss the institutional values found in both statements. Initially, Library X's mission read as follows:

> Library X provides materials and services to satisfy the informational, educational, recreational, and cultural needs, both expressed and anticipated of the residents of Township X.

The new mission statement reads as follows:

> As the information center of the community, Library X strives to deliver the highest level of timely service to library users of all ages as it promotes literacy, lifelong learning, personal fulfillment, and the principles of intellectual freedom.

As a tool, the mission statement attempts to present an image of who and what the organization is. Boulding (1961, p. 11) points out that images of "fact" can also be images of "value" in an organizational context. How someone presents a concept basically reflects values that underlie that concept.

Boland (p. 11) also writes, that "…the image of value is concerned with the rating of the various parts of our image of the world, according to some scale of betterness or worseness." Thus the assumption is made here that, since the members of Library X changed their mission statement, it was felt that the new one was in some way either better or more appropriately fitting to Library X's current state of being.

In order to understand the values (or the change therein), it is necessary to understand the image (and, the change therein) that these two documents portray. Table 5.11 is an effort to further expand upon the notions set forth within the context of the two mission statements.

In the old mission statement Library X's name is simply stated as a proper noun. In the new statement, Library X's name is qualified by a simile in terms of who they are. Also denoted is the library's place and purpose within the community – it is not just "Library X" anymore, but an "information center of the community." It is not just a place, but a place with a relationship and purpose that serves a non-specified community (e.g. it doesn't read "information center of township X").

The primary change in the new mission statement reflects the view of what the institution thinks it is. In the earlier years, the library was a library. With the advent of the new mission statement the institution is now referred to as an "information center." Such a change reflects a perception of what Library X believes it is and the "face" or image that it intends to present to the public. Such a change in image suggests that a change in values also occurred somewhere along the way.

The way an institution describes itself reflects the way it perceives its role, as well as how it wants to be perceived by others. In the new mission statement, the term "library" as a descriptor of the purpose of Library X was not sufficient and the concept of "information center" was selected. This reflects a fundamental shift in how Library X perceives its products, role and services. It should also be noted that the word "library" still appears on all formal documents, logos, stationary, and basically anything that leaves the administrative domain of Library X. Still, with respect to the new mission statement, there appears to be a distinctive shift in perception away from the role of "library" to that of "information center."

In general, the notion of "information center" suggests a more dynamic, proactive environment than the concept of "library." Not because it is necessarily true, but because of the image that the respective concepts evoke. In this case it might be argued that an image is, indeed, a value and a change in image suggests a change in values.

To "provide," as in the old statement, means "to procure beforehand; to get, collect or make ready for future use…"(Webster). It is a statement of pro-activity that suggests preparation for future interaction. In the new statement, to "deliver" means to "give or transfer, to put into another's possession or power, to commit; to pass from one to another" (Webster). This change suggests that there is more responsibility placed on users within the new vision of service than with the old. The idea of "provision" suggests security and that "someone" will take care of things (like parents are providers for children) while the notion of "delivery," suggests that objects are passed by one to another.

In the old statement the "library" provided a service, whereas in the new mission statement the "information center" delivers. The images evoked from the word "provide" suggest a more nurturing but, not necessarily demand driven environment. Parents, for instance, provide for their children yet children often don't have much voice in the situations where they are provided for. On the other hand, to "deliver" suggests that "we will get it to you." It is a word often used in television commercials where a company makes a promise by stating that they will deliver "X" to you no matter what. As a value statement, the word deliver suggests a stronger commitment to the effort than provide.

In the old mission statement what is provided are "materials and services – a basic statement of "what." In the new statement, materials are not mentioned while there is a much stronger emphasis on the service orientation qualified by adjectives "timely" and "highest level."

"Materials and services" were the focal point of the old mission statement while the new mission statement places a higher value on service. Interestingly, materials are not mentioned. Service is both a product and a means to an end. The new statement reads that the "highest level of timely service" to promote "literacy, lifelong learning, personal fulfillment, and the principles of intellectual freedom." The mission statement not only encompasses the values of the library but also projects values upon users (e.g. it is assumed that users pursue literacy, personal fulfillment, etc).

To satisfy means to "gratify fully the wants, wishes or desires of…to make content." Satisfaction, as a measure of information system success, has been measured in many library studies over the years. In many ways it is an ambiguous term. To ask "are you satisfied?" doesn't really get to the heart of the user's activities within the system (see Dervin & Nilan, 1986 for further criticism). Satisfaction of needs, as a facet of information provision, suggests that "needs" can actually be satisfied and accounted for. The image suggested here is one of a stimulus/response. If you have a question, I will answer it.

In reality, however, there may not necessarily be a "right" or "wrong" answer in such a process thus rendering the notion of "satisfaction" as being relatively useless. In contrast, the concept to "promote" means "to forward; to advance; to contribute to the growth, enlargement or excellence of." There is a shift in perspective that suggests a vision of cultivating an ongoing relationship with users. The image evoked is one of engagement in a process.

This difference between "satisfaction" and "promotion" represents a subtle, albeit probably unintended, shift in values from more of a user driven (in a "traditional" sense – as per Dervin and Nilan's (1987) definition) perspective to more of a provider driven point of view. In the old mission, it was the goal to "satisfy informational, educational...needs..." while in the new mission statement the providers envision themselves as being there to "promote" values and ideals of the institution such as "literacy, lifelong learning, personal fulfillment..."

This shift illustrates a distinct change in how the providers view themselves and their role in the community with respect to both function and values. In the old statement the focus was on function (or a fulfillment/satisfaction of a function). It described what the information providers did. In the new mission statement there is an emphasis on Library X's ideological vision as determined and written by the current group of librarians.

The old mission statement defines users as residents of Township X. Users are defined with respect to geographic boundaries. However, this is not entirely accurate since there are other people who are allowed to use the library who are not residents of the township (i.e. people who work there, or others who want to pay a membership fee.) In the new statement users are bounded by the institution. That is, the focus is placed on "library [emphasis mine] users."

An interesting dynamic emerges from the new mission statement. The library, as an institution, has selected services that it chose to "promote" to a population of people who are considered "library users." The language of the new statement indicates that the institutional priorities are focused on those who are already participants in the institutional domain. This statement is in conflict with some of the values presented earlier that state access should be as wide as possible. It is not always possible to create a system that can be accessed by all. Instead the institution needs to focus its services in a manner that best fits the population and the institution.

In this context, the mission statement, as it had evolved within the life cycle of Library X, represents an institutional effort to describe its ideological role and purpose (as they see it) within a particular community.

Library X's purpose and conditions and circumstances that are particular to its specific community bound values.

It has been determined that Library X's priority will be to deliver the "highest level of timely service" to its constituency. Of all the possible priorities "timely service" was stressed. This suggests that it is believed that time/efficiency is important to the user population.

The mission statement also suggests that literacy; lifelong learning, personal fulfillment, and intellectual freedom are values that should be shared with the user contingency. The library is a promoter of such values, a statement that implies that their services, goals, policies, procedures, etc. will probably attempt to support these higher level aims. These values are outlined in Table 5.12.

Reference Manual

The reference manual is organized to present guidelines for the Reference Services department. It is intended to serve as a guide, a basis for staff evaluation and "a description of services offered by the department and the extent to which they are provided, including any priorities or limitations" (Reference Policy Manual, p. 4). It is stated that users can obtain copies of this manual "upon demand." It is assumed that users would know that such a manual exists and that they would understand that copies could be obtained.

The goals can be translated into values, as expressed in the written statements. The values here are viewed as priorities that are established by the providers for themselves with respect to the user community. The priorities (as reduced in Table 5.13) are explicitly stated.

The mission of the Reference Services department appears to be focused around the notions of service and maximization of use. On the one hand, the providers determine, a priori, how they will serve the public. On the other hand, assumptions are made about what the public requires and how they require it. For instance, it is stated that "accuracy, efficiency and courtesy" are important. Yet, in a realistic setting it is not clear who defines what is accurate, efficient and courteous. Thus, seemingly objective criteria become rather subjective when projected into a "real life" environment.

Table 5.14 outlines the values associated with the general guidelines for provision of reference services. It is the goal of Library X to keep the Reference desk adequately staffed. At least one professional librarian is required to be present, and the second person there can be an intern, trained paraprofessional or professional librarian. It is a priority to provide as much staff as necessary to maintain the level of service required. It is assumed that service should attempt to match the volume of requests. It is also assumed that more staffing will give people a higher level of service. The assumption is that there should be enough people to provide adequate service. Those who work at the desk should have an appropriate attitude and manner, as set forth by the policy. It is assumed here that policy can dictate attitude/manner.

Inquiries, as they are presented to the reference desk, are prioritized by the nature of the user's proximity. Face to face encounters take priority over phone calls. The importance or urgency of individual requests is not considered in the manual.

Reference Services staff members are responsible for handling emergencies and reporting problems to proper authorities. Reference staff is also responsible for maintaining order in the "Quiet Study" room. The fact that order needs to be maintained suggests that there is a potential for disorder. Much of what is "patrolled" is not defined. For instance, what would constitute noise?

Another major area of the responsibility for Reference services includes requests for materials indicated in Table 5.15. The three primary values that emerge, once again, are privacy, service and security. Reference librarians are required to assist users in finding materials that are in the collection using the resources within the library. They are allowed to check status of various resources but never can reveal the borrower's identity. If an item is not in the collection then it can be obtained from other libraries or purchased for the user. It appears to be a given that certain titles are prone to mutilation or theft so the library must make provisions to "protect" those items. In short, the greater good appears to be served by focusing on the "exception" to the norms (vandalism). Protection of property is clearly a priority. As a result there is a breech in trust between provider and user in that users must submit formal documents (license or library card) to access certain parts of the collection.

On the one hand, providers must protect their resources. On the other, they must ensure user access and privacy. The priority here appears to be resource location and provision to the user. At the same time, there is concern for resource protection and security, and there is an explicit requirement that whatever is requested needs to comply with the Materials Selection Policy. It is very succinctly stated that "Under no circumstances are the identities of current or previous borrowers provided to users" (Source: Reference Policy Manual, p. 6).

According to the reference manual there are two types of requests presented to the Reference Desk: "Requests for Materials" (as depicted in

Table 5.15) and "Requests for Information" (as depicted in Table 5.16). There is a distinction between materials (physical artifacts, or containers of information) and information that entails some sort of verbal discussion between user and librarian with respect to the information-seeking problem/ question the user brings to the system.

Reference librarians can either provide specific information or guide users toward sources of information. The manual is quite clear on this issue. For "short answer" responses, librarians can actually respond directly to the query. For "longer, more detailed answers, extensive searching or interpretation of materials" reference staff can assist users to find the appropriate resources.

It is of some interest to note that librarians do not assume responsibility for the "answers" given. Responses are source generated. Furthermore, there is an assumption that "answers" are sought. Perhaps this is a general way of looking at a reference situation, but the information-seeking process is not always one that specifically requires an "answer."

Use is specifically defined in relation to the perceived role of the Reference division. Use of this segment of the information retrieval system is classified into two categories, each being related to a particular type of query – specific or general. Specific queries are "answered" while users with more complex inquiries are offered "guidance."

The reference process is not without limitations. Table 5.17 outlines search parameters for user inquiries. The first parameter mentioned is that of time. The reference librarian's time is limited by needs of other users, complexity of materials, users' library experience, and staff availability.

Librarians are not allowed to give appraisals though they can refer users to a print source for further information. This is a protocol that repeats itself throughout the course of this section. The librarian's role is seen as being "objective", and responses are aimed at being non-subjective. Yet, it can be argued that the act of selection (at least according to my values centered approach) suggests some level of subjectivity because one resource is selected over another. In the policy, however, it is presented as being an objective action.

It is also departmental policy not to recommend titles for purchase. Users are expected to make such determinations on their own. Librarians can, however, locate reviews and evaluations. Reviews and evaluations are not exactly "objective", so, it could be argued, that the source the librarian selects is not neutral. If the object is not neutral, it is arguable that the gesture that connects user to object is value laden, albeit it is unintentional.

With respect to medical questions, the staff is supposed to provide "short factual information from the library's resources..." but offer no interpretations or opinions. The same goes for legal questions. Advice or interpretations are not acceptable. Such parameters make sense from the perspective of liability. However, from a reference perspective they may be limiting because librarians might be more bounded in such situations from asking certain types of questions which could result in a situation where the user's request was either misunderstood or not adequately understood to provide relevant materials.

Similar parameters apply to genealogical, trivia and contest questions. If a request is specific, then an answer can be given, if not, the user is directed to resources. The reference staff can answer trivia and contest questions if the questions require "factual" responses from a standard source.

With respect to translations, staff provides the proper dictionaries and will attempt to locate a translator if needed. Student assignments are treated like any other request unless there are other instructions given by the teacher. Again, providers attempt to maintain neutrality while defining their roles.

Providers are allowed to give users advice with respect to their knowledge of the collection or by directing them to appropriate resources. They are constrained by the collection and the resources within the library.

It is of interest to note that the search parameters previously outlined are an effort to create a neutral field within which the providers should operate. The nature and role of the reference librarian, as depicted in this section, is one that attempts to link users with resources. There appears to be little room for personal opinion and judgment calls in a formal sense. It is difficult to say how such neutrality and objectivity are maintained nor is it the goal of this section to do so. However, the values that emerge from this section stress, over and over, such traits.

When the Reference Department cannot respond to an inquiry then the request is then processed through a library network. The Reference librarians can also refer users to relevant agencies but do not assume the role of mediator between user and agency.

Telephone Reference

The following section of the manual was designed to specifically address the issues involving telephone reference requests. Although many of the parameters are similar to the previous discussion of in-person requests there are some basic differences between how the providers address the specific issues.

Table 5.18 outlines the areas that will be further discussed in this section. In-person requests take priority over telephone inquiries. It seems reasonable to give the person who makes the effort to come to the system priority over the one who does not. On the other hand, it is certainly more convenient for users to not have to physically go to a library to get information. The manual makes it clear that inquiries will be answered; however, there is a particular order that is set forth for providers to follow. Priority is not given to long distance callers and the burden of paying for the call is placed upon the user. In a way, this discourages a particular type of use, but, in another way, it does not stretch the library's budget.

Reference services are only provided for "short, factual inquiries." Lengthier, more involved inquiries are clearly discouraged. There is a distinct priority given to inquirers with short questions, while the user who comes to the library may have a lengthier and more involved interaction with the librarian (but not without parameters, as discussed in previous section). It is also specifically stated in the manual that sources that are consulted will be cited to the caller. The librarians are instructed to give no interpretation, however, of the sources but to encourage users to come to the library in order to pursue the interpretation on their own.

The primary priority for telephone inquiries appears to be time and quantity of information to be distributed. The pragmatics of providing information services dictate efficient operation due to a high volume of transactions that take place. Only short responses are allowed in telephone interactions. These priorities certainly make sense from the providers' point of view. Although every effort is focused on responding to users' queries, the parameters limit and define the very nature of the interaction before it even takes place.

Referring users to resources is more important within this structure than providing information based on personal knowledge. Information seeking is viewed from two perspectives. People seek either "short factual" answers or their requests are more complex. If complexity becomes an issue, then librarians refer users to resources. Such protocols appear to be efforts to put librarians into positions of non-involvement or objectivity. Furthermore, a higher priority is placed on information that is obtained from a source than that of a librarian's personal knowledge. Librarians' opinions and interpretations are not valued. Efforts to remain neutral suggest that neutrality is a strong value.

Database Searching

Besides general reference services, the library also provides database searching for users. These services are classified under "ready reference" or "fee based" categories.

If the required materials are determined not to be in the library then the librarian can pursue an online search. Another criterion for performing a search is whether doing so will save time. It is stipulated that such searches will be accomplished within one working day. It should be noted that no other types of searches have such a specific time requirement. It is also stipulated that trained professionals perform all searches. Table 5.19 summarizes the handling of reference searches.

Fee Based Services

Online searches are performed only when time for search formulation and execution does not exceed one hour. Lengthy searches are referred to commercial services. Three working days are required for search completion.

The primary concern with fee-based searches is financial. Another point to note is that users must wait three days for search results. This almost seems like a deterrent to those who might use this service. It is also not clear how users are informed of this service. Table 5.20 summarizes the requirements.

Typically, reference materials are not circulated. As pointed out in the policy manual "most reference tools cannot be taken from the building without causing severe inconvenience to other potential library users. The reference needs of the majority are given priority over the needs of any individual" (Reference Policy Manual, p. 11).

The conditions for loaning reference materials are summarized in Table 5.21. In the situation where reference materials are made available for circulation the priority of the Reference department is to ensure in any way possible that items will be returned promptly within the time restraints set forth. All of this is made with the stated and implied intent of providing equitable access to eligible users.

Other Reference Services

Besides handling inquiries and responding to information requests, the Reference Services area manages numerous public displays of various kinds of informative material.

Table 5.22 summarizes the other services provided by the reference department. The key priority involving these reference displays is that the librarians in charge act as filters for what information is selected versus what is omitted. The criteria for such selection are not clear. As I was observing the various parts of the library I did notice these displays as well as the information bearing objects that were on them. My primary observation was that there was a lot of material on these stacks and that the objective of the display seemed random.

The reference services department is also responsible for other areas that are sometimes not directly related to reference service. For example, they instruct patrons on the use of photocopying machines. They are also responsible for the public typewriters. It is also stipulated in the manual that "individuals may not use their own typewriters or portable microcomputers in the building" (Reference Manual, p. 14) so that other users are not disturbed. Apparently separate rooms are provided for typing.

Other tasks include reserving materials for school assignments, providing tours and formal bibliographic instruction. Reference is also handled via correspondence. Every effort is made by the library to provide "extraordinary personal service" (Reference Manual, p. 15) to handicapped individuals so that they can obtain equal access to the library's resources. Also available are special services for deaf users. The library also attempts to service homebound users (providing they have valid library cards) by mailing books and providing return postage (with the provision that the library is reimbursed for the cost).

Service to Other Libraries

Library X provides services to other libraries that are members of a particular regional library cooperative. Such a relationship is the result of a contractual relationship of various libraries in the network. Table 5.23 illustrates the priorities stated that pertain to services Library X provides to other libraries. Professional cooperation and resource sharing are juxtaposed with the notions of maximization of use as well as gaining broader access to a larger variety of resources.

The Reference Collection

It is specified in the Reference Manual that the holdings of the Reference department are collected and "maintained and developed to meet specific information needs of the public" (p. 16). The criteria for selection are "utility, currency, quality, affordability and relation to existing collection" (p. 16). The head of reference as well as the staff is responsible for collecting the materials. Public participation is encouraged although it is not clear how this is accomplished. A text is classified as a reference item primarily if its utility is determined to meet "...specific, recurrent information needs of users." The priorities are outlined in Table 5.24.

Circulation Policy and Regulations of Library X

Another important library function and public service is that of circulation. Circulation of materials is a critical measure of libraries' success. Access, use and borrowing are actively encouraged. The policy and regulations set forth the rules and infrastructure within which such activity can take place.

User confidentiality and privacy are stressed. All information remains confidential unless the library needs to contact a user to return borrowed materials. Table 5.25 highlights the key points of the circulation department's policy pertaining to users.

Regulations

Most of this section basically sets forth the rules that govern the library and the consequences of breaking such rules. The values in this section are similar to those of the reference manual. However, there are monetary values assigned to materials in the circulation policy that place a weight on the "value" of the materials.

The library card is the primary key to accessing the information environment and its uses, restrictions, and distribution are closely monitored. Residents of Township X have full access to the library. Users with cards from libraries that have entered into a reciprocal agreement with Library X have borrowing privileges for print materials only. Others have to purchase cards. At different levels fees are charged. In this sense, the library, through service prioritization, actually places a value per user per year upon use of the library. Card distribution and use is closely monitored and revocation of privileges results if users do not comply with rule structure. Some cards can be shared with other family members or household residents, while others cannot (e.g. student or worker cards). Fees are not related to content. They appear to be more related to format rather than utility, subject matter, availability, and so forth. Such priorities are summarized in Tables 5.26 and 5.27.

Materials Selection Policy

The goal of Library X is to "develop collections of materials to meet the public's diverse and ever-changing library needs: for information, research, learning and recreation." (Materials Selection Policy, p. 1). The purpose of the selection policy statement is to provide a framework that will guide staff in the process of selection of materials. It is also the purpose of this policy to provide a statement to the public that will enable them to understand the rationale behind selection decisions made by the staff.

There is a commitment to being as objective as possible in the selection process. Standards for selection are supposed to determine what is chosen rather than personal bias. Public use, as measured by circulation, determines what is to be duplicated within the older portion of the collection. Utility is determined by the following criteria: merit, quality, excellence, significance, personal interest, needs, and the purposes of users. There is an effort here to determine what is useful from a user's point of view.

Materials that are selected are also compared to those already in the collection. For instance, it might be determined that a particular item is not necessary because there is already sufficient subject coverage in the collection. Timeliness is both a goal and a criterion. To maintain a current collection the librarians are aware that critical reviews, etc. may not be available. Selection will take place if requested with the understanding that better quality materials will replace poorer quality in the future once more materials on the subject are made available.

It is clearly stated in the criteria for selection that there will be no bias based on reputation and status of author. Selection criteria are highlighted in Table 5.28.

Maintenance and Collection Development

Since Library X views itself as a "dynamic community resource" rather than a "static repository" (Materials Selection Policy, p. 3), use is the major criteria for retention of materials. Certainly exceptions do occur but, for the most part, use is the key value in the process. Demand is a criterion that is used to determine what portion of the collection might require duplication or reduction. Accuracy is also another criterion that is applied to objects in the collection when it affects the "general health and safety of potential users" (Material Selection Policy, p. 4). When accuracy is not essential, then other criteria can be applied.

Library X is focused on continual improvement based on the criteria of Timeliness, Quality, Style of Presentation, and Accuracy. If individuals have concerns about some aspect of the collection they are required to fill out a "Statement of Concern" for reconsideration of materials. Gift materials are treated according to the same criteria as stated for selection and purchase of materials. Table 5.29 presents the key criteria used for maintaining and developing the collection.

Library Exhibit Policy

With respect to the placement of objects into the physical environment that are not part of the actual circulating collection, Library X has an Exhibit Policy that outlines the rules for this process. The policy specifically states that the exhibits are selected to represent "students, amateur and professional artists, hobbyists, collectors, and museum collections" (Library Exhibit Policy, p. 1). It is not clear as to whether exhibits are limited to these specific groups. Table 5.30 summarizes the priorities of Library X with respect to Exhibits Values in Documents that address Public Behavior

The Library User Bill of Rights

A Library User Bill of Rights was adopted by the Board of Trustees in September, 1995. It very generally outlines what providers believe that users should be doing in the library and how users should be treated and viewed by the institution. Table 5.31 outlines the values presented in this document. This document presents formal parameters for what should be expected of the library with respect to its services to users.

Library X Code of Conduct

As an antithesis to what the users should expect of the library (as noted in the prior paragraphs) the Library X Code of Conduct outlines what behavior is unacceptable in the library environment. The primary goal is to create and maintain an environment that can adequately sustain user activities without infringing on others space and rights. The main theme in this document illustrates the importance of maintaining public order and protecting public space and property. Since the library is a public space, regulations set forth in the Code of Conduct are deemed necessary as a vehicle in the goal of environmental control.

Violation of the Code of Conduct will result in denial of access, defined as a "privilege." Legal measures can also be taken to penalize a person who has crossed a regulatory line. Children are a specifically defined and protected group. If a child is left alone without a guardian then an entire set of rules exists according to which guardians are held accountable. Table 5.32 outlines these priorities

Other Documents

User's Guide
The User's Guide is a small pamphlet that is prepared by Library X that attempts to tell people what the library is all about. Library X is described as "Your place to know, your place to grow" (User's Guide, p. 4). The presentation of the organizational "self" in this portion of the document is geared not so much at regulation and control as it is towards telling the public why they should come and use the library. In this instance, the "relationship to users" is really an "image" that is presented to them by Library X about itself and its services. Table 5.33 highlights the values extrapolated from the introduction to the brochure.

Contained within the User's Manual is the library's mission statement, instructions on how to get a library card, what to do if cards are lost, overdue fines, about the catalog, renewals, reserves, requests to purchase materials and information pertaining to gifts and memorials. The next section introduces the programs offered by the library. It is followed by a list of phone numbers, parking information, collection information, description of services and hours.

There are no specific instructions that tell users (or potential users) how to get to the library. An address is given yet specific coordinates in the context of a map are not. The assumption here is that either people will know how to get there or will be able to figure a way to get information pertaining to the specific geographic location of the library.

Long-Range Plan, 1995–2000
When an organization undertakes a long range planning process, they take a serious look at their current mission, goals, objectives, and so forth in an effort to position and prepare themselves adequately for future pitfalls and opportunities. Such a planning process requires a strong organizational commitment and effort in order to be effective. Library X made such a commitment in 1989 and the result was a Long-Range Plan that was adopted in July of 1994.

Service Goals and Objectives

In this category the primary priorities are efforts geared towards increasing accessibility to collections and services. Increases in time and quantity of items circulated as well as access to electronic resources are specifically noted.

Increasing user awareness of resources is the second objective in this category. Two groups have been specifically targeted for this effort: users of meeting rooms and "special populations" – a category that remains undefined.

The third goal has to do with increasing use of the library. Since there are no "new" objectives noted, it is assumed that the ongoing objectives are sufficient to support this goal. Overall, the library's goal is to increase use with respect to the numbers of people who patronize the facility. Certain user groups that were perhaps previously ignored are targeted. Overall the objective is quantitative.

With respect to efficiency pertaining to checking, renewing and handling materials, Library X has prioritized speed and convenience for its service goals. Table 5.34 summarizes these priorities.

Collections and Resources

The next primary concern in the long-term plan is the library's collection and its resources. For the most part, the library wants to increase collection size and format due to their perception and anticipation of future public demand. One area that is also prioritized is that of foreign language items. Some of the objectives in this section are linked directly to the library's objectives pertaining to use. Table 5.35 summarizes the objectives and goals.

Facilities

The primary goal is to have a building that will support the library's growth, mission, and plan. The objectives pertaining to the current status of the library building suggest that there has already been discussion of a future site for library X. With respect to facilities for individual use, the objectives are geared toward improving and increasing space. For group use, there is a desire to increase the level of accommodation as well. Once the new objectives for increasing staff space are listed, it becomes apparent that it is perceived that more space is a need. Ideally, the physical space would be readily accessible, comfortable and materials would be within reach. Using the library would be a convenience. Table 5.36 summarizes the library's goals with respect to facilities.

Staff

It is the goal of the library to provide staffing that is adequate to perform the functions required by the specified services. The specific priorities are outlined in Table 5.37. The main goal here is to provide enough staff to add services that are believed to be of value to the community.

Administrative and Directional

Staff communication is a primary objective with respect to administrative goals and objectives as well as enhancing and maintaining solid community and political relationships. Table 5.38 outlines the priorities set forth in this section.

DISCUSSION

Once the values/priorities were organized into spreadsheet format and sorted by both frequency of occurrence and by their source (data available upon request) it was found that the data sources fell into three general categories.

The general categories of values derived are as follows: Symbolic, Ideological, and Functional. These categories are primarily related to the data source from where the values initially appeared. For example, "Ideological" values were found in data sources such as those that were imported from the

American Library Association and those that appeared in Library X's mission statement. The nature of such documents is basically visionary and laden with cultural ideologies.

In contrast, the "Functional" categories of values are found mainly in documents that are policy and goal oriented such as the Reference Policy Manual, the User Code of Conduct, etc. The "Functional" Category was further broken down into the following subcategories "operational," "regulatory," and "future-orientated." These subcategories further define the nature of the data sources. Using the previous examples of the Reference Policy manual and the User Code of Conduct document, it can be stated that the former is more operationally oriented because it defines the manner by which the Reference area should operate. The latter is more regulatory in nature in that it is an effort to define, control and regulate user behavior within the system. The final category, "Future-oriented", simply describes Library X's Long Range Plan in that it is a document that is concerned with the future shape and operation of the library.

The "symbolic" category was perhaps the most difficult to label because of the nature of the data source. These values are those that I, through my systematic description and observation of the system, interpreted from my activities within the system. These values are "symbolic" in that they were derived from my interaction with the physical artifact. The values are derived from a text, of sorts. That text came from my "reading of" (Thomas, 1996) that library and the values were extracted from that process. Some of those values were very explicit while others were more tacit. Figure 4 shows the breakdown of the value categories.

It was also found that the context from which values were derived affected the types of values discovered. The source of data tended to affect the meaning of values. For instance, "use" as it was represented in the artifact related to objects placed in that environment that facilitated use, explained a resource, presented a place to work, etc. "Use" as it was interpreted from the reference function related to location, presentation and utilization of resources. While in circulation "use" tended to be referred to as a count of items distributed. In the mission statement, on the other hand, "use" is a more general and assumed term. It is not explicitly discussed or defined.

Also it was found that how priorities manifested themselves in the various data sources tended to differ. For example, "security" was instantiated in the artifact as a presentation of warnings, antitheft devices and prevalence of surveillance features. Security, in an ideological context is not mentioned. In operational/functional formats it appears as a form of managerial control. It is an effort to protect public property.

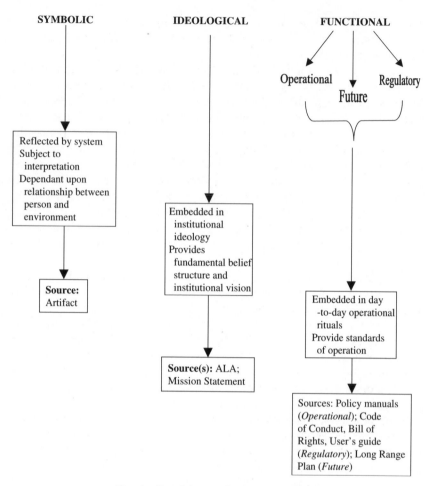

Fig. 4. Breakdown of value categories.

The data were further broken down into a spreadsheet that listed the values discovered and marked the frequency of their appearance in the different sources examined. The most commonly recurring values were use, security, service, users, control, public order, convenience, objectivity, and education. The fact that these values emerged with greater frequency does not suggest that they are more important than any other values, just simply that they were discovered in more than one data source.

For example, "use" was observed as being a priority in 13 locations/ objects in the information space. In the mission statement there was one observation of use as it was stated in Library X's general priorities. There is really no way to suggest that the 13 observations are more important than the one because of the context within which those values appeared and the meaning of that context within the form of this study. Furthermore, it is noted that there is no explicit mention of use in the statements adopted from ALA even though every statement presented supports users and use in a variety of ways. Use; in this case is not really a value, but an assumption, as Schein (1984) pointed out, that is so obvious that it remains unstated. Such assumptions are powerful because they have actually become a part of the cultural identity of that institution and embedded in its ideology to the point where they are virtually not articulated. "Literacy" is another such value that is probably more of an assumption as is "Reading."

Values in Relation to their Source

Artifact

The primary values that emerge from the analysis of the artifact are use and users. The other values that emerge are those of control and security. Some of the values in the public space relate to how the library defines its identity and purpose whiles others have to do with how that space should be navigated and used.

Yet, when the values those are not counted as being derived from the artifact are examined, it can be argued that some also appear in the artifact though in perhaps more tacit ways. For example, it can be argued that technology, youth, literacy, and currency are values that are embedded in the infrastructure of the artifact. However, those terms did not emerge through my description and analysis of the artifact. I did note that children were a highly valued user group within the Library's public space but also noted that youth were not. This could be a simple issue of semantics or it could be viewed as an inconsistency within the environment. The values in this category tended to be geared more toward user orientation and appeal.

American Library Association (ALA)

The values stated in this section are in line with those that underscore the basic rights of citizens in a democracy. Certain human freedoms are highlighted as being paramount. There are fewer values listed in this category but they are greater in scope and implication. The greater the scope, the more general the value statement becomes. The values listed underscore the library professionals' beliefs and commitment to the basic freedoms as set forth in the constitution. Those freedoms are specifically applied to the process of reading (as indicated by the high value placement upon books) as being a fundamental right for every citizen. This concept becomes the focal point of information provision in the library environment and from it stems the emphasis on books, learning, open mindedness – all values found within the library environment – but grounded within the ideological structure adopted from ALA.

Mission Statement

Library X's ideological identity begins to take shape within the boundaries of its Mission Statement. Elements of ideological foundations appear within the mission statement (e.g. Intellectual freedom; education; literacy). But also, the pragmatic elements of what Library X believes to be its role appear (e.g. information provision, service, and efficiency). More clearly defined is the Library's role within the context of its community (e.g. recreational) and in the community itself (e.g. users). More specifically stated in the mission statement is the term "library users" for whom its services and products are designed. On the one hand, this can be viewed as a generic concept for its community, but on the other it is really a more specific focus upon a group of people from within Library X's potential community. Functional elements of use and scope of service and process are defined within this context.

Reference Policy Manual

Besides having ideological values in place, an institution needs to have a pragmatic approach to its operational functions. To say that the library is an open place for everyone all the time is really, not the most practical way to operate an establishment. The actual practice of information provision is laden with rules and boundaries.

Reference is one of the primary services provided by Library X. With respect to the policies that guide reference service provision, among the most commonly occurring values were: service, security, objectivity, time and use. Although a few "visionary" values appear within the reference policy, for the most part the objectives of the values derived are of an operational nature. The reference area also places a higher priority on subject matter as well as the relevance of the service to the user. Furthermore, there are considerable criteria that are set forth defining the parameters within which it is acceptable for the reference staff to operate. Again, these are predominately priorities of an operational/functional nature. The value of control is a key aspect of provision of reference services in that both the materials and the space need to be adequately organized and regulated to operate within the stated value of timeliness.

The values of objectivity and neutrality are important in the parameters that define reference service and provision. They also, specifically, define the acceptable actions of information providers with the context of reference service provision. Since this is a fundamental point of interaction between users and system, the importance and implications of the values supported within such an environment should not be overlooked.

Another interesting element emerges from the examination of the Reference Service Policy is that the librarian, is defined as a conduit for information. The source itself is considered to be the authority and almost all responses must accommodate that priority. The Librarian's role is one of neutrality and objectivity. It is stated in the policy that personal opinions should not be given as a source of information.

Reference Collection Policy
With respect to the Reference Collection, it can be seen that most of the values are directed towards use and nature of the collection. It is the first area where the value of relevance becomes verbalized. The priority of this area is to create a collection that will have meaning to users and fall into the collection parameters set forth by the institution.

Circulation Policy
The primary values stated in the circulation policy are use, access, privacy, collection, and, circulation. Confidentiality, with respect to user identity, is strongly protected. The operational values in a circulation area are primarily control and processing (efficiency). Use is a value that relates to materials that are borrowed. Again, this is closely connected with regulation, protection, and control of resources and members' actions in relation to those resources.

Library Card Policy
With respect to library membership as it is outlined for library cardholders, the values are more regulatory in nature: control, rules, regulation, and cost. Courtesy suggests an operational approach towards service.

The library card, itself, is a symbol of membership. The values set forth in the policies and rules governing the distribution and use of library cards are predominately control oriented. The process of becoming a member is really a process of understanding disclosed rules and organizational objectives.

Membership is based on a variety of criteria that basically define sectors of users (e.g. local residents; residents of other townships; business members; etc). Membership is not fundamentally equal for all citizens in that there must be some means for control and accountability.

Selection Policy

With respect to selection of materials for Library X, the predominant values are use, quality, relevance, and objectivity. These values relate content to use. There are priorities that are grounded in pragmatics (e.g. cost, timeliness, durability) as well as those that make an effort to relate to the demand side of the institution (e.g. significance, relevance, user needs). The values that relate most to providers are those that make an effort to define the ideological context within which selection takes place. For instance, the notions of objectivity, neutrality, and non-discrimination in resource selection are values that promote an ideological framework with the selection process. That said, the ideological values are still positioned within the pragmatic constraints of information selection and dissemination.

Collection Development Policy

The primary values that emerge from the Collection Development Policy are primarily use and service oriented. Use is the basic criteria against which holdings are evaluated. Quality of materials and format are among the functional values that define this process. Although use is a primary criterion it cannot be said, given the scope of this study, how it is measured in relation to the issues/policies in question.

The Exhibit Policy

The Exhibit Policy is a very general code of priorities that loosely defines the nature of library visual experience. The emphasis is on community while values include safety, visual experience and variety. This is a way in which the community can participate in the physical environment through artistic representation, among other media. Exhibits reflect certain values, in and of themselves.

User Bill of Rights

The User Bill of Rights makes the effort to define, for users, what they should expect of the library. Interestingly, this document outlines a value structure that by design attempts to establish priorities and expectations for users. On the other hand, it is also a document that makes an effort to define what the system is all about, albeit from the providers' point of view.

The primary values that are outlined in this document are service, safety, use, equity, comfort/convenience, and providing what is believe to be "popular" or in demand. This focus also establishes boundaries around user expectations in that it makes the effort to define what users should expect to do or not to do. From the values perspective this is a double-edged sword: to define is to limit, but to limit and control (in an operational context), one must define parameters.

User Code of Conduct

The User Code of Conduct defines public order, as well as the sanctions that could be imposed if the codes are broken. It further stipulates behavioral codes for users, and the focus is on order, security, safety, and control. Users are not a priority in this document, but control of users is.

User's Guide

The purpose of the User's Guide is to introduce the user to the products and services of the library. One part of this process is a marketing effort, while the other is an outline of rules and membership expectations. For the most part, the guide reads as an "information about" Library X tool. However, implicitly it begins to shape the user's image of the library through the process of defining what the library is as well as the requirements set forth to access the environment.

Long Range Plan

As a planning document, the Long-Range Plan's focus is on targeting areas of future development. Values such as design, functionality, growth, technology and (generally speaking) development are explicit priorities and most of these values are unique to this category. Convenience, service, education (of staff), communication, and use are among the most frequently mentioned values in this category. Organizational growth is an intrinsic goal to this process as is the concept of improvement of the physical space and service program provided within.

Values and Core Values

Values are not always explicit but can be inferred through detailed understanding of institutional preferences, choices, and priorities as well as how those choices are reflected in institutional artifacts. What was discovered through the course of this study was that the findings are in fact representations of what was valued by Library X. This list of values is a subset of a much broader set of values defined as "core values:"

> Human values are conceptualized as consisting of a relatively small number of core ideas or conditions…that are capable of being organized to form different priorities. (Rokeach, 1970, p. 49)

The core values identified during this study are not particularly surprising but do serve an important role as an inherent reality check on the nature of the data derived. Table 2 identifies the core values identified during analysis.

Use

As much as the Library is a free space, it does not follow that users are free to do whatever they want in this space. What can be done is outlined very clearly in the rules of the institution as well as in the structural component of the institution (the public space). Users are a highly valued sector of the library environment, specifically children. There is a strong institutional effort to reach out and get more people to use the library. This is more of a commitment to the educational and ideological beliefs of the library than an effort to reach out to any particular individual or group. Needs are "identified" by the library.

Service

Service is what the library does. The values listed in this category are those that support the actions of the library in direct relation to the users. Service is somewhat of an interface between the ideological presentation of the library and those who must functionally navigate it. Service is how the ideology of a system is translated into a process that makes the institutional goals possible.

Personal Liberty and Growth

There is a strong value of protecting personal freedoms and rights within the library environment. These rights are integrated into the ideological vision of information provision.

Control

The value of control is one of the strongest values and functional priorities in the library environment. It is one thing to have a public space that is open for use and another to protect that space and ensure it is kept in good operating condition. To control is also to define. Library X defines for users what they can and should expect. They also tell users that there are more

Use	Service	Personal Liberty & Growth	Control	Literacy	Community	Information
Affordability	Accuracy	Due process	Gatekeepers	Education	Communication	Materials
Fun	Answers	Equity	Boundaries	Learning	Culture	Popular collections
Interaction	Collection	Freedom	Order	Reading	Diversity	Popular culture
Accessibility	Comfort	Ideas	Organization		Leadership	Printed material
Membership	Confidentiality	Intellectual freedom	*Procedures*		Welcoming	Source as authority
Recreation	Convenience	Open mindedness	Property		Marketing	Technology
Familiarity	Courtesy	Privacy	Regulation		Promotion	Variety
	Durability	Tolerance	Rules		Needs	Visual experience
	Efficiency	Creativity	Safety		Children	Books
	Facts	Achievement	Security		Special needs	
	Quality		Social order			
	Quantity		Space (control of)			
	Relevance		Territoriality			
	Simplicity		Financial			
	Style		Quiet			
	Time					
	Timeliness					
	Excellence					
	Experience					
	Improvement					
	Neutrality					
	Objectivity					
	Productivity					
	Professional cooperation					
	Staff					

rules to enforce than potential tasks being done in the library. But, looking at the larger picture, it can be seen that without control there could be a lack of order.

The other "image" that the library presents is that of organization. To be organized is to be in control and there are meticulous methods in place to ensure this is possible on an operational level. In turn, this reflects upon the image that defines what this library is. Control is accomplished on both an operational level and an "intellectual" level. Part of the library's function is to ensure processes flow smoothly. The other part is maintaining control of intellectual content. From this stem the elaborate classification and organizational schemes.

Literacy

Literacy, in this context, incorporates the emphasis Library X places on reading, learning, and education. Much of what is in the environment is focused towards those goals, particularly those elements that directly attempt to communicate messages to users (e.g. banners, posters, notes, etc). There is an ideologically oriented vision that literacy is a freedom and right for all. Yet, in the physical environment there are elements of literacy that are defined and, as a result, bounded by institutional visions and actions.

Community

Community, as a core value, more specifically refers to Library X's efforts to reach out to, and communicate with its users as well as residents and businesses of Township X. Efforts are made to appeal to a variety of ethnic and cultural groups. There are small collections geared towards certain groups (e.g. ESL, Chinese, etc). Such gestures suggest that there is at least an effort to identify and serve those communities. The level of service, however, is a question for another study. In general, the rhetoric of Library X is welcoming. Yet, the reality of defining collections and the levels of information provision creates a situation where it is not possible to serve all members of the community equally.

Information

Information provision, as a value, essentially defines what information providers do. There is an inherent belief that information is important. In this context, information is not one type of resource. In fact, information ranges from tiny posters taped to pillars, to notes given to users, to pamphlets and guides, to informal and formal interactions with the system. The library is a place for exchange or retrieval of information and that is how it posits itself.

The library strongly values its product. The library's product, even given the latest technological advances within the system is still linked to the book and to the process of reading. This is a link between product and ideology. There is a strong image in both the general cultural contexts as well as in the specific case of Library X of libraries being the places to go for books. Other products such as "information" are less specifically defined, while books are a much more recognizable entity that can symbolically be used to represent the institution's identity in a variety of ways (e.g. logos, marketing, etc.)

Relationships Between Values: Inconsistencies, Tensions, and Constraints

Through the course of examining the values with respect to their sources, I began to notice inconsistencies amongst the institutional priorities discovered. There appears to be a natural tension between offering an environment for public use and controlling that environment. The same types of conflicts arise from ideological and visionary components of an institutional structure and the pragmatics of operationalizing those values and objectives. This section will discuss those issues.

Service/Access to All Versus Actual User Base

The ideological values that fundamentally define the culture of librarianship are firmly grounded in the philosophy that presents library use and service as a right available to every person. In theory this is a noble cause, but in reality it is a benchmark that is difficult to reach. First of all, operationally it is not possible to serve every single person in equal ways. There is a distinct hierarchy of use where certain groups are given certain privileges over others. These are mostly pragmatic distinctions (e.g. township residents use the library for free versus residents of other towns who must pay a fee), and such functional values or priorities serve to limit the otherwise generally broad-based ideological values.

From the perspective of the artifact (the library's actual physical locale) there are certain constraints that implicitly limit access. For instance, because of the Library's location it becomes difficult to access without owning a vehicle or perhaps having access to bus routes. It is likely that some constituencies of the township population do not own vehicles or have access to buses.

Presenting Services Versus Pragmatics of Provision

The Library User's Manual, a promotional brochure, states the following: "There is so much to see and do at the Library! Learn about any subject that interests you…Have any question answered in person or by phone…" The intent of such a manual is to inform potential clients about the benefits and services provided by the library. But in some ways such statements can be misleading. Ideologically there is a framework in place within the culture of Library X that suggests people have the right to any kind of information they require. Yet, in reality the parameters set forth in the reference manual (operational objectives) very clearly stipulate what can and cannot be provided to users. For instance, questions that require "short answers" are preferable to those that are more complex. Questions pertaining to certain topics cannot be "answered" by the librarian. They must be located and sited from a source. By default, if a question is asked for which a source does not exist then the question cannot be answered. Furthermore, economic constraints are surely a factor in limiting the scope of the items collected by any particular library. Another implicit issue has to do with the nature of the collection itself and how it is created. The simple act of choice suggests that some things were selected over others, and perhaps the "answer" to a users' query rests in a source that was not considered to be credible by the library in its collection development efforts.

Privacy
Privacy is a strong value in Library X. It is valued in both an ideological and operational way. User identity is strictly guarded in the circulation policy, reference area and indirectly in the Code of Conduct. Juxtaposed to what was examined and revealed by the artifact, certain inconsistencies emerged. It was observed that user privacy was not a priority in the public space of the library.

One example of this is in the reference area. In order to ask a question, users typically queue up at the front of the desk and the reference transaction takes place in an area than can, at times, be densely populated. This type of environment is not particularly inviting to anyone who might have a question that is of a sensitive nature. There is often more than one librarian stationed behind the desk as well and it is not uncommon for the librarians to ask for each other's assistance. The user's inquiry essentially becomes part of the public space. This method of user assistance also negates the "promise" made in the user's manual that claims any question can be answered. If a comfort zone is necessary within which to ask questions then certain people, simply by default of the design of the reference area, will probably not bring their queries into that domain.

Another example of the lack of priority for user privacy is embedded in the way that the reading areas and chairs are set up in the library. There are some study carrels for individual use but for the most part the furniture is set up in ways that chairs are place side by side. My observations were supported by Sommer's (1969a) research on territoriality in that I noticed that users typically do not want to sit next to others. The way in which the reading chairs are set up is also not conducive to task related privacy. The chairs are situated in an area where there is often a stream of traffic (between the magazine racks) and it is difficult to get a sense of comfort in that area since there seems to always be someone behind one's shoulder. The areas with tables are also clustered together as opposed to placing tables individually throughout the library there tend to be separate reading areas.

This type of design brings together all users who require table space into one place. With respect to user tasks, it is highly probable that some of the users will require space to perform individual tasks while others will use it for group related activities and tasks. Elements of privacy do not appear to be a consideration within this type of public organization of space.

There is a distinct effort in the public space of the artifact to delineate the personal/professional space of the library personnel from that of the users. Use of physical barriers such as counters, doors, shelves and file cabinets is evident throughout the space. Space is definitely allocated and defined for the providers' use within the public space of the library. Users, on the other hand, are left to their own means and methods of territorial marking which accounts for Sommer's (1960) findings as well as my own observations of coats, books and other personal paraphernalia strategically placed around users' perceptions of their personal space. It may also explain why people often will not take a seat right next to someone.

Privacy and Space
In Library X's Long-Range Plan, as well as in other supplementary sources of data (minutes of Board of Directors meetings and conversations with library administration) space, or lack thereof, is discussed as a concern within the context of Library X. In the previous section it was pointed out that often, given the physical layout of user space in the library, much of the available space was not occupied. One short-term fix to the space issue might be a simple reconfiguration of the current user workspace in an effort to maximize use of that space.

Neutrality and Objectivity Versus Selection Criteria
In the Reference and Selection policies there is a strong emphasis placed on the values of objectivity and neutrality in the provision of services. Yet, by default selection of materials for the library are subjected to selection

criteria, and ultimately certain items are selected over others. Certain areas in collection development are given priority over others. There is an interesting relationship between values that promote objectivity and the actual practice of information provision.

On the one hand, the Reference Manual clearly states that librarians must defer to the authority of a printed source. In turn, that source is considered as being objective. Yet, the existence of that source in the library suggests that some criteria were applied to some selection process by which that source was selected over another. Neither a source nor the process by which it comes to be part of a collection are particularly objective.

Thinking of this relationship in terms of an example could lead to the following scenario. A person has a question that relates to understanding how a certain disease might come about. A typical reference question response would be to lead the user to a medical dictionary or some other such resource in the collection. The primary medical resources are based in Western medical processes and ideologies (as juxtaposed to eastern or homeopathic practices that, in some cultures, are considered more valid than the western models). A typical inquiry would not lead to a response that presents all views on medical perspectives, but would be limited to the dominant one within the environment. By definition, as set forth in the policy manual, this is considered to be a neutral/objective response. On the other hand, looking at it from a perspective that focuses on values, it can be seen that one viewpoint is more strongly represented over others. This, in my analysis, is not considered to be objective. It is simply a response that is embedded within an institutional design that accumulates objects based on certain criteria.

Use Versus Control

It is one thing to say that anyone can have access into a particular public space and yet another to maintain order and control within that space. Ideologically the library is positioned as being a place for all people, but operationally design mechanisms must be in place to maintain order and control within that space. Rules are created to shape and define what is acceptable activity within the space and, by default, define what should be counted as appropriate behavior within. Such elements are discussed in the Bill of Rights and the Code of Conduct. There will always be an underlying tension between ideological images of what library use should be and the pragmatics of everyday operation of a public environment.

Access, Literacy, and Use

Literacy and access are related in that the level of literacy affects the way an environment will be accessed and used. Physical access is different from cognitive access in an environment. A homeless person may access the library for physical comfort while a student may attempt to work on a homework assignment. The degree to which a project is accomplished is related to the degree to which a person understands the system that is being navigated for the purposes of his objectives.

The values of literacy and reading are presented in a variety of formats in the artifact itself as well as in the texts of the institutional policies. Ironically, the value of literacy is actually a barrier to it, as much as it is a goal of library operation. It is a barrier because a person must have a certain level of literacy to make the system have some meaning. If a person does not speak English or has a poor verbal command of the language, there is probably very little chance that he or she will find the library a useful resource in their lives.

Chatman (1991) found this to be true in her study of janitors. Other groups, specifically ethnic minorities, have established their own information networks located in local bodegas, sausage shops, travel agencies and the like. One only needs to go to an ethnic neighborhood to find that the primary source of information for such groups is not always located in the local public library. On the one hand, books are a strong value in Library X. On the other, perhaps that type of source of information does not or cannot fulfill certain kinds of information needs. In and of itself, this is not a problem but when positioning libraries in public forums it is perhaps a bit misleading to say that the library can provide all people with any type of information.

Even if language was not a problem for an individual it still does not guarantee that access to the environment would be successful. For one thing, just because someone knows how to read and write, it does not necessarily follow that that person understands that which is written or implied within the framework of the language. There is a certain culture that surrounds the presentation and storage of information resources that is not particularly simple. With respect to the intellectual space of Library X, there are a variety of assumptions made about users and their ability to understand the logic of the system.

The fact that some of the items in the library are alphabetically organized and located in the catalog while others are not in the catalog is confusing. The popular literature section in the central portion of the library is not cataloged. Therefore, if a person is looking for a particular book it may actually exist in the library but not in the resource used to look for it. It is assumed that serendipity and browsing would be the primary modes of access and use of this collection. And, given the location of the collections, it is reasonable to assume that people will figure it out.

This, of course, gets down to the level where certain cultural common-alties between user and provider are assumed by the system. Like, for instance, "we" would both agree that Star Trek books would be considered as items to be placed in the popular fiction section. This is perhaps a fair assumption, given the fact that both of us have similar cultural experiences. In an ethnically diverse community one would have to stop and wonder whether the user population does, indeed, have a similar definition of what the providers believe to be "popular." It would even be questionable whether or not such items would even be considered of interest within certain groups and/or cultures.

Within the collection, what is "popular" is defined by the library staff and labeled as such. Underlying this seemingly simple process is a fundamental assumption that suggests we all somehow share a similar culture and that we should know what Star Trek novels are all about. The term "popular" is quite subjective and based in certain socio/cultural experience and often assumed that "everyone" knows about an object that is defined within that category. A certain level of cultural literacy on the part of users is assumed by Library X.

"Quiet" Versus Activity

There is a concerted effort on the part of information providers to define and control the activities within the library environment. There is both a spoken and unspoken rule as well as a priority that suggests that a quiet environment needs to be maintained. In reality, given the way that the built environment is configured and the nature of many of the activities going on in the public space, it would be impossible to keep the environmental noise to a low level.

First of all, there are three major stations within which a consistent level of interaction must take place. Circulation, Reference, and Media Services areas are all open for users to come and to ask questions, obtain materials, etc. Since the library is basically an open space and these areas are not enclosed, it is not possible to control noise level. Furthermore, the children's area is not enclosed, and between stories and children's voices and other normal everyday activities, the noise level is relatively high. The existence of a "Quiet Study" room suggests that the providers already know that this is a problem and are at least trying to provide a small, enclosed area where the no talking rule is enforced. There is still a culturally bounded issue in that many people who bring their children to the environment tend to tell them to be quiet, etc. And, to a limited extent, there is an institutional effort to contain noise.

In the User's Guide the providers declare what they believe the library is:

> "The Library offers more than just materials and programs: it is also a place to be a part of your community...The Library has been called "the closest thing to Main Street" – the place where you are welcomed and helped by friendly expert staff, where you can get the information you seek, and perhaps even meet a friend or two."

There is little question that the values stated here are positioning the library as a place for social encounters. Ideologically Library X has made the shift from the stereotypical, static environment to that of a dynamic social meeting place for its community. However, within the confines of the public space there are conflicting messages sent to users that suggest that certain behaviors are not appropriate (e.g. talking, boisterous behavior, etc). In fact, it was pointed out in some of the minutes of the Library Board Meetings that the behaviors of teenagers, many of whom came to the library to socialize, were disruptive and required greater control.

User Equity and Time

The values of timeliness and efficiency are prevalent in Library X's definitions of itself and its services. They are operational objectives and measures of success in service provision. In certain areas, such as reference services, these values are combined with the importance of maintaining user equity. For instance, in some circumstances short answer questions are a preferred priority over those that require more in depth work (as noted in the discussion of the reference policies) so that more people can be helped with their information problems. This is done to ensure that everyone has his turn with the reference librarian. With respect to circulation, there are limits set forth on how long and by whom an item can be borrowed. These are basically straightforward operational rules that attempt to maintain user equity. On the other hand, in some circumstances they can also serve to affect how a person uses the library or how he asks his question at the reference desk. Time is simply one-way by which use can be defined, and possibly restricted.

Values and Users

Although this study did not focus on users, per se, the final research question asks "what do the values that are discovered suggest about perceptions of users and use of the system?" Although my observations were not focused on user activity I found that some inferences and observations could be made with respect to how the system perceives and represents users in the public space and institutional policy.

Defining Users

To be a library user, one must somehow first come to or contact the library. Users are people who use the library. It was shown that Library X's mission statement refers to "library users of all ages" rather than "residents of township X," that the older version addressed.

There are various levels of use, as defined by the rules of Library X, depending on who the individual is and where he lives. At some level, this suggests that the library is geared towards those who are active participants in its environment. If a person is already a user, then the library staff and the system will hear the person's opinions, requests, etc. and will respond by purchasing the relevant materials, providing a particular type of service etc.

This view makes a large assumption about a community's knowledge and perception of what a library is all about. It suggests that people know what the library is and what it does. But, on the other hand, Chatman's (1991) work found that certain groups, such as janitors, do not find the library a useful resource for their day-to-day needs. This issue raises a circular type of argument that says if a person is a user, the system will respond to their needs, but making those people users requires that there be something in the library to attract individuals in the first place.

Most information-oriented artifacts in the library are text based. There is a fundamental assumption made about users of the system. It is assumed that they can read. It is also assumed that the user can understand the way that the system is organized and classified and that the user will have some idea as to how to navigate a complex system that is organized in various ways. Some items are arranged alphabetically and not noted in the card catalog while other items are in the card catalog and are grouped by Dewey classification. Certain holdings are situated in non-circulating stacks. Some are grouped by genre while others are grouped by alphabetical order. Some things are in filing cabinets while others need to be requested at the desk. This is a lot of information to expect a user to process or understand. It is unclear how users are supposed to know such details. Part of Library X's success, it seems, may depend on how it utilizes the public's already existing knowledge about classification, etc. within its environment (for instance, the media section organizes videos in ways that are used in video stores, etc.).

It is also assumed that users will ask for help when needed. Yet, the reference area is located off to the side rather than in the central area into which people first enter. Instead, there is a large information kiosk that people are supposed to use to find out about the library. More importantly, it is assumed that the users will know how to ask a question or, at least, to get started with an interaction. The system is bounded by parameters while the users worlds and queries can span an unlimited range.

User Types

The library is organized by user type (Adult, Young Adult, and Children); by what the users might like to read (mysteries, science fiction); by type of service; by type of artifact (book, audio, etc); and by activity, etc. There is a definite favor toward children in this library, and the adult collection is quite adequate. Interestingly, the Young Adult area is very underdeveloped and not very relevant based on the nature of the collection that I observed that was labeled as the "young adult" collection. The system essentially defines and labels how the space "should" be used and by whom.

It is relatively easy to distinguish an adult from a child, but when one is a "young adult" one becomes part of that gray area that becomes more difficult to define. It is difficult in a setting where a "rigid mindset" (Zerubavel, p. 34) rules to account for "gray" areas and incorporate them into the existing structure. Interestingly, there was a lot of discussion about the "young adults" who tended to wreak havoc in Library X in the minutes of the Board Meetings. This was clearly viewed as a problem user group, and it is pointed out in the literature that young adult populations are difficult to serve. In this instance the physical manifestation of a collection is a rather symbolic representation of an underlying issue with a particular user group.

Conflicting Messages Sent to Users

While ideologically the library is posited as a social place, users are, in reality, constrained by rules that govern behavior within the public space. "Quiet" is a value that emerges from the Code of Conduct. The image of "Main Street" conflicts with that of the rules of the public space. This is one example of conflicting messages sent to users.

In another section of the User's Manual the text says that users can find out about "any subject that interests you." Yet, in reality, as previously discussed, there are very specific parameters that define the nature of reference services as well as those of collection policy.

Preaching to the Converted

Throughout Library X there are messages posted that encourage reading, or membership in the environment. There are many "READ" posters hung on sides of stacks as well as signage that praises the accomplishments of libraries and those who use libraries. It's interesting that such reinforcement of ideology is perceived to be of importance since those who will likely be exposed to such messages are already part of the "system" in that they can probably read and have library cards.

Trusting Users/Controlling Users

A public library is a rare entity in that it collects and circulates publicly owned materials. This system is based on trust and control. Unfortunately, the assumption about the public that is most obvious is that of distrust by the system. There are a variety of security mechanisms visibly in place that suggest wrong-doing is assumed, and such measures are important to protect the public's property from potential damage by individuals.

The library wants to position itself as a happy and helpful environment in which users feel comfortable. On the other hand, it needs to employ tight rules of control and restriction within the space in order to ensure the space remains undamaged.

Conveying Information to Users in the Public Space

It appears that the information providers want to communicate messages to users in the public space. The assumption is that users require certain kinds of information that is there to express institutional rules, define elements of the system, and provide community resources and information etc. The walls, shelves, tables, and basically any exposed areas are covered with paper, flyers, posters, etc.

The problem with this design is, simply stated, information overload. There is no real structure to the messages posted within the artifact and the random structure, not to mention quantity of information, makes it relatively difficult to notice. Some of the messages posted could potentially be of importance to users but the way they are displayed suggests a low priority in terms of creating a system of user-friendly messages. The utility of the written communication from provider to user is questionable. Basically, the papers, etc. become part of the décor.

It was also observed that much of the "signage" in the public space was either directional or rule oriented, an effort to label elements of the library. Less visible were signs that made an effort to explain to the user about elements of the system.

Users as Variables that Need Control

Systems are built for users and, without users, systems would not exist. Yet as much as a system exists to meet the needs of users, users can also be a potential risk to the system. Users bring an element of uncertainty into the system and, in turn, the system must have mechanisms of control that maintains order within the system. The order desired within the public space is one that is defined by providers.

CONCLUSIONS

The research problem that motivated this study was that people do not use information systems/libraries to the extent that the providers think is appropriate. It was hypothesized that such situations could occur because the values and priorities that underlie the system's design may not be congruent with those of the users of the system. This study begins to explore this problem by focusing on the values that define the system in an effort to understand their role within.

A public library, as an information system, was investigated with respect to how its public space reflected it values. Institutional values were also identified and analyzed. Institutional values and values reflected by the artifact were compared. The results yielded tensions, incongruities and conflicts between those values.

Values and Mismatches

It was found that a variety of value structures coexisted within the physical environment of Library X. Library X was very clear in setting its parameters with respect to the nature and level of service it could provide to users in an institutional context. Yet, in its presentation of itself to users, it was not that clear. It was also found that many incongruities existed in the various value structures identified that could potentially lead to mismatches between those value structures. The conflicts could be between the institutional language and its practice; or between what their practice parameters are and how they define those parameters. Simple, unintended, tacit messages could potentially be communicated to users that do not conform to the rules of the public space.

Values play a key role in defining boundaries because it is not possible to do everything for everyone. Functionally speaking, Library X is quite clear about those boundaries as they are set forth in institutional processes and operations. It also attempts to convey rules, restrictions, procedures, etc. to users. However, the manner by which this is accomplished tends to be ineffective because of the volume of messages that bombard people as they enter the environment. Furthermore, the actual arrangement of the physical space is often in conflict with the priorities set forth within Library X's rule structure. This type of mismatch, once again, leads to a misunderstanding of how space should be used. On the one hand, Library X wants to accommodate everyone and everyone's tasks; on the other hand it needs to maintain order and control. Yet, their space simply is not configured in a way that will make such goals easy reach.

The following is a synopsis of the various observations that were made in this study that pertain to values and mismatches between value structures:

Values Affect the Shape of the Information System

Information systems are created by people. Choices are made with respect to what should or should not be in a particular environment and how that environment should be configured. Over time, choices define the shape of an institution. In order to include something, something else must be excluded. Each choice and decision is guided by institutional perceptions of what is important and needed within that space.

A Variety of Value Structures Coexist within the Public Space of the Library

It was found that different sources exhibited different values and that the same value could potentially have different meanings as it was discussed in relation to its source. This element of multiplicity of meaning holds a potential for misinterpretation and misunderstanding.

There are Mismatches Between Ideology and Function

It is one thing to believe in an ideology and another to put it into practice. In fact, the process of putting an ideological vision into practice is value laden in that everything cannot be included in the final outcome. It is one thing to say that everyone should have access, yet another to have the required space to accommodate that value. When positioning an institutional image in a public domain, limitations and exclusions should be taken into account.

There are Mismatches Between Library X's Values and those that are Reflected Through the System

There is an inherent contradiction in priorities and values between what Library X says about itself and the values reflected in the physical space.

These contradictions should not be underestimated and require even more rigorous investigation. The image created needs to match with what is encountered in the actual physical space. If not, there will be a mismatch between user expectation and the reality of use.

There are Mismatches Between What is Expected of Users and How those Expectations are Communicated to Users
Expectations of users (order, behavior, types of use) are not clearly communicated within the public space. Confusing and conflicting messages result.

All Users are not Equal
In the public space of Library X there are distinct differences in how resources are allocated according to use. The strongest mismatch identified is between the Children's and Young Adult areas. The former is colorful, fun, well-staffed, bright and designed very much to appeal to children. The latter is in the back of the library, with a relatively small collection of book and a few chairs. Children are encouraged to interact with the space, while young adults are often pointed to as being a problem group. The Children's area tends to be noisy and that appears to be acceptable. Much more emphasis is placed on making the library a fun and lively space for children but not so much for adults. The transitional group, the teenagers, rest in the gray area between the two groups. The collection and physical space reflects this tension.

Environments Communicate Values and Affect Use
From the previous discussion it can be inferred that children are a more valued user constituency than young adults. This is because a greater emphasis is placed on the development of programs and services for this group. (This is also true for other elements of information as well). As children become Young Adults they are no longer valued as they were when they were children. The way that they were taught, initially as young children to act in the Library context is no longer acceptable as they pass the line that divides children from young adults. The system has expectations of this user group yet the physical environment barely begins to communicate those expectations.

The library defines how it should be used. It also defines the nature of use. For instance, the system defines how and where questions should be asked, how those questions should be answered, and, even more importantly, and what objects will be placed within its locale. By limiting scope and defining resources, the system limits user options. It would appear that the system can potentially affect and shape use.

Mismatches Between How Providers Define Use of Public Space and the Values that the Space Conveys to Users

While providers had very specific priorities with respect to managing how space should be used, the physical environment reflected other priorities that did not always correspond to the providers' intents. For example, individual privacy is not a high priority in Library X. Though they will protect what a person reads (as per circulation records), queries are voiced in open environments such as the reference area. Such a forum is not particularly conducive to inquiries of a more private nature.

Users are told to feel comfortable, yet the environment constrains them from interacting. In order to make the place comfortable for all, constraints need to be put in place and certain environmental elements need to be controlled (e.g. noise, interaction, etc). On the other hand, the system is configured in a way that requires people to sit next to one another, thus creating a perfect environment for potential communication.

Values Define and Exclude

Jackson (1984) writes that "every traditional public space, whether religious or political or ethnic in character, displays a variety of symbols, inscriptions, images, monuments, not as works of art but to remind people of their civic privileges and duties – and tacitly to exclude the outsider." (p. 18) Although one would not immediately suspect a public library of being "exclusive," it is a notion that perhaps should not be dismissed. This study found that Library X directs its services towards a relatively specific audience. It was also found in this study that the system's priorities are directed towards specific groups and areas of interest. Certain objects are brought to the foreground of the library suggesting that providers assume those objects are important to users (e.g. popular paperback collections; "did you miss?" section, etc). By defining and bringing what is important into the foreground, other elements must naturally fall into the background, a position of less importance.

Formally, Library X does not state that only certain users can enter its premises. On the contrary, in publicly distributed documents it invites everyone to its locale under the assumption that something is offered for everyone. However, it can be inferred that perhaps the environment is built around those who tend to frequent and participate in that environment.

This can be a very effective way to run an information service and energies can be focused on those who actually utilize the resources.

On the other hand, what about the people who do not frequent the library? It could be argued that, if they are not interested in the system, then why should the system guess as to what needs they might have. Perhaps they would use the system if there were some way to more clearly understand the elements of their requirements. Or, perhaps their requirements are so far removed from the realm of information provision in a library context that their participation in the system would be futile. Perhaps the public library is really not the place for everyone nor does it necessarily follow that the library should be such a resource as it has been shown that the system must operate within realistic parameters.

Values Define Use

Use and users were the most frequently valued aspects of Library X's priorities identified in this study. In retrospect, it is observed that most of the values related to use and users define various groups and artifacts that are perceived to be of value. It is interesting to note that the process of use is not defined in terms of how providers understand users' search processes but in terms of restrictions in how the system responds to demands.

For example, in the reference policy the values that are geared toward helping users understand the system are very general. The objective is to provide accurate, efficient and courteous assistance; to "facilitate optimal use," etc. Yet, as the policy becomes more specific in terms of operation, the values become more restrictive in terms of what the librarian cannot provide as a response or service.

The service objectives are defined in terms of impartiality and neutrality of the providers and the system. Yet the act of defining what can or cannot be given to users is neither impartial nor neutral.

Implications for further Research

Potential Site-Specific Investigations

It is important to note, that this study focused only on the values of information providers and those that were interpreted from the objects located in the public space of Library X. User perspectives were not examined directly as a source of data. The objective was to focus on the role that values have in the process of information provision. Future research could easily build upon the value framework identified.

A logical future investigation could focus on investigating the user community of Library X in terms of their values and priorities. In this case the user community would be defined as those people who actually use the library. It would be important to characterize such users with respect to their priorities and values as they relate to their activity and presence in the library. Those values could then be compared to the ones discovered by this investigation in order to see how they compare. Such data could really supplement the notion of mismatches between users and systems priorities.

The other group, though more difficult to locate, that could be examined are the non-users, those people who do not go to Library X. This type of investigation would perhaps be more aligned to a study of information-seeking behavior, though more specifically oriented to identifying values and priorities as opposed to focusing on problem solving issues. Again, these values could be compared with already existing data in order to see what types of similarities and differences would exist. The objective would be to explore whether differences in values might account for non-use.

The nature of this investigation is such that new products and spaces could be added to the main portion of the study. For example, this study focused only on the public space of the library in the interest of defining investigational boundaries. Library X, on the other hand, has information services that are located beyond the physical environment of the Library. Such services include web pages, outreach programs, bookmobiles, and so forth. Each of these extensions could be studied using the same methods and frameworks that were developed here. Each area could potentially offer new insights into Library X's priorities.

Finally, it would be of much interest to study the current group of information providers with respect to their values. Even though they operate within the "organizational" perspective, their perspectives would add a valuable insight to the elements identified in this work. It cannot be assumed that they naturally would have the same values as those that were identified in this study. Follow up interviews could yield valuable information pertaining to Library X's value structures.

Methodological Implications

The results of this study cannot be generalized to other libraries. The findings are specific to Library X. However, the methodological framework developed can readily be transferred to the study of other environments and libraries. This could offer the opportunity to compare various structures by using values and priorities as common denominators.

More pragmatically, the framework could be utilized as basis for institutional self-study. It allows practitioners to look at themselves in terms of what they say is important versus what they discover as being important within the boundary of their information system. The framework developed here could also be used as a tool for evaluation of services in terms of institutional priorities. Institutional priorities can be compared to the priorities in the actual practice of information provision. In other words, what they say they do can be compared to what is actually done and reflected in the information product. The results could support institutional objectives or shed light on discrepancies discovered.

SUMMARY

Values are an important component in the design of information environments. Defining what should be in the system limits the potential of what could be. Values limit and define. There is always a tension between ideology and the functional elements of operation. Putting beliefs into practice is a value-laden process.

Libraries as information retrieval systems are neither neutral nor objective. There is a strong effort in Library X's policies and procedures to maintain a level of objectivity and a position of neutrality. These types of values are not possible to attain in an operational reality because the process of design and selection require choices to be made. Such choices are value laden and, therefore, not neutral and neither is the system that results from those choices.

Boland (1987, p. 376) writes that "designing an information system is a moral problem because it puts one party, the system designer, in the position of imposing an order on the world of another." It was found that sometimes design priorities are not reflected by the system to users in ways that were intended by information providers. Such mismatches between instantiation and intent are the result of conflicting values. Perhaps the design of an information system is also a problem of structuring values and priorities in a manner that is consistent within structures of institutional priorities as well as reflective of an order that is understandable to users. Ideology needs to be reflected in the pragmatics of system operation because discrepancies can send conflicting messages to users, limiting the use of the system.

REFERENCES

Banbury, J. (1987). Towards a framework for systems analysis practice. In: R. J. Boland & R. A. Hirschheim (Eds), *Critical issues in information systems research* (pp. 79–95). New York: John Wiley & Sons.

Bazillion, R. J., & Braun, C. (1994). Academic library design: Building a "teaching instrument". *Computers in Libraries, 14*(2), 14–16.

Becker, F. D. (1973). Study of spatial markers. *Journal of Personality and Social Psychology, 26*(3), 439–445.

Becker, H. S., & McCall, M. M. (Eds) (1990). *Symbolic interaction and cultural studies.* Chicago: University of Chicago Press.

Belkin, N. J. (1980). Anomalous states of knowledge as a basis for information retrieval. *The Canadian Journal of Information Science, 5,* 133–143.

Belkin, N. J., & Vickery, A. (1985). *Interaction in information systems: A review of research from document retrieval to knowledge-based systems.* London: The British Library.

Berg, P. O., & Kreiner, K. (1990). Corporate architecture: Turning physical settings into symbolic resources. In: P. Gagliardi (Ed.), *Symbols and artifacts: Views of the corporate landscape* (pp. 41–68). New York: Aldine de Gruyter.

Blumer, H. (1969). *Symbolic interactionism: Perspective and method.* Berkeley, CA: University of California Press.

Bodker, S. (1991). *Through the Interface: A human activity approach to user interface design.* Hillsdale, NJ: Lawrence Erlbaum Associates.

Boland, R. J. (1987). The in-formation in information systems. In: R. J. Boland & R. A. Hirschheim (Eds), *Critical Issues in information systems research* (pp. 363–380). New York: John Wiley & Sons.

Boulding, K. E. (1961). *The image.* Ann Arbor: University of Michigan Press.

Borgman, C. L. (1996). Why are online catalogs still hard to use? *Journal of the American Society for Information Science, 47*(7), 493–503.

Brown, R. A. (1992). Students as partners in library design. *School Library Journal, February, 1992,* 31–34.

Canter, D. (1975). An introduction to environmental psychology. In: D. Canter & P. Stringer (Eds), *Environmental interaction: Psychological approaches to our physical surroundings.* New York: International Universities Press.

Chang, S. J., & Rice, R. E. (1992). Browsing: A multidimensional framework. In: M. E. Williams (Ed.), *Annual review of information science and technology, Vol. 28* (pp. 231–276). Medford, NJ: Learned Information, Inc.

Chatman, E. A. (1991). Life in a small world: Applicability of gratification theory to information seeking behavior. *Journal of the American Society for Information Science, 40*(5), 329–333.

Chatman, E. A. (1996). The impoverished life-world of outsiders. *Journal of the American Society for Information Science, 47*(3), 193–206.

Ciborra, C. U., & Lanzara, G. F. (1990). Designing dynamic artifacts: computer systems as formative contexts. In: P. Gagliardi (Ed.), *Symbols and artifacts: Views of the corporate landscape* (pp. 147–168). New York: Aldine de Gruyter.

Connor, E., & Patton, R. (1995). Partnering with architects or how do you get what you thought you wanted? *Colorado Libraries, Winter 1995,* 25–26.

Curry, A., & Henriquez, Z. (1998). Planning public libraries: The views of architects and librarians. *Library Administration & Management, 12*(2), 80–90.

Curry, A., & Schwaiger, U. (1999). The balance between anarchy & control: Planning library space for teenagers. *School Libraries in Canada, 19*(1), 9–12.

Dervin, B. (1980). Communication gaps and inequities: moving toward are conceptualization. In: B. Dervin & M. Voight (Eds), *Progresses in Communication Sciences, 2* (pp. 73–112). Norwood, NJ: Ablex.

Dervin, B. (1992). From the mind's eye of the user: The sensemaking qualitative-quantitative methodology. In: J. D. Glazier & R. R. Powell (Eds), *Qualitative research in information management* (pp. 61–84). Englewood, CA: Libraries Unlimited.

Dervin, B., & Nilan, M. (1986). Information needs & uses. In: M. E. Williams (Ed.), *Annual review of information science and technology, Vol. 21* (pp. 3–33). White Plains, NY: Knowledge Industry Publications.

Dewdney & Ross (1994). Flying a Light Aircraft: Reference service evaluation from a user's viewpoint. *Research Quarterly, 34*(2), *Winter 1994,* 217–230.

Dougherty, D., & Kunda, G. (1990). Photograph analysis: A method to capture organizational belief systems. In: P. Gagliardi (Ed.), *Symbols and artifacts: Views of the corporate landscape* (pp. 185–206). New York: Aldine de Gruyter.

Eaton, G. (1991). Wayfinding in the library: Book searches and route uncertainty. *Research Quarterly, Summer 1991,* 519–527.

Gagliardi, P. (1992a). *Symbols and artifacts: Views of the corporate landscape.* New York: Aldine de Gruyter.

Gagliardi, P. (1992b). Artifacts as pathways and remains of organizational life. In: P. Gagliardi (Ed.), *Symbols and artifacts: Views of the corporate landscape* (pp. 5–38). New York: Aldine de Gruyter.

Geertz, C. (1973). *The Interpretation of cultures.* New York: Basic Books.

Georgia Librarian. (1993). From the architects point of view. *The Georgia Librarian (Winter 1993),* 98–103.

Glaser, B., & Strauss, A. (1967). *The discovery of grounded theory: Strategies for qualitative research.* Chicago: Aldine.

Graham, C. (1998). Libraries in history. *The Architectural Review, 203*(1216), 72–75.

Hall, E. T. (1976). The anthropology of space: An organizing model. In: H. M. Proshansky, W. H. Ittelson & L. G. Rivli (Eds), *Environmental psychology: People and their physical settings,* (2nd ed) (pp. 158–170). New York: Holt, Rinehart & Winston.

Havard-Williams, P., & Jengo, J. E. (1987). Library design and planning in developing countries. *Libra, 27*(2), 160–180.

Jackson, J. B. (1984). *Discovering the vernacular landscape.* New Haven, CT: Yale University Press.

Jones, D. J. (1993). Staying smart: Challenges of library design in the 1990s. *The Australian Library Journal (August 1993),* 214–227.

Konar, E., Sunderstrom, E., Brady, C., Mandel, D., & Rice, R. W. (1982). Status demarcation in the office. *Environment and Behavior, 14*(5), 561–580.

Kuhlthau, C. C. (1991). Inside the search process: Information seeking from the user's perspective. *Journal of the American Society for Information Science, 42*(5), 361–371.

Larsen, J., & Schultz, M. (1990). Artifacts in a bureaucratic monastery. In: P. Gagliardi (Ed.), *Symbols and artifacts: Views of the corporate landscape* (pp. 281–302). New York: Aldine de Gruyter.

Line, M. B. (1998). Designing libraries round human beings. *ASLIB Proceedings, 50*(8), 221–229.

Lushington, N. (1976). Some random notes on functional design. *American Libraries, January 1976*, 92–96.

Lushington, N. (1993). Order and freedom in public library design. *The Unabashed Librarian, 88*, 15–17.

Lyytinen, K. (1987). A taxonomic perspective of information systems development: Theoretical constructs and recommendations. In: R. J. Boland & R. A. Hirschheim (Eds), *Critical Issues in information systems research* (pp. 3–41). New York: John Wiley & Sons.

Martin, J. (1992). Planning a library: An interview with architect Hugh Hardy. *Wilson Library Bulletin, May 1992*, 38–40.

Morgan, G. (1986). *Images of organization.* Newbury Park: Sage Publications.

Parker Pearson, M., & Richards, C. (1994a). Ordering the world: perceptions of architecture, space and time. In: M. Parker Pearson & C. Richards (Eds), *Architecture and order: Approaches to social space* (pp. 1–37). NewYork: Routledge.

Parker Pearson, M., & Richards, C. (1994b). Ordering the world: perceptions of architecture, space and time. In: M. Parker Pearson & C. Richards (Eds), *Architecture and order: Approaches to social space* (pp. 1–37). New York: Routledge.

Parker Pearson, M., & Richards, C. (1994c). *Architecture and order: Approaches to social space.* New York: Routledge.

Raspa, R. (1990). The C.E.O. as corporate myth-maker: Negotiating the boundaries of work and play at Domino's Pizza company. In: P. Gagliardi (Ed.), *Symbols and artifacts: Views of the corporate landscape* (pp. 273–302). New York: Aldine de Gruyter.

Rizzo, J. (1992). Ten ways to look at a library. *American Libraries, 23*(4), 322–327.

Rockwell, E. (1989). The seven deadly sins of architects; gluttony and lust aren't on the list – but ignorance and myopia in library design are. *American Libraries, 20*(4), 307–310.

Rokeach, M. (1970). *Understanding human values.* New York: Free Press.

Rophlf, R. H. (1986). Library design: What not to do. Successful library building programs avoid these common pitfalls. *American Libraries, 17*(4), 100–107.

Rosen, M., Orlikowski, W. J., & Schmahman, K. (1990). Building buildings and living lives: A critique of bureaucracy, ideology and concrete artifacts. In: P. Gagliardi (Ed.), *Symbols and artifacts: Views of the corporate landscape* (pp. 69–84). New York: Aldine de Gruyter.

Sassoon, J. (1990). Colors, artifacts, and ideologies. In: P. Gagliardi (Ed.), *Symbols and artifacts: Views of the corporate landscape* (pp. 169–184). New York: Aldine de Gruyter.

Schein, E. H. (1984). Coming to a new awareness of organizational culture. *Sloan Management Review, Winter 1984*, 3–16.

Scholz, C. (1990). The symbolic value of computerized information systems. In: P. Gagliardi (Ed.), *Symbols and artifacts: Views of the corporate landscape* (pp. 233–254). New York: Aldine de Gruyter.

Shibutani, T. (1955). Reference groups as perspectives. *American Journal of Sociology, 60*, 562–569.

Shibutani, T. (1986). *Social processes: An introduction to sociology.* Berkeley, CA: University of California Press.

Sommer, R. (1969a). Studies in personal space. *Sociometry, 22*, 247–260.

Sommer, R. (1969b). *Personal space: The behavioral basis of design.* Englewood Cliffs, New Jersey: Prentice-Hall.

Sutton, R. K. (1996). New world forces libraries to adapt. *School Planning and Management, 35*(6), 1–4.

Taylor, R. S. (1986). *Value-added processes in information systems.* Norwood, NJ: Ablex.

Thomas, N. P. (1996). *Reading libraries: An interpretive study of discursive practices in library architecture and the interactional construction of personal identity.* Rutgers: The State University of New Jersey, School of Communication, Information and Library Studies, New Brunswick, New Jersey.

Turner, J. A. (1987a). Understanding the elements of system design. In: R. J. Boland & R. A. Hirschheim (Eds), *Critical issues in information systems research* (pp. 97–111). New York: John Wiley & Sons.

Turner, J. A. (1987b). Understanding elements of system design. In: R. J. Boland & R. A. Hirschheim (Eds), *Critical issues in information systems research* (pp. 97–112). New York: John Wiley & Sons.

Underhill, P. (1999). *Why we buy: The science of shopping.* New York: Simon & Schuster.

Weick, K. E. (1991). *Sensemaking in organizations.* Thousand Oaks, California: Sage Publications.

Williams, R. M. (1979). Change and stability in values and value systems: A sociological perspective. In: M. Rokeach (Ed.), *Understanding human values: Individual and societal* (pp. 15–70). New York: The Free Press.

Winograd, T., & Flores, F. (1986). *Understanding computers and cognition: A new foundation for design.* Reading, MA: Addison-Wesley.

Wolcott, H. F. (1995). *The art of fieldwork.* Walnut Creek, CA: Alta Mira Press.

Zerubavel, E. (1991). *The fine line: Making distinctions in everyday life.* New York: Free Press.

Zerubavel, E. (1997). *Social Mindscapes: An invitation to cognitive sociology.* Cambridge, MA: Harvard University Press.

APPENDIX. CONSOLIDATED LIST OF TABLES FROM SECTION "EXAMINING THE ARTIFACT"

Table 5.1. Values of General Architectural Layout.

Values – Priorities	Instantiation
Library	Logo on building distinguishes library from the other buildings
Reading books	Logo
Convenience	Book drops, garbage cans, ashtrays
Order; rules	Allocation of parking spaces
Convenience	Allocation of parking spaces
Community	"Ordinary" façade that fits into the landscape
Boundaries territoriality	Rectangular layout (distinguishing tasks, functions, and access)

Table 5.2.   Values in the Entranceway (Transitional Space).

Values – Priorities	Instantiation
Reading	Banners and "read posters"
Community	Exhibits, letters, announcement of events
Children	Banner (best give to give children)
Convenience	Shopping baskets
Culture	Art exhibits of local artists, schoolchildren
Security	Presence of security gate, theft warnings, security guard during certain hours
Library membership	Solicitation of library cards, friends of the library, etc.
Service	Signage, general presentation of artifacts in entranceway.
Rules	Presence of literature that establishes user protocol
Library	Patron praise letters, etc.
Security	Presence of security
Information	Presence of a lot of information in this area

Table 5.3.   Values in Interior Design.

Values – Priorities	Instantiation
Organization	Effort made to label all spaces
Order (social/ territorial)	Using furniture and objects to mark private versus public territories
Circulation	Prominent location of circulation desk in exit direction
Marketing use	Placement of stacks (slanted, Did you miss?) in prominent areas
Territoriality	Use of doors, walls, furniture to keep traffic in designated locations
Use	Large signs defining general areas
Security	User access restricted from areas containing expensive items (e.g. media services and circulation desk areas)

Table 5.3. (*Continued*)

Values – Priorities	Instantiation
Comfort	Cushioned chairs in reading areas
Use of resources convenience	Tables and chairs as designated work areas baskets, return baskets
Efficiency	Maximizing seating in small areas by arranging tables in most efficient way
Children	Colorful and child friendly design of children's section
Interaction	Placement of chairs in relation to each other
Achievement	Display of artwork
Creativity	
Users	
Containment of noise	Effort to isolate noisy areas (restrooms, phones, etc.)
Order	Order of objects more important than aesthetics (e.g. color scheme, etc)
	Encouraging users to place items in return baskets rather than on shelves

Table 5.4. Values in Visual Artifacts.

Values – Priorities	Instantiation
Book	Logo
Open mindedness	Logo
Learning	Logo
Ideas	Logo
Culture	Logo
Order	Signage that defines space – user type, function, subject, type of material; community function
Order	Signs located by objects in library that make an effort to identify the object
Use, equity in	Limiting use of popular items
	Establishing fines based on what is perceived to be of greater value to the public

Table 5.4.   (*Continued*)

Values – Priorities	Instantiation
Public order	Signs reinforcing adherence to rules e.g. "No Smoking," "Quiet"
Users	"Ask for a cozy blanket" if user feels chilly
Comfort	
Convenience	
Rules procedures	Signs posted at most work stations
Marketing	Ranging from New York Times best sellers list to
Promotion	advertisement of newspaper holdings of library
Use	
Reading	Read posters
Popular culture	Celebrity images promoting libraries and reading
Community	Posting community events
Information	Bulletin boards with issues that are perceived to be of value (e.g. men's health)
Service	Tax returns; tax services; postage stamps
Library promotion	Patron praise; posters showing the importance of librarians
User orientation	General value

Table 5.5.   Values in the "Front-Line".

Values – Priorities	Instantiation
Users	Foreground location of signs; information kiosk, catalog
Marketing	"Did you miss?"
Convenience	
Circulation	
Use	
Users special needs	Foreground presentation of large print books, ESL collection; etc.

Table 5.5. (*Continued*)

Values – Priorities	Instantiation
Promotion Marketing Circulation	Placement of popular reading materials in the front area
Users special needs	"Slanted" book section

Table 5.6. Values in the Central Reading Area.

Values – Priorities	Instantiation
Popular collections Users order	Placement of collection in central area of library Categories of classification (e.g. horror, science fiction, etc.)
Circulation/use	Prominence of popular collection

Table 5.7. Values in Organization of Media Services.

Values – Priorities	Instantiation
Use	"Familiar" ordering of items, similar to music stores
Order Use User, familiarity	Organization by item type
Simplicity	Alphabetical organization
Use, ease	Presentation of popular subject headings as classification structure
Circulation Marketing	Did you miss popular items?
Security	Keeping items behind the media services counter
Access	Making costly items available for a reasonable fee

Table 5.8. Values in Intellectual Organization of Youth Services Area.

Values – Priorities	Instantiation
Users	Diverse display/organization of items; using familiar symbols (e.g. Peanuts posters, etc.)
Reading	Colorful and whimsical displays, objects, signs
Learning	
Fun	
Familiarity	
Simplicity in organization	Color coding of spines; familiarity with objects
Utility	Integration of items into the work areas, maximizing displays
Education	Explicit effort made to educate users regarding classification system, item use, etc.
Control	Self contained environment; all amenities within designated space
Protection of users	
Users	Giving children a sense of "ownership" and belonging in the environment
Children	Effort in design/organization

Table 5.9. Values in the Reference Area.

Values – Priorities	Instantiation
Information	Extensive collection; large number of miscellaneous resources and papers containing various types of information posted upon bulleting boards, etc.
Interaction	Primary place in library where users get direct access to providers
Service	Various products and services available
In house use	Mostly non circulating collection
Assistance/service	Provides a place where users can present their information requirements
Librarian as authority	Some information here can only be accessed via librarian
Users	Face to face contact

Table 5.10. Values Adopted from External Sources (ALA).

Values – Priorities	Instantiation
Freedom (s): speech, religion, press, right to assemble, petition for grievances	First amendment
Due process	Fourteenth amendment
Books for all No exclusion based on origin, background, views of creator Materials should present all points of view Materials should not be removed because of partisan disapproval Libraries should challenge censorship Libraries should support freedom of expression and ideas Access should not be denied because of origin, age, background or views Exhibit spaces should be equitably available (regardless of beliefs or affiliations)	Library bill of rights
Libraries should be against censorship Libraries should provide broadest access to materials Liberty of circulation ensures freedom of expression Protect user confidentiality Materials should represent diverse views Selection≠approval Producers of materials should not be prejudged Libraries should contest public's freedom to view	Freedom to view statement
Should not predispose attitudes towards materials by affixing prejudicial labels	Statement on labeling

Table 5.10.   (*Continued*)

Values – Priorities	Instantiation
Opposition to criteria for judgment (of objectionable publications)	
Ratings of private agencies should not be enforced	
Does not condone censorship	Freedom to read
People should decided what they should read, not censors	statement

Table 5.11.   Change of Values with respect to Change in Image.

	Old Mission Statement	Old Image/ Values Presented	New Mission Statement	New Image/Values Presented
Who we are	Identity/role as proper noun (library)	Static institution "Traditional" norms; beliefs	Identity/role as information center	Dynamic Environment "Modern"
What we do	Provide	"Nurturing" environment	Deliver	Interactive "Productive environment"
Product	Materials and services	Both (materials and services) are given equal weight	Service orientation	Emphasis on providing "timely" and "highest level" of service High value on service
Purpose	Satisfy "to gratify fully the wants…"	Stimulus/ response relationship	Promote "to forward; to advance; to contribute to growth…"	Cultivation of ongoing relationship To participate in a process

Table 5.11. (*Continued*)

	Old Mission Statement	Old Image/ Values Presented	New Mission Statement	New Image/Values Presented
What users require	Functional view of what users require: Education Recreation Culture	Material Orientation	Ideological-conceptual view of user wants	Ideological orientation toward what users require: Literacy Lifelong learning Personal fulfillment Intellectual freedom
Users	Users geographically bounded	Residents of Town X given priority	Users "institutionally" bounded	Library users given priority

Table 5.12. Values in the Mission Statement.

Values – Priorities	Instantiation
Timely service Literacy Lifelong learning	Definition of service Definition of objectives
Personal fulfillment Intellectual freedom	Definition of rights

Table 5.13. Values of Reference Department as set forth by Library X.

Values – Priorities	Instantiation
Accuracy Efficiency Courtesy	Provision of information

Table 5.13.   (*Continued*)

Values – Priorities	Instantiation
Access Optimal use	Defining space
Needs, current/anticipated Uses, current/prospective	Selection, acquisition, organization
Professional cooperation	Interlibrary cooperation Utilization of external resources

Table 5.14.   General Guidelines for Reference.

Values – Priorities	Instantiation
Service	Staffing
Service	Attitude: respect & willingness to assist
Interaction (in person) Users	Query prioritization
Public order	Managing emergencies & noise

Table 5.15.   Requests for Materials.

Values – Priorities	Instantiation
Privacy	Not able to reveal borrower identity

Service	Finding materials in collection as
	    well as outside of the library's
	    collection

Security	Placing certain items from collection
Property	into secure space

Table 5.16. Requests for Information.

Values – Priorities	Instantiation
Facts Resource as authority	Focus on short/factual answers Provision of guidance in location of information sources Defer to resource authority for queries requiring long responses

Table 5.17. Search Parameters.

Values – Priorities	Instantiation
Equity Time Efficiency	Time: related to perception of user need and level of expertise
Objectivity Source authority	Appraisals: connect user with source; cannot give appraisals
Objectivity Source orientation Source is authority	Librarian cannot recommend sources for purchase; refers users to printed sources
Objectivity Source is authority	Medical questions: only short factual responses; cannot provide interpretations or opinions
Impartiality	Legal questions: locate specific citations, show how resources are used; cannot give advice or interpret
Neutrality	Genealogical questions: locate sources; assist in use of collection; cannot engage in research
"Facts" not details	Trivia and contest questions: provide factual information
Intermediary role	Translations: librarian as intermediary, a link to resource (referral)

Table 5.17.   (*Continued*)

Values – Priorities	Instantiation
Objectivity Neutrality, etc.	Student assignments: treated like any other request unless special requests made
Sources as authority	Reader's advisory: can recommend based on personal knowledge; can also refer to guides and sources

Table 5.18.   Telephone Reference Search Parameters.

Values – Priorities	Instantiation
Equity Short inquiries Time	Time limit: 5-min limit
Service Equity	Reserves; 3 per caller
Facts	Contest, Lottery and Race results
Source as authority Objectivity	Medical questions: Only short definitions or descriptions provided
Time	Verbatim quotes
Time Objectivity	Legal questions: Reading specific short citations/ definitions
Quantity Time (implied)	Street address directory: 3 per caller
Print source Time	Consumer product recommendations: printed source only; if source is lengthy, user must come to library
Objectivity Time	School Assignments: 3 factual answers per student Long passages cannot be read

Table 5.19. Ready Reference Searches.

Values – Priorities	Instantiation
Time Service	Complete searches within one day
Levels of use	Use of service, e.g.: Free for member
Experience	Fee based for outsider Search performance
Cost reduction	Cost: If it is "quick" then it is free; if not, it becomes a fee based service

Table 5.20. Database Searching: Fee-based Searches.

Values – Priorities	Instantiation
Time	Scope of service: priority to users from specified service area
Membership	Searches cannot exceed 1 hour
Use by location	Population served: use limited by geographic boundaries
Quality of service Expertise of searcher Time Money	Searchers: effort to provide most experienced person to perform the task to save time and money (both parameters set by information providers)
Cost reduction	Cost: user pays; Half of estimated fee must be left for deposit Payment is due regardless of search success
Protection monetary interests	Payment: cash; cashier's check; certified check Over $25 no cash accepted

Table 5.21.   Conditions for Loans of Reference Materials.

Values – Priorities	Instantiation
Security Protection of resources Equity in use	Eligibility: must have particular user status and must leave library cards as security, except for Township employees who only need give department name and phone number
Control	Number of items to be loaned: 1. Book 2. State documents 3. Mail order catalogs quantity Limitation
Control	Loan periods: users can borrow items for one week
Control	Renewal of loans: an additional week may be granted
Control Financial Protection of resources	Fines: fines are per diem and privileges are revoked if fines exceed $5 and users do not pay

Table 5.22.   Other Reference Services.

Values – Priorities	Instantiation
Education	Reference bulletin boards
Informing users	No commercial ads Must be approved by staff Material should be "educational, cultural, and recreational"
Limiting scope Information Education	Information stands and displays No commercial ads Contain only copies of "educational, cultural, and recreational activities" Occasional distribution of political brochures

Table 5.22. (*Continued*)

Values – Priorities	Instantiation
Community	Community Calendar (dissemination of information for particular social events)
Users Use Education	Tours: Effort to orient users to environment
Education	Formal instruction
Service	Photocopiers: Instruct users on use
Service Environmental regulation	Public typewriters: rules created for use (first come, first serve); no personal equipment allowed in building
Service	Voter registration
Service	Reference by correspondence
Service	Paging of Patrons
Security	Public use of library phones
Service	Reserve collection for school assignments (only students in Township X schools)
Special services	Handicapped users
Service – fee-based	Photocopy, fax, mailing

Table 5.23. Service to Other Libraries.

Values – Priorities	Instantiation
Professional cooperation	Telephone reference and reference referral: responsibility to regional reference contract
Maximizing resources Professional cooperation Resource sharing	Interlibrary loan: loan only if books on shelf and not circulating

Table 5.23.   (*Continued*)

Values – Priorities	Instantiation
Maximizing use	Phone requests for ILL: user must have proper documentation
Service	Photocopy requests: 20 pages no charge 15 cents per page extra

Table 5.24.   Criteria for Reference Collection.

Values – Priorities	Instantiation
Utility Currency Quality Affordability Relevance: Relation to existing collection	Criteria for development Public recommendation encouraged
Utility	Classification
Utility Manageability	Size and growth of collection – direct relationship to what is considered most
User needs	Evaluation

Table 5.25.   General Policy of Circulation Process.

Values – Priorities	Instantiation
Use Circulation Access	Vision
Privacy Confidentiality Collection of materials	Goal

Table 5.26. Library Cards.

Values – Priorities	Instantiation
Access	Distribution: residents, township X – privileges without cost
Monetary measure of service	Distribution: non-residents (hierarchy of use); different services for different values
Control	Card replacement: fee required One card per use
Regulated utility	User type: some cards can be shared some cannot

Table 5.27. Notifications and Restrictions.

Values – Priorities	Instantiation
Regulation Control	Rule compliance
Control Protection property	Lost cards: user liability until notification
Rule conformity	Fines: immediate payment, if not, revocation of privileges
Rule conformity	Nonpayment for services: if not, privileges revoked
Rule conformity	Privilege restoration: must settle accounts
Rule conformity Control	Revocation of family privileges: if fines exceed specified amount, family privileges are suspended

Table 5.28.   Criteria for Selection.

Values – Priorities	Instantiation
Neutrality Objectivity	Selection process: Non-partisan Non-doctrinal Non-judgmental
Public use (circulation)	Standard for selection: assumptions about what is of interest to the public
Merit Quality Excellence Significance Personal interests Purposes of users Needs	Utility: effort to determine what is useful in relation to users
Objectivity (in selection) Assessment of quality	Critical reviews: makes connection between public interest and external critical reviews
Suitability to use (Use) Durability	Physical format
Replacement Augmentation Relevance Relativity	Relationship to extant collection
Timeliness	Timeliness: selection made when criteria are not available
Objectivity Non discriminatory	Reputation and status of author: effort to establish non partisan collection
Users (non discriminatory)	Age level: age restrictions not made
Cost effectiveness Professional cooperation	Availability in other libraries: borrowing when possible from other libraries

Table 5.29. Collection Development and Maintenance Criteria.

Values – Priorities	Instantiation
Use Demand	Retention: focus on what people request/ borrow
Use Demand	Duplication
Timeliness Quality Style Accuracy	Continual improvement
Use	Reconsideration: a forum for users to express concern about some aspect of the library's holdings

Table 5.30. Library Exhibit Policy.

Values – Priorities	Instantiation
Variety Visual experience Safety	Exhibits

Table 5.31. Values Reflected in the Library User Bill of Rights.

Values – Priorities	Instantiation
Use, defining of	What users should do: research, homework, prepare reports, browse, use computers, think, daydream or read; suggest new materials
User equality Non discrimination	Children: treated with same courtesy as adults

Table 5.31. (*Continued*)

Values – Priorities	Instantiation
Defining expectation	What users should expect of library:
Service; defining	Purchase current best sellers and popular
Popular culture	materials (according to selection policy and
Service	budget)
Comfort	Borrow materials
Convenience	Help
Efficiency	Timely resolution of complaints and problems
	Cleanliness
	Safety
	Courteous treatment
	Efficient service

Table 5.32. Library X Code of Conduct.

Values – Priorities	Instantiation
Safety	Creating environment: to create an
Protection of library	environment that will promote "legitimate"
goals	library business
Space	Protection of users, staff, property
Social order	
Control	
Tolerance	Users should accept each other
Space	Obstruction of passage and entrance ways
Control	
Security	
Control	Dress/person:
Space	Proper dress (footwear/shirts) required
Courtesy	Proper hygiene
Safety	No weapons (real or play)
Law	
Protection of property	No eating, smoking, drinking; soliciting
Order	

Table 5.32. (*Continued*)

Values – Priorities	Instantiation
Quiet	No noisy behavior
Security Public order Safety	No harassment (sexual, physical, verbal, assault)
Public rights Privacy	No formal public interactions (such as research surveys)
Children Safety	Children cannot be left unattended
Law Safety Security	Any illegal acts forbidden

Table 5.33. Introduction to User Brochure.

Values – Priorities	Instantiation
Answers to any question To learn about any subject	What users can expect
Popular appeal Marketing	What users can borrow
Variety	What users can engage in: Book discussions Foreign film showings English improvement skills Accompany children to story time; craft or music program
Social Community Interaction	Library X positioned as meeting place Library as "Main Street"

Table 5.33. (*Continued*)

Values – Priorities	Instantiation
Welcoming Friendly Expert	Providers
Getting what you seek	Information

Table 5.34. Collection and Service Accessibility.

Values – Priorities	Instantiation
Access	Make collection and service more accessible
Technology	Expand hours
Increase resources	Increase number of books that can be borrowed
Growth	Provide electronic directory of services Provide access to electronic sources
Outreach	Increase awareness of library resources and services
Diversity	Focus on meeting room users and "special populations"
Increase use	Increase percentage of residents who are registered borrowers Increase number of patrons using library Increase circulation Increase use of reference and information services Extension of library services into community Increase attendance of children and young adults
Speed Efficiency Convenience	Improve checkout ease and efficiency and, general handling of materials Institute express checkout Self service stations Integrate technology

Table 5.34. (*Continued*)

Values – Priorities	Instantiation
Access Service Accuracy Efficiency	Provide accurate and efficient reference and information services Increase access through print and electronic resources
Efficiency	Deliver information in person, phone, fax or other electronic means
Education	Expand services to children and young adults Provide homework assistance Provide regularly scheduled programs
Communication Informing community	Provide Community news and information Community bulletin board; expand informational programming; provide video production support to municipal departments
Communication	Increase information about community and local activities and resources
Convenience Service	Provide ancillary services to the public e.g. Notary public at all hours of operation

Table 5.35. Collections and Resources.

Values	Instantiation
Needs Diversity Circulation Utility	Develop collections to meet public's diverse and ever-changing needs Increase size Increase money spent Develop collections in new formats (anticipating public needs) Develop collection in languages other than English (foreign language)

Table 5.36. Facilities.

Values – Priorities	Instantiation
Space	Provide a library building that will fulfill its mission and plan Feasibility of current building Determine suitable sites Secure consultant Develop public support
Space Territoriality Design Function Use	Provide adequate facilities for individual use Increase seating, table space, study carrels Improve quiet study Increase equipment (special considerations; equipment; comfort)
Increase space Comfort, convenience Users (work style)	Provide adequate facilities for group use Important to create physical environments that will accommodate group use
Comfort Convenience	Provide adequate space for basic library collections and services Increase space Drive up bookdrops
Convenience Patron comfort Space	Provide space for ancillary library services Special room for equipment – copy, fax, chance machines; telephones Snack area – convenience
Improvement of workflow (productivity) Functionality Staff satisfaction	Provide adequate work space for the staff to perform the functions required by the services provided Media services: provide larger circulation area and staffed reference function Periodicals circulation station Video studio Conference room for the board Staff room Work space for graphic artist, maintenance, custodial, and storage functions

Table 5.36. *(Continued)*

Values – Priorities	Instantiation
Communication	Provide optimal physical access to the library and its resources
Assistance	Directional signage
Improvement	Shelving non fiction in sequential order
Access	Shelving materials at a reasonable height
Convenience	Reorganize young adult collection
Outreach	Increase parking
	Encourage initiation of community bus or van service

Table 5.37. Staff.

Values – Priorities	Instantiation
Service	Provide adequate staff:
Security	Provide staff to circulate through the collection
Education	Make notaries available
	Provide a security monitor from mid-afternoon until closing on weekdays and all day on weekend days
	Provide a training officer to coordinate staff training and orientation, volunteer staff, conference attendance, and continuing education

Table 5.38. Administrative and Directional.

Values – Priorities	Instantiation
Staff	Develop staff creativity, skills, and commitment; maintain good morale
Service	
Communication	Institute interdepartmental cooperation and communication
	Provide in-house staff development activity

Table 5.38.   (*Continued*)

Values – Priorities	Instantiation
Interlibrary cooperation Leadership Intercommunity cooperation	Maintain and enhance relationships with other libraries at all levels and assume a leadership role in planning cooperation and innovation; maintain relationships with township officials; local agencies, schools; volunteer program; friends of the library and organizations
Timeliness Education	Maintain knowledge of changing political, social, economic conditions
Finance	Secure adequate funding to meet current and future needs
Communication	Broaden funding base for local station by developing business sources

MARKETING: A NEW WAY OF DOING BUSINESS IN ACADEMIC LIBRARIES

Melissa Cox Norris

INTRODUCTION

Why does the idea of marketing generate such negative reactions from many in the academic library world? Research on the word "marketing" in the Oxford English Dictionary (OED) reveals that usage of the term can be traced back to 1561 when it meant simply "to buy or sell" (Oxford English Dictionary, 2004, http://dictionary.oed.com/). As early as 1884, the meaning began to change to "bringing or sending (a commodity) to market," which encompasses not just the selling of a product, but the "systematic study of all the factors involved in marketing a product" (Oxford English Dictionary, 2004, http://dictionary.oed.com/). Is it the idea of "selling" that offends so many in libraries? Or do some dislike the suggestion of libraries having "products" much as companies do?

Libraries, especially those in academe, hesitate to compare themselves to the corporate world. Traditionally, college and university libraries have left marketing to their public-library counterparts. Why is it viewed as acceptable for public libraries to market and not for academic libraries? Perhaps, it is the perception that public libraries have less well-defined user populations than do academic libraries, which see students and faculty as built-in audiences needing their services and resources. Or worse, it may be a case of

Advances in Library Administration and Organization
Advances in Library Administration and Organization, Volume 22, 275–295
Copyright © 2005 by Elsevier Ltd.
ISSN: 0732-0671/doi:10.1016/S0732-0671(05)22006-0

snobbery that leads some to believe that marketing is an endeavor not worthy of those in higher education.

Academic libraries must begin to embrace and integrate marketing into the way they do business. They can no longer afford the "build it and they will come" philosophy that has long prevailed. With the Internet and popular search engines such as Google^{TM} and Yahoo!$^{®}$, libraries are facing competition like never before. Today's college students, having grown up with computers, are experts at using technology and are more comfortable gathering their own research. As a result, they increasingly do not see libraries as necessary gateways to information. To stay relevant and successful in today's environment, academic libraries must embrace marketing to develop and package the products and services users want and to promote them in a way that will both attract users and convince them to use and value the library. Marketing not only increases the use of the library, it also can help to address certain challenges facing the library. Along with competition, libraries are facing an economic crisis with government funding of higher education steadily decreasing. Marketing will help libraries face challenges and beat competition as it provides the means to develop and package the services users want and to communicate the worth and importance of the library to users and the public-at-large (Weingand, 1999, pp. 2–3).

WHAT IS MARKETING?

Marketing is no longer viewed as merely the selling of a product, but more "an approach to product design that reflects the identified needs of the target populations" (Weingand, 1999, p. 2). Marketing involves the process of creating products that consumers want. In terms of libraries, marketing can be defined as the process of planning, promoting, and advertising library services and resources created and packaged to fit users' needs and expectations. In essence, marketing gives libraries the tools to determine what services users want, and then to develop, package, and promote those services and resources in a way that will entice users to use the library effectively.

WHY MARKET?

Obvious Reasons to Market

An obvious reason to market is to create more informed users. Judging by gate counts from many libraries, the need is not necessarily to bring more people into the library, but rather to inform users better on how to use the library once they are there. Although some libraries are experiencing high visitation, declining circulation statistics from many libraries may indicate that while users are coming to the library, they are not necessarily using the resources and collections. Therefore, another obvious reason to market is to increase the use of resources, collections, and services – both new services introduced as well as existing resources. Libraries and their services and resources are constantly changing. Marketing helps users stay informed and aware. A final obvious reason to market is to bring non-users into the library – physically and virtually. Libraries should find non-users and target marketing efforts to them, whether the goal is to encourage them to visit the library or to use the myriad of available online resources.

Less-Obvious Reasons to Market

Along with obvious reasons to market are some less-obvious ones. First, it is imperative that the library gains the support of university administration. It is not news that many libraries are facing economic hardships. Marketing the library to those who make funding and staffing decisions is essential. Through marketing, the library can inform university administration just how key the library is to the success of the university. Not only do libraries support the academic needs of students, they are also key factors in the research endeavors of faculty – faculty who bring important research dollars into the university. A strong library helps attract high quality faculty.

In addition to marketing to university administration, libraries should strive to gain the support of local and state government officials. Government officials, too, need to know just how important the library is to the academic and financial strength of the university and the general well-being of the community. Another important marketing audience is library donors. Libraries can no longer rely on the government for funding, and donors bring key financial support to libraries. They need to know both the strengths and the needs of libraries.

The final less-obvious reason to market is to create a more informed and satisfied staff. A well-informed staff that has pride in the library will not only help to market the library, but will also be a more productive staff. It is essential that staff know about the services, resources, and accomplishments of the library as they are one of the key marketers of the library and should be as informed as possible.

Marketing to Challenges

Another important reason to market libraries is to address challenges – both the known challenges such as rising competition, and those unknown crises that can occur such as a natural disaster or controversy. The more the public, university administration, and other leaders know about the library before a challenge, the more they can support it during a challenge.

A current example of marketing to address challenges is competition. While the Internet creates many possibilities for research and plays a large role in a library's daily work, it also is one of the main competitors libraries face. Many students do their primary research on the Internet and much of that research is poorly done with faulty and inferior resources. Internet research can also contribute to the rise in plagiarism – both intentional and unknowing. Libraries should play a lead role in teaching users how to use the Internet effectively as a research aid. Libraries should instruct users how to evaluate resources found on the Web, how to avoid plagiarizing, and how to combine the use of these resources with other more traditional forms of research found in the library. However, before the library can guide users in the proper way to use the Internet for research, they must get users' attention away from the Web and into the library. Libraries must market their importance and the role they play in students' academic success. As Stephen Abram and Judy Luther point out in their article "Born with the Chip," "we must focus on helping them [students] develop the ability to evaluate sources of information effectively to ensure that they determine the quality of information upon which they will base life decisions" (Abram & Luther, 2004, p. 34).

Libraries are Already Marketing, so they Might as well do it Right

Believe it or not, libraries market on a daily basis. Everyday, libraries send messages to users, some positive, some negative. Being aware of everyday marketing activities can assist libraries in improving the messages they send to audiences. The following are examples of daily activities that market the library.

First, the library staff serves as key marketers of the library. Daily interaction at service desks between library staff and users plays a vital role in marketing the library. In addition to providing information about services and resources (thus, promoting them), library staff presents an image of the library as being knowledgeable and helpful and adding value to the research process. Along with interacting with users, library staff members market the library through work with colleagues both within and outside the university. The way in which they represent the library, both in actions and specific comments, will have an impact on how colleagues form opinions and gather information about the library. Getting involved in campus activities provides an effective vehicle for marketing. Some library staff members market their library by serving on faculty committees, curriculum boards, and other academic programs, or through social interaction with faculty colleagues.

Library staff members who conduct library instruction are also key marketers of the library. When librarians teach users how to use a service or resource, they are in essence promoting that service and the library. Library instruction is positive promotion of the library in that it creates an image of the library staff as being knowledgeable and helpful. To the extent possible, marketers should be involved in library instruction. They can provide promotional materials to have available at instruction sessions, as well as promote the library's instruction program so as to heighten awareness and increase attendance. Marketers should also be aware of what services and resources are being taught so that they can include these subjects in marketing materials.

Second, the various signs, both directional and informational, placed throughout the library market to users. Both their clarity and design portray an image of the library. Unfortunately, signs are often produced quickly with little thought to their design or tone, both of which create impressions and send messages. The conditions of signs also make an impression with library visitors. Signs should be clean, absent of dirt and graffiti, and not appear worn. Too often, signs are negative in tone telling users not to do something. When requesting that users not do something, word it in a positive way. Instead of saying, "No Eating, Drinking, or Smoking," the sign might say, "Please discard food and beverages before entering the library." The sign will have the same affect but seem less harsh and authoritative. In an effort to be helpful, libraries are often guilty of over signing, which can overwhelm library visitors and create an over-bearing tone. Signs should be kept to a minimum and take care that the language is clear, concise, and positive.

Third, a significant way libraries are already marketing is through their Web site. The Web is a major vehicle for marketing and should be treated as such. The library's site should contain informative as well as promotional information such as press releases, news and events pages, and images of the library or pictures taken of its collections. Space should also be devoted to the library's exhibits or other outreach activities. The look of the Web site markets an image of the library to the world. Often, the Web site is the first or only way some people visit the library; therefore, its design plays an important role in introducing the library and influencing opinions. The site should be attractive with an up-to-date look, and it should be refreshed regularly. It should follow information architecture, navigation, and accessibility standards, as well as be easy to use. It is also good practice for the library's Web site to resemble that of its college or university so that it is obvious to visitors that the two entities are part of the same organization. An example of an academic library that has incorporated marketing into their Web site is that of the Ritter Library at Baldwin–Wallace College (http://www.bw.edu/academics/libraries/). "News & Events" and "Library News" are key menu items on their site. Also, the photograph and the introductory paragraph about the library serve to both introduce visitors to the library and to portray a very welcoming image. Another library site that markets itself well is that of the Indiana University Libraries (http://www. libraries.iub.edu/). Here, they have an entire section called "About IUB Libraries" where general promotional information is included, as well as "Welcome Information" where visitors will find the libraries mission, a fact sheet, and how to contact the library.

Another key way to market the library on the Web is not through the library's site, but through that of its university. Studies show that the Web is the primary first resource many prospective students use when considering a university. Therefore, it is essential that there be a prominent link to the library's Web site from the university's homepage and that it appears as a main menu item. Also, if the university includes promotional items on their homepage such as photographs from around campus or highlights of university news, the library should be included. Send photographs of the library to the university's Webmaster. Make sure that those responsible for posting university news receive a copy of all library press releases. The University of Missouri Library offers a good example of a library that is well marketed on its university's homepage. The library is featured in the Web site's "Did You Know" segment that includes interesting and noteworthy facts about the university. The library's "Did You Know...about Mizzou's comic book section?" highlights a fun collection from the libraries' Special Collections division (http://www.missouri.edu/didyouknow/programs/comics.htm).

WHO TO MARKET TO?

Obvious Audiences

Central to the question of "why market?" is "who to market to?" Two of the obvious audiences are students and faculty. Both audiences, however, must be divided into sub groups in order to tailor marketing messages to the characteristics and unique wants and needs of each group. "Students" can be broken down into such sub groups as undergraduates, graduates, international students, non-traditional students, and distance-learners. "Faculty" can be further divided into: full-time, part-time, adjunct, humanities, sciences, and professional (law, medicine, business, etc.). How far a group is subdivided depends on both the size and complexity of the group. When marketing to faculty at larger universities with many departments and colleges, for example, the group "faculty" should be subdivided as much as possible in order to reach those various faculty members. By contrast, when marketing at a university with only a hundred or so faculty, those faculty members will have much in common with each other and interact regularly, and, therefore, may not need to be as subdivided as faculty members from a larger institution.

Less-Obvious Audiences

Following the less-obvious reasons to market are those less-obvious audiences to market to: the university administration, government officials, community leaders, donors (both actual and potential), and library staff. Another less-obvious audience to address, and one that may include people from all audience types, are opinion leaders. Opinion leaders are not necessarily defined by position or label, but rather are those around campus and the community who have a voice and to whom people respond. This may include the local radio personality, the editors of the city and campus newspapers, student leaders, even popular faculty and staff on campus. Opinion leaders permeate all organizations, including universities, and while they cannot necessarily be labeled, they can be found throughout every constituency group and should be sought out. Getting opinion leaders on the library's side can have lasting marketing benefits as they serve as positive ambassadors of the library. Having a third party of this sort who is not officially linked to the library, speaking positively on its behalf can often have more of an impact than promotional material will ever have.

It is important to note here the difference between "audience" and "users." While they may appear to be one and the same, users are those people who actually use the library. The audience reaches beyond users to encompass everyone the library sends messages to, including: users (current, potential, and future), as well as library staff members, university administration, government officials, opinion leaders, donors, and the general public.

Target Marketing

It is impossible to reach all audiences at the same time with the same message. Therefore, to market effectively, it is essential to do "target marketing," which means to tailor messages to particular groups. When targeting a message to one group, it is important not to alienate another. There are often vast cultural differences and varying wants and needs between audiences. For example, take the differences in preferences and ideas often found between undergraduate students and traditional donors. What might attract the attention of one group may alienate the other.

When doing target marketing to one audience, other audiences may hear and respond to the message, resulting in what can be termed "residual marketing." Examples of residual marketing occurring naturally are when the library sends a donor an invitation to an event and that donor then shows the invitation to a neighbor; or, when the library target markets a new resource to faculty members who, in turn, share the information with their students, thus spreading the library's message to a different audience. While these secondary viewers were not the intended target audience, they received the message through no effort of the library, thus resulting in residual marketing. While residual marketing can occur naturally, it should be viewed as a bonus, not a strategy.

Getting to Know You

In order to target market to the various library audiences, it is essential to know as much as possible about their wants and needs, likes and dislikes, and library usage patterns. The more the library knows its audience and users, the easier it is to create messages that will resonate with them. There are numerous ways through market research to gather information about the library's audiences. This data will indicate what services and resources are of value to users and how best to communicate to various audiences. Market research can either be "self-reported," where users say directly what they want or think, or "observational," where users are observed to note their preferences and work habits (Kirk, 2003, p. 30). Both methods have merit, and a combination of the two should be performed in order to gather the most complete information.

Self-Reported Market Research

An example of self-reported market research is surveying both current users and non- or future users (such as high school students). Both of these groups will provide vital information as to their wants and needs, which may vary greatly between and within user groups. When using surveys as market research, existing surveys performed for other purposes than gathering market data, such as LIBQual, can provide valuable information to aid in the marketing effort. Upon obtaining a survey, review it for information about the services the users said they most valued or wished the library had, or those services users were least satisfied with and why. This information will determine both the services users want, and those that need promoting. New surveys can be created with the sole purpose of gathering marketing information. Surveys can be in print or electronic form. They can be mailed or e-mailed to respondents, or put in pre-existing communication mediums such as a newsletter or Web site. There are free and subscription-based survey-creation tools such as Zoomerang (http://info.zoomerang.com/) and Survey Monkey (http://www.surveymonkey.com/) that provide the means to create and administer surveys and to analyze the data they collected.

Interviews are another valid means to collect market research. They can be administered either on the spot, via the telephone, or by leaving the library and visiting users and non-users on and off campus. Interviews can be formal, such as when a library representative pre-arranges a session with users to ask them about certain aspects of the library or its services. Informal interviews that occur naturally, such as when a librarian is assisting a user and takes the opportunity to seek their opinion on a particular library matter, can also garner useful market research data. When interviewing users, libraries can also utilize existing relationships. They can organize lunches with librarians and users to ask them what they want, or take advantage of the relationship between librarians and faculty and have librarians ask the faculty with whom they correspond with on a regular basis what services they want or most value.

Closely related to interviews are focus groups, which are small gatherings of users (usually 8–10) brought together and surveyed about their general thoughts or feelings about the library (Kirk, 2003, pp. 34–35). Focus groups can also be an effective means of gathering user input on new library services. Participants can test and react to services, as well as provide insight into how and when they think they will use those services or how best to communicate information about new services. When organizing focus groups, it is best to hold more than one so that results can be compared and contrasted. It is equally important that focus groups be comprised of users from only one user group (Kirk, 2003, p. 36). When attempting to survey both students and faculty members, for example, separate focus groups should be held for each category of user. Mixing participants working at different academic levels and with different interests will skew results, as group dynamics will negatively affect the participants' ability to give honest feedback. Likewise, as dissimilar audiences have varying preferences and wants, all of which can impact their input, it is best not to mix audiences in the same focus group so that those likes and dislikes do not compete with each other.

Another effective way to gather market data from users is to have them test services as they are being developed and after they are introduced. One example of doing this is through usability testing of the libraries' Web site. Usability testing involves actual users performing certain tasks on the Web site such as locating a title in the catalog, finding the library's hours of operation, or asking a reference question. Those tasks they find easy to perform or complete quickly indicate the strengths of the Web site. Where users have difficulties performing tasks can indicate weaknesses in the design or functionality of the Web site (US Department of Health and Human Services, 2004, http://www.usability.gov/methods/usability_testing.html). Usability testing can also be applied to other library services such as self-checkout, book locations, interlibrary loan, and other services either being introduced to the library or are being altered or enhanced in some way. Not only does usability testing help to improve services by showing areas needing correction, it also provides important insight into user needs and their overall knowledge of the library and its services and resources. By analyzing what services tested well, the library can gain information on those services that are most valued and used and, therefore, should be marketed. Services that do not test well may not be because of faulty design or problems with the Web site, but rather can be an indication that users are uninformed about the service. If the library sees value in these unknown services, it can increase marketing to improve use.

Observational Market Research

Observational market research involves simply watching users or gathering and analyzing pre-existing data to ascertain what services users need or their usage preferences (Kirk, 2003, p.30). One key advantage of observational market research is that usually it is a very cost-effective method of gathering information. It can be as simple as a librarian reporting how she or he sees patrons using the library. Observational market research can often be more reliable than self-reported data in that the users do not necessarily know they are providing information and, therefore, are not biased in their responses. However, it is important that the person doing the observation not add his or her own bias to the analysis. Having at least two people observe users can be beneficial in that the information they provide can be weighed against each other to ensure biases are discarded.

A key observational method used in market research that will allow libraries to find out what users want and, thereby, what services should be developed and marketed to them is to go where the users are. Visit classes and speak both to faculty and students about their library needs. Or, simply observe a class to see what they are studying. Visit dorms and cafeterias or have a "Tell the Library What You Want" open session. Get involved in students activities. The objective here is to visit the invisible or non-users. Not only will going where the user is provide the opportunity to ask and observe what they want, it will also help library staff get to know its audience. Getting to know users will also market to them as they will begin to see the library in a different light.

Observational market research could also involve the gathering of data and statistics from other sources such as admission statistics, census reports, and consumer indexes. Knowing such information as the number of students attending the university, their gender, where they come from, their ages, and other attributes will help in making marketing decisions as to what services to promote and how best to communicate with the user population.

Self-reported and observational market research both have pros and cons. Utilizing a combination of the two to gather user information will provide a more thorough and well-rounded look at users' needs and preferences.

Besides being essential in gathering facts on audiences so as to develop and package and then market library services and resources, market research has an added bonus of being a form of marketing in itself. While asking users what they want and need, such as in surveys, focus groups, and the like, the library is marketing to them by educating them about the library and giving them the opportunity to know the library better.

BEFORE ADVERTISING—KEY MARKETING TIPS

There is much research and planning that goes into marketing before an ad is ever placed or a brochure designed. Following a few key marketing tips will prepare the library to market to its highest potential.

Prioritize Marketing

Typically, marketing has been the last stage in the process of developing a service or resource. Instead, libraries should move marketing to the beginning of the process. When developing new services, marketing staff should be invited to attend the earliest development meetings. This will give the marketers a complete understanding of the service they are charged with promoting. Involving marketers early on in the process will also allow for the service's implementation and marketing to coincide.

Along with moving marketing to the beginning of the process, libraries should also involve marketing in the development of new services. In other words, create new services that users want. Too often libraries try to convince users why they should use a service; instead, libraries should develop and package services to fit what users want. That is not to say that libraries must create all new services. They should, however, develop and market services that users want as a priority – not those that libraries feel users need. As Douglas B. Herron notes in his book Marketing Nonprofit Programs and Services, "Try to blend both needs and wants into your marketing program. Find out what people's problems are and help to solve them" (Herron, 1997, p. 12). Along that line of thinking, libraries should market to users' wants, rather than solely to their needs, and they should address existing service problems and shortcomings rather than creating new ones for which they have a solution at hand. Marketers can help when creating or repackaging services as they conduct market research to determine user wants and preferences. This will result in the creation of consumer-focused services and thus the increased likelihood of those services being used.

Speak their Language

Libraries should know their audience, not just who they are as previously discussed, but also how best to reach them and when. Questions to ask include: Where do users get their news? Do they read newsletters? Do they notice and remember print advertisements? Do they respond better to their peers or librarians telling them about a resource? Knowing how users communicate will show how best to reach them and with what message.

Today's college students are part of what is referred to as the "millennial generation." Students of this group were born roughly between 1982 and 2002. They grew up with computers and technology and never knew a world without the two. Therefore, they are very comfortable with technology and adapt to and expect new technological developments and changes to emerge faster than older generations do. Students of the millennial generation are accustomed to working in groups and prefer electronic communication. They are community-minded and tend to be environmentally conscious and apt to volunteer (Abram & Luther, 2004, pp. 34–37). Knowing these traits of a large population of library users can serve as a guide in both developing and promoting new library services. When marketing the library to students of this generation, communicate via e-mail, try an electronic newsletter, or Instant Message them. Since they expect to work in groups, ensure that the library is equipped to accommodate this by having an adequate number of group-study rooms, tables, and computer workstations that are conducive to group work and collaboration.

The challenges and competition the Internet poses represent just one side of how new technologies have impacted libraries. It is also accurate to say that the Internet provides great opportunities when marketing library services. When targeting the millennial generation, for example, the Internet can be used to gather market-research data on this group by visiting the sites aimed at them. Also, investigate the idea of a library portal or Weblog as other means of marketing the library to current undergraduate students.

It is equally important when communicating to users to speak their language and avoid library jargon. All users may not understand library terms such as "interlibrary loan," "circulation," and "reference," so it is better to word library functions and services in terms that each user group will understand. For example, rather than instructing users to, "Access indexes and databases online," say, "Find journal articles online."

In addition to writing marketing messages in a language that appeals to users, the audience should always be paramount when designing promotional materials. In other words, when creating marketing materials, design and write with the audience in mind. What are their tastes? What are their needs? What are their priorities? What the designer, library staff, and administrators may want should come after consideration of the wants and preferences of the intended audience.

Along with speaking their language, marketing messages should be packaged into benefits users will experience from using the library. This relates back to marketing to their wants rather than to their needs and speaks to the library's capacity to add value to the educational experience. Therefore, when promoting a service such as e-reserves to undergraduate students, do not say, "We have E-reserves;" instead say, "Access course materials in your pajamas." This markets to the way in which students often prefer to use the library and demonstrates that the library has a real understanding and appreciation for their wants. In addition, determine what benefits are unique to the library and highlight those in marketing efforts (Herron, 1997, p. 39). Does the library, for example, have a café? Is the building known for its architecture? Cornell University Library found a creative way to highlight typical library services along with unique library features with their "Great things about the library" list that appears on their Web site (http://campusgw.library.cornell.edu/about/greatthings.html). Here, they mention everyday library services such as wireless networks and electronic databases, but also encourage visitors to take advantage of the library's bird-watching station. Highlighting what makes the library unique or how it can benefit users is a powerful way to market its worth.

Branding

Another key marketing tip is to develop an identity (a.k.a. a brand) and be loyal to that brand. Branding involves both the visual design used in promotional items and the overall image users have of the library. As Herron states, "Brand image affects people's desire to affiliate with your organization" (Herron, 1997, p. 209).

A useful example from the corporate world of a company that employs a powerful use of design branding is Nike. The Nike swoop and "Just Do It" slogan are instantly recognizable symbols and appear on everything the company produces from tennis shoes to sports apparel and equipment to commercials and print ads. Along with providing a visual i.d. for the company, this visual branding of Nike helps to tie together all the various products and services they produce. Libraries can use this example of branding as an approach to helping audiences package together the various services, resources, and often numerous locations that make up a library system.

University Libraries at the University of Cincinnati (UC) provides an example of how libraries can use visual branding. Recently, UC underwent branding efforts in which they created a new brand for the university that included language, colors, design graphics, and a new logo. Along with the new logo, they established guidelines for its use in design of all publications. The objective of the new logo and branding guidelines was to create a distinct identity for UC and its various colleges, departments, and branch campuses. In the past, the various groups had their own identities – all of which competed against each other and confused audiences. The goal with branding was that each piece passes the "envelope test," meaning that, upon pulling a publication out of an envelope, audiences will recognize it immediately as belonging to UC. Along with branding to the university, departments and colleges are allowed to have a sub-brand to help identify themselves to their own audiences. University Libraries created its own sub-brand with the use of a book graphic used along with UC's other branding elements on library signage, the Web site, and all promotional publications. The effect is a strong identity to the university, as well as a look of their own that users relate to as belonging to the library. Other units at UC have used such tactics as choosing a color or repeating particular language to represent their uniqueness to their audience while still making it clear that they are part of the university as a whole (University of Cincinnati, 2002, http://www.uc.edu/branding/).

Branding allows for the creation of a strong, positive identity. Constantly changing design, colors, and graphic elements in publications only confuses audiences. Branding also helps to create a consistent identity and foundation for each promotional piece to build upon. When creating a branded image for the library, it is important to note that looks matter. It is often said that 95% of the message is in the packaging. While this may be a slight exaggeration, the point is that libraries should look closely at the design of promotional items and what impression they make. A well designed brand will also help you to get and maintain an audience's attention as busy people tend to read or listen to things that feel as if they are well thought out and well done, while discarding things that appear poorly done. Just as important as promotional material in creating an impression and communicating a message, is the physical appearance of the library itself. Libraries should examine: Is the library clean? Is it inviting to use? What are the conditions of the signs? Is the furniture too worn and outdated? The look of both promotional pieces and the physical aspects of the library play a key role in visually branding the library.

The second part of branding involves the thoughts, opinions, and general attitudes audiences have of a product or company. Consistent communication, publicity, and personal experiences are all ways in which audiences form an opinion about a library. Thoroughly knowing and communicating the library's message will help create a positive and accurate image of the library. A company that is successful in this aspect of image branding is Sony, which has built a reputation of high-quality products and was recently voted the "best brand" for the fifth consecutive year by U.S. consumers in a Harris Poll (The Harris Poll[®], 2004). Coke, Johnson & Johnson, Tide, Q-tips, and Kleenex are other examples of products with very strong brand identities. This aspect of branding is less concrete than the visual aspect of branding, and it often takes years of concentrated efforts in which to build an image. However, the library's reputation will impact marketing efforts as it influences how audiences receive library messages. Knowing the library's image amongst its audiences will indicate what message to send and also what services and resources to promote. If the library is known to be on the forefront of technology, for example, capitalize on this image by promoting its various electronic and online services. If the library has a bad reputation with faculty for providing poor service, find out where service is lacking, improve that service, and then target market it to faculty.

KISS – Keep It Simple Stupid

A common phrase in marketing is KISS, or "Keep It Simple Stupid." Many users find libraries to be complex organizations offering a myriad of services and resources to a diverse user group. When marketing the library, simplify the message down to the core of what the library is about, and then target marketing messages to meet individual wants. Do not try to promote all the library has to offer to every audience. Let the user know what the library is so that they will act to discover all the library can provide. For example, use campaigns such as: "Come Discover the Library," "The Library. A World of Possibilities," "Library is to research as A is to paper."

Repetition

The last marketing tip is to repeat, repeat, repeat. Marketing is never complete. An audience must hear a message multiple times before they act or even remember it. It is also important to assess marketing efforts constantly, including the strategies, message, audience, and the goals in marketing. There is always room for improvement and ways to freshen a message or better target an audience.

WHAT LIBRARIES HAVE GOING FOR THEM TO MAKE MARKETING EASIER

Now that the importance and the enormity of marketing have been established, there is good news in that libraries have a lot going for them that makes marketing easier. First, libraries have an engaged audience in students, faculty, and university staff in need of library services and resources. Second, libraries have tangible products and services to offer users. Things such as chat reference, electronic databases and journals, and interlibrary loan are all services that research and experience have shown that users both value and use. Third, libraries are a bargain. Through tuition and fees, students have already paid for most library services and resources. Use this angle when marketing the library. Fourth, for the most part libraries have a good reputation of providing quality service and of being information gateways. Even the joke of librarians wearing sensible shoes and shushing users can be used positively if packaged creatively. The New Jersey Public Library system has gone against the traditional librarian stereotype in their marketing campaign centered on a "Super Librarian" character. Through cable television spots, their Web site, and other marketing mediums, the library system uses the superhero to send the message that libraries are not dull places and to illustrate that "librarians are fun and approachable" (Keresztury, 2004, pp. 32–34). Do not be afraid to think creatively when developing marketing strategies. Often breaking a mold or going against type can be very powerful and have a big impact on audiences.

In addition to the library-focused benefits listed above, libraries also benefit by being members of a larger organization in their colleges and universities. Aligning the library with an organization that has positive things to offer is always strength when marketing. Among the college or university's strengths that libraries can draw upon when marketing are name recognition and reputation. Promoting the library's relationship with the college or university with a good reputation will aid marketing efforts as it associates the library with a positive organization and gives the audience an automatic introduction to the library. In addition, libraries can share in their institution's marketing efforts by using materials the college or university produces for various services and resources. Perhaps the library can customize the university's marketing materials to add their name and contact information. Most colleges and universities have marketing and public relations staff where their library may not. In some instances, these staff members are assigned to help promote the library. Get to know these staff members and partner with them to help promote the library. Feed them information on new services and resources or tell them anecdotes of satisfied library users that they may want to use as a way to promote the university and, in turn, the library.

Along with aligning the library to its college and university to aid in marketing efforts, seek other organizations with which to partner. The

American Library Association (ALA) has created a comprehensive marketing plan called "@ your library®" that can be customized and used to promote individual libraries while also drawing on the strengths and reputation of ALA. According to the campaign's Web site, the program's objective is to "showcase the value of libraries and librarians in the 21st century," and to give libraries the tools and resources to target this message to their own audiences (American Library Association, 2004, http://www.ala.org/ala/pio/campaign/aboutyourlibrary/welcome.htm). The Association of College and Research Libraries (ACRL), in collaboration with ALA, customized the campaign to meet the specific marketing challenges and objectives of academic libraries. Information about the "@ you library®" campaign and a toolkit are available at ALA's Web site at http://www.ala.org/ala/pio/campaign/campaignamericas.htm.

In Ohio, members of OhioLINK, a consortium of 85 college and university libraries, have joined together to form the OhioLINK Marketing Task Force. The charge of the group is "to enable Ohio's academic libraries to more effectively market their resources and services by providing customizable tools and information." (OhioLINK Marketing Task Force, 2003). To date, the group has created a communications plan and marketing toolkit, a Web site with examples and best practices of effective marketing samples, and started a marketing list serve to discuss and provide marketing information. The group gave workshops around the state to give libraries the tools and knowledge to market to their respective audiences. Not all states will have an organization like OhioLINK in which to organize a marketing task force, so marketers must look to partner with other academic libraries in the area, or with library colleagues regardless of their location, who share their interest in promoting library use. There is strength in numbers. Collaborating with organizations and colleagues will provide opportunities to share resources, ideas, and expand horizons.

WHAT IS REQUIRED TO MARKET?

Other than a basic understanding of the main concepts of marketing, there are certain steps required in order to market effectively.

Planning

Marketing should be included in the library's strategic plan, both to show its importance in the direction of the library and to allow a venue in which to plan how to market. In addition to the strategic plan, the library should also create a comprehensive marketing or communications plan well before developing advertising strategies. In the plan, the library should include the marketing goals, the target audiences, and challenges facing the library (both internal and external) that marketing can help address. Next, the plan should list marketing strategies as well as a work plan explaining how and who will complete the marketing efforts. The plan should include a budget, workflow and timeline, personnel, and lastly, an assessment strategy to monitor and judge marketing efforts.

Time

A library can have the best intentions to market itself, but unless a commitment is made it is hard to find the time necessary to market well. Therefore, dedicate a percentage of a staff person(s) job to marketing. Also, administrators should carve out time in their own schedule to strategize about marketing and to meet with those responsible for doing the marketing. Sufficient time should be devoted to planning, executing, and assessing marketing strategies.

Staff

While marketing is a group effort involving everyone in the library, it is imperative that someone has the responsibility for marketing the library. Ideally, every library would have a communications professional whose sole responsibility would be to promote the library and communicate its message to all audiences. Unfortunately, this is not the reality in most libraries. To be successful at marketing, libraries should identify a staff member(s) to lead and organize marketing initiatives, even if that represents only a portion of their job responsibilities, and then provide them with the necessary marketing training to do the job well.

Budget

Marketing can be done inexpensively, and a lot of marketing is free (such as how library workers interact with users at service desks). However, money is needed to support basic marketing efforts such as: producing promotional materials like brochures and newsletters; organizing outreach events such as student orientation, exhibits, and lectures; and creating advertising such as ads in university newspapers. It is hazardous to be too frugal with the marketing budget, however, as things done too cheaply are unlikely to be noticed and result in a waste of time and money.

Buy-in

It is essential that all stakeholders support the libraries' marketing efforts. They need not necessarily be involved in all marketing decisions, but should be in support of the overall idea and goals of marketing. Library staff, especially, should support the marketing efforts and clearly understand their particular roles, whether it be as market research data collectors or ambassadors of the library. Marketing should be an accepted part of library culture. In order to do this, marketing has to be something that everyone who works in the library thinks about and realizes that it is not a one-time initiative, but an everyday function of work in the library.

CONCLUSION

As Herron argues, "due largely to an increasingly competitive environment, our program services must be more market sensitive and purposeful today" (Herron, 1997, p. 7). Academic libraries can no longer afford the belief that, because they are part of a "public good" with resources and services people value, users should and, therefore, will always continue to value and use the library (Weingand, 1999, p. 2). Instead, by considering a more updated definition of marketing as the creating and packaging of products users want, marketing should be viewed as an essential tool that will help libraries be more successful. By knowing users and their expectations, as well as how best to communicate with them, marketing can give the library the means to better serve and communicate with users. Marketing, therefore, should not be a bad word in academic libraries, but rather a part of the management style of the library. Just as administrators know the processes of information delivery, they should also know the basics of marketing and that when applied to the library, can better prepare it to serve users and to inform all audiences of the value and benefit of academic libraries to the general well-being of all involved.

REFERENCES

Abram, S., & Luther, J. (2004). Born with the Chip. *Library Journal*, *129*(8), 34–37.
American Library Association. (2004). Available: http://www.ala.org/ala/pio/campaign/ aboutyourlibrary/welcome.

Harris Poll Interactive. (2004). The Harris Poll[®], 2004, #50, July 7, 2004. Available: http://www.harrisinteractive.com/harris_poll/index.asp?PID=479.

Herron, D. B. (1997). *Marketing nonprofit programs and services: Proven and practical strategies to get more customers, members, and donors.* San Francisco: Jossey–Bass Publishers.

Keresztury, T. (2004). *Super librarian to the rescue! Library Journal, 129*(9), 32–34.

Kirk, B. C. (2003). *Lessons from a chief marketing officer.* New York: McGraw–Hill.

OhioLINK Marketing Task Force. (1997). Unpublished document. Communication Plan Workbook: *A Customizable Plan for OhioLINK Libraries.*

Oxford English Dictionary. (2004). Available: http://dictionary.oed.com/.

University of Cincinnati. (2002). Available: http://www.uc.edu/branding.

U.S. Department of Health and Human Services. (2004). Available: www.usability.gov/methods/usability_testing.html.

Weingand, D. E. (1999). *Marketing/Planning Library and Information Services.* Englewood, Colorado: Libraries Unlimited, Inc.

HOW CAN ACADEMIC LIBRARIANS CREATE VALUE? ☆

Mark L. Weinberg, Marsha Lewis, Hugh D. Sherman, Julia Zimmerman and Eleni A. Zulia

In the past three years, the OhioLINK budget has been reduced $640,000 (8.3%).

Users are more sophisticated and expect more from both the library and the university.

It may be difficult to give good customer service that results in user satisfaction without adequate staff to provide the service.

INTRODUCTION

Like other public and nonprofit leaders, academic librarians face multiple challenges (McGregor, 2000) such as tight and declining budgets, technology-savvy users, higher performance expectations from clients and overseers, complex production networks, rapid technological change, and increased competition (Stoffle, Allen, Morden, & Maloney, 2003). These challenges require new leadership roles, skill sets, and techniques for academic librarians, as well as restructuring the library organization. A discussion of their changed roles and organizations contextualizes the discussion of how academic librarians should meet the challenges of a

☆ Based on a presentation at the OhioLINK Directors' Meeting, November, 2003.

Advances in Library Administration and Organization
Advances in Library Administration and Organization, Volume 22, 297–314
ISSN: 0732-0671/doi:10.1016/S0732-0671(05)22007-2

changed service environment (Stoffle et al., 2003). However, a void in the discussion is the failure to suggest a leadership role best suited to governing complex academic libraries, as well as the lack of a coherent strategic framework to guide academic librarians in formulating, implementing, and assessing strategy to create additional value (Gilreath, 2003).

We argue the challenges of managing complex organizational networks, along with the academic librarian's new role, require a strategic framework that integrates performance measures to deal with change. The specific strategic framework we believe will help academic librarians create public value and navigate change is Mark Moore's Strategic Triangle. This model focuses managerial attention on three key strategic components of public and nonprofit management: public value creation, political management of the authorizing environment, and building operational capacity to deliver value (Moore, 1995). We also suggest organizations develop performance measures for each component of the triangle to improve strategy implementation. The arguments for this framework follow a discussion of the change issues, challenges, and prescriptions for academic libraries and the broader public and nonprofit sectors. Although the focus here is on academic libraries in the public and nonprofit sectors, this approach also is useful for academic librarians at private universities (Moore, 1999).

CHANGES, CHALLENGES, AND OPTIONS FOR ACADEMIC LIBRARIANS

Stoffle et al. (2003) describe the changing environment for academic libraries throughout the United States. First, the economic climate for academic libraries has deteriorated as state funding for higher education has been significantly reduced, making future library funding uncertain. Second, academic libraries face increased "commercial competition" for the provision of services (Stoffle et al., 2003). Third, decreased funding and increased competition has brought increased accountability and performance expectations as "boards of trustees and legislatures" have mandated performance measures (Stoffle et al., 2003). Finally, changes in technology significantly impacted academic libraries in the areas of electronic collections, library portal developments, content databases, and other innovations (Stoffle et al., 2003). Stoffle et al. (2003) argue an increasing number of organizational, personnel, value, and service issues must be addressed in light of these major changes. For example, with respect to organizational change, the authors cite Roy Tennant who states "rapid change in libraries" means librarians should adopt a process called "zooming" that enables them to make small changes constantly (Tennant, 2002, as cited in Stoffle et al. (2003).

Similarly, Lin (2001) claims "society, economics, politics and technology have had a profound effect on the organizational structure of academic libraries" and the role of academic library directors. Library functions, operations, and services also have undergone major changes. Library organizations are flatter, have fewer staff, and are constantly learning. The academic librarian is now a manager and a leader, meaning expectations associated with the scope and complexity of the task expanded to include marketing, community outreach, consensus building, and fundraising activities (Lin, 2001).

McElrath (2002) also sees dramatic changes in academic libraries over the last 20 years. Some of the major challenges facing librarians are increased expectations from the library and the university, users with extensive technology knowledge, the ability to maintain adequate staffing, the skyrocketing cost of serials, and the rate of organizational change (McElrath, 2002). These challenges impact libraries in a number of ways, including the application of business ideas to their organization. Patkus and Rapple (2000) argue competition and technology changes have led to new models of work for libraries that move the library organization closer to a business organization. Following Collins and Porras's (1996) discussion on core values for business, they state it is not enough to focus on making libraries more customer service oriented, instead directors must understand and advocate for the organization's "core values" in order to change libraries. These core values then can be communicated and acted upon by employees throughout the organization, thereby creating a common vision.

Hernon, Powell, and Young (2001) suggest shifting the library directors' focus from their internal environment to their external environment. This external focus means directors need to be creative, digital, "politically savvy," innovative, flexible, and increasingly, risk takers (Hernon et al., 2001). In fact, the next generation of academic library directors truly must be multi-faceted, as they need to be

flexible, adaptive, stable, of equitable temperament, have endurance, a vision, knowledgeable about scholarly communication, plan with stakeholders, good communicators, advocate for library, know technologies, committed to resource sharing, support staff development, put together management teams, empower staff, be open minded, approachable, embrace change, seek external funding, have a public service focus, develop partnerships, compromise, delegate responsibility, and understand libraries as complex organizations (Hernon et al., 2001).

Hence, library administrators, like their counterparts throughout the public and nonprofit sectors, experience more demanding role expectations that require different skill sets, and they are charged with leading and managing much different organizations than those of the past.

Implicit in this discussion of the changing role of academic librarians and changes for libraries is the leader's centrality to organizational performance during periods of change. Soete (1998) argues the director's leadership is the key to a library's success: "Directors have leadership responsibilities for envisioning the future of their organizations and setting goals to achieve that future, choosing and leading the best possible staff, managing resources wisely, fundraising, seeing that exciting new programs get implemented, and assuring that the technology is there to support these programs." Soete also lists 11 key leadership roles to assess the library director's performance, including serving as "chief representative and spokesperson, campus administrator, liaison, monitor, negotiator and advocate, fund raiser, leader of planning and operations, leader of staff, communicator, change agent and entrepreneur, and finally resource allocator" (Soete, 1998). This view is consistent with emerging literature on "strategic leaders" and their role in organizational change as well as with the renewed interest in public management leadership and organizational performance (Doig & Hargrove, 1990).

Although strategic leadership theory acknowledges strategies may emerge from any level of the organization, top managers are uniquely positioned to have the most impact on the organization's strategy (Sherman, Lewis, Weinberg, & Schermerhorn, 2004). In an influential article by Ireland and Hitt (1999), strategic leadership is redefined for the 21st century as an effort to "anticipate, envision, maintain flexibility, think strategically, and work with others to initiate changes that will create a viable future for the organization." In the current uncertain and changing environment, leaders cannot identify, prioritize, and analyze all of the available information to develop strategies to increase organizational value. Leaders rely more on the organization's members to identify critical information and serve as partners by participating in the strategic formulation and implementation processes. For this practice to be effective, members must understand and share a commitment to the organization's purpose. This purpose is a major focus for the leader and is reflected in Ireland and Hitt's (1999) description of the strategic leader's tasks, specifically the development of an organization's vision and culture, as well as the skills and abilities of its members.

Strategic leadership increasingly is important throughout the public sector (Doig & Hargrove, 1990). Doig and Hargrove (1990) suggest "entrepreneurial executives" have to "identify new missions and programs," "develop and nourish external constituencies," "create internal constituencies to support new goals," "enhance the organization's technical expertise," "motivate and provide training to members of the organization," and "scan organizational routines and points of interests to identify areas of vulnerability." This certainly applies to academic librarians and the environment they lead their organizations.

This literature on new leadership roles and new organizations is useful because it provides a context for the discussion of what academic librarians should do to face change. Many libraries have done quite well responding to change. For example, the development of OhioLINK, "a consortium of the libraries of eighty-four Ohio colleges and universities and the State Library of Ohio," and similar consortia throughout the United States shows how academic libraries have responded successfully to change (Ohio Library and Information Network, 2004). There are many talented and dynamic academic library leaders, but writings on leadership for both academic librarians and for those in the broader public and nonprofit sectors are limited in the recommendations on leadership roles and organizational change. First, academic librarians too often are viewed as leaders of organizations, rather than as public leaders charged with governing complex networks seeking socially valuable goals for society (Feldman & Khademian, 2002). Second, academic librarians face multiple reporting and performance requirements and often are judged on their contributions to "improved organizational performance" or "managing change." We argue the standard of performance for governing academic libraries should be public value creation. With this as the librarian's primary leadership responsibility, they need a coherent strategic framework that fits their needs.

ACADEMIC LIBRARIANS, PUBLIC LEADERSHIP, GOVERNANCE, AND PUBLIC VALUE

We suggest it is useful for academic librarians to think of themselves as public leaders charged with governing complex networks toward the creation of public value. The concepts of public leadership, governance, and value inform leadership tasks in numerous ways. First, public leadership implies the central role of politics in organizational leadership. Public sector executives must engage the "politics surrounding their organization" to seek out what is publicly valuable, as well as anticipate a "world of political conflict" and changing technology in which they constantly restructure their organizations (Moore, 1995). This role means executives are participants in political processes and coalition politics, and like elected officials they are "goal seeking actors in their own right" (Lynn, Heinrich, & Hill, 2000b). Second, since politics defines what is valued, public leaders must address political questions regarding the fair distribution of privileges and burdens. Since politics involves decisions regarding collective judgments as opposed to individual private decisions, questions of justice always are involved (Moore, 1995).

While business, public, and nonprofit leaders all are concerned with governance, public governance is fundamentally different from governance in the private sector. Although there are multiple and complex definitions of the term, it is defined here as "regimes of laws, administrative rules, judicial rulings, and practices that constrain, prescribe and enable government activity, where such activity is broadly defined as the production and delivery of publicly supported goods and services" (Lynn, Heinrich, & Hill, 2000a). Governance structures can be viewed as sets of "dynamic relationships that are influenced by the decisions and actions of public managers, and governance is about the way these interactions are structured" (Feldman & Khademian, 2002). The latter portrayal represents a view of government increasingly focused on the production and delivery of services in networked as opposed to bureaucratic systems.

A central argument in the public administration governance literature is on the role of the public manager as a leader. This literature focuses on both the outcomes and the processes of service delivery in government because managers are accountable not only for policy outcomes, but also for the appropriateness of the structures and relationships they create and support (Feldman & Khademian, 2002). Also, since the literature argues that management, or the processes organizations engage in, matters in achieving outcomes, a new empirical research stream (discussed in detail later) on the logic of governance is yielding evidence supporting the use of strategic management by public sector executives (Heinrich & Lynn, 2000; Nicholson-Crotty & O'Toole, 2004; Rainey & Steinbauer, 1999). This type of governance research examines normative theories about public management by examining aspects of processes, technology, and organizational structure (Lynn et al., 2000a).

Public leaders often operate in governance networks where their own agencies interact with others over whom they have little control. As public sector work increasingly is delivered through these networks, it is crucial public leaders possess "the knowledge of how to concert action" among "actors in networks of negotiation, implementation, and delivery" (O'Toole, as cited in Lynn et al., 2000a). If we define academic librarians as public leaders charged with governing complex networks, and if we are concerned with both the outcomes and process in the production of library goods and services, then we can establish a standard for judging public leader performance. We argue here this standard contains strategy, a public value framework, and performance measures to deal with change.

THE IMPORTANCE OF USING A STRATEGY AND PUBLIC VALUE FRAMEWORK TO DEAL WITH CHANGE

Businesses typically respond to demands for change by developing and implementing a new or revised strategy. Strategy helps a firm position itself by differentiating its products or services from the competitors (Porter, 1996), provides congruence amongst the organization's vision, goals, policies, and activities (McGregor, 2000), and does this all in an effort to provide greater value to its shareholders (Treacy & Wiersema, 1995). In the public sector, organizational strategy management has become increasingly important due in part to the "grater devolved responsibility" of "acquiring resources and achieving results" to the local organization (Llewellyn & Tappin, 2003). Many approaches to formulating strategy exist (Niven, 2003), and the development of strategy in the public and nonprofit sectors focuses on strategic management as opposed to strategic planning (Poister & Streib, 1999). However, a major limitation of strategy in the public sector at both the institutional and managerial levels is the lack of focus on value.

For strategy to be successful in the public and nonprofit sectors, it must be focused on "how public value is best produced" (McGregor, 2000). At the institutional level, Smith and Huntsman (1997) argue the role of government is to create incremental value for citizens. In *Creating Public Value: Strategic Management in Government* (1995), Mark Moore argues forcefully that "the aim of managerial work in the public sector is to create public value." These are both substantive and normative arguments of what practitioners should do and what the public should expect from public and nonprofit managers (Moore, 1995). To meet these demands of strategy in the public and nonprofit sectors, the strategic framework we suggest is the Strategic Triangle.

The Strategic Triangle focuses managerial attention on three key areas of public and nonprofit sector management: public value creation, political management of the authorizing environment, and building operational capacity to deliver value (Moore, 1995). Public value creation concerns what is valuable for the agency to do in relation to its public sector mission. Therefore, strategy in the public sector must accomplish substantive value to overseers, clients, and beneficiaries because public value satisfies community as opposed to individual preferences (Moore, 1995). Political management relates to the expectations of various political stakeholders, as well as how the manager and agency manages the political environment so resources and authority continually flow. Operational capacity relates to what is achievable for the manager to push the organization to accomplish and what capacities need to be developed to move value creation forward. Also, strategy must facilitate an operationally and administratively feasible production model (Moore, 1995). The three integrated components of the model imply successful public strategists must not only develop public, or "substantive value" strategies and an operational model to deliver public value, but they also must develop political strategies and the operational capacity to engage the authorizing environment. In the public and nonprofit sectors, political analysis and strategy are essential because value creation resides in the act of governing by seeking socially valuable goals for society (Feldman & Khademian, 2002), and politics serves as the forum for deciding questions of value (Moore, 1995).

In practice, public and nonprofit managers strategically "manage upward to the authorizing environment, outward to the task environment, and downward to the organization" (Moore, 1995, O'Toole, Meier, and Nicholson-Crotty, 2003). Clearly, variations exist amongst government and nonprofit entities in terms of mission, authorizing environments, and production processes, but the model generally is applicable to all public and nonprofit organizations (Moore, 1999). The utility of the framework is illustrated through a case study about the Learning Commons at Ohio University. The case is presented from the standpoint of the library's director:

"Alden Library is the main library at Ohio University. When I became director, we were celebrating the building's thirtieth birthday. Like many academic libraries built in the late sixties, it is inadequate for today's library services. In particular, the library's second floor needed renovating. While it was a large area, it was cut into odd spaces. It had ancient orange carpeting and original furniture, making it neither attractive nor functional. From the time I arrived at Ohio University, I had petitioned the administration for renovation funding, but my pleas were unsuccessful as the project was nowhere on the university's priority list. Around this time, Ohio University was preparing for a university-wide fundraising campaign, and my staff and I decided to make the second floor renovation the centerpiece of the library campaign. We hoped to raise enough private funds to renovate the floor into an Information Commons, which many academic libraries have created.

One of our goals was to design the floor so it could be closed off from the remainder of the building in order to keep the Commons open when the rest of the library was closed. This would allow extended service hours with minimal staffing costs, and when students got wind of this, they were extremely excited since they had begged for round-the-clock library access for years. We then formed a student advisory board and began to learn about what students wanted and needed, and it did not always match our assumptions. Through this exercise, we realized the opportunities for innovative services were huge.

The university hired a new provost who wanted to transform the undergraduate experience into a model of active and engaged learning. During his first year, he focused on academic areas at the exclusion of the library. But when the library staff worked closely with students on planning the project, and when we established a faculty advisory committee to link campus learning initiatives with the potential services of the new facility, he began to take notice. He realized the renovated space would be a unique and much-needed learning environment on our campus. At that point we adopted the name 'Learning Commons' to piggy-back on the university-wide interest in learning.

We continued to raise funds and ultimately raised over half the amount needed for the project. Then through loans and internal savings, we found the rest of the necessary project money. Some of the university's most active donors contributed to the project, and their interest had a beneficial effect. While nobody gave a darn about my aversion to orange carpet, the support of influential alumni captured the attention of the university's administration.

This attention influenced the project positively with the library receiving a half-million dollar base-budget increase to hire staff and support technology in the Learning Commons. This is a huge budgetary increase for us, especially in a bad budget year. Why did we get it? Because we 'created public value.' Renovating an ugly and non-functional floor of the library, even though it was needed badly, was not a high priority for my 'authorizing agency.' But when we:

- programmed it to address previously unmet student and faculty needs,

- incorporated the provost's agenda of active and engaged learning, and
- attracted the attention and support from influential alumni,

we received significant support from the university's administration. This is a concrete example illustrating Moore's Strategic Triangle by:

- managing downward – improving the library's facilities, thereby improving our ability to operate efficiently,
- managing outward – innovating and improving service to our users, and
- managing upward – meeting political expectations and needs."

This case illustrates the strategic components forming the core of Moore's Strategic Triangle, along with the necessity of developing a strategy that touches all three areas. In addition to case examples of organizations using the Strategic Triangle, there also is quantitative research indicating the model's utility throughout the public and nonprofit sectors.

CASE AND EMPIRICAL EVIDENCE OF THE STRATEGIC FRAMEWORK'S EFFECTIVENESS

A recent research stream examining governance has provided evidence supporting the use of the Strategic Triangle by public sector executives (Heinrich & Lynn, 2000; Nicholson-Crotty & O'Toole, 2004; Rainey & Steinbauer, 1999). This research tests normative theories of public management, thereby helping to fill the "black box" between what leaders do and program outcomes. It also suggests the most successful public managers are deliberate in their approach to internal and external management issues, such as re-organizing and managing their operational capacity as well as managing their stakeholder and network relationships within the policy environment. These two functions are equivalent to the Strategic Triangle's operational capacity and political management components. An example of this research is Nicholson-Crotty and O'Toole's (2004) study of 570 police departments in the United States. They analyzed data related to the internal management processes of the agencies such as human resource management, training, technology investments, clear directives, and other activities. The study indicated internal management activities were positively and significantly related to performance outcomes (Nicholson-Crotty & O'Toole, 2004).

Another key study in this area is O'Toole, Meier, and Nicholson-Crotty's (2003) examination of the Strategic Triangle's impact on program outcomes.

They examined the management activities of 500 Texas school superintendents in three directions: upward (to their boards and authorities), downward (to internal district management), and outward (to the larger network and policy environment). Their research found managing outward to the larger network consistently associated positively with organizational performance (O'Toole et al., 2003).

Quantitative studies are not the only evidence of the model's utility in the public and nonprofit sectors. Case-based evidence also supports the usefulness of the Strategic Triangle across a wide range of policy areas (Weinstein, Jacobowitz, & Siegel, 2003; Sherman et al., 2004). Case evidence for the model also comes from Ohio University's Voinovich Center for Leadership and Public Affairs, which since 1998 has used the Strategic Triangle along with strategic performance measures as the model for its seminars. The Center has trained over 1000 public sector and nonprofit executives and has conducted intensive interviews with approximately 100 graduates of the Institute. Graduates were asked what components of the model they tried to implement and what, if any, impact the model had on organizational success. Public and nonprofit managers report the primary uses and advantages of the model are: (1) as a decision making tool to ensure all the internal and external components important to implementing strategic decisions are considered, (2) as a tool to maintain an appropriate focus on communicating the agency's value to its important stakeholders, (3) as a common framework for the management team to evaluate new opportunities and make decisions about existing programs and directions, and (4) as a way to focus the organization on measuring key strategic performance indicators. These reasons point to the necessity of strategy and a strategic framework for public and nonprofit organizations. These elements also must be suited properly based on the organization's sector, mission, and policy area.

THE IMPORTANCE OF INTEGRATING EVIDENCE AND PERFORMANCE MEASURES IN THE FRAMEWORK TO IMPROVE STRATEGY IMPLEMENTATION

To be successful, strategy must "mirror the realities of the organization's environment," and the "resource allocation process must mirror strategy" (Christensen, 1997). According to Moore, bad strategy or strategic failure results when the organization produces something that does not mirror the community's desires (politics), the organization is unable to produce the desired good or service (operational capacity), or what is produced has no long term value (public value) (Moore, 2003). Kaplan and Norton (2001) found strategic failure primarily results not from the formulation of bad strategy, but from good strategy that is poorly implemented. Implementation failure can occur due to a lack of data on strategic activities, a disconnect of activities across the organization's "value chain" (Epstein, 2001), or a deficiency of strategy acceptance throughout the organization (Kaplan & Norton, 2001).

Increasingly, problems related to strategic implementation are solved by developing and deploying performance measures within a strategic framework (Kaplan & Norton, 2001, 2004; Simons, 1995; Epstein, 2001; Saul, 2003). Three viable approaches of integrating performance measures into a strategic framework aimed at improving strategy implementation include logic models for organizational value chains (Epstein, 2001), an often "controversial approach" to performance measurement such as CompStat (McKay, 2003) or CitiStat (Henderson, 2003), and specialized forms of value chains popularly known as scorecards (Kaplan & Norton, 1996, 2001, 2004). Carolyn Heinrich (2003) also makes the argument that public and nonprofit organizations can use performance measurements to better implement strategy. She argues performance measures should be used to help public managers understand both how policy and management decisions are linked to outcomes and how systemic and situational factors affect performance (Heinrich, 2003). To develop effective models for performance measurement, the organizational context, processes, and the necessary level of analysis must be taken into account. She suggests a number of models to measure performance including logic models (Heinrich, 2003).

Using scorecards is a useful model for improving strategy implementation by developing performance data on important strategic components, testing connections between strategic activities, and gaining acceptance of strategy throughout the organization all with the aim of developing "strategy-focused organizations" (Kaplan & Norton, 2001). Numerous public and nonprofit organizations use the Balanced Scorecard or a modified version of the scorecard as a tool to improve strategy implementation, and we agree it is valuable at measuring some of the key concepts for public and nonprofit sector organizations. In recent years academic libraries have begun to use the Balanced Scorecard (BSC), and the University of Virginia is a leader in this effort. The BSC organizes performance measures into four categories, or perspectives, key to generating value for the organization. These perspectives include financial, customer value, internal business practices, and learning and growth measures (Kaplan & Norton, 2001). In 2001, the University of Virginia implemented the BSC to gain control of statistical operations, introduce balance into statistical work by examining relationships between finance and internal processes as well as between data and information on user (customer) services, obtain a clearer picture of organizational performance (Self, 2003), and to focus the library (Willis, 2004).

The BSC also has been used by major academic libraries in Germany. The traditional BSC places the financial perspective at the top of the scorecard, but in this case the libraries put customers, defined as "users," at the top (Poll, 2001). The German libraries implemented the system to measure and improve service quality, along with translating the libraries' mission, vision, and goals into a system of performance indicators. Both the University of Virginia and the academic libraries in Germany using the BSC found it helped them visualize the relationship between cause and effect among target values, evaluation data, and actions taken (Poll, 2001).

When public and nonprofit organizations use a balanced scorecard, they often follow Kaplan and Norton's (2001) suggestion to alter its setup and place mission at the top versus the business model of placing finances at that point. Even with this change, there are fundamental differences to take into account between the private and the public and nonprofit sectors in terms of their organizational reality and the impact this has on the development and implementation of both strategy and performance measures. Unlike business strategy, public and nonprofit strategy is embedded in politics (Moore, 2002; Parhizgari & Gilbert, 2004), and this dynamic creates a complex reality for public sector management (Meier & O'Toole, 2002). Also, a large-scale study comparing measures of organizational effectiveness in public and private organizations found that, while some performance measures appropriately are applied to both sectors, others are "based on invalid assumptions" (Parhizgari & Gilbert, 2004). These differences reinforce the need for public and nonprofit organizations to create both strategy and performance measures appropriate for their organizational sector, mission, and policy area.

We suggest that nonprofit and public organizations use the Strategic Triangle with performance measures to address implementation issues arising from the absence of data on the strategy, a lack of connection among strategic components, and the need for strategy integration throughout the organization. Moore (2002) presents the "Public Value Scorecard" as a modified version of the Balanced Scorecard that is more applicable to public and nonprofit work. He points out similarities between the Balanced Scorecard and the Public Value Scorecard such as the focus on measurement, the emphasis on measuring more than just financial statistics, and the idea that measures should fit into the "execution of a future oriented strategy of value creation" (Moore, 2002). Moore asserts, and we agree, that a "Public Value Scorecard" is better suited for public and nonprofit organizations because it "aligns more neatly with the ambitions of a nonprofit organization" whose "…ultimate goal is not to capture and seize value for themselves, but to give away their capabilities to achieve the largest impact on social conditions that they can, and to find ways to leverage their capabilities with those of others" (Moore, 2002).

Using the Public Value Scorecard to address the lack of data on strategy, measures are developed for the value, political management, and operational capacity components. This enables managers to monitor progress on all necessary components for accomplishing a strategic goal. Moore (2002) suggests various value, political, and operational capacity measures for public and nonprofit organizations. Value measures include social objective outcomes such as "bringing relief to distressed humans," as well as measures of "output, process and input measures that allow them [organizations] to recognize the value of what they are doing and to improve performance" (Moore, 2002). Measuring outcome, process and output measures of value is useful since value resides in both organizational outcomes and the organization itself (Moore, 2002).

Political measures focus on measuring the strength of the relationships between the organization and its "supporters and legitimaters" (Moore, 2002). An example of a political measure is sources of revenue. Moore (2002) argues organizations should view them as "accounts" the organization is trying to maintain and further by making choices about which accounts are the most strategically important to maintain. Operational capacity measures look at both the capacity of the organization and the organization's partners in the production process or network. Measures can include core competencies of employees, technologies and organizational policies and processes.

Another value of using the Strategic Triangle and performance measures is the opportunity to test for strategic alignment. The model not only creates a monitoring system for the strategy, but it also serves as a framework to test hypotheses and relationships between the organization's strategic components. For example, are the organization's operational activities actually resulting in increased value? Are political management actions leading to increased access to operational resources? Asking these types of questions and using performance measurement data to draw out the conclusions helps organizations reformulate and shift strategy in order to accomplish its goals.

The strategic performance model's integration into the organization's everyday activities promotes strategy acceptance, and it serves as an "internal control system" (Kaplan & Norton, 2001; Simons, 1995). Even though CompStat is not a scorecard, the New York Police Department's (NYPD) creation and use of the system is an example of integrating performance measures into a strategic framework. As NYPD Commissioner, William Bratton followed Kaplan and Norton's directive to "Measure the strategy!" by making performance measures a centerpiece of the department's strategic efforts (Kaplan & Norton, 2001; Buntin, 1999). Both the distribution of performance measures and the regular meetings on CompStat-generated statistics promoted strategy integration by requiring everyone in the organization to think about the measures and their relationship to department strategy, communicated measures quickly, and facilitated innovation and strategy evaluation (Buntin, 1999).

One point to consider is even with elements in place to promote strategy acceptance, there are limits to this acceptance. This limitation in the public and nonprofit sectors stems from its orientation toward the citizen versus the private sector orientation toward the consumer (Moore, 1995). The citizen emphasis creates an open system in which minority opinions and disagreement are part of the political process deciding questions of value (Moore, 1995). While the NYPD was successful attaining many of their goals, they experienced difficulties encouraging their strategy due to the need for including political minorities in the process (Buntin, 1999).

The approach of using the Strategic Triangle along with performance measures is relatively new and just starting to be used by public and nonprofit organizations, meaning there is limited evidence of its utility. For example, there are a number of state arts organizations using the Strategic Triangle as a scorecard by developing measures based on each component (Patterson, 2003). As more organizations adopt this strategic framework, there is a necessity to study the approach to determine its usefulness and effectiveness for public and nonprofit organizations.

SUMMARY

In sum, this essay argued academic librarians need to redefine their roles, manage complex governance networks, employ a strategy and public value framework to deal with change, and integrate performance measures into a public value strategic framework. We maintain that the key to managing change is the development and implementation of organizational strategy.

To improve this process of strategy implementation and development, we presented a model appropriate for public and nonprofit organizations that incorporates public value and strategic performance measures. We also presented evidence of the model's utility for public and nonprofit organizations. While research provides evidence of the Strategic Triangle's value, our work with public and nonprofit executives leads us to the conclusion it is enhanced further with sector-appropriate performance measures that gauge implementation success at all three points of the triangle.

REFERENCES

Buntin, J. (1999). *Assertive policing, plummeting crime: The NYPD takes on crime in New York City*. Case number C16-1530.0, 1–24. Cambridge: John F. Kennedy School of Government.

Christensen, C. (1997). Making strategy: Learning by doing. *Harvard Business Review, 75*(6), 141–149.

Collins, J. C., & Porras, J. I. (1996). Building your company's vision. *Harvard Business Review, 74*(5), 65–77.

Doig, J. W., & Hargrove, E. C. (1990). "Leadership" and political analysis. In: J. W. Doig & E. C. Hargrove (Eds), *Leadership and innovation: Entrepreneurs in government* (pp. 1–22). Baltimore, MD: Johns Hopkins University Press.

Epstein, P. D. (2001). The performance value chain: A valuable tool for learning "what works". *The Bottom Line, 19*(1), 9–14.

Feldman, M. S., & Khademian, A. M. (2002). To manage is to govern. *Public Administration Review, 62*, 541–554.

Gilreath, C. (2003). ACRL/Harvard Leadership Institute. *College & Research Libraries News, 64*(2), 90–91.

Heinrich, C. J. (2003). Measuring public sector performance and effectiveness. In: G. Peters & J. Pierre (Eds), *The handbook of public administration* (pp. 25–37). London: Sage Publications.

Heinrich, C. J., & Lynn, L. E. (2000). Means and ends: A comparative study of empirical methods for investigating governance and performance. *Journal of Public Administration Research and Theory, 11*, 109–138.

Henderson, L. J. (2003). The Baltimore CitiStat program: Performance and accountability. *The Business of Government*, (Summer), 1–43.

Hernon, P., Powell, R. R., & Young, A. P. (2001). University library directors in the association of research libraries: The next generation, part one. *College and Research Libraries, 62*, 116–145.

Ireland, D., & Hitt, M. (1999). Achieving and maintaining strategic competitiveness in the 21st century: The role of strategic leadership. *Academy of Management Executive, 13*(1), 43–57.

Kaplan, R. S., & Norton, D. P. (2001). *The strategy-focused organization: How balanced scorecard companies thrive in the new business environment*. Boston: Harvard Business School.

Kaplan, R. S., & Norton, D. P. (2004). *Strategy maps: Converting intangible assets into tangible outcomes.* Boston: Harvard Business School.

Kaplan, R. S., & Norton, D. P. (1996). *The balanced scorecard: Translating strategy into action.* Boston: Harvard Business School.

Lin, C. (2001). Changes in stated job requirements of director positions of academic libraries in the U.S. *Journal of Information, Communication and Library Science, 8*(1), 9–25.

Llewellyn, S., & Tappin, E. (2003). Strategy in the public sector: Management in the wilderness. *Journal of Management Studies, 40,* 955–982.

Lynn, L. E., Heinrich, C. J., & Hill, C. J. (2000a). Studying governance and public management: Challenges and prospects. *Journal of Public Administration Research and Theory, 10,* 233–261.

Lynn, L. E., Heinrich, C. J., & Hill, C. J. (2000b). Studying governance and public management: Why? How? In: C. J. Heinrich & L. E. Lynn (Eds), *Governance and performance: New perspectives* (pp. 1–33). Washington, DC: Georgetown University.

McElrath, E. (2002). Challenges that academic library directors are experiencing as perceived by them and their supervisors. *College & Research Libraries, 63,* 304–321.

McGregor, E. B. (2000). Making sense of change. In: J. L. Brudney, L. J. O'Toole & H. G. Rainey (Eds), *Advancing public management: New developments in theory, methods, and practice* (pp. 127–151). Washington, DC: Georgetown University.

McKay, J. (2003, November). Continuing the revolution: Crime tracking concept evolves into powerful government management tool. *Government Technology, 16*(14), 18–53.

Meier, K. J., & O'Toole, L. J. (2002). Public management and organizational performance: The effect of managerial quality. *Journal of Policy Analysis and Management, 21,* 629–643.

Moore, M. H. (1995). *Creating public value: Strategic management in the public sector.* Boston: Harvard University.

Moore, M. H. (1999). Managing for value: Organizational strategy in "for-profit," "nonprofit" and governmental organizations. Unpublished manuscript.

Moore, M. H. (2002). A rejoinder and an alternative to "Strategic performance measurement and management in nonprofit organizations" by Robert Kaplan. Unpublished manuscript.

Moore, M. H. (2003, July). Recognizing public value: The challenge of measuring performance in the public sector. Presentation at the meeting of the Start 1 Project Midwest Arts Organization, Columbus, OH.

Nicholson-Crotty, S., & O'Toole, L. J. (2004). Public management and organizational performance: The case of law enforcement agencies. *Journal of Public Administration Research and Theory, 14,* 1–18.

Niven, P. R. (2003). *Balanced scorecard: Step by step for government and nonprofit agencies.* Hoboken, NJ: John Wiley & Sons.

Ohio Library and Information Network. (2004). *Ohio Library and Information Network.* Retrieved September 16, 2004, from http://www.ohiolink.edu/about/what-is-ol.html.

O'Toole, L. J., Meier, K. J., & Nicholson-Crotty, S. (2003). Managing upward, downward and outward: Networks, hierarchical relationships and performance. Paper presented at the meeting of the American Political Science Association, Philadelphia.

Parhizgari, A. M., & Gilbert, G. R. (2004). Measures of organizational effectiveness: private and public sector performance. *Omega, 32,* 221–229.

Patkus, R., & Rapple, B. A. (2000). Changing the culture of libraries: The role of core values. *Library Administration and Management, 14,* 197–204.

Patterson, A. (2003). Compilation of performance measures as of August 5, 2003. Arts Midwest Start program, Minneapolis, MN.

Poister, T. H., & Streib, G. D. (1999). Strategic management in the public sector. *Public Productivity Review, 22,* 308–325.

Poll, R. (2001). Performance, processes, and costs: Managing service quality with the Balanced Scorecard. *Library Trends, 49,* 709–717.

Porter, M. (1996). What is strategy? *Harvard Business Review, 74*(6), 61–78.

Rainey, H., & Steinbauer, P. (1999). Galloping elephants: Developing elements of a theory of effective government organizations. *Journal of Public Administration Research and Theory, 9,* 1–32.

Saul, J. (2003). *Nonprofit business intelligence: How to measure and improve nonprofit performance.* (Available from B2P Commerce Corp, 445 West Erie, Suite 208, Chicago, IL 60610).

Self, J. (2003). Using data to make choices: The balanced scorecard at the University of Virginia Library (ARL Bimonthly Report 230/231). Retrieved September 17, 2004, from http://www.arl.org/newsltr/230/balscorecard.html.

Sherman H., Lewis M. S., Weinberg M. L, & Schermerhorn, J. (2004). Developing a strategy focused organization and the importance of strategic performance management. Paper presented at the meeting of the Irish Academy of Management, Dublin, Ireland.

Simons, R. L. (1995). Control in an age of empowerment. *Harvard Business Review, 73*(2), 80–88.

Smith, G. E., & Huntsman, C. A. (1997). Re-framing the metaphor of the citizen government relationship: A value perspective. *Public Administration Review, 4,* 309–318.

Soete, G. (1998). Evaluating library directors: A study of current practice and a checklist of recommendations (Occasional Paper 21). Retrieved September 2, 2004, from http://www.arl.org/olms/checklist.html.

Stoffle, C. J., Allen, B., Morden, D., & Maloney, K. (2003). Continuing to build the future: Academic libraries and their challenges. *Libraries and the Academy, 3,* 363–380.

Treacy, M., & Wiersema, F. (1995). *The discipline of market leaders.* Boston: Addison-Wesley.

Weinstein, M. G., Jacobowitz, R. L., & Siegel, D. E. (2003). Applying Moore's strategic triangle to implementation of school-based budgeting in New York City. Paper presented at the meeting of the American Educational Research Association, Chicago.

Willis, A. (2004). Using the balanced scorecard at the University of Virginia Library: An interview with Jim Self and Lynda White. *Library Administration and Management, 18*(2), 64–67.

CAREER PATTERNS OF AFRICAN AMERICAN WOMEN ACADEMIC LIBRARY ADMINISTRATORS

Barbara Simpson Darden and Betty K. Turock

Within 21st century issues confronting the United States reside the seeds of major challenges for library, and information science education, and practice. The demographic ballasts of our country are shifting, even as our professional moorings remain static and the people of our nation age. Population referred to as minorities throughout the 19th and 20th century is becoming the emerging majorities of today. Diversity concerns pervade the multi-cultural, social, economic, and political domains of a world connected by electronic advances that have closed distances and made possible millisecond communication. At the same time, the graying of America is more than a catchy phrase. For the first time the average age of librarians is the key factor in the projection of a shortage some estimate to last as long as 20 years (Pungitore, 2002).

The confluence of the challenges posed for librarianship by the convergence of diversity and aging as a new century gets underway provide the opportunity for a leap forward in the profession's attempts to make significant gain in cultivating diversity among tomorrow's librarians.

Advances in Library Administration and Organization
Advances in Library Administration and Organization, Volume 22, 315–360
Copyright © 2005 by Elsevier Ltd.
ISSN: 0732-0671/doi:10.1016/S0732-0671(05)22008-4

CHALLENGES DEFINED

For over two decades, we have known from melding fertility and immigra-
tion data, that the population of the United States would become steadily
more diverse. Throughout the 1990s it was reported that one in four persons
in the nation was a minority. By the time we entered the new millennium,
that figure increased to one in three. Now it is predicted that in the year
2030, the emerging majority of Americans will be people of color. No matter
the type of library or information agency, in this century all will face the
challenge of providing service to population within the context of an entirely
new order of pluralism.

Yet data on enrollment in American Library Association (ALA) accredited master's programs by ethnic origin, taken from the Association for
Library and Information Science Education (ALISE) web site show that the
population remains predominantly white. With 50 library and Information
Science (LIS) programs reporting, the total of 10,478 white students constitute 79.1% of the enrollment. Black students comprise 4.9%, while they
constitute 12.3% of the nation's 2000 population, as determined by the
Census Bureau. Hispanic students and Asian or Pacific Islanders comprise
3.3% and 2.7%, respectively, compared to their 12.5% and 3.7%. The 80
American Indian or Alaskan Natives account for 0.4% of the total.

White students constitute 50.7% of all doctoral students enrolled. Their
lower percentage is not accounted for, by increased enrollment of other U.S.
ethnic groups, but by the higher percentage of international doctoral students. Black students comprise 5.2%, Hispanics students 1.9 percent and
Asian and Pacific Islanders 1.7%. (Association for Library and Information
Science Education 2002). Overall the involvement of all non-white ethnic
groups at the doctoral level, calculated at 9.2%, is fairly characterized as
minimal.

A second stream of data demonstrates that a large percentage of the
current workforce will soon retire, but new recruits are not entering the
profession in sufficient numbers to fill vacant positions. With a median age
of 47, more than 46% are expected to leave the profession by the close of
2006. This trend holds across all library types. Reports indicate difficulty in
filling open positions (Dohm, 2000). In January 2003 the American Library
Association (ALA) reported, "40% of library directors will be retiring in the
next seven years" (Livengood, 2003, p. C2). At the same time the number of
master's level graduates from ALA accredited schools, "remains relatively
flat, about 5,000 a year and fluctuates insignificantly from year to year"
(Jacobson, 2000, p. 14).

Taken together these two challenges – increasing diversity so that the library workforce is more responsive to the communities served and the aging of the profession – offer an opportunity for diversity to become an educational cornerstone in the recruitment and retention of a new generation of librarians. Without that focus it is not clear that libraries will continue to support diverse populations, or understand their experiences, their needs, their languages, or their perspectives.

Betty J. Turock and E. J. Josey have consistently emphasized the importance of bringing greater diversity to the profession. Turock stresses that:

> Greater diversity in leadership has become more than a social and moral issue. Increasing diversity will not only capture unique leadership talents, it will also yield benefits in innovation and creativity that arise as a result of seldom tapped perspectives being brought to problems from different backgrounds and life experiences.
>
> (Turock, 2001, p. 112)

E. J. Josey highlights the need for more minority staff members to ensure the development of programs and collections to meet the information needs of a multi-cultural population.

> A library workforce that represents many nationalities, cultures, and languages brings with it special sensitivities that give a powerful edge in our ability to serve our customers. The library and information profession must reflect the communities that our libraries...serve.
>
> (Josey, 2002, p. 15)

In her article, "Diversity and the Color of Leadership", Camilla Alire (2001) notes that people of color within the profession can: (1) Recognize and root out obstacles to achieving diversity and press for an organizational culture in which change thrives and discrimination ends; (2) serve as mentors, role models, leaders, and spokespersons; and (3) provide the necessary linkages to diverse communities of service. Isaura Santiago (1996), in the book *Achieving Administrative Diversity*, reminds us that professionals of color bring cultural competency to their positions through knowledge of minority history, evidence of supporting services to minorities, and needed linguistic abilities.

Turock reasons that:

> A new generation of library workers is on the horizon, if we conscientiously make diversity a priority. For the face of the profession to reflect the face of the nation, the recruitment of people from diverse populations is essential. But until now that recruitment has eluded education for library and information careers. Recently developed recruitment theory and research supply evidence of factors that have an impact on career choices and their relationship to the ability of the profession to recruit emerging

majorities. From extant research it is clear that a good deal more is known about recruiting emerging majorities than is systematically applied in the profession.

(Turock, 2003, p. 2)

The purpose of the research basic to what is reported in this chapter is to meet the challenges posed for librarianship by the convergence of diversity and aging as the new century gets underway. The study concentrates on one segment of the emerging majority populations, the African American woman, within one type of setting, the academic library, to propose a model for recruitment and advancement based on evidence gathered on:

1. Vital factors that impact the choice of librarianship as a career.
2. Career paths that lead to top administrative posts within academic libraries.
3. Elements that contribute to professional growth once a professional position is attained.
4. Facilitators and barriers that advance or retard career trajectories, particularly in the quest for leadership positions.

LITERATURE REVIEW

By 2008 women will comprise at least 50% of the workforce (Monthly Labor Review, 2000). Most of the increase will be in female intensive occupations. Data on advancement to top leadership positions does show substantial gains for white women. Laura Liswood embraces this rise in her book, Women World Leaders: Fifteen Great Politicians Tell Their Story. Relying on the findings of her research, she describes the powerful influence women bring to the leadership role and the diversity it lends to organizational decision-making, (Liswood, 1995, p. 5). She concludes that while women in leadership roles are still a minority, their existence manifests possibility.

Judy B. Rosner's earlier work advanced the concept that women's increasing success in reaching administrative positions adds credence to the claim that a non-traditional leadership style is well-suited to the conditions of some work environments (e.g. library directors) and can increase an organization's chances of surviving in an uncertain world. It "supports the belief that there is strength in a diversity of leadership styles." (Rosner, 1990, p. 120).

In organizational settings, however, the expectation is that leaders will think and act according to institutional dictates. Parker's (2001) research on

African American leadership within dominant culture organizations gives evidence that this expectation places African Americans at a disadvantage because they are drawn from white norms. Based on her experiences as an African American administrator along with the results of her studies, she further posits:

> I find it difficult to view leadership as a set of universal constructs derived from a select few and generalized to all groups because those generalizations often do not fit my experience as a Black woman within dominant-culture institutions. Rather, I see leadership as a localized, negotiated process of mutual influence that would theoretically accommodate multiple view points and diverse situational challenges.
>
> (Parker, 2001, p. 42)

In 1991, the U.S. Department of Labor first brought to our attention the barriers that women and minorities face prior to meeting the invisible, but ever-present glass ceiling. These barriers encompass not only gender and race, but also stereotyping; lack of management commitment to established systems, policies, and practices for achieving workplace diversity and upward mobility; and limited opportunities for advancement to decision-making positions. The Women's Research and Education Institute Report, The American Women 2001–2002: Getting to the Top (Costello, 2001), has predicted that, given these barriers, it might take from 75 to 100 years for African American females to obtain parity in employment opportunities.

The literature has documented the expansive attention given to examining the status of women and minorities in professions other than librarianship. Management studies have repeatedly shown that men, especially white men, predominantly populate higher level positions. As late as 1997 and 1999 within librarianship, the educator, Suzanne Hildenbrand, noted that, "while the data certainly show some advances for women in librarianship, there remains a puzzling persistence of inequity…including an under representation at the top" (Hildenbrand, 1997, p. 44, 1999, p. 46).

Deborah Hollis adds other dimensions to Hildenbrand's conclusions. She notes that a default definition of women is in use in research in librarianship based on the disclaimer accompanying the majority of gender studies that "underrepresented groups are not the focus of the work" (Hollis, 1999, p. 51). This default definition leaves us with little hard data to substantiate the progression of the career of African American women in librarianship. Further research by the same author showed that by 1997, a 25% increase in the number of female library heads was evident, bringing the total of female library heads to a sizeable 43%. This was a significant increase from 1986 when they represented only 18% of the total (Hollis, 1997, p. 67). In later research Hollis observed the data documented that:

White women have made substantial gains in the last twelve years with promotion to the top level ranks in eighty-six major academic libraries. Keeping in mind that only a certain number of positions actually became vacant during the twelve years, these findings are actually quite impressive for women. Women and men of color continue to have a very small presence in this arena.

(Hollis, 1999, p. 70)

Using data from Hollis and the Research and Education Institute Report along with the implications of current recruitment programs emanating from education institutions, the trajectory for African American women is clearly an even longer uphill battle for parity in library administration.

Eitzen (1988) emphasizes the influence of the status characteristics of administrative positions on individual and group social identity. The differential rewards given these positions in organizations, including higher salaries and the prestige connoted by leadership has thus far eluded African American librarians. The head of a library assumes not only a challenging leadership role, but also has attained the highest rank in the organization with commensurate authority, responsibility, remuneration, and prestige. While the career of librarianship is not one sought for its financial rewards, it is rightfully perceived by some African American women initially attracted to it as exemplifying a glass ceiling that acts as an effective barrier to a prestigious and desired social and professional identity. This, coupled with the lack of financial rewards, makes the career even less attractive than the lack of financial rewards alone.

Isolating the Factors in Success

The literature points to a series of studies, beginning more than two decades ago and continuing to the present, that suggest factors leading to success in the quest for the highest academic library posts. Edward Mapp, who found the informal network an important ingredient, noted "It is axiomatic that job mobility, especially at the highest echelon, depends to a large extent upon direct personal and professional contacts and political connections" (Mapp, 1970, p. 376). Parson (1976) in his study, "Characteristics of Research Library Directors, 1958 to 1973," corroborated the trend toward library heads obtaining their positions via informal networks.

Schiller's (1969) sample of 2,000 librarians revealed that women obtained their goal of becoming academic library heads at a later age than men. In her study "Career Patterns of Academic Library Administrators," Moran (1981) culled the data on the career advancement of a selected group of academic library heads to ascertain professional characteristics affiliated with their success. A distinct pattern emerged: women obtained their promotions mainly via internal institutional upgrades, rather than selection from outside through search committees. Karr's (1984) study of "The Changing Profiles of University Library Directors, 1966–1981," added the idea that mentors were significant factors in facilitating the climb for both women and men.

Smith (1990) found that role models influenced career selection. Additional studies like those of Kermit Davis, Hubert Field, and William Giles corroborate the importance of internships and co-op programs in providing role models for career decisions. They advised that those counseling potential recruits should urge them to consider the possibility of internships and co-op programs to provide interaction on a daily basis with managers in their area of interest. This interaction, the authors advise, will "do much toward providing a realistic picture of organizational life and the rewards it brings as well as allow for the development of role models and mentors." (Davis, Field, & Giles, 1991, p. 89)

AFFIRMATIVE ACTION

From its early days, affirmative action was a major force in assisting women's advancement. Studies over time have documented gender discrimination in librarianship toward those seeking top level administrative positions (Fennell, 1978; Moran, 1981; Irvine, 1985; Squire, 1991; Sullivan, 1996; & Jossey, 1999). Still the controversy continues on the importance of affirmative action in the success of minorities in the workplace. Has affirmative action fulfilled its mission? And is it no longer needed? Are the basic questions at the root of the controversy. Library literature has documented affirmative action as a potent element in the amelioration of historic barriers against emerging majorities in hiring and moving up within the ranks. But there is little systematic evidence concerning what remains for affirmative action to accomplish.

Born of the civil rights movement three decades ago, the history of the influence of affirmative action on the success of African American women's vertical job mobility stretches back to 1965 when the phrase was first promulgated during President Lyndon Johnson's tenure in office. A compilation of legislative initiatives brought together as Title IX, it was designed to help eliminate past and present discrimination based on race, color, religion, sex, or national origin that legally and illegally denied the right to exercise full U.S. citizenship. Today affirmative action protects African Americans, American Indians/Native Alaskans, Hispanics, Asian/Pacific Islanders, women, Vietnam era veterans and people with disabilities. Teresa Neely, a new young and prominent voice among African American administrators, has charged, however, that beginning "with the wider emphasis on diversity and multi-culturalism, which has appeared in the library literature, beginning in 1993, the primary issues of black librarians have been diluted or forgotten." (Neely, 2000, p. 132).

DeEtta Jones stresses the importance of distinguishing between the influence of affirmative action and equal opportunity, as we attempt to define the future of affirmation action within libraries. She denotes that "affirmative action is an aggressive program which seeks to set goals and objectives, and establish and enact policy to redress discrimination" (Jones, 1999, p. 12). Equal opportunity, on the other hand, in a more passive fashion, addresses the avoidance of discrimination. She concludes that the main import of equal opportunity is in the hiring process, while affirmative action has more lasting significance in addressing conditions in the workplace for the duration of the time those hired are on the job.

Research by Carol L. Kronus, Betty Jo Irvine and Corrine O. Nelson has validated that affirmative action and equal employment opportunities enhanced career mobility for women, and to some lesser extent for African American women who have been traditionally by-passed for library administrative positions (Irvine, 1985, p. xii). A more recent study by Nelson (1997) with Evan St. Lifer, "Unequal Opportunity: Race Does Matter", which gathered perceptions about ethnicity's relationship to advancement, showed that not much had changed over the years. It concludes that affirmative action has paved the way for women to enhance their career options in academic libraries and to become more than "feminine tokens" in a male dominated academic library administrators world. However, the authors remind us that minority female librarians continue to occupy few top administrative positions and have not experienced the full measure of reward from affirmative action. Their article concludes that there is a significant difference in perceptions of the current state of diversity in academic libraries, "Librarians of color see a major problem: whites do not" (St. Lifer & Nelson, 1997, p. 44).

Although affirmative action did yield positive results in the past, recent legislation and court rulings have affected it negatively. Within librarianship, it is possible to conclude that while white women have made in-roads in managerial positions, African American women's careers in the profession have not shown a similar trend and that, to date, affirmative action has been of limited benefit to them. This research attempts to determine the facts about benefits and barriers borne of affirmative action and their association with success through information collected from the people in question, the top African American women administrators in academic libraries.

RECRUITMENT

An editorial, *"News and Views,"* (1997, p. 53) in the Journal of Blacks in Higher Education, made it clear that African Americans are overdue at graduate schools of library science. It declared that:

> Decisions as to what books and journals are to be acquired at the nation's university libraries are made almost exclusively by white officials. As long as few blacks enter the field of library science the best they can expect is a world in which white people will decide what reading material is best for black people as well as what works of black intellectuals and political commentators are to be placed on library shelves

Recruitment is pointed to in the literature as the essential factor requiring major change if the profession is to become more diverse and, therefore, more responsive to the changing demographics of the United States. Recruitment appears repeatedly in studies and in comments by experts as a continuing barrier rather than a facilitator of progress.

Winston (2001), who has focused on developing a theory of recruitment, conducts the most current research on the topic. His work, ongoing at Rutgers University, has found that common themes emerge across the literature of the professions. One proven premise is that the reasons individuals have chosen their professional specialties provide worthwhile principles for the development of recruitment strategies, since, similarities exist between those currently employed in a given profession and those who are likely candidates for recruitment into it. His data give raise to a number of factors, including the support of family, friends, teachers, and colleagues and work experience in libraries prior to entering master's programs, tested in this research to see if the theory holds true for African American women in academic libraries.

Maurice B. Wheeler's dissertation research supplied convincing evidence about reasons for the limited presence of emerging majorities in librarianship. His data place the cause squarely in the corner of library education. He found that:

> When administrators were asked to suggest reasons for the low percentage of African American in their ranks, without exception, each response made reference to the low

percentage of African American students pursuing the M.L.S and the even lower number of doctoral students.

(Wheeler, 1994, p. 147)

de la Pena McCook's (1993) research indicates that even the small number of minorities present in the profession is dwindling. The low count of current African American students reduces the number who might be ready for administrative positions in the future. Melody M. McDowell has underscored the urgency of the diminishing numbers when she writes:

Black librarians are growing scarce. Black librarians are disappearing. These gatekeepers of African American culture, around whom many community activities revolve, are exiting the profession in droves, with few replacements in sight, and the decimation of the ranks is leaving a cultural vacuum that gets increasingly hard to fill.

(McDowell, 2001, p. 78)

W. Lee Hisle has called intense recruitment one of the top issues facing academic libraries. He advises that, "the need to find and retain quality leadership for libraries is a core issue for the future. Even as retirements increase, fewer librarians are entering the profession as a whole, and fewer librarians are entering the academic library field in particular" (Hisle, 2002, p. 14).

While the need for recruitment is clear, according to the work of Eileen McElrath, few current academic library administrators see increasing the diversity of staff and their access to administrative position as pressing issues within recruitment. McElrath's (2002) research has shown that chief academic officers to whom library administrators report ranked diversity as either their number two or number three most pressing problem. Yet, chief library administrators did not rank diversity within their three most pressing challenges. A lack of commitment to achieving workplace diversity becomes apparent.

The reputation of the organization and its treatment of its employees is seldom considered as a factor in recruitment, but the studies done by Albinger and Freeman (2000) give credence to its importance. They found that job seekers not only make decisions based upon their own personal values, but also on the organization's reputation for providing employees with an accommodating work environment. Previous to this work, Buttlar and Caynon (1992) recommended the systematic development of factors affecting the selection of minorities as part of recruitment, including the institution's reputation for their treatment and support. Joyce K. Thornton's research on the job satisfaction of African American women led to the identification of many factors that pertain to the reputation of academic libraries where:

> African American librarians were often in a unique situation. Many times they were in libraries where they had additional pressures on them…including questions about their ability to perform a job well and endure other stresses and anxieties solely based on race.
> (Thornton, 2001, p. 14)

Other evidence that could lead to a new perspective for recruitment arises from an independent study conducted by Tracy Paler, a master's student at Rutgers University. Her data point to interdependence between the university and the field as an untapped force for recruitment and retention. Paler developed and pilot tested a questionnaire, then sent it to a systematic sample of 141 ALISE members. From the data collected and analyzed, she found that interdependence exists on an individual and local basis in the production of research. The precedent for working together appears well ingrained in the careers of educators and practitioners. But the same interaction was not found in recruitment initiatives. Instead two tracks were found: One originating in the field and the associations supporting practice and the second originating in library education and the associations supporting it (Turock, 2003). The research reported on here focuses on interdependence as a factor that offers hope for developing a more diverse profession in the 21st century.

Table 1 brings together in one alphabetical list the 25 factors, described in the literature prior to this study that were perceived to influence the career path of African American women in the top administrative positions of academic libraries.

SIGNIFICANCE AND LIMITATIONS OF THE STUDY

Few studies exist that concentrate on racial minorities in library administrative positions. Lelia Rhodes (1975) compiled the most comprehensive research to date on successful African American women in librarianship. Their biographical profiles were the subject of her Ph.D. thesis, "A Critical Analysis of the Career Backgrounds of Selected Black Female Librarians." Fifteen African American librarians, whose median age was 64, and who were or had been in administrative library positions, were a part of the study. Five of them had earned the Ph.D. in library science. Rhodes analyzed their career backgrounds to determine roadblocks encountered and

Table 1.   Factors Influencing Career Paths.

Affirmative action
Conference attendance
Continuing education
Early experience in libraries
Education
Ethnicity
Expected leadership styles
Family, friends, teachers
Field – university interdependence
Gender
Hourly work week
Institutional politics
Interesting classes
Lack of institutional commitment to diversity
Landmark years
Limited opportunities for advancement
Membership in professional organizations
Mentors
Networking, formal and informal
Organization reputation
Personal attributes
Political connection
Promotions from within
Recruitment practices
Role models
Supportive colleagues

differences in their educational backgrounds and career experiences. But 30 years have passed since the completion of her work.

More recent research concerning management career models in librarianship has often focused on gender and sometimes related gender to the influence of affirmative action, but there is an absence of research on racial minorities in library and information administrative positions. In a profession predominantly populated by women, rectifying this omission becomes increasingly important as the demographics of the nation change significantly.

The limited existing data on African American women administrators imply differences between their career experiences and the career experiences of white women, which suggest that factors influencing the career choices, paths, and patterns of white women may not be appropriate for women of color. The assumption that generalization about men could be applied to women led also to the misapplication of some earlier career paths information. One such generalization was that the career advancement for men was in direct relationship to hard work: the harder they worked the more career advancement. Futas (1991) disputed that generalization for women in her research on career paths of male and female librarians. Although she found that hard work was necessary for women, it was not one of the major determining career advancement factors as it was among men. She documented that sex discrimination was the biggest deterrent. Identifying relevant factors in present day African American women's elevation to administrative positions, the unique problems they face, and the advantages and disadvantages they might encounter adds a unique dimension to prior studies that considered only gender.

With threats surrounding affirmative action programs growing due to recent court rulings and perceptions of reverse discrimination, this door may close before it has completely opened. This research asks African American academic library heads the significance of affirmative action in their rise. It also explores: career selection factors in choosing librarianship; the pressure, stresses, and anxieties African American academic library administrators experience based on race; the role of networking, within the institution and external to the organization, mentors, professional organizations, and institutional politics.

The initial need for this study was predicated on a series of current conditions affecting the profession, including:

1. The dwindling numbers of African American academic librarians and library administrators in a time when the national demographics are moving toward greater diversity.
2. The glaring lack of sufficient numbers of African American students recruited to graduate programs of library and information science and to academic librarian positions.
3. The necessity for libraries to continue serving as centers for African

American culture with African American librarians as knowledgeable gatekeeper, collection managers and builders cognizant of that culture.

4. The leadership talents African American librarians bring to their jobs based on their unique backgrounds and experiences.
5. The special cultural competencies of African American librarians, which enable them to respond better to the needs of emerging majority populations along with other populations the library is chartered to serve.

This research not only renders data specifically on the career paths of African American women library administrators, it also adds information on women's career development, where research specific to emerging majority population is scarce; contributes to the literature on recruitment; and provides the basis for the creation of a model depicting factors influencing career paths of African American library administrators. It expands knowledge fundamental to increasing the diversity of the profession of librarianship and to assist African American women in becoming more successful in their quest for vertical mobility.

The nature of this research imposes certain limitations. First, it is constrained by the scarcity of African American women administrators in academic libraries. The largest and most prestigious institutions are represented by their membership in the Association of Research Libraries (ARL). Among over 120 ARL members, only one African American woman headed the entire system. As a result, though still leading to the small number of seven subjects, this investigation did include the entire population of African American women who serve in top administrative positions. A possibility does exist that some members of the population were not located, since no list is extant for them in either print or database form.

The paucity of subjects available for this work combined with the paucity of research literature and statistics related to ethnicity in librarianship posed difficulty for building on prior concepts or results, systematically drawn. Since, this is an exploratory and descriptive qualitative study, its findings cannot be generalized to African American library administrators overall. With the small number of participants, even transferability to other African American women in similar work situations must await confirmation from future studies, perhaps broadened to all African American women in administrative positions at any level. The final limitation of this work arises for all research, that is, the limitation based on the availability and willingness of those solicited to participate in a timely and accurate fashion.

METHODOLOGY AND METHODS

This study relied on instrumentation that included a mail survey, vita-resume analysis and taped telephone interviews, for further probing and clarification. The survey asked six open ended questions. The follow-up interviews picked up the threads of the survey with further open ended questions similar for all respondents. Once dialog was initiated, the interviews took varied directions depending on the responses given. Pattern matching that is, looking for recurring themes found in responses and/or repeatable regularities, was the principle research method utilized.

The respondents for this study were drawn from the African American female administrators listed in the Directory of Ethnic Professionals in Library and Information Sciences and The Black Caucus of the American Library Association Membership Directory. The snowball technique was used to gather referrals from African American library leaders. The initial focus was on African American women heads of libraries with membership in the Association of Research Libraries (ARL).

Deborah Hollis lamented in her 1999 research that only in the Big 10 Conference of Mid-western states was an African American woman head of an ARL library. In the initial search for this study in 2000 once again only one ARL member library was discovered that had an African American woman as the chief. Clearly research cannot be based on one respondent. The population located was not sufficient for generating useful data for African American librarians who wished to seek top administrative positions.

To increase the size of the participant pool the focus shifted to the entire population of African American females who held the top library administrative positions in institutions of higher education. The small population of African American women leading academic libraries led to the further addition of an assistant chief from an historically black ARL institution. Current status and positions of the population were verified by returned mail surveys and resumes. The total population of seven African American women located in top academic library administrative positions became the subjects for this study.

RESEARCH QUESTIONS

To fill the gaps identified in previous studies and to contribute to the literature on leadership in libraries, the research questions guiding this work were:

1. What is the profile of the academic libraries administered by African American women?
2. What is the profile of African American women in top administrative positions in academic libraries?
3. What are their career paths?

4. What factors influenced their career choices?
5. What factors influenced their professional growth?
6. What facilitators and barriers to leadership positions did African American women academic library administrators perceive?

Table 2 shows the research questions and the instrumentation used to gather data for each question.

The resumes, mail survey questions and interviews: collected information about the characteristics of the respondents' libraries; developed librarians' profiles; explored career patterns; identified factors that influenced librarians to choose librarianship as a career; examined elements that influenced

Table 2. Instrumentation.

Research Questions	Survey	Interview Schedule	Document Review
1. What is the profile of academic libraries administered by African American Women?	1, 2, 3, 4, 5, 6		
2. What is the profile of African American women in top administrative positions in academic libraries?			Resume
3. What are the career paths of African American women in academic administrative library positions?	7, 8, 9, 10, 11, 12, 13		Resume
4. What factors influenced career choice of African American women academic library administrators?		1, 3, 6	
5. What factors influenced professional growth of African American women in academic administrative library positions?		2, 4, 5,7, 8, 9, 10, 11, 12	
6. What facilitators and barriers to leadership positions were perceived by African American women academic library administrators?		13, 14, 15, 16, 17	

Table 3. Carnegie Classification/Higher Education.

Carnegie Classification	Definition
Doctoral/research universities – extensive	Typically offer a wide range of baccalaureate programs: committed to graduate education through the doctorate; awarded 50 or more doctoral degrees per year across at least 15 disciplines.
Doctoral/research universities – intensive	Typically offer a wide range of baccalaureate programs; are committed to graduate education through the doctorate; awarded at least ten doctoral degrees per year across three or more disciplines.
Master's Colleges and universities I	Typically offer a wide range of baccalaureate programs: committed to graduate education through the master's degree; awarded 40 or more master's degrees per year across three or more disciplines.
Master's colleges and universities II	Typically offer a wide range of baccalaureate programs: committed to graduate education through the master's degree; awarded 20 or more master's degrees per year.
Baccalaureate colleges – liberal arts	Primarily undergraduate colleges with major emphasis on baccalaureate programs; awarded at least half of their baccalaureate degrees in liberal arts fields.

professional growth; and provided information on perceived barriers and facilitators to advancement.

The Carnegie Classification of Institutions of Higher Education, grouping colleges and universities according to their missions, was applied to the institution from which the population was drawn. Table 3 briefly presents the basic operational similarities and differences among the institutions employing the study participants.

FINDINGS

Presentation of the findings is organized around the themes inherent in each of the six research question. The data charted arise from the most frequent responses given by the study participants to initial queries and follow-up probes.

Career Choice

Factors that influenced the career choice of African American women administrators are summarized in Table 4. The forces at the top of the list were

Table 4.   Career Choice.

Respondents	Librarian's Initial Professional Choice	Influenced by	Prior Library Work Experience
A	Yes	College librarian	Yes
B	Yes	Going to the library	Yes
C	No	University librarian	No
D	Yes	High school librarian	Yes
E	Yes	Prior education	Yes
F	Yes	Going to the library	Yes
G	Yes	College librarian	Yes

library connected. "Librarians encountered early in life" was the most prevalent response with "going to the library" in second place.

All but one respondent had work experience in libraries prior to entering an education program for the master's degree. The six agreed that it was a major factor in their career selection and concurred that it afforded them an opportunity to observe libraries in action. Later they were able to base their decision to enter the profession on their experiences in the actual day-to-day world of their future careers. The six found that it was an advantage to come to their first position knowing what to expect on the job. Three expressed the view that on the job experience also afforded them an opportunity for greater success in the courses they took in pursuit of the master's degree. Connections with the university that lasted past the receipt of the master's were depicted as bringing mentoring and contacts that influenced success once a library position was obtained. Taken together, these findings make a strong case for developing interdependence between the university and the field. The perception was that libraries were not only first rate sites for attracting to the profession those already interested in librarianship, but also that long time university-field connections led to advantages throughout the career.

In response to probing when discussions of recruiting arose, four of the seven characterized current practices in library education programs as ineffective and called the efforts on the part of library educators to bring diversity to the profession insufficient. The necessity to look at recruitment from new perspectives was accentuated, if it was to lead to an enlarged pool of emerging majorities available in the future for administrative posts.

Targeted recruiting was perceived as a major key to diversity. Five described instances in their lives or in the lives of other African American administrators where it was of critical importance. The former Title II-B from the U.S. Department of Education was pointed to as bringing many influential African American colleagues to the profession. The respondents compared that now defunct program to the current ALA Spectrum Initiative and portrayed the two as influential largely because they both provided financial support to many who could not have afforded the expense of the educational experience.

Six respondents chose librarianship as their initial profession. Only one did not. She believed this was an advantage. Coming into librarianship after a successful career as a scientist, she claimed, provided her with experiences that prepared her for the challenges of library administration, especially dealing successfully with the politics and prejudices of the academic environment.

PROFILE OF ACADEMIC LIBRARIES

The profile of academic libraries administered by African American women is summarized in Table 5. Among the institutions five were within the Carnegie Doctoral/Research Classification, four were extensive and one was intensive. One study participant administered a library in an institution where the master's was the highest degree granted; another headed a library classified as residing in a baccalaureate college. Libraries in Doctoral/Research-Extensive settings were the top four with regard to budget, staff and collection size. Three of the four Doctoral/Research-Extensive institutions were public universities and members of the Association of Research libraries (ARL). In addition to the one African American woman heading the entire library system of an ARL library, another was found who administered the undergraduate library alone. The third was an Assistant Chief at a special library within a library system. Significantly, public universities employed five members of the total population.

The title of Dean, regardless of the Carnegie classification, was the predominant one used by academic institutions for heads of libraries. Four at Doctoral/Research institutions held the title of University Librarian or Dean with only one titled Director. The top library administrative position of the master's college was also termed Director.

Four of the seven respondents agreed that their present title gave them appropriate recognition within the University. The Director at the Doctoral/Research institution did not believe that her classification accorded her a commensurate level of recognition. Reasons supplied by the respondents for

Table 5. Library Profiles.

Respondents	Carnegie Classification	Title	Public or Private	Collection Size	Annual Budget ($)	Staff	ARL
A	Baccalaureate College	University librarian	Private	203,600	481,844	11	No
B	Doctoral/research – extensive	Dean	Public	1,004,000	6,078,000	106	No
C	Doctoral/research – extensive	Dean	Public	2,123,257	12,901,160	211	Yes
D	Doctoral/research – extensive	Assistant Chief	Private	2,465,152	13,517,653	149	Yes
E	Doctoral/research-intensive	Dean	Public	288,671	978,481	26	No
F	Master's college	Director	Public	188,213	841,301	17	No
G	Doctoral/research – extensive	Director	Public	9,647,652	30,457,637	397	Yes

the Dean as the appropriate title for their position were that:

- Library heads in academic institutions were in charge of faculty.
- Librarians who held academic rank, like teaching faculty, should report to deans.
- Library heads administratively interacted with deans and had duties, such as, evaluating faculty librarians for tenure and promotions, that equated with dean responsibilities.
- Deans had professorial rank while Directors did not.

In view of the size of the population available for this study four of the respondents raised questions about whether institutions of higher education were committed to their stated intentions to seek a more diverse workforce.

Finally, study participants agreed that risks were great when they pursued career in academic library administration, regardless of the institution in which they found themselves. The comfort zone resided in lower level librarian positions. Unlike library administrators, librarians have greater job security, including tenure, multi-year contracts and/or union membership. The necessity for confidence to take risks, especially in making tough and unpopular decisions for the betterment of the institution was reinforced here as crucial for success.

PROFILE OF LIBRARY ADMINISTRATORS

The profile of African American women in top administrative positions in academic libraries is summarized in Table 6. All had earned master's degrees from ALA accredited library schools. Four of the seven respondents had doctorates. Three of the four held the doctorate in library science. Two of four ARL institutions had top administrators who held doctorates; two did not. This finding runs counter to the widely accepted norm that the Ph.D. is essential for becoming head of an ARL library.

Data on the profiles of these top administrators documented that five had published; one of the five had authored or edited 11 books. All had

Table 6. Administrators' Profiles.

Ph.D.		Member Professional Organization		Publications		Required Study of Management	
Yes	No	Yes	No	Yes	No	Yes	No
3	4	7	0	4	3	7	0

membership in professional organizations, including membership in the ALA division, which specifically advances the concerns of academic libraries, the Association of the College and Research Libraries (ACRL).

In both surveys and interviews it was clear that the participants possessed or developed and honed personal attributes that could be subsumed under the term self-reliance. In this vein, the seven spoke of personal qualities that they felt were essential as they sought leadership positions including self-confidence, daring, firmness, courage to follow convictions, grit, boldness, backbone, openness, fearlessness when making unpopular decisions, and the ability to take risks without fear of reprisal.

While the consensus was that continuing education kept knowledge updated and was beneficial in reaching top level posts, six commented that few courses offered by professional library associations met their needs. Their perception was that most offerings concentrated on the public library environment and were not as applicable for academic library administration. These respondents also stated that most continuing education programs and institutes did not address areas of concern that were problematic for African American women library administrators. They did, however, praise the conferences of ALA's Black Caucus, which concentrate on issues germane to the realities of their work life.

This group of administrators unanimously noted that continuous growth in their knowledge of management was an essential element in their successful rise to top administrative positions. They recommended a mandatory management course for all receiving library education. Five of seven, however, suggested a departure from present instructional programs. They believed that library students should take that course in business schools or be taught by business school faculty. They based their opinions on the fact that academic library administrators competed for library resources with non-library colleagues who often used management principles and terminology emanating from the business view point and educational experience. One respondent observed that the management terminology she learned placed her at a disadvantage when she was trying to communicate with or persuade her non-library colleagues to support resources for the library.

CAREER PATHS

Table 7 summarizes the career paths of the African American woman who were study participants. Some landmark years arose from the data. All entered library education for the master's degree between 1 and 10 years

Table 7. Career Paths.

Respondent	Years between Degrees (yr)	Age Entering Profession	Salary Range ($)	Hours Per Week	Number of Promotions
A	1–10	34	61,000–79,999	45	2
B	1–10	34	>100,000	60	5
C	1–10	40	>100,000	55	1
D	1–10	42	60,999	40	1
E	1–10	41	61,000–79,999	50	3
F	1–10	40	61,000–79,999	55	1
G	1–10	30	61,000–79,999	45	2

after the bachelor's degree was conferred. They entered academic librarianship between the ages of 30 and 40. The respondents concurred that, in their experience, assuming the head-of-the-library duties prior to age 30 placed the incumbent at a high risk of failure due to insufficient experience. According to the respondents, experience and maturity obtained working in the library field and in lower level administrative posts were requisites to overcoming career barriers and becoming successful when they assumed the top leadership spot. All respondents had received at least one promotion prior to their present position. The promotional range was from a high of a five to a low of one, although not all were within the same institution, as the literature suggests.

Although administrators' salaries were, for the most part, still modest, they had advanced significantly from meager beginnings. Current salaries ranged from a low of $60,999 to a high of more than $100,000. The Assistant Chief listed a lower figure than the other top officials, as might be expected. The modal range was from $62,000 to $79,999. The two respondents who cited salaries of over $100,000 headed libraries at public Doctoral/Research-Extensive Carnegie classified institutions.

Participants reported that work weeks were long throughout their careers. Currently they ranged from a low of 40 h in one case to a high of 60 h in another. Administrative heads at large research libraries had the longest work weeks ranging from 55 to 60 h per week. The Assistant Chief was the only one who worked less than 45 h. The pattern showed that the majority of the respondents spent more than the normal 35 h work week at their jobs. It can be stated that librarians whose goal is to become the top administrator at an academic library should anticipate long work hours.

PROFESSIONAL GROWTH FACTORS

Table 8 summarizes professional growth factors that contributed to the successful advancement of study participants. All stressed the importance of attending professional conferences at least annually to keep up-to-date professionally. Two attended from one to three conferences; two attended from four to six; and three from seven to nine. Administrators who worked at private institutions attended one to three conferences per year, whereas, those who worked at public institutions attended four to nine. The latter were influenced by the fact that they were given 100% reimbursement for their attendance. None of the respondents who worked at private institutions received a similar level of financial support.

The respondents also agreed that going to professional conferences was critical not only for the educational programming, but also for the opportunities to interact with other colleagues. This was especially important to these African American women, since none of them reported belonging to a formal network that had career advancement as a goal, although all indicated that they were aware of such networks. They had no knowledge, however, of any formal network that specifically assisted in and promoted the advancement of African American women to top academic library administrative positions. Two respondents did note an awareness of informal networks that took on this mission, which they defined as "word of mouth" networks with no formal structure or name.

Fewer African American women administrators meant fewer role models for those aspiring to the top jobs. Five of the respondents did report having mentors, when moving through the career ranks, however, two others who worked at ARL libraries had non-library connected mentors. One was the early supervisor of the administrator who came into librarianship as a second career. This chief scientist, who believed that it was important to have several viable career options, frequently described the advantages he had gained from obtaining his secondary career as an information science expert.

Table 8. Professional Growth Factors.

Professional Conference Attendance		Informal Network		Formal Network		Mentors	
Yes	No	Yes	No	Yes	No	Yes	No
7	0	2	5	0	7	7	0

The second non-library mentor was a respondent's mother who had a strong affinity for libraries and wanted her daughter to go to "library school" to become a librarian. She encouraged working toward becoming a library administrator. The majority of respondents had mentors, connected to the profession who were supportive library colleagues and administrators to whom the study participants had once reported.

BARRIERS

The barriers to leadership positions considered significant by the African American women academic library administrators, based on the frequency with which they were mentioned by respondents, are brought together and summarized in Table 9. The patterns found point to race and gender as the primary obstacles.

If the goal was to move up to an administration position or find success as a library administrator, the consensus of the respondents was that race was a major barrier. Their assessment included the charge that on the job perpetuation of ethnic and racial stereotypes continues today.

The presence of institutional racism in the work place was variously described by respondents. On the individual level, it was recorded as at the root of considerable staff dissension and mistrust of each other, as well as mistrust of the organization as a whole. The result, five of these top administrators agreed, was that too often staff members who once thought of librarianship as a career, began to think of it as only a job. They were also united in their perception that racism was fueled by assumptions and misconceptions about emerging majority cultures.

Racism, four posited, too frequently infused the fabric of organizations in which they had at one time worked with the notion that diversity was not welcome and collections and services to non-majority constituencies were not important, lowering the quality of service to emerging majority populations. Four respondents found merit in the observations of Neely, who in

Table 9. Barriers.

Affirmative Action		Race		Gender	
Yes	No	Yes	No	Yes	No
4	3	7	0	6	1

a conference presentation, related the history of librarianship to evidence of racism, the precedence of bigotry and hatred and the perpetuation of ethnic and racial stereotypes (Neely, 1998). These shortcomings still exist, the four concluded.

Five of the seven respondents believed that if it were not for their race they would have advanced faster and further in their careers. To support their views, all five volunteered that they had applied for positions to which others, less qualified, were appointed. In some cases those appointed did not even meet the minimum required qualifications.

Six respondents agreed that, based on their ethnicity, they were too often viewed negatively and taken less seriously than their white colleagues. They described situations in which they were marginalized and unable to move ahead with ideas and directions that would have benefited service for constituents. Early career plateaus were characterized as creating struggles and cycles of frustration that had to be overcome to regain the momentum required to move up the administrative ladder. They termed their potential and skills, when they began their professional lives, as seldom utilized or acknowledged with awards or other forms of recognition.

Respondents supplied instances when their suggestions were not considered, but the same suggestions were given attention when Caucasians in lesser ranks reiterated them. They also stated that when confronted with negative encounters with white colleagues and students, they often asked themselves the question, "Am I treated in a disparaging manner because of my race?" All participants thought that they not only had a much harder journey on the road to career success, but also continued to experience less job satisfaction due to racism.

Six concurred that gender was a factor in their career progression. They believed that being female negatively affected their chances for promotions. The consensus was that all males, but African American males to a lesser degree than Caucasian males, had a better chance of becoming heads of libraries. Women hit a glass ceiling that eliminated or at best deterred promotions. In addition, men usually had positions with the power to select library administrators and tended to appoint those who fit into the "old boy network." The data demonstrated that, while gender is a deterrent to career success, being female and African American was a double detriment.

A concern was shared by four administrators that the original intent of Affirmative Action, to assist African American, Native American, and Hispanic populations, was weakened by redefining minorities with a concentration on diversity as the key element. According to the four, this change has resulted in reports citing numbers for minorities that do not reflect a picture of the African Americans employed, since figures are frequently combined for all racial groups as an aggregate minority complement, but not supplied for specific racial groups. The result was that, in some cases, institutional data might show a larger number of minority hires yearly, when the number of African American added together, the total was actually lower. They noted that there were fewer African American female fouryear academic library administrators now than there were 10 years ago.

Two respondents stated that Affirmative Action laws did not assist them in obtaining their present positions. One was from an historically black institution where all administrators were of African descent. The other, who worked in a majority institution, offered that, "If Affirmative Action laws were of assistance, I would have been chosen for other positions that I applied for. I know that my credentials and experience were more impressive than the candidates that were hired." The majority of the respondents made clear their belief that unless the original intent of Affirmative Action laws was restored, it might unwittingly become a significant barrier to leadership positions for African American women who are academic library administrators.

Concepts of leadership were also perceived as barriers by four of the respondents who concluded that the expected style was the one that led to advancement. Five of the respondents determined that little room existed for the addition of talents and perspectives arising from backgrounds and experiences that differed from those currently in positions when decisions are made about who will advance in the organization. Four commented that they received little on the job coaching as they progressed through the ranks of library administrators. They advised anyone aspiring to a top spot to concentrate on developing the ability to stand alone, willing and unafraid, when making difficult decisions.

FACILITATORS

The chief facilitators of paths that led to leadership positions put forth by the respondents are summarized in Table 10. Professional growth factors perceived as within the control of the study participants were endorsed by them as facilitators.

Conference attendance through which they obtained, maintained, and updated their managerial skills was mentioned by all seven. Agreement also came among all respondents that Affirmative Action is still necessary to

Table 10.   Facilitators.

Affirmative Action Still Needed		Conference Attendance		Organizational Reputation	
Yes	No	Yes	No	Yes	No
7	0	7	0	5	2

counteract leadership obstacles, although only four of the seven believed that it was beneficial to them in obtaining positions. One participant was adamant that without Affirmative Action laws; she would have missed a chance for career advancement. She related an instance in which she was promoted only because the selection committee had to submit a ranked, racially balanced interview list to the Affirmative Action Director. Although she was number two on that list, when the number one ranked candidate declined the offer, the search committee skipped her and recommended the third ranked candidate, who was Caucasian. The Director intervened and officially asked the committee to follow the practice of recommending in rank order.

Data showed that working in a public institution was a career facilitator. All respondents whose professional home was a public academic library, regardless of whether it possessed ARL status, reported better salaries, more staff to supervise, and larger collections and budgets to manage. Public academic libraries were also cited as the place where advancement and support for professional growth were more prevalent.

Time and again throughout interviews, organizational reputation for just and fair treatment, unlimited by discriminatory practices arose in the participants' discussions. The respondents paid attention to reputation when they searched for new positions throughout their careers. They sought environments denoted as conducive to the successful fulfillment of their career aspirations.

The majority of career barriers and facilitators converged around professional growth, where conflicts were in ample evidence. Facilitators, whom respondents deemed crucial to their advancement, were also seen as barriers. This division was in evidence when these factors were divided into those within the control of the administrators and those outside of it, which depended on intervention by others. Factors outside their control were considered barriers by more than half of the participants. Role models, mentors, network opportunities, and political connections, cited as influential in successful advancement to top positions, were not available in quantities that met the need. Either those who could fill in the blanks were unwilling to step into the breach, or they did not see the need for them to do so.

In summary, study participants put particular emphasis on three factors they considered barriers, which caused them to:

1. Lament that Affirmative Action is not as effective as it once was in espousing its original intent due to court challenges, charges of reverse discrimination, and the emphasis on diversity.
2. Emphasize that institutional racism is the most detrimental factor in hindering the career progression of African American women.
3. Stress that the lack of role models, mentors and networking are not only major hindrances to the career advancement of African American librarians, but are also detrimental to recruiting African Americans to library education.

THE SUCCESSFUL ADMINISTRATOR

Characteristics of the African American women who were successful in navigating the path to the top leadership position in academic libraries present a profile for other with similar aspirations. These women administer budgets over $203,000; are active members of professional associations, attend professional conferences, continue their education, particularly in management, work long hours, cultivate political connections, possess supportive colleagues, family, and friends, and work in libraries in public institutions of higher education (Table 11).

Table 11. Characteristics of Successful African American Women
Academic Library Administrators.

Administer annual budget ≥ 203,000
Maintain active membership in professional associations
Attend professional conferences
Continue growth in management knowledge
Work long work hours
Cultivate political connections
Work in public institutions
Develop essential personal attributes
Possess supportive colleagues, family, and friends

FACTORS UNCOVERED AND REAFFIRMED

For the final analysis, data were divided into facilitators and barriers uncovered in this work and those reaffirmed from prior studies to determine whether this research had met its goals of making contributions to knowledge and suggesting new directions for the future that would: assist in enriching the profession by increasing its diversity, and help African American women in their quest for vertical mobility. These data are brought together in one pattern in Table 12.

Facilitators Uncovered

Seven influential facilitators were uncovered from the data collected and interpreted in this research.

University–Field Interdependence: The ongoing leverage that results for recruiting when the university and the field realize the import of their interdependence was an advantage to the women in the study throughout their career. It is fair to say that not only are the administrators of tomorrow working in libraries today, making them a fertile place for recruitment, but also that, when the university-field connection is made, the advantage realized continues through the counseling and connections some former professors might supply.

Public University Advantage: Most of the subjects for this study were top administrators in public institutions. Throughout the study, in library and administrators' profiles and in the respondents' career paths, it became evident that a professional home in a public institution offered the most favorable work environment, especially those which were also ARL members. Work effort, signified by hours on the job in this study, were not only equally long regardless of the institution in which the respondents were employed, but also increased with the level of responsibility attained.

Reputation of the Institution: Among the factors these administrators attended to when they sought new positions was the reputation the institution had as a place conducive to the growth and development of emerging majority librarians, not just in administration, but throughout its ranks. Once again, the public university had the advantage.

Title: The top administrators in this study all had the responsibility for securing needed resources for the libraries they led. The title their positions bore was considered significant, not only in the remuneration and rank that

Table 12. Factors Uncovered and Reaffirmed to Administrative Positions.

Facilitators/ Barriers	Career Choices	Library Profiles	Administrators' Profile	Career Paths	Professional Growth
Facilitators uncovered	☐ University—field interdependence	☐ Public university advantage ☐ Reputation of the institution ☐ Title	☐ Education ☐ Personal attributes	☐ Pattern of promotions ☐ Age entering profession	
Barriers uncovered	☐ Current recruitment practices	☐ Little feedback on performance ☐ Expected leadership style			☐ Affirmative action
Facilitators reaffirmed	☐ Early experiences libraries ☐ Librarian contacts ☐ Targeted recruitment ☐ Financial support	☐ Budget, staff, and collection size	☐ Membership in professional organizations ☐ Publications	☐ Hours worked	☐ Affirmative action ☐ Conference attendance ☐ Political connections ☐ Supportive colleagues, family, and friends
Barriers reaffirmed		☐ Institutional racism ☐ Lack of commitment To diversity	☐ Gender ☐ Ethnicity		☐ Insufficient: ☐ Role models ☐ Mentors ☐ Network opportunities

accompanied it, but also in the recognition it was accorded in negotiation with others who were seeking resources for the units they supervised. The designation Dean was the preferred title.

Education: This study led to the explosion of the myth surrounding the education needed for a top position in a major academic library. An examination of the resumes of these administrators demonstrated that the Ph.D. is not essential if the goal is to head an ARL library in either a public or a private institution, but that the master's degree from an ALA accredited program was absolutely indispensable. All members of the study group, however, placed emphasis on the necessity to keep up with the latest developments in the field through continuing education.

Personal Attributes: From follow-up interviews with the study participants, personal attributes were brought together that top administrator thought were critical. They centered on self-reliance. The respondents indicated that at times they observed characteristics in other administrators that connoted leadership. When they did not possess these characteristics, they set about to acquire them. They offer proof that leaders are made, not born.

Landmark Years and Patterns of Promotions: The identification of landmark years for career progression and the pattern of promotions associated with them supplied guide posts for others aspiring to academic library leadership. The number of promotions to the top spot varied, but the general agreement was that experience in significant administrative positions was essential for success as an organizational leader. While the literature suggests that women advance more in the same institution than they do if their careers take them to a number of professional homes, these data did not substantiate that claim.

Barriers Uncovered

The identification of barriers to the success of African American women who aspire to top administrative posts was considered of critical importance to improve their chances of reaching their career goals. Along with influential facilitators, barriers were uncovered not previously recorded in the literature. Four were noted as most significance based on the attention they received from the respondents in both the survey and the interviews.

Current Recruitment Practices: The word misguided was frequently associated by the study participants with current recruitment practices. Educators, four related, held fast to the same tactics even though they showed little or no success. Most surprising to the administrators was that little movement has occurred in the number of emerging majority students now in master's programs, since the faculty of the programs were researchers whose forte was finding innovative answers to questions that contained challenges as yet unresolved. If educators were sufficiently committed to greater diversity in the student body and, therefore, greater diversity in the field, they reasoned, more effective recruitment means would have been found long ago to reach that end.

Expected Leadership Style: Advancement depended on perceptions of the leadership style of the candidates for promotion, these administrators claimed. The expected standard was built from the view point of white middle-class culture. Most management research, texts, and popular literature are written from that perspective without reference to the resultant strengths that differences in style and skill would bring to the job. It becomes the norm, which all organizational members are expected to personify, if they want to move up in the management chain. But the expectations associated with this style of leadership are also often in conflict with stereotypical assumptions about African American women. These assumptions too frequently leave African American women out of the promotional loop, even though they bring skills the organization is short of and even when their managerial style is, in fact, built on the models espoused as the organizational norm.

Feedback on Performance: While five study participants described the importance they place on day-to-day feedback on job performance for those they are grooming for top leadership spots, they were firm in their conviction that they received less coaching as they worked their way through the ranks than did their white colleagues. They described feedback as limited and less than what they wanted or needed. They noted further that their contributions to the organization were seldom recognized nor were they coached sufficiently to help them further their management abilities.

CONTROVERSY IN FACILITATORS AND BARRIERS

The remaining factors influential in the career paths of African American academic library administrators were reaffirmed from prior research. The documentation of professional growth contributed a series of such influences around which controversy swirled. They were simultaneously described as facilitators and barriers by respondents. The most important of these was the growing controversy over the status of Affirmative Action.

The administrators feared that its more recent interpretation emphasizing diversity obscured the prior positive influence it had on opportunities for African Americans. While all respondents applauded its past influence and considered it essential for future progress, they were concerned that, without a return to its original intent, the benefits of Affirmative Action for African American women would disappear before the parity that it promised was achieved.

Other factors conceived of as both facilitators and barriers included: role models, mentors, and network opportunities. They were considered facilitators critical to obtaining and maintaining a successful career. But the study participants denoted that, for the most part, they acted as barriers, since they were not as available to them as they were to their white colleagues. They felt that the lack of this meaningful support hindered their development of political connections that in turn hampered their career progress. The conflict between supply and demand surrounding the three forces was made painfully evident from participants' comments.

Facilitators Reaffirmed

Early experiences in libraries, including work experience and contact with librarians who acted as mentors and counselors, found in prior research were strongly reconfirmed here as major determiners of future career choice, as were targeted recruitment campaigns. Financial support also came to the fore in the comments of four of those responding. One of the major deterrents to entrance in master's programs was the lack of money needed to pay the costs. The prospect of obtaining loans to become qualified for a profession that offered only moderate remuneration was not considered an incentive to enter librarianship. The presence of financial support became a deciding factor in the decision to seek the education required.

Active membership in professional organizations was reaffirmed as a facilitator. Professional affiliations of the respondents included memberships in library associations at the national, state and/or regional level. One of the benefits they all stated that accrued from this affiliation was the opportunity to attend conferences where continuing education was part of the venue. Publications were perceived as a secondary benefit of the conferences. Committee work often led to extended study of a topic. Discussing publications around these ideas with publishers was facilitated at the meetings. Finally, the ongoing support of colleagues, family and friends was reinforced as a facilitator that contributed to the motivation to continue the struggle for advancement opportunities.

Barriers Reaffirmed

Barriers repeated over decades as detrimental to the advancement of African Americans in the profession were reaffirmed in this research. Respondents alluded again and again to gender, race, and lack of commitment to the advancement of emerging majorities not only within the institutions in which they were once employed, but also within the field generally as well as among educators, professional associations, and their library leaders.

But the respondents reserved the denotation as the greatest barrier to their success for institutional racism, which occurred when an organization privileged one group over another through its formal and informal policies, and practices. Looking at race in a biased manner impedes the success of African American women by adhering to assumption that result in negative conclusions concerning their selection for positions at the top of the organization. Institutional racism was also perceived as responsible for decreasing their opportunities to be hired.

The burden of institutional racism was exacerbated when a small number of African American women were employed in predominantly white institutions. There, work in a profession that is officially characterized as occupationally segregation, that is, where 70% or more of its members are of one gender, collides with the barriers of gender and ethnicity, putting the African American woman at an disadvantage that brings only minimal chance for reaching the career goal of leadership.

Although past research suggested that teachers, interesting jobs and job benefits were influential factors in the career path and direction of African American women administrators, this study found no data that substantiated that claim.

SIMPSON'S CAREER PATH MODEL

A Model of the Career Patterns of African American Women Academic Library Administrators was developed from the research data reported on here. This model depicts the factors considered of greatest influence in the career advancement of African American female academic library administrators' career. It has implications for setting and implementing paths that lead to the attainment of leadership positions in academic libraries.

The model is divided into three components, beginning with recruiting through the factors that operate as facilitators and barriers to career progress. The facilitators denote those factors useful in the climb. The recruiting factors and the barriers are recommended as an agenda for all members of the profession to pursue in their places of influence, whether that is in the work place, in educational programs, or in professional associations. Gathering the attention of others in librarianship to the critical need for change can affect the work environment of colleagues long into the future.

CONCLUSIONS

The study that was the basis for this chapter replaces the prevailing conventional wisdom with systematically drawn evidence. It suggests new directions, which come when the time is right to address some long time professional challenges that have evaded solutions. The nation's minorities are rapidly becoming emerging majorities. The number of retirements anticipated in the next decade makes critical the need for them to fill many of the jobs now open and those projected. A new generation of librarian is on the horizon for academic and all types of libraries, where the recruitment of diverse population to beginning and leadership positions is essential.

The academic library chiefs who participated in this research made known their belief that their unique needs as African American women administrators were largely ignored by the professional associations in which they were members. While these associations could respond, they had not yet chosen to do so. Four elements uncovered or reaffirmed in the research can become pivotal departures in the response they seek. These departures can serve as the basis for the development of a national action plan that grows in scope to supply solutions that address the challenges that remain. Interdependence, lack of sufficient attention to professional growth issues, and institutional racism demand concerted effort now.

Interdependence

Educators and practitioners can each continue to design and execute programs that address recruiting and retaining emerging majorities and developing more diverse leaders for the profession and the discipline. But that course negates the advantages of interdependence between the two, which this research demonstrates is required for progress.

In the recent past at the national level the major example of interdependence between practitioners and educators is ALA's Spectrum Initiative.

Its thrust was to establish within ALA a Diversity Office and Officer to coordinate and sustain an intense, targeted recruiting effort, oversee the annual selection of diverse scholars, and ensure the provision of financial support for them. Put in place in 1996 with the first scholarships awarded in 1998, this program has now educated more than 250 students. But advocacy is essential to continue ALA's response at a level that will make a difference. It is also essential to generate the commitment to programs that improve cultural competencies and diversify leadership.

The Spectrum Initiative should make a locus for action the 20 programs of library and information science that, to date, have not matched or contributed to the funding of Spectrum Scholars entering their programs, as well as those that have not actively sought Spectrum Scholars. Since the Initiative offered its first scholarships more than 6 years ago, this connotes a sluggish record of response from educators to ALA's gift to the profession and to library education. The leaders of ALA need to place an emphasis on making a substantial effort to enlist the commitment of ALISE in establishing a combined interdependent organizational goal with appropriate incentives to encourage all programs of education to participate in and contribute to the Spectrum.

The Institute of Museum and Library Service (IMLS), under the inspired leadership of Dr. Robert Martin, has funded statewide model programs that are developing and testing the success of interdependence in recruiting and educating the next generation librarians. In these models recruits are drawn from the ranks of the field for education in library programs not only at the master's level, but also at the doctoral level. Library and information science needs professors who are African American as desperately as the field needs them in libraries. This IMLS program should be watched to determine whether it is worthy of emulation in states across the country. At the same time the IMLS should consider funding a combined ALA–ALISE initiative to gather data on best practices from library and information science programs that have successfully attracted and retained African Americans. This compilation can act as a guide for all LIS educators.

Institutional Racism

Racism cannot be corrected if society is not willing to admit that it exists and does not understand that it causes harm, not only to the people that are targeted, but also to those who do the targeting. As long as racism remains unaddressed in either society or librarianship, institutional racism will remain an immutable barrier. The African Americans study participants document that they have faced exclusion from participation, full status and opportunity because of institutional racism, which is often less than obvious because it is implicit, indirect, residual, and perpetuated by acts of omission as well as commission.

The point of departure here is an educational program beginning from the evidence supplied by this study that improved communication is essential to dispense with the pervasiveness of institutional racism. From the perspective of the African American library administrators who were study respondents, most whites tend to believe, communicate, and act as though few or no race-based motivations are present, whereas, most African Americans tend to believe, communicate, and act as though most race-based actions are deliberate. The profession needs to document racial injustices and what members of emerging majorities perceive as points of action as a precursor to building a multi-organizational effort that will correct similar responses in the future. This is another agenda for interdependence.

Together ALA and ALISE can develop a strategic plan that seeks to identify the knowledge and skills needed to increase the cultural competencies of LIS professionals, including their understanding of their role in a society of emerging majorities. Together the two organizations can become lightning rods for the curricular revisions that prepare all graduates for work in a society of emerging majorities. Enlisting ARL in this effort will strengthen it even further. The three associations can institute a series of programs that work to end institutional racism by: supplying participants with learning experiences about histories and cultures other than their own; producing familiarity with the countless acts of exclusion and devaluation that occur from culture to culture; dispelling negative myths and stereotypes; making clear that self-esteem for all cultures is a non-negotiable tenet of acceptable professional behavior, and, through this activity, contribute to progress in assuring professional equity at a national level.

Role Models, Mentors, and Networks

Three factors were noted in this investigation as critical for professional growth: role models, mentors, and networking. They are interrelated. Role models become mentors who create networks. More African American academic library women administrators can seek these three roles, but their minimal numbers make it difficult. The numbers who request their guidance has already overwhelmed some.

To move forward, the myth that the ideal role model must be of the same ethnicity needs to be laid to rest. Role models serve to guide and influence by example another's personal, educational, or career aspirations. The essential quality of the role model is not her or his ethnicity but that she or he possesses knowledge, skills and operational techniques, which the professional initiate lacks and from which, by observation and comparison with her own performance, those new to librarianship can learn. All librarians, but especially Caucasian women who have been the major beneficiaries of Affirmative Action laws, should take on the challenge of becoming role models and mentors to African American women.

Networking encourages members to share with others the hints they learned that enhanced their entry into professional life. Networks allow identification and bonding between those that can help a career grow and those who want to pursue career growth. Ultimately new members can branch out from the networks they originally joined to form their own, where other role model and mentor relationships emerge. Associating with networks outside the profession is an option. The Executive Leadership Council (ELC), the nation's premiere network of African American corporate executives whose mission is to prepare "the next generation of African American business leaders for success" is a suitable environment for African American women who aspire to academic library administration. The Black Caucus could create a formal link with the ELC that would open wide the opportunity for a new group of role models and mentors. The Caucus can also search out similar networks that are dedicated to the successful preparation of African American female leaders in other fields. They are viable substitutes for the networking opportunities that do not now exist within the profession.

Study participants stressed mentors as essential ingredients for success. They were seen as making it possible for emerging majorities to bypass the hierarchy, to get inside information, to short-circuit cumbersome procedures, and to cut red tape. The major components of mentoring are divided among tasks associated with teaching, counseling, intervention, and sponsorship. In the teaching phase, mentors present organization's politics and expectations. In the counseling stage, they advise on work-related challenges and, to the degree they are able, listen to and help resolve personal problems interfering with successful professional performance. When snags hit, as they eventually do, mentors offer encouragement to stay the course. In phase three, intervention, mentors rescue from mistakes those whom they are assisting to grow professionally, support them when they take risks that could lead to failure, recommend them for key assignments, and help them get the resources they need to succeed. In the last stage, sponsorship, mentors nominate them for leadership positions.

The role of the mentor is so varied that no one person can take on all of its dimensions. They can, however, select those that best fit with their talents and interests. The role of mentor is made to order for previous association leaders – Past Presidents and former Board members – as part of their ongoing development of the profession.

National models exist for creating successful networks where role models, mentors and networking opportunities converge, among them those of the Oregon chapter of the American Leadership Forum and the U.S. Small Business Administration, which has set up a program specifically geared to the needs of women and minorities. But the African American administrators in this research were looking for leadership in the creation of this type of program from organizations within librarianship. This is another opportunity for the development of an initiative that brings the talents of the appropriate professional associations together.

Within ALA two models exist, which could function as points of departure for a more comprehensive, interdependent national program geared to the needs of emerging majorities. The first of these was ALA's Emerging Leaders Institute, which was discontinued after only a year of successful operation. To set it up the membership was canvassed for volunteer role models, mentors, and network members while a national call went out for the identification and nomination, including self-nomination, of emerging leaders. The goal was to select 35 diverse participants for the Institute with follow-up Institutes to be held semi-annually. Over 300 nominations were received from which the 35 were selected. That response alone is a signal that there is a need for the rebirth of Emerging Leaders.

The second model, Advocacy Now, exists for the way in which a new network of Emerging Leaders, combining role model, mentor, and networking activities, can be promoted nationally. The lead factor in this model is education. Training sessions, lead by consultants from outside ALA with established reputations for excellence, were employed for the program's introduction, each trained participant pledged to go back to his or her state and offer a similar work shop, using materials made available for the training, and offered primarily through programs at state and local library conferences. The participants there pledged to take the program and materials back to their libraries and continue the training.

The design of a program on a national scale to promote, implement, and support professional growth for African American women who seek career in administration could once again arise from ALA, ALISE, and ARL by making its development the responsibility of a cross-association task force composed of librarians from all parts of the country and all types of libraries with careful selection to ensure representation of the new face of America. With a mentoring initiative in place, those ready now to become mentors could be put into immediate action and those seeking greater skill in mentoring across ethnic lines could receive the training they want and deserve. Lack of adequate compensation and significant recognition for the work such a program would require are the reasons identified by the respondents in this study that might preclude its success. A compensated program, they recommended, could overcome the competing obligations that would prevent its successful completion. Funds could be used to hire a part time employee to free the participants from other duties and responsibilities to provide uninterrupted time for national program members. The IMLS might be tapped for funding the development and initial test of the proposed national program with a compensated component included.

FURTHER RESEARCH

This study made noticeable the lack of prior investigations with African American women as the focus, not just in academic libraries and not just in the area of administration, but in librarianship in general. The literature review verified a growing body of research on women and their career choices, but the unique situation and history of African American women make questionable the transferability of these findings or the resultant models to them. Correcting the situation affords little plumbed topics with the opportunity for critically needed attention in the future.

The size of the current group of African American women in top library positions in academe suggests that further study should not only continue on the same group, but also shift to the entire population of African American women in administration, regardless of the level of the post they occupy in the administrative chain. That population could first be limited to the administrators found in academic libraries with subsequent studies based in other types, including public, special, and school libraries. One investigation might also sample all of these populations with the goal of determining if the factors found in the research presented here operate in all environments. Such an approach could determine if one environment is more favorable to the success of African American women than others. Clearly a study of this kind would also be amplified by data on all African Americans in administrative roles, both men and women, to determine if the same factors operate, regardless of the gender of the administrator.

Each of the themes fundamental to this study and the ensuing data analysis – career choice, library and administrator profiles, career paths, and professional growth – deserve the attention of researchers interested in their applicability to the wider groups. The factors uncovered and reaffirmed here, for example the interdependence of the university and the field, affirmative action, the effect of the presence or absence of role models, mentors, and networking, found within the profession, could become the singular subject of multiple studies to determine their effect at various career stages.

The process of attracting African American women to the profession, then moving them into top level positions will take a collaborative effort supported and engaged in by the entire profession. We need studies that will discover what is missing from current environments that, if added, would render librarianship more appealing to a larger number of career seekers. While the comparatively low salaries for beginning positions, coupled with the amount of education required to qualify for entry are most frequently assumed as the cause of the limited number of African American recruits, no substantive data exist to give credence to this supposition. The proposed investigation could take on the approach of market research, specifically targeted at African American youth.

Even more compelling is an emphasis on retention once the recruits are in the library. So far this topic has received more rhetoric than research. We need a variety of programs with differing variables that are backed by measurable outcomes on which data are gathered to determine the factors that encourage successful retention. This type of investigation is not currently part of the targeted funding available for library research. It needs to be added as a focus. It is not enough to attract to programs of education African Americans who have or acquire a desire for administrative positions only to find that they become drop-outs further into their career.

Mentoring is another topic frequently discussed in the literature. It has become the subject of many conferences as well, but locating mentors within the profession remains an unresolved issue for the African American women who find the search for them arduous. This research demonstrates the importance placed on mentors. The field cannot wait until there are enough African American librarians available to mentor new recruits of similar ethnicity. A study, built on a sample of current members of the field regardless of ethnicity, is needed that clearly delineates the role of the mentor in our profession, along with the time and tasks it requires to fill the role.

This work could also serve as a way to find those willing to become mentors in the future.

Library educators must be a sub-group within such research. Mentoring is part of their world. Determining those willing to specifically mentor African Americans women would also lead to the identification of programs most suitable for the women when they decide to initiate study for the master's degree. It is important to know if a faculty is lacking educators who understand the importance of adding more Africans American women to the profession or who are unwilling to make part of their mission taking on some responsibility for the growth and development of these women during their education and beyond. It is not likely that the programs lacking mentors are suitable places for African Americans to attend.

Research that begins with the aspirations of African American women when they enter library education performed longitudinally would supply data on how these aspirations are changed by the experiences they encountered over time. Studies of African American female librarians who want to become academic library administrators could encompass the reasons the aspirations have or have not been achieved. Data such as these, if later applied in the field, can reduce the barriers and increase the facilitators that make aspirations a reality, while also serving as a basis for motivating African American female librarians to enter academic library administration. The data may serve as a guideline to assist with research on recruitment theory as well.

Several further questions arise specific to the audience for this study, which dictate future research. What are the career aspirations, goals, and expectations of African American women when they enter academic library administration? Do they expect to attain them? What sacrifices do they anticipate as a result of their career choices? What can be done to increase the African American female applicants to the administrative job pool? When African American women academic library administrators excel in their jobs, are organizational plans and mechanisms in place to ensure their promotion? How can the facilitators and barriers uncovered or reaffirmed in this study be applied to the library environment to allow African American women to experience the success they are pursuing?

This research found that white colleagues do not see the problems African Americans perceive as barriers to their career progression in academic library administration. While knowledge of another group's perceptions does not automatically guarantee insight or understanding, it is important that colleagues have an understanding of each other's perception, in this case knowledge of what constitutes institutional racism. Such recognition cannot break down all barriers to communication but it can help reduce the chances of misinterpreting behavior. Research directed toward operationally defining and uncovering institutional racism can lead to its recognition by all members of the academic library work force, particularly recognition of what constitutes it. This, in turn, can form the basis for the creation of subsequent programs that lead to its eradication. Libraries cannot move forward, if immutable institutional racism is allowed to continue.

Declaring support for diversity without commitment to put research findings into practice is detrimental to the future of the profession. Library staff in the 21st century must reflect the diversity of the communities served, not only because it raises the level of service to that community, but also because growth in emerging populations means that without their interest in the profession, enough librarians may not be available to continue service at a suitable level for anyone. African American women should be in academic library administrative positions because everyone benefits. They bring a knowledge base, skills, unique experiences, and varied creative approaches to problem solving that assist the institution in fulfilling its mission. Their recruitment and career development is crucial for academic and all libraries.

To date a dearth of research and limited attention have been devoted to the status of African American administrators of both genders in all types of libraries. It is imperative that more studies are undertaken to illuminate what is needed to make the library open and welcoming to African Americans so their aspirations to lead libraries are not thwarted. The results of these investigations must then be placed into action in the field. The perceptions of the participants in this study about professional barriers cannot be ignored. We must all work to overcome them and create the library that makes their career aspirations a goal worth pursuing. A viable future for the profession depends on it.

REFERENCES

Albinger, H., & Freeman, S. J. (December 2000). Corporate social performance and attractiveness as an employer to different job seeking populations. *Journal of Business Ethics*, *28*, 243–253.

Alire, C. A. (2001). Diversity and leadership: The color of leadership. In: M. D. Winston (Ed.), *Leadership in the library and information science professions: Theory and practice*. New York: Haworth.

Association for Library and Information Science Education. (2002). *Statistical Report*. (Electronic). Retrieved November 1, 2004 from the World Wide Web: http://ils.unc.edu/ALISE/2002/Students/Students01.htm.

Buttlar, L., & Caynon, W. (1992). Recruitment of librarians into the profession: The minority perspective. *Library and Information Science Research, 14,* 259–280.

Costello, C. B. (2001). *The American Women 2001–2002: Getting to the top.* Washington, DC: The Women's Research and Education Institute.

Davis, K., Field, H., & Giles, W. (September 1991). Recruiter–applicant differences in perceptions of extrinsic rewards. *Journal of Employment Counseling, 28,* 82–90.

de la Pena McCook, K. (1993). Diversity deferred: Where are the minority librarians? *Library Journal, 118*(18), 35–38.

Dohm, A. D. (2000). Gauging the labor force effects of retiring baby-boomers. *Monthly Labor Review, 123*(7), 2081–2085.

Eitzen, S. D. (1988). *In conflict and order understanding society.* Boston: Allyn and Bacon.

Fennell, J. C. (1978). *A career profile of women directors of the largest academic libraries in the United States: An analysis and description of determinants.* Tallahassee: Florida State University.

Futas, E. (September 1991). The faculty vanishes; accelerating retirements and difficulty in attracting new educators could spell disaster for the profession as a whole. *Library Journal, 116,* 148–152.

Hildenbrand, S. (March 1997). Still not equal closing the library gender gap. *Library Journal, 122,* 44–46.

Hildenbrand, S. (April 1999). The information age vs. gender equity. *Library Journal, 124,* 44–47.

Hisle, W. L. (November 2002). Top issues facing academic libraries. *College & Research News,* 714–715.

Hollis, D. (1997). In our own voices: Ethnically diverse librarians and librarianship in the 1990s. Paper presented at the American Library Association Annual conference. San Francisco.

Hollis, D. (1999). Affirmative action or increased competition: A look at women and minority library deans. *Journal of Library Administration, 27*(1–2), 49–75.

Irvine, B. J. (1985). *Sex segregation in librarianship: Demographic and career patterns of academic library administrators.* Westport, Connecticut: Greenwood.

Jacobson, J. (2002). *A shortage of librarians. Chronicle of Higher Education Career Network* [Electronic] (8) 14. Retrieved November 4, 2002 from the World Wide Web: http://chronicle.com.jobs/2002/08/2002081401htm.

Jones, D. (1999). The definition of diversity: Two views. A more inclusive definition. *Journal of Library Administration, 27*(1–2), 5–15.

Jossey, E. J. (1999). Diversity: Political and societal barriers. *Journal of Library Administration, 27*(1–2), 191–202.

Josey, E. J. (2002). Why diversity in American libraries. *Library Management, 23*(1–2), 10–16.

Karr, R. D. (July 1984). The changing profile of university library directors, 1966–1981. *College and Research Libraries, 45,* 282–286.

Livengood, R. (January 2003). Librarians expected to be in shortsupply in the future. *The Post Standard (Syracuse, NY),* C2.

Liswood, L. (1995). *Women world leaders: Fifteen great politicians tell their story.* San Francisco: Pandora.

McDowell, M. M. (March–April 2001). Help wanted at our libraries: Black librarians are growing scarce just like black teachers. *Book Issues Book Review, 3*(2), 78–79.

McElrath, E. (July 2002). Challenges that academic library directors are experiencing as perceived by them and their supervisors. *College & Research Libraries, 63*(4), 304–320.

Mapp, E. (November 1970). The invisible librarian. *Library Journal*, 3745–3747.

Monthly Labor Review. (February 2000). Women's share of labor force to edge higher by 2008. Monthly Labor Review Online.

Moran, B. (1981). *Career patterns of academic library administrators*. Unpublished doctoral dissertation, University of New York, Buffalo.

Neely, T. (October 1998). *Unequal opportunities: Race does matter*. Paper presented at a conference at Penn State Libraries. Available: http://www.libraries.psu.edu/divers/conf/unequal.htm.

Neely, T. (2000). Effects of diversity on black librarianship: Is diversity divergent? In: E. J. Josey & M. L. DeLoach (Eds), *Handbook of black librarianship*. Lanham, Maryland: Scarcrow.

Nelson, C. O. (September 1997). Continuing the struggle. *Library Journal*, *122*, 44–46.

News and Views. (Summer 1997). African Americans are overdue at graduate schools of library science. *The Journal of Blacks in Higher Education*, No. 16, 53.

Parker, P. S. (2001). African American women executives' leadership communication within dominant-culture organizations. *Management Communication Quarterly*, *15*(1), 42–82.

Parson, J. L. (1976). Characteristics of research library directors 1958–1973. *Wilson Library Bulletin*, *50*, 613–617.

Rhodes, L. (1975). *A critical analysis of the career background of selected black female librarians*. Unpublished doctoral dissertation. Florida State University, Tallahassee.

Rosner, J.B. (November–December 1990). *Ways women lead*. Harvard Business Review.

St. Lifer, E., & Nelson, C. O. (November 1997). Unequal opportunities: race does matter. *Library Journal*, *122*, 42–46.

Santiago, I. (1996). Increasing the Latino leadership pipeline: Institutional and organizational strategies. In: R. C. Bowen (Ed.), *Achieving administrative diversity*. San Francisco: Jossey-Bass.

Schiller, A. R. (1969). The widening sex gap. *Library Journal*, *94*, 1098–1100.

Smith, P. (March 1990). The choice of a sex-nontraditional occupation: The female headed household effect – a research note. *Youth & Society*, *21*, 399–406.

Squire, J. S. (Fall 1991). Job satisfaction and the ethnic minority librarian. *Library Administration and Management*, *5*(4), 194–203.

Sullivan, C. J. (1996). *Affirmative action and women in academic libraries: How far have we come?* Unpublished master's thesis. University of North Carolina at Chapel Hill.

Thornton, J. K. (2001). African American female librarians: A study of job satisfaction. In: T. Neely & K.-H. Lee-Smeltzer (Eds), *Diversity now: People, collections, and services in academic libraries*. New York: Haworth.

Turock, B. J. (2001). Women and leadership. In: M. D. Winston (Ed.), *Leadership in the library and information science professions: Theory and practice*. New York: Haworth.

Turock, B. J. (2003). *Diversity: For recruiting a new generation to the library workforce in urban libraries*. A proposal submitted to the Institute for Museum and Library Services. Washington, DC.

Wheeler, M. B. (1994). *African American faculty perceptions of recruitment, retention, and tenure processes and practices in US ALA accredited library information science programs: A descriptive study*. Unpublished doctoral dissertation, University of Pittsburgh.

Winston, M. D. (2001). Recruitment theory: Identification of those who are likely to be successful as leaders. In: M. D. Winston (Ed.), *Leadership in the library and information science professions: Theory and practice*. New York: Haworth.

ABOUT THE AUTHORS

Melissa Cox Norris is the Director of Library Communications at the University of Cincinnati. She is a founding member of the OhioLINK Marketing Task Force. Prior to joining the University of Cincinnati in 2002, she worked for three years at the University of Virginia Library as the Director of Communications and Publications.

Odin L. Jurkowski is an Assistant Professor of Library Science at Central Missouri State University. After 8 years working in academic libraries in positions ranging from access services librarian to director, he completed his Doctorate from Northern Illinois University and made the switch to teaching. The courses he teaches are online or hybrid in nature and his research interests cover the many aspects of technology use in libraries.

Pamela Kindja Ladner has served as Technical Services Librarian and Library Director at Mississippi Gulf Coast Community College. Upon completion of her undergraduate and graduate studies in Library and Information Science, she earned a Ph.D. in Educational Administration with an emphasis in Higher Education. She is currently the Assistant Dean of the Learning Resources Center at Mississippi Gulf Coast Community College – Jackson County Campus.

Marsha Lewis is a Senior Research Associate at Ohio University's Voinovich Center for Leadership and Public Affairs. She currently manages applied research projects related to public sector strategy development. For the past five years, Lewis directed and led the curriculum development for the Ohio University Executive Leadership Institute. Lewis has a master's degree in public administration from Ohio University and is currently pursuing a Ph.D. in educational research and evaluation.

Tara Lynn Fulton has been in university libraries since 1981, and at Lock Haven University since 2000. She has published and presented on various topics related to library leadership, including mentoring, ethics, collaboration, reorganization, change, recruitment, and training. She was a Visiting Professor at Long Island University's Palmer School LIS program in 1998.

She has been teaching part time at Rutgers University's LIS program since 1991 and completed her doctoral work there in 2003.

Charles B. Osburn is Dean and Professor Emeritus of University Libraries at the University of Alabama, where he teaches part time in the School of Library and Information Studies. He is the author or editor of several books and a number of articles.

Lilia Pavlovsky's early research experience was in legal and financial areas related to corporate finance. Later work involved managing and directing information centers in non profit and management consulting environments. Has taught courses at Rutgers and Long Island Universities MLIS programs that included Information Seeking Behavior, Management and Research Methods. Doctoral work completed in 2003 at Rutgers University.

Barbara Simpson Darden has been a Library Director for twenty years. She served as chair of the following organizations: Council of Library Administrative and Management Association Affiliates, New Jersey Academic Library Network and the Council of Library Directors, Deans and University Librarians. She also served on numerous boards such as the Rutgers University Board of Governors' Library Advisory Committee, Library State Advisory Council, and Library Services and Technology Act Council. She served as Assistant Program chair for the First National Conference of African American Librarians. She is known for her consulting expertise in the following areas: Library public relations, staff development motivation, and library buildings and design.

Hugh D. Sherman serves as Associate Director for the Voinovich Center for Leadership and Public Affairs at Ohio University, and he is an Associate Professor of Strategy and Chair of Management Systems at the Ohio University College of Business. He received his Ph.D. from Temple University in 1995 in strategy and international business. His research interests are corporate governance, international management, entrepreneurship and economic development. His most recent publications have appeared in Journal of International Management, Journal of Teaching International Business, Economic Development Quarterly, Long Range Planning, and Corporate Governance: An International Review.

Betty K. Turock is Professor and Dean Emerita of the School of Communication, Information and Library Studies at Rutgers University. She has also served as the President of the American Library Association (ALA), and during her tenure she focused on Equity on the Information Super-highway, just and equitable access to electronic information and elimination of the digital divide widening the gap between the information rich and the information poor both in our nation and around the world. Turock was the force behind the creation of the Spectrum Initiative.

Mark L. Weinberg directs the Voinovich Center for Leadership and Public Affairs at Ohio University, and he teaches in Ohio University's Department of Political Science Master's of Public Administration program. His teaching and research interest is in how public and nonprofit organizations are strategically managed to create public value. Dr. Weinberg also serves as the Whisman Scholar of the Appalachian Regional Commission.

Julia Zimmerman has served as Dean of Libraries at Ohio University since 1999. Before coming to Ohio University, she served on the staff of libraries at Georgia Institute of Technology, Pennsylvania State University, Wake Forest University School of Law, and Florida State University. She is one of the founders of GALILEO, Georgia's multi-type library consortium, and currently chairs OhioLINK's Library Advisory Council. She holds degrees from Florida State and Emory University.

Eleni A. Zulia serves as a Research Associate at the Voinovich Center. Her main research areas include strategy and performance measurement related to the public and nonprofit sectors. She has a master's degree in public administration from Ohio University.

AUTHOR INDEX

SUBJECT INDEX

SET UP A CONTINUATION ORDER TODAY!

Did you know that you can set up a continuation order on all Elsevier-JAI series and have each new volume sent directly to you upon publication? For details on how to set up a **continuation order**, contact your nearest regional sales office listed below.

To view related series in Sociology, please visit:

www.elsevier.com/sociology

30% Discount for Authors on All Books!

A 30% discount is available to Elsevier book and journal contributors on all books (except multi-volume reference works).

To claim your discount, full payment is required with your order, which must be sent directly to the publisher at the nearest regional sales office above.